The Rough G

Bangkok

written and researched by

Paul Gray and Lucy Ridout

ROUGH
GUIDES

www.roughguides.com

Contents

Bangkok by Boat colour section following p.80

Thai Cuisine colour section following p.176

Colour maps following p.272

3

◄◄ Tuk-tuk driver ◄ Statues at the Grand Palace

Introduction to
Bangkok

**The headlong pace and flawed modernity of Bangkok
match few people's visions of the capital of exotic Siam.
Spiked with scores of high-rise buildings of concrete and
glass, it's a vast flatness which holds a population of at
least nine million, and feels even bigger. But under the
shadow of the skyscrapers you'll find a heady mix of chaos
and refinement, of frenetic markets and hushed golden
temples, of early-morning alms-giving ceremonies and
ultra-hip designer boutiques.**

Bangkok is a relatively young capital, established in 1782 after the Burmese sacked Ayutthaya, the former capital. A temporary base was set up on the western bank of the Chao Phraya River, in what is now Thonburi, before work started on the more defensible east bank, where the first king of the new dynasty, Rama I, built his fabulously ornate palace within a protective ring of canals. Around the temples and palaces of this "royal island", there spread an amphibious city of shops and houses built on bamboo rafts moored on the river and canals.

Ever since its foundation, but with breakneck acceleration in recent years, Bangkok has attracted internal migration from all over Thailand, pushing the city's boundaries ever outwards in an explosion of modernization that has seen the canals on the east side of the river concreted over and left the city without an obvious centre. The capital now sprawls over 330 square kilometres and, with a population forty times that of the second city, Chiang Mai, and four-fifths of the nation's automobiles, it's far and away the country's dominant city. In the make-up of its population, however,

Bangkok bucks world trends, with over half of its inhabitants under thirty, so helping to consolidate its position as one of Asia's liveliest and most fashionable cities.

What to see

Rama I named his royal island **Ratanakosin**, and it remains the city's spiritual heart, not to mention its culturally most rewarding quarter. No visit to the capital would be complete without seeing the star attractions here – if necessary, the dazzling ostentation of **Wat Phra Kaeo** and the **Grand Palace**, lively and grandiose **Wat Pho** and the **National Museum**'s hoard of exquisite works of art can all be crammed into a single action-packed day.

One of the other great pleasures of the city is a ride on its remaining waterways; the majestic **Chao Phraya River** is served by frequent ferries and longtail boats, and is the backbone of a network of canals, floating markets and waterside temples – including the striking five-towered **Wat Arun** – that remains fundamentally intact in the west-bank **Thonburi** district. Inevitably the waterways have earned Bangkok the title of "Venice of the East", a tag that seems all too apt when you're wading through flooded streets in the rainy season.

Bangkok began to assume its modern guise at the end of the nineteenth century, when the forward-looking Rama V relocated the royal family to a neighbourhood north of Ratanakosin called **Dusit**. Here he commissioned grand European-style boulevards, built the new Chitrlada Palace (still used by the royal family today), had his charming, teakwood **Vimanmek Palace** reconstructed nearby, and capped it all with the erection of a sumptuous new temple, **Wat Benjamabophit**, built from Italian marble. When political modernization followed in 1932, Dusit was the obvious choice of home for Thailand's new parliament, which now sits in Parliament House.

Bangkok's commercial heart lies to the southeast of Dusit, where sleek glass towers and cool marble malls lend an air of energy and big-city drama to the districts of **Silom**, **Siam Square** and **Sukhumvit**. These areas shelter a few noteworthy tourist sights, too, best of which is **Jim Thompson's House**, a small, personal museum of Thai design. **Shopping** downtown varies from touristic outlets selling silks and handicrafts to international fashion emporia and boutiques showcasing Thailand's increasingly desirable home-grown contemporary designs. For livelier scenes, explore the dark alleys of the bazaars in **Chinatown** or the Indian district, **Pahurat**, or head out to the enormous, open-air **Chatuchak Weekend Market**. Similarly, the city offers wildly varied entertainment, ranging from traditional dancing and the orchestrated bedlam of Thai boxing, through hip bars and clubs both downtown and in the backpackers' enclave of **Banglamphu**, to the farang-only sex bars of the notorious Patpong district.

North and west of the city, the unwieldy urban mass of Greater Bangkok peters out into the vast, well-watered central plains, a region that for

▼ Wat Phra Kaeo

centuries has grown the bulk of the nation's food. The atmospheric ruins of Thailand's fourteenth-century capital **Ayutthaya** lie here, ninety minutes' train ride from Bangkok and, together with the ornate palace at nearby **Bang Pa-In**, make a rewarding excursion from the modern metropolis. Further west, the massive stupa at **Nakhon Pathom** and the floating markets of **Damnoen Saduak** are also easily manageable as a day-trip, and combine well with a visit to the historic town of **Phetchaburi**, famous for its charming old temples. Riverside **Amphawa** is similarly evocative and makes a perfect escape from the city, with its genuine floating markets and traditional canalside neighbourhoods. An overnight stay at **Kanchanaburi** is also well worth the effort: impressively sited on the River Kwai, it holds several moving World War II sights, including the notorious Death Railway.

Rat or raja?

There's no standard system of transliterating Thai script into Roman, so you're sure to find that the Thai words in this book don't always match the versions you'll see elsewhere. Maps and street signs are the biggest sources of confusion, so we've generally gone for the transliteration that's most common on the spot; where it's a toss-up between two equally popular versions, we've used the one that helps best with pronunciation. However, sometimes you'll need to do a bit of lateral thinking, bearing in mind that a classic variant for the town of Ayutthaya is Ayudhia, while among street names, Thanon Rajavithi could come out as Thanon Ratwithi – and it's not unheard of to find one spelling posted at one end of a road, with another at the opposite end. See p.247 for an introduction to the Thai language.

When to go

Bangkok's climate is governed by three seasons, though in reality the city sits firmly within the tropics and so enjoys warm days and nights year-round. The so-called **cool season**, which runs from November to February, is the most pleasant time to visit; days are invariably bright and clear, and temperatures average a manageable 27°C (though they can still reach a broiling 31°C at midday). This is high season for the tourist industry, so rooms and flights are at a premium and well worth booking in advance; prices shoot up further for the Christmas and New Year period. March sees the beginning of the **hot season**, when temperatures can rise to 36°C, and continue to do so beyond the end of April. During these sweltering months you may find yourself spending more money than at other times, simply in order to secure the benefits of air-conditioning, whether in hotel rooms, restaurants, taxis or buses. The daily downpours that characterize the **rainy season** can come as a

City of Angels

When Rama I was crowned in 1782, he gave his new capital a grand 43-syllable name to match his ambitious plans for the building of the city. Since then 21 more syllables have been added.

Krungthepmahanakhornboworn-ratanakosinmahintarayutthaya-mahadilokpopnopparatratchathani-buriromudomratchaniwetmahasath-anamornpimanavatarnsathitsakka-thattiyavisnukarprasit is Guinness-certified as the longest place name in the world and roughly translates as "Great city of angels, the supreme repository of divine jewels, the great land unconquerable, the grand and prominent realm, the royal and delightful capital city full of nine noble gems, the highest royal dwelling and grand palace, the divine shelter and living place of the reincarnated spirits". Fortunately, all Thais refer to the city simply as Krung Thep ("City of Angels"), though plenty can recite the full name at the drop of a hat. Bangkok – "Village of the Plum Olive" – was the name of the original village on the Thonburi side; with remarkable persistence, it has remained in use by foreigners since the 1660s, when the French built a short-lived garrison fort in the area.

welcome relief, though being hot and wet is a sensation that doesn't appeal to everyone. The rainy season varies in length and intensity from year to year, but usually starts with a bang in May, gathers force between June and August, and comes to a peak in September and October, when whole districts of the capital are flooded. Rain rarely lasts all day however, so as long as you're armed with an umbrella there's no reason to reschedule your trip – and you'll get more for your money, too, as many hotels and airlines drop their prices right down at this time of year.

Average daily temperatures and rainfall

	Jan	Feb	Mar	Apr	May	Jun	Jul	Aug	Sep	Oct	Nov	Dec
Bangkok												
Max/min (ºC)	28/21	28/21	29/21	30/22	31/23	31/23	30/23	31/23	31/23	30/23	29/23	28/22
Max/min (ºF)	82/70	82/70	84/70	86/72	88/73	88/73	86/73	88/73	88/73	86/73	84/73	82/72
Rainfall (mm)	11	28	31	72	190	152	158	187	320	231	57	9

20

things not to miss

It's not possible to see everything Bangkok has to offer on a short trip – and we don't suggest you try. What follows is a subjective selection of the highlights, from extravagant palaces and frenetic markets to tranquil neighbourhoods and cutting-edge shopping, plus great day-trip destinations around the city. They're arranged in colour-coded categories to help you find the very best things to see, do and experience. All entries have a page reference to take you straight into the guide, where you can find out more.

01 The Grand Palace Page **59** • Sheltering Thailand's holiest temple, Wat Phra Kaeo, and its most sacred image, the Emerald Buddha, this huge complex is a beautiful kaleidoscope of strange colours and shapes.

02 Thanon Khao San Page **74** • Legendary hub for Southeast Asian backpackers: the place for cheap sleeps, baggy trousers and tall tales.

03 Ayutthaya Page **133** • Razed by the Burmese, the old capital is a grassy, brooding graveyard of temples, an hour to the north by train.

04 Wat Arun Page **97** • The Temple of Dawn looks great from the river – and even better close up.

05 **63rd-floor sundowner** Page **189** • Fine cocktails and jaw-dropping views, especially at sunset, at The Sky Bar and Distil.

06 **Songkhran** Page **40** • Thai New Year is the excuse for a national waterfight – don't plan on getting much done if you come in mid-April, just join in the fun.

07 Jim Thompson's House
Page **107** • An elegant and very personal museum of Thai crafts and architecture.

08 Contemporary design
Page **205** • Traditional East meets minimalist West.

09 Cycling the city Page **31** •
Venture beyond the downtown gloss on a bicycle tour through the capital's rural fringes.

10 Vimanmek Palace Page **101** • This elegant late-nineteenth-century summer palace was built from golden teakwood, without a single nail.

12 Erawan Shrine Page **111** •
The full spiritual monty: Buddhism, Hinduism and animism, dancing, lottery tickets and enough jasmine and gold to knock you out.

11 Thai cookery classes
Page **48** • Insider tips on everything from five-star cuisine to fruit-carving and vegetarian curries.

13 Wat Pho Page **66** • This lavish and lively temple is home to the awesome Reclining Buddha and a great massage school.

14 **Traditional Thai Puppet Theatre** Page **197** • The last troupe of its kind, this is the only authentic form of Thai dance-drama performed to a high standard every night of the week.

15 **Chatuchak Weekend Market** Page **122** • Bangkok's top shopping experience features over eight thousand stalls selling everything from hill-tribe jewellery to designer lamps.

16 **Thai boxing** Page **198** • Nightly bouts at the national stadia are accompanied by live music and frenetic betting.

17 **Traditional massage** Page **200** • Combining elements of acupressure and yoga, a pleasantly brutal way to help shed jet lag, or simply to end the day.

19 **National Museum** Page **70** •
The cornucopia of Thailand's artistic heritage, ranging from sculptural treasures to fantastic royal funeral chariots.

18 **A boat trip on the Thonburi canals** Page **95**
• The best way to explore the city's old-fashioned waterside communities.

20 **Muang Boran Ancient City** Page **130** • Escape from the city to this attractively landscaped open-air museum, which features beautifully crafted replicas of Thailand's finest monuments.

Basics

Basics

www.roughguides.com

Getting there

At the time of writing, all international flights into Bangkok are using the capital's new Suvarnabhumi Airport (coded "BKK"); there is however talk of resurrecting the old Don Muang Airport ("DMK") for low-cost flights in the future. See p.26 for more information about both airports.

Air fares to Bangkok generally depend on the **season**, with the highest being from approximately mid-November to mid-February, when the weather is best (with premium rates charged for flights between mid-December and New Year), and in July and August to coincide with school holidays. You will need to book several months in advance to get reasonably priced tickets during these peak periods.

Flights from the UK and Ireland

The fastest and most comfortable way of reaching Bangkok **from the UK** is to fly nonstop from London with Qantas/British Airways, Thai Airways or Eva Airways, a journey time of about eleven and a half hours. These airlines usually keep their prices competitive, at around £500/730 plus tax in low season/high season. Fares on indirect scheduled flights to Bangkok are always cheaper than nonstop flights and start at £380/550 plus tax, though these journeys can take anything from two to twelve hours longer.

There are no nonstop flights from any **regional airports** in Britain or from any **Irish airports**, and rather than routing via London, you may find it convenient to fly to another hub such as Frankfurt (with Lufthansa), Zurich (with Swiss), Abu Dhabi (with Etihad) or Dubai (with Emirates), and take a connecting flight from there. Return flights from Newcastle upon Tyne with Emirates, for example, with good connections in Dubai, currently start at around £530, including taxes. Flying from Dublin via Amsterdam with Aer Lingus and China Airlines costs around €800.

Flights from the US and Canada

There are no nonstop flights **from North America** to Bangkok, as Thai Airways recently abandoned its "ultra-long-haul" services from New York and Los Angeles and now only flies from LA via Osaka (5 weekly). However, plenty of other airlines run daily flights to Bangkok from major **East and West Coast cities**, with only **one stop** en route; it's generally easier to find a reasonable fare on flights via Asia than via Europe, even if you're departing from the East Coast. From New York expect to pay around US$1150/1350 return in low season/high season, including taxes; from LA US$950/1150. Air Canada has the most convenient service to Bangkok from the largest number of **Canadian cities**; from Vancouver, expect to pay around Can$1450/1600 in low season/high season; from Toronto, Can$1650/1825. Cheaper rates are often available if you're prepared to make two or three stops and take more time.

Minimum **flying times**, including stopovers, are twenty hours from New York or Toronto (westbound or eastbound), nineteen hours thirty minutes from LA, eighteen hours from Vancouver.

Flights from Australia and New Zealand

There's no shortage of **scheduled flights** to Bangkok **from Australia**, with direct services from major cities operated by Thai Airways, Qantas/British Airways, Jetstar and Emirates (around nine hours from Sydney and Perth), and plenty of indirect flights via Asian hubs, which take at least eleven and a half hours. There's often not much difference between the fares on nonstop and indirect flights, which start from around Aus$700/1200 (excluding taxes) in low/high season from Sydney and most major eastern Australian cities. Fares from Perth and Darwin are up to Aus$100/200 cheaper.

From New Zealand, Thai Airways runs nonstop twelve-hour flights between Auckland and Bangkok, charging from NZ\$1100/1700 (excluding taxes) in low/high season. Qantas/British Airways and Emirates flights from Auckland make brief stops in Sydney, adding at least a couple of hours to the trip, and other major Asian airlines offer indirect flights via their hubs (from seventeen hours): fares for indirect flights also start at about NZ\$1100/1700. From Christchurch and Wellington you'll pay NZ\$150–300 more than from Auckland.

Flights from South Africa

From South Africa, Thai Airways, code-sharing with South African Airways, operates three nonstop flights a week from Johannesburg to Bangkok, taking eleven and a half hours and costing around ZAR10,500 return in low season or ZAR12,000 in high season, including taxes. Otherwise, you'll be making a stop either in the Middle East or in Hong Kong or Southeast Asia, with fares starting at around ZAR7500/10,000 in low/high season.

Airlines

Aer Lingus Ⓦ www.aerlingus.com
Air Canada Ⓦ www.aircanada.com
Air New Zealand Ⓦ www.airnewzealand.com
Bangkok Airways Ⓦ www.bangkokair.com
Berjaya Air Ⓦ www.berjaya-air.com
British Airways Ⓦ www.ba.com
Cathay Pacific Ⓦ www.cathaypacific.com
Emirates Ⓦ www.emirates.com
Etihad Airways Ⓦ www.etihadairways.com
EVA Air Ⓦ www.evaair.com
Firefly Ⓦ www.fireflyz.com.my
Jetstar Ⓦ www.jetstar.com
Korean Air Ⓦ www.koreanair.com
Krabi Airline Ⓦ www.krabi-airline.com

Rough Guides online

Find everything you need to plan your next trip at Ⓦ www.roughguides.com. Read Rough Guides content on destinations worldwide, make use of our unique trip-planner tool, book transport and accommodation, check out other travellers' recommendations and share your own experiences.

Lufthansa Ⓦ www.lufthansa.com
Malaysia Airlines Ⓦ www.malaysiaairlines.com
Qantas Airways Ⓦ www.qantas.com
Qatar Airways Ⓦ www.qatarairways.com
Silk Air Ⓦ www.silkair.com
Singapore Airlines Ⓦ www.singaporeair.com
South African Airways Ⓦ www.flysaa.com
Swiss Ⓦ www.swiss.com
Thai Airways Ⓦ www.thaiair.com
Tiger Airways Ⓦ www.tigerairways.com

Airline offices in Bangkok

Aeroflot ☎ 02 251 0617–8; **Air Asia** ☎ 02 515 9999; **Air Canada** ☎ 02 670 0400; **Air France** ☎ 02 635 1191; **Air India** ☎ 02 653 2288; **Air New Zealand** ☎ 02 235 8280–3; **Bangkok Airways** ☎ 1771 or 02 265 5555; **British Airways** ☎ 02 627 1701; **Cathay Pacific** ☎ 02 263 0606; **China Airlines** ☎ 02 250 9888; **Druk Air** ☎ 02 237 9201–3; **Emirates** ☎ 02 664 1040; **Etihad** ☎ 02 253 0099; **Eva Air** ☎ 02 269 6288; **Finnair** ☎ 02 634 0238–9; **Garuda** ☎ 02 679 7371–2; **Gulf Air** ☎ 02 254 7931–4; **Japan Airlines** ☎ 02 649 9500; **KLM** ☎ 02 635 2400; **Korean Air** ☎ 02 635 0465–9; **Lao Airlines** ☎ 02 236 9822; **Lufthansa** ☎ 02 264 2400; **Malaysia Airlines** ☎ 02 263 0565–71; **Pakistan International (PIA)** ☎ 02 234 2961–5; **Philippine Airlines** ☎ 02 633 5713; **Qantas Airways** ☎ 02 627 1701; **Royal Brunei** ☎ 02 637 5151; **Singapore Airlines** ☎ 02 353 6000; **Sri Lankan Airlines** ☎ 02 236 8450; **Swiss** ☎ 02 204 7744; **Thai Airways** ☎ 02 356 1111; **United Airlines** ☎ 02 353 3939; **Vietnam Airlines** ☎ 02 655 4137–40.

Travel agents and tour operators worldwide

Creative Events Asia Thailand Ⓦ www.creativeeventsasia.com. Wedding specialists for everything from paperwork to the ceremony and guest accommodation.
Flight Centre US ☎ 1-866/967-5351, Canada ☎ 1-877/967-5302, UK ☎ 0870/499 0040, Australia ☎ 13 31 33, New Zealand ☎ 0800/243 544, South Africa ☎ 0860/400 727; Ⓦ www.flightcentre.com. Guarantee to offer the lowest international air fares.
North South Travel UK ☎ 01245/608 291, Ⓦ www.northsouthtravel.co.uk. Competitive travel agency, offering discounted fares worldwide. Profits are used to support projects in the developing world, especially the promotion of sustainable tourism.
Origin Asia Thailand Ⓦ www.alex-kerr.com. Cultural programmes that teach and explain Thai arts such as dance, music, martial arts, textiles, flower

offerings and cooking. Courses last from one day to a week and are held in Bangkok.

STA Travel US ☎1-800/781-4040, UK ☎0871/2300 040, Australia ☎134 782, New Zealand ☎0800/474 400, South Africa ☎0861/781 781; ⒲www.statravel .com. Worldwide specialists in independent travel. Good discounts for students and under-26s.

Telltale Travel UK ☎0800/011 2571, ⒲www .telltaletravel.co.uk. Tailor-made tours that aim to offer as authentic an experience as possible, with accommodation mainly in upscale homestays in Bangkok and beyond.

Trailfinders UK ☎0845/058 5858, Republic of Ireland ☎01/677 7888, Australia ☎1300/780 212; ⒲www.trailfinders.com. One of the best-informed and most efficient agents for independent travellers.

Travel Cuts US ☎1-800/592-CUTS, Canada ☎1-866/246-9762; ⒲www.travelcuts.com. Popular, long-established specialists in budget travel, including student and youth discount offers.

USIT Republic of Ireland ☎01/602 1906, Northern Ireland ☎028/9032 7111, with branches in Athlone, Belfast, Cork, Dublin, Galway, Limerick and Waterford; ⒲www.usit.ie. Ireland's main outlet for discounted, youth and student fares.

Travel agents and tour operators in Bangkok

Asian Trails 9th Floor, SG Tower, 161/1 Soi Mahadlek Luang 3, Thanon Rajdamri ☎02 626 2000, ⒲www.asiantrails.net. Sells flights and tours and runs scheduled and private transfers from Bangkok hotels and the airport.

Diethelm Travel 12th Floor, Kian Gwan Building II, 140/1 Thanon Witthayu ☎02 660 7000, ⒲www .diethelmtravel.com. Especially good for travel to Burma, Cambodia, Laos and Vietnam.

ETC (Educational Travel Centre) Ground floor, Royal (Ratanakosin) Hotel, 2 Thanon Rajdamnoen Klang, Banglamphu ☎02 224 0043; 180 Thanon Khao San, Banglamphu ☎02 629 1885; and 5/3 Soi Ngam Duphli ☎02 286 9424; ⒲www.etc.co.th. Sells air tickets and Thailand tours.

Jysk New Road Guest House, 1216/1 Thanon Charoen Krung, between Sois 34 and 36 ☎02 630 6994–8, ⒲www.jysktravel.com. A reliable agent for train, bus and air tickets, as well as their own unusual tours.

Olavi Travel Opposite Gullivers' Tavern at 53 Thanon Chakrabongse, Banglamphu ☎02 629 4711–3,

---

Six steps to a better kind of travel

At Rough Guides we are passionately committed to travel. We feel strongly that only through travelling do we truly come to understand the world we live in and the people we share it with – plus tourism has brought a great deal of **benefit** to developing economies around the world over the last few decades. But the extraordinary growth in tourism has also damaged some places irreparably, and of course **climate change** is exacerbated by most forms of transport, especially flying. This means that now more than ever it's important to **travel thoughtfully** and **responsibly**, with respect for the cultures you're visiting – not only to derive the most benefit from your trip but also to preserve the best bits of the planet for everyone to enjoy. At Rough Guides we feel there are six main areas in which you can make a difference:

- Consider what you're contributing to the **local economy**, and how much the services you use do the same, whether it's through employing local workers and guides or sourcing locally grown produce and local services.
- Consider the **environment** on holiday as well as at home. Water is scarce in many developing destinations, and the biodiversity of local flora and fauna can be adversely affected by tourism. Try to patronize businesses that take account of this.
- Travel with a purpose, not just to tick off experiences. Consider **spending longer** in a place, and getting to know it and its people.
- Give thought to how often you **fly**. Try to avoid short hops by air and more harmful night flights.
- Consider **alternatives to flying**, travelling instead by bus, train, boat and even by bike or on foot where possible.
- Make your trips "**climate neutral**" via a reputable carbon offset scheme. All Rough Guide flights are offset, and every year we donate money to a variety of charities devoted to combating the effects of climate change.

Ⓦ www.olavi.com. Sells air tickets and budget transfers.

Royal Exclusive 9 The Place, 18/2 Thanon Chan ☏ 02 676 4182–7, Ⓦ www.royalexclusive.com. Good for travel to Burma, Cambodia, Laos and Vietnam, and also sells air and train tickets.

STA Travel 14th Floor, Wall Street Tower, 33 Thanon Suriwong ☏ 02 236 0262, Ⓦ www.statravel.co.th. The Bangkok branch of the worldwide chain is a reliable outlet for cheap international flights.

Thai Overlander 407 Thanon Sukhumvit, between sois 21 and 23, ☏ 02 258 4778–80, Ⓦ www .thaioverlander.com. Helpful place selling flights, train tickets and day-trips.

From neighbouring countries

Sharing **land borders** with Burma, Laos, Cambodia and Malaysia, Thailand works well as part of many overland itineraries, both across Asia and between Europe and Australia. Bangkok is also one of the major regional flight hubs for Southeast Asia.

The main restrictions on overland routes in and out of Thailand are determined by **visas**, and by where the permitted land crossings lie. For a guide to Thai visa rules see p.24. Details of visa requirements for travel to Thailand's immediate neighbours are outlined below, but should be double-checked before you travel. Contact details for **Asian embassies** in Bangkok are given on p.49. Many Khao San tour agents offer to get your visa for you, but beware: some are reportedly **faking the stamps**, which could get you in pretty serious trouble, so it's safer to go to the embassy yourself.

From Burma

At the time of writing, there is no overland access from **Burma** into Thailand and access in the opposite direction is mostly restricted to day-trips. There are, however, numerous flights between Bangkok and Burma, and tourists who intend to enter Burma by air can buy four-week tourist visas at the Burmese embassy in Bangkok for B800; apply to the embassy and you can collect the next day.

From Cambodia

At the time of writing, six overland crossings on the **Thai-Cambodian border** are open to non-Thais, but regulations are changeable so check with the Cambodian Embassy in Bangkok and consult Ⓦ www.talesofasia .com/cambodia-overland.htm and Ⓦ www .thaivisa.com for travellers' recent experiences. All Cambodian borders open daily from 7am to 8pm. Numerous **flights** operate between Bangkok and Cambodia.

Visas for Cambodia are issued to travellers on arrival at Phnom Penh and Siem Reap airports, and at all land borders; you need US$20 and two photos for this. If you do need to buy an advance thirty-day visa, you can do so online or from the Cambodian Embassy in Bangkok. This costs about B1000; apply before noon and you can collect your visa the following day after 5pm.

The most commonly used land crossing is at **Poipet**, which lies just across the border from the Thai town of **Aranyaprathet** and has public-transport connections with Sisophon, Siem Reap and Phnom Penh. There are two trains a day from Arany-aprathet to Bangkok (about 6hr), departing at 6.35am and 1.35pm, and two in the opposite direction, departing Bangkok at 5.55am and 1.05pm. Tuk-tuks will take you the 4km between the train station and the border post. Buses also run from Arany-aprathet to Bangkok's Northern (Mo Chit) Bus Terminal (at least hourly until 7pm; 4hr 30min). In Aranyaprathet you'll need to take a tuk-tuk from the bus station to the border. It's also possible to buy a **through-ticket to Siem Reap** from Bangkok from almost any travel agent in Banglamphu for B400–600 but this option is dogged by **scams** (including a visa "service charge" scam, described in detail at Ⓦ www.talesofasia .com/cambodia-overland-bkksr-package .htm), can take up to ten hours longer than doing it independently, often travels via the less convenient Pailin or O'Smach border crossings instead, and nearly always uses clapped-out buses or even pick-ups, despite the promised "luxury" bus.

The other main border crossing is from **Koh Kong** (with transport to and from Sihanoukville and Phnom Penh) across the Dong Tong River estuary to **Hat Lek** near Trat on Thailand's east coast; this is the fastest option if you're travelling nonstop from Bangkok to Cambodia. Minibuses run from

Hat Lek to Trat, 91km northwest (1hr–1hr 30min; B120), where you can pick up a bus straight to Bangkok's Eastern or Northern Bus Terminal (4hr 30min–6hr). In the reverse direction, buses run frequently from Bangkok to Trat, where minibuses depart for Hat Lek every 45 minutes between 6am and 5pm.

From Laos and Vietnam

Tourists can cross into Thailand at five points along the **Lao** border, all of which have frequent bus connections with Bangkok's Northern (Mo Chit) Bus Terminal: Houayxai (for Chiang Khong; 10 daily buses to and from Bangkok; 13–14hr); Vientiane (for Nong Khai; frequent buses to and from Bangkok; 11hr; and 3 trains daily; 11–13hr); Khammouan (aka Tha Khaek, for Nakhon Phanom; frequent buses to and from Bangkok; 12hr); Savannakhet (for Mukdahan; frequent buses to and from Bangkok; 11hr); and Pakxe (for Chong Mek; daily buses to and from Bangkok; 11hr). In addition there are numerous **flights** between Bangkok and Laos.

Visas are required for all non-Thai visitors to Laos. A thirty-day **visa on arrival** can be bought for US$30–42 (depending on your nationality), plus one photo, at Vientiane, Louang Phabang and Pakxe airports, and all the above-listed land borders. Or you can buy one in advance from the Lao Embassy in Bangkok (B400–1700 if collected the following day, or an extra B200 to collect it within the hour).

If you have the right Lao visa and Vietnamese exit stamp, you can travel **from Vietnam** to Thailand via Savannakhet in a matter of hours; you'll need to use Vietnam's Lao Bao border crossing, west of Dong Ha, where you can catch a bus to Savannakhet and then another bus across the Mekong bridge to Mukdahan. All travellers into Vietnam need to buy a **visa in advance**. Thirty-day visas can take up to four working days to process at the embassy in Bangkok and cost B1000.

From Malaysia and Singapore

Travelling between Thailand and **Malaysia and Singapore** has in the past been a straightforward and very commonly used overland route, with plentiful connections by bus, minibus, share-taxi and train, most of them routed through the southern Thai city and transport hub of Hat Yai. However, because of the ongoing sectarian **violence in Thailand's deep south**, all major Western governments are currently advising people not to travel to or through Songkhla, Pattani, Yala and Narathiwat provinces, unless essential (and consequently most insurance companies are not covering travel there). This encompasses Hat Yai and the following border crossings to and from Malaysia: at Padang Besar, on the main rail line connecting Butterworth in Malaysia (and, ultimately, Kuala Lumpur and Singapore) with Hat Yai and Bangkok; at Sungai Kolok, terminus of a railway line from Hat Yai and Bangkok, and at adjacent Ban Taba, both of which are connected by road to nearby Kota Bharu in Malaysia; and at the road crossings at Sadao, south of Hat Yai, and at Betong, south of Yala. (The routes towards Kota Bharu and Betong pass through particularly volatile territory, with martial law declared in Pattani, Yala and Narathiwat provinces; however, martial law is not in effect in Hat Yai itself nor the districts of Songkhla province through which the Bangkok–Butterworth rail line and the Hat Yai–Sadao road pass.) For up-to-the-minute advice, consult your government travel advisory (see p.44).

Nevertheless, the provinces of Trang and Satun on the west coast are not affected, and it's still perfectly possible to travel **overland via Satun**: by ferry to Satun's Thammalang pier from Kuala Perlis (45min) or the island of Langkawi (1hr), or by air-con minibus between Kangar and Ban Khuan. There are five daily buses from Satun to Bangkok's Southern Bus Terminal and the journey takes sixteen hours.

In addition, there are numerous daily **flights** from Malaysia and Singapore to Bangkok.

Most Western tourists can spend thirty days in Malaysia and fourteen days in Singapore without having bought a **visa** beforehand, and there are useful Thai embassies or consulates in Kuala Lumpur, Kota Bahru, Penang and Singapore (see p.25).

Visas

There are three main entry categories for visitors to Thailand; for all of them, under International Air Travel Association rules, your passport should be valid for at least six months. As visa requirements are subject to frequent change, you should always consult before departure a Thai embassy or consulate, a reliable travel agent, or the Thai Ministry of Foreign Affairs' website at ⓦ www.mfa.go .th/web/2637.php. For further, unofficial but usually reliable, details on all visa matters, go to ⓦ www.thaivisa.com and especially their various moderated forums.

Most Western passport holders (that includes citizens of the UK, Ireland, the US, Canada, Australia, New Zealand and South Africa) are allowed to enter the country for short **stays** without having to apply for a visa – officially termed the **tourist visa exemption**. You'll be granted a thirty-day stay at an international airport but, in a recent change, only fifteen days at an overland border; the period of stay will be stamped into your passport by immigration officials upon entry. You're supposed to be able to somehow show proof of means of living while in the country (B20,000 per person, B40,000 per family), and in theory you may be put back on the next plane without it or sent back to get a sixty-day tourist visa from the nearest Thai embassy, but this is unheard of. You are also required to show proof of air tickets to leave Thailand again within the allotted time, though this is not often checked by Thai immigration authorities. However, if you have a one-way air ticket to Thailand and no evidence of onward travel arrangements, it's best to buy a tourist visa in advance: some airlines will stop you boarding the plane without one, as they would be liable for flying you back to your point of origin if you did happen to be stopped.

If you're fairly certain you may want to stay longer than fifteen/thirty days, then from the outset you should apply for a **sixty-day tourist visa** from a Thai embassy or consulate, accompanying your application – which generally takes several days to process – with your passport and two photos. The sixty-day visa currently costs, for example, US$35 or £28 in the UK; multiple-entry versions are available, costing

US$35 or £28 per entry, which may be handy if you're going to be leaving and re-entering Thailand. Ordinary tourist visas are valid for three months, ie you must enter Thailand within three months of the visa being issued by the Thai embassy or consulate, while multiple-entry versions are valid for six months. Visa application forms can be downloaded from the Thai Ministry of Foreign Affairs' website (see opposite).

Thai embassies also consider applications for **ninety-day non-immigrant visas** (£45 or US$65, for example, single entry, £100 or US$175 multiple-entry) as long as you can offer a reason for your visit, such as study, business or visiting family/friends (there are different categories of non-immigrant visa for which different levels of proof are needed). As it can be a hassle to organize a ninety-day visa, it's generally easier to apply for a thirty-day extension to your sixty-day visa once inside Thai borders.

It's not a good idea to **overstay** your visa limits. Once you're at the airport or the border, you'll have to pay a fine of B500 per day before you can leave Thailand. More importantly, however, if you're in the country with an expired visa and you get involved with police or immigration officials for any reason, however trivial, they are obliged to take you to court, possibly imprison you, and deport you.

Border runs, extensions and re-entry permits

Setting aside the caveats about proof of funds and onward tickets above, it's generally possible to get a new fifteen-day tourist visa exemption by hopping **across** the border into a neighbouring country such as Cambodia and back. Tourist visa exemptions can be **extended** within Thailand for up to a further ten days, or sixty-day tourist visas for a further thirty days, at the discretion of immigration officials; extensions cost B1900 and are issued over the counter at immigration offices (*kaan khao muang*; ☏1111 for 24hr information in English, ⓦwww.immigration.go.th). You'll need two photos as well, plus two photocopies of the main pages of your passport including your Thai arrival card, arrival stamp and visa. Immigration offices also issue **re-entry permits** (B1000 single re-entry, B3800 multiple) if you want to leave the country and come back again while maintaining the validity of your existing visa.

The **immigration office in Bangkok** is on the northern outskirts of the city, southwest of Don Muang airport (see map, p.123), inside Building B, Bangkok Government Centre, Thanon Chaeng Watthana (Mon–Fri 8.30am–4.30pm; ☏02 287 3101–10); the nearest overground train station is Lak Si (from Hualamphong) or it's a 15min taxi ride from either BTS Mochit or Chatuchak Park subway. Many Khao San tour agents offer to get your visa extension for you, but beware: some are reportedly faking the stamps, which could get you into serious trouble.

Thai embassies and consulates abroad

For a full listing of Thai diplomatic missions abroad, consult the Thai Ministry of Foreign Affairs' website at ⓦwww.mfa.go.th/web/10.php.

Australia 111 Empire Circuit, Yarralumla, Canberra ACT 2600 ☏02/6206 0100, ⓦcanberra.thaiembassy.org; plus consulate at 131 Macquarrie St, Sydney, NSW 2000 ☏02/9241 2542–3, ⓦthaiconsulatesydney.org.

Burma 94 Pyay Rd, Dagon Township, Rangoon ☏01/226721.

Cambodia 196 Preah Norodom Blvd, Sangkat Tonle Bassac, Khan Chamcar Mon, Phnom Penh ☏023/726306–10, ⓦwww.thaiembassy.org/phnompenh.

Canada 180 Island Park Drive, Ottawa, ON, K1Y 0A2 ☏613/722-4444, ⓦwww.magma.ca/~thaiott; plus consulate at 1040 Burrard St, Vancouver, BC, V6Z 2R9 ☏604/687-1143, ⓦwww.thaicongenvancouver.org.

Laos Vientiane ⓦwww.thaiembassy.org/vientiane: embassy at Avenue Kaysone Phomvihane, Saysettha District ☏021/214581–2, consular section at Unit 15 Bourichane Rd, Ban Phone Si Nuan, Muang Si Sattanak ☏021/453916; plus consulate at Khanthabouly District, Savannakhet Province, PO Box 513 ☏041/212373.

Malaysia 206 Jalan Ampang, 50450 Kuala Lumpur ☏03/2148 8222, ⓦwww.thaiembassy.org/kualalumpur; plus consulates at 4426 Jalan Pengkalan Chepa, 15400 Kota Bharu ☏09/748 2545; and 1 Jalan Tunku Abdul Rahman, 10350 Penang ☏04/226 9484.

New Zealand 2 Cook St, PO Box 17226, Karori, Wellington ☏04/476 8616–9, ⓦwww.thaiembassynz.org.nz.

Singapore 370 Orchard Rd, Singapore 238870 ☏6737 2158, ⓦwww.thaiembassy.sg.

South Africa 428 Pretorius/Hill St, Arcadia, Pretoria 0083 ☏012/342 5470, ⓦwww.thaiembassy.co.za.

UK and Ireland 29–30 Queens Gate, London SW7 5JB ☏020/7589 2944, ⓦwww.thaiembassyuk.org.uk. Visa applications by post are not accepted here, but can be sent to various honorary consulates, including those in Hull (ⓦwww.thaiconsul-uk.com) and Dublin (ⓦwww.thaiconsulateireland.com).

US 1024 Wisconsin Ave NW, Suite 401, Washington, DC 20007 ☏202/944-3600, ⓦwww.thaiembdc.org; plus consulates at 700 North Rush St, Chicago, IL 60611 ☏312/664-3129, ⓦwww.thaichicago.net; 611 North Larchmont Blvd, 2nd Floor, Los Angeles, CA 90004 ☏323/962-9574, ⓦwww.thai-la.net; and 351 E 52nd St, New York, NY 10022 ☏212/754-1770, ⓦwww.thaiconsulnewyork.com.

Vietnam 63–65 Hoang Dieu St, Hanoi ☏04/823-5092–3; plus consulate at 77 Tran Quoc Thao St, District 3, Ho Chi Minh City ☏08/932-7637–8, ⓦwww.thaiembassy.org/hochiminhcity.

Arrival

Unless you arrive in Bangkok by train, be prepared for a long trip into the city centre. Suvarnabhumi Airport is 25km out and the three long-distance bus stations are not much closer in, though at least the Northern Terminal is fairly near the Skytrain and subway, while the Eastern Terminal is close to a Skytrain station.

By air

Bangkok's main airport is **Suvarnabhumi** (coded "BKK" and pronounced "soo-wanna-poom"; flight information ☎02 132 0000, airport information counter ☎02 132 9324–9; ⓦwww.bangkokairportonline.com), 25km east of central Bangkok between Highways 7 and 34. At the time of writing, the only scheduled flights using the old **Don Muang Airport** (coded "DMK"; domestic departures ☎02 535 1192, domestic arrivals ☎02 535 1253; ⓦwww.donmuangairportonline.com), 25km north of the city, were Nok Air and One-Two-Go's domestic services. However, there's been a fair bit of politically motivated toing and froing of domestic airlines between the two airports over the past few years: it may well be that the woefully underused Don Muang will again close to scheduled flights altogether, or it might, conceivably, be allowed to handle a greater range of low-cost flights. If you do wind up at Don Muang, the best way to get into the city centre is by licensed, metered taxi from the desk outside Arrivals (about B300–350).

Suvarnabhumi Airport

At Suvarnabhumi, which bears more of a resemblance to a shopping mall than an airport, you'll find plenty of 24-hour exchange booths, ATMs, cafés and restaurants, as well as several bookshops, pharmacies and internet cafés. In the **arrivals hall** on Floor 2, there's a tourist police booth; two TAT information desks, which are helpful but marooned at the hall's far east and west corners (daily 8am–10pm; ☎02 134 0040); and Thai Hotels Association accommodation desks, with prices generally cheaper than rack rates. Car-rental companies, including Avis and Budget

(see p.48), have booths beside the luggage conveyor belts (though you'll have to pick your car up from the Public Transportation Center – see opposite). There are pricey, 24-hour left-luggage depots, charging B100 per item per day, both in arrivals and in the **departures hall** on Floor 4, which is also home to a post office. On Floor 3, there's a 24-hour clinic run by Samitivej Hospital.

Airport transport

On the other side of the huge airport complex from the terminal building stands the Public Transportation Center, accessible via a free, ten-minute ride on an Express shuttle bus from Gate 5 outside arrivals or Gate 10 outside departures – be sure not to confuse these with the much slower Ordinary shuttle buses, which ferry airport staff around the complex. However, because of the inconvenience involved, taxis and many buses now pick up and drop off at the terminal building, as detailed below. The high-speed Suvarnabhumi Airport **rail link** (SARL), that's currently reported to be opening in early 2010, will be the quickest means of getting downtown from the airport terminal. Nonstop Airport Express trains to the City Air Terminal at Makkasan Station (which connects with the subway system at Phetchaburi station) are planned to take about fifteen minutes and cost B150, while stopping Airport City Line services to Phaya Thai (an interchange with the Skytrain system), including stops at Makkasan and Thanon Rajprarop, should take around thirty minutes and cost B45. The TAT offices in the arrivals hall have full details of all airport transport.

The most economical way of getting into the city is by **public air-con bus** (B22–34) or **minibus** (B40–70), with the following routes, mostly 24-hour, likely to be useful to visitors:

#551, from Gate 1 or 8, Floor 1 of the terminal building, to Victory Monument, which has a Skytrain (see p.34) station; #552 from the **Public Transportation Center** along Thanon Sukhumvit via Ekamai (for the Skytrain), turning left along Thanon Ratchadapisek to Khlong Toey via Queen Sirikit Convention Centre (for the subway); and #556 from Gate 8, Floor 1 of the terminal building to Democracy Monument, Thanon Rajdamnoen Klang (for Banglamphu guest houses) and the Southern Bus Terminal.

The dedicated, air-conditioned **airport bus** (daily 5am–midnight; at least every 30min; B150) is fine for lone travellers, but at most times of the day, the convenience of a taxi is going to be cheaper for a group of two or more, or at least not much more expensive. These buses depart from outside Gate 8, Floor 1 of the terminal building, covering four routes: #AE1 terminates at Sala Daeng Skytrain station, via Pratunam, Thanon Rajdamri and a circuit west along Thanon Suriwong and east along Thanon Silom; #AE2 goes to Thanon Khao San in Banglamphu, via Pratunam, Thanon Phetchaburi, Democracy Monument, Sanam Luang, Thanon Phra Arthit, Thanon Phra Sumen and Thanon Chakrabongse; #AE3 runs the length of Sukhumvit and Ploenchit roads, via Ekamai Skytrain, to the Erawan Shrine, before doubling back via Thanon Phetchaburi to Sukhumvit Soi 3; and #AE4 runs to Hualamphong Station, via Victory Monument, Siam Square, Thanon Phrayathai and Thanon Rama IV.

Taxis to the centre are comfortable, air-conditioned and reasonably priced, although the driving can be hairy. Walk past the pricey taxis and limousines on offer within the baggage hall and arrivals hall and ignore any tout who may offer a cheap ride in an unlicensed and unmetered vehicle, as newly arrived travellers are seen as easy prey for robbery, and the cabs are untraceable. Licensed and metered public taxis are operated from clearly signposted, official counters, outside the arrivals hall's Gates 3 and 10. Even including the B50 airport pick-up fee and around B70 tolls for the overhead expressways, a journey to Thanon Silom downtown, for example, should set you back around B350, depending on the traffic.

Airport accommodation

With time to kill and money to spare before your onward journey, you might want to rest and clean up in one of the **day rooms** in the airport's transit area (US$80 for one person, US$87 for 2 people, for 4hr). Day rooms (B4500 from 8am–6pm, or B3000 for 4hr) are also available at the airport **hotel**, the four-star *Novotel Suvarnabhumi* (℡02 131 1111, ⓦwww.accorhotels.com; ➒). Offering Thai, Japanese, Chinese and international restaurants, a swimming pool and fitness centre, the *Novotel* is a ten-minute walk from the terminal building – or catch the shuttle bus from outside Gate 4, Floor 2. Just outside the airport complex, to the north near Highway 7, *Queens Garden Resort* (℡02 172 6114, ⓦwww.queensgardenresort.net; ➎) is a more economical choice, providing hot water, air-con, minibar and satellite TV in all bedrooms and 24-hour pick-ups (B150).

By train

Travelling to Bangkok by **train** from Malaysia and most parts of Thailand, you arrive at **Hualamphong Station**, which is centrally located, at the southern end of the subway line. The most useful of the city buses serving Hualamphong is the #159 (non-air-con), which runs west to Democracy Monument, Rajdamnoen Klang (for Banglamphu) and the Southern Bus Terminal, and east to MBK, Siam Square, Chatuchak and the Northern Bus Terminal. See box on p.32 for other bus routes via Hualamphong.

Station **facilities** include an exchange booth, several ATMs, an internet centre and a makeshift **left-luggage** "office", actually just bags piled up in a corner (daily 4am–11pm; B30–80 per day, depending on size). A more economical, and possibly more secure place to store baggage is the *TT2 Guest House* (see p.164), about fifteen minutes' walk from the station (B15–20 per item per day).

One service the station does not provide is itinerant tourist assistance staff – anyone who comes up to you in or around the station concourse and offers help/information/transport or ticket-booking services is almost certainly a **con-artist**, however many official-looking ID tags are hanging round their neck. This is a well-established scam to fleece new arrivals and should be avoided at all costs (see p.42 for more details). For train-related questions, contact the 24-hour "Information" counter close by the departures board. The station area is also fertile ground for **dishonest tuk-tuk drivers**, so you'll need to be extra suspicious to avoid them – take a metered taxi or public transport instead.

By bus

Buses come to a halt at a number of far-flung spots. All services from the north and northeast terminate at the **Northern and Northeastern Bus Terminal (Mo Chit)** on Thanon Kamphaeng Phet 2 (though a move to Thanon Chaeng Watthana, even further to the north, is being talked about); some east-coast buses also use Mo Chit, including several daily services from Pattaya, Rayong (for Ko Samet), Chanthaburi and Trat (for Ko Chang and the Cambodian border). The quickest way to get into the city centre from Mo Chit is to hop onto the Skytrain at Mo Chit Station, or the subway at the adjacent Chatuchak Park Station, fifteen minutes' walk from the bus terminal on Thanon Phaholyo-thin, and then change onto a city bus if necessary. Otherwise, it's a long bus or taxi ride into town: city buses from the Northern Bus Terminal include ordinary #159 to Siam Square, Hualamphong Station, Banglamphu and the Southern Bus Terminal; and ordinary and air-conditioned #3, and air-conditioned #509 and #512 to Banglamphu; for details of these routes see p.32.

Most buses from the east coast use the **Eastern Bus Terminal (Ekamai)** between sois 40 and 42 on Thanon Sukhumvit. This bus station is right beside the Ekamai Skytrain stop and is also served by lots of city buses, including air-conditioned #511 to Banglamphu and the Southern Bus Terminal (see box on p.32 for details), or you can take a taxi down Soi 63 to Tha Ekamai, a pier on Khlong Saen Saeb, to pick up the canal boat service to the Golden Mount near Banglamphu (see p.33). There's a left-luggage booth at the bus terminal (daily 6am–6pm; B30 per day).

Bus services from Malaysia and the south, as well as from Phetchaburi, Kanchanaburi, Damnoen Saduak, Nakhon Pathom and Samut Songkhram use the huge, airport-like **Southern Bus Terminal** (Sathaanii Sai Tai; ☎02 434 7192) at the junction of Thanon Borom Ratchonni and Thanon Phutthamon-thon Sai 1 in Taling Chan, an interminable 11km west of the Chao Phraya River and Banglamphu. Most drivers on these services make a stop to drop passengers towards the eastern end of Thanon Borom Ratchonni, much nearer Phra Pinklao Bridge and the river, before doing a time-consuming U-turn for the terminus; if you're heading across the river to Banglamphu or downtown Bangkok you should get off here, along with the majority of the other passengers.

This is also a better place to grab a **taxi** into town, as rides are faster and cheaper when started from here. **City buses** serving both this stop and Sathaanii Sai Tai include #124 for Banglamphu, #511 for Banglamphu and Thanon Sukhumvit, and #516 for Thewet and Banglamphu (see box, p.32). The bus terminal itself has lots of facilities, including a food hall, internet access, ATMs and scores of shops. The left-luggage office is beside the Black Canyon Coffee Shop, near the Information booth on the ticket-sales floor (5am–9pm; B20–60 per day).

Orientation

Bangkok can be a tricky place to get your bearings as it's huge and ridiculously congested, with largely featureless modern buildings and no obvious centre. The boldest line on the map is the Chao Phraya River, which divides the city into Bangkok proper on the east bank, and Thonburi, part of Greater Bangkok, on the west.

The historical core of Bangkok proper, site of the original royal palace, is **Ratanakosin**, cradled in a bend in the river. Three concentric canals radiate eastwards around Ratanakosin: the southern part of the area between the canals is the old-style trading enclave of **Chinatown** and Indian **Pahurat**, linked to the old palace by Thanon Charoen Krung (aka New Road); the northern part is characterized by old temples and the **Democracy Monument**, west of which is the backpackers' ghetto of **Banglamphu**. Beyond the canals to the north, **Dusit** is the site of many government buildings and the nineteenth-century palace, which is linked to Ratanakosin by the three stately avenues, Thanon Rajdamnoen Nok, Thanon Rajdamnoen Klang and Thanon Rajdamnoen Nai.

"New" Bangkok begins to the east of the canals and beyond the main rail line and Hualamphong Station, and stretches as far as the eye can see to the east and north. The main business district and most of the embassies are south of **Thanon Rama IV**, with the port of Khlong Toey at the southern edge. The diverse area north of Thanon Rama IV includes the sprawling campus of Chulalongkorn University, huge shopping centres around **Siam Square** and a variety of other businesses. A couple of blocks northeast of Siam Square stands the tallest building in Bangkok, the 84-storey **Baiyoke II Tower**, whose golden spire makes a good point of reference. To the east lies the swish residential quarter off **Thanon Sukhumvit**.

Bangkok addresses

Thai **addresses** can be confusing, as property is often numbered twice, firstly to show which real-estate lot it stands in, and then to distinguish where it is on that lot. Thus 154/7–10 Thanon Rajdamnoen means the building is on lot 154 and occupies numbers 7–10.

A minor road running off a major road is often numbered as a **soi** ("lane" or "alley", though it may be a sizeable thoroughfare), rather than given its own street name. Thanon Sukhumvit, for example, has minor roads numbered Soi 1 to Soi 103, with odd numbers on one side of the road and even on the other; so a Thanon Sukhumvit address could read something like 27/9–11 Soi 15, Thanon Sukhumvit, which would mean the property occupies numbers 9–11 on lot 27 on minor road number 15 running off Thanon Sukhumvit.

City transport

Transport can undoubtedly be a headache in a city where it's not unusual for residents to spend three hours getting to work – and these are people who know where they're going. However, the recent openings of the subway system and the elevated train network called the Bangkok Transit System, or BTS Skytrain, have radically improved movement in downtown areas of the city. Unfortunately for tourists, these systems do not stretch as far as Ratanakosin or Banglamphu, where boats still provide the best means of hopping from one sight to another.

The main form of transport in the city is **buses**, and once you've mastered the labyrinthine complexity of the route maps you'll be able to get to any part of the city, albeit slowly. Catching the various kinds of **taxi** is more expensive, and you'll still get held up by the daytime traffic jams. **Boats** are obviously more limited in their range, but they're regular and as cheap as buses, and you'll save a lot of time by using them whenever possible – a journey between Banglamphu and the GPO (General Post Office), for instance, will take around thirty minutes by water, half what it would usually take on land. The **Skytrain** and **subway** each have a similarly limited range but are also worth using whenever suitable for all or part of your journey; their networks roughly coincide with each other at the east end of Thanon Silom, at the corner of Soi Asoke and Thanon Sukhumvit, and on Thanon Phaholyothin by Chatuchak Park (Mo Chit), while the Skytrain joins up with the Chao Phraya River express boats at the vital hub of Sathorn/Saphan Taksin (Taksin Bridge). **Walking** might often be quicker than travelling by road, but the heat can be unbearable, pavements are poorly maintained and the engine fumes are stifling.

Buses

Bangkok is served by over four hundred bus routes, reputedly the world's largest bus network, on which operate three main types of bus service (though controversial plans, opposed by the transport unions and poorer commuters, to do away with non-air-con services are under discussion). On **ordinary** (non-air-con) buses, which are either red and white, blue and white, or small and green,

fares range from B7 to B8.50; most routes operate from about 4am to 10pm, but some maintain a 24-hour service (see box, p.32). **Air-conditioned** buses are either blue, orange or white (some are articulated) and charge between B12 and B25 according to distance travelled; most stop in the late evening, but a few of the more popular routes run 24-hour services. As buses can only go as fast as the car in front, which at the moment is averaging 4km per hr, you'll probably be spending a long time on each journey, so you'd be well advised to pay the extra for cool air – and the air-conditioned buses are usually less crowded, too. It's also possible to travel certain commuter routes on yellow or pink, air-conditioned private **microbuses**, which offer the certainty of a seat (no standing allowed) and generally charge a flat fare of B30.

Some of the most useful city-bus routes are described in the box on p.32; for a comprehensive roundup of bus routes in the capital, buy a copy of Bangkok Guide's *Bus Routes & Map* (see p.36), or log on to the Bangkok Mass Transit Authority website (Ⓦ www.bmta.co.th), which gives details of all city-bus routes, except microbuses and airport buses.

Boats

Bangkok was built as an amphibious city around a network of canals – or **khlongs** – and the first streets were constructed only in the second half of the nineteenth century. Many canals remain on the Thonburi side of the river, but most of those on the Bangkok side have been turned into roads. The Chao Phraya River itself is still a major transport

Tours of the city

The Bangkok Metropolitan Administration tourist office (see p.36) runs year-round **tours** of the city's historic centre in a "tram" (more like an open-sided bus), which covers a forty-minute circuit from the Grand Palace down to Wat Pho, up to Banglamphu and back to the palace (daily 9am–5pm, every 45min; B30). From mid-December to mid-January, the same office has in previous years offered night-time tours by bicycle or open-topped double-decker bus, and may do so in future years too. As part of the BMA's greening of the city, it's also possible to pick up bicycles and maps from this office, and seven other locations in and around Ratanakosin, for a self-guided tour along clearly marked cycle lanes (Aug–April Mon–Fri 10am–6pm, Sat & Sun 10am–8pm; free, passport required as deposit); unfortunately, local drivers tend to block or ignore the lanes, which makes the prospect a lot less enticing. Real Asia (℡02 665 6364, ⓦwww.realasia.net) does full-day canal and walking tours through Thonburi and leads outings by train to the historic fishing port of Samut Sakhon (both B2000, including lunch and boat trips).

Unlikely as it sounds, there are several companies offering **cycle tours** of the city's outer neighbourhoods and beyond; these are an excellent way to gain a different perspective on Thai life and offer a unique chance to see traditional communities close up. The most popular, longest-running bicycle tours are the ABC Amazing Bangkok Cyclist Tours, which start in the Thanon Sukhumvit area and take you across the river to surprisingly rural khlong- and riverside communities; tours operate every day year-round, cover up to 30km depending on the itinerary, and need to be reserved in advance through Real Asia (see above; B1000–2000 including bicycle). Bangkok Bike Rides (℡02 712 5305, ⓦwww.bangkokbikerides .com or ⓦwww.spiceroads.com; B1000–2500 per person, minimum 2 people) also operates from the Sukhumvit area and runs a programme of different daily tours within Greater Bangkok, including Ko Kred, as well as to the floating markets and canalside neighbourhoods of Damnoen Saduak (see p.144). Velo Thailand runs two different bike tours out of its cycle shop at 88 Thanon Samsen Soi 2 on the edge of Banglamphu (℡02 629 1745, ⓦwww.velothailand.com). The 1pm tour goes to Thonburi (3–4hr; B1000), while the after-dark tour (6–9pm; B1100) takes in floodlit sights including Wat Pho, Wat Arun and the Pak Khlong Talat flower market.

For details of Thonburi canal tours, see p.95; for Chao Phraya Express tourist boats, see p.32; and for dinner and cocktail cruises along the Chao Phraya River, see p.182.

route for residents and non-residents alike, forming more of a link than a barrier between the two halves of the city.

Express boats

The Chao Phraya Express Boat Company operates the vital **express-boat** (*reua duan*; ⓦwww.chaophrayaboat.co.th) services, using large water buses to plough up and down the river, between clearly signed piers (*tha*); see the colour map at the back of this book. Tha Sathorn, which gives access to the Skytrain network at Saphan Taksin Station, has been designated "Central Pier", with piers to the south of here numbered S1, S2, etc, those to the north N1, N2 and so on

– the important stops in the centre of the city are outlined in the box on p.34 and marked on our colour maps at the back of the book. In future, express-boat services may be extended downriver to Samut Prakan.

No-flag, local-line boats call at every pier between Wat Rajsingkorn, just upriver of Krung Thep Bridge, in the south, and Nonthaburi, ninety minutes away to the north, but only operate during rush hour (Mon–Fri roughly 6–8.40am & 3–6pm, every 20min). Boats do not necessarily stop at every landing – they only pull in if people want to get on or off, and when they do stop, it's not for long – so when you want to get off, be ready at the back of the boat in good time for your pier. The only boats to

Useful bus routes

For buses from Suvarnabhumi Airport, see p.26; for more details on Banglamphu bus stops and routes, see p.78.

#3 (ordinary and air-con, 24hr): **Northern Bus Terminal**–Chatuchak Weekend Market–Thanon Phaholyothin–Thanon Samsen–Thanon Phra Arthit (for **Banglamphu guest houses**)–Thanon Sanam Chai (for **Museum of Siam**)–Thanon Triphet–Memorial Bridge (for **Pak Khlong Talat**)–Taksin Monument (for **Wongwian Yai**) –Wat Suwan.

#15 (ordinary): Thanon Ratchadaphisek–Krung Thep Bridge–Thanon Charoen Krung–Thanon Silom–Thanon Rajdamri–**Siam Square**–Thanon Lan Luang–Sanam Luang–Thanon Phra Arthit (for **Banglamphu guest houses**).

#16 (ordinary and air-con): Thanon Srinarong–Thanon Samsen–**Thewet** (for guest houses)–Thanon Phitsanulok–Thanon Phrayathai–**Siam Square**–Thanon Suriwong.

#25 (ordinary and air-con, 24hr): Pak Nam (for **Ancient City** buses)–Thanon Sukhumvit–**Eastern Bus Terminal**–Siam Square–**Hualamphong Station**–Thanon Yaowarat (for **Chinatown**)–Pahurat–**Wat Pho**–Tha Chang (for the **Grand Palace**); some #25 buses (ordinary only) only go as far as Hualamphong Station, while during rush hours some #25 buses take the expressway, missing out Siam Square.

#53 circular (also anti-clockwise; ordinary): Thewet–Thanon Krung Kasem–**Hualamphong Station**–Thanon Yaowarat (for **Chinatown**)–Pahurat–Pak Khlong Talat–Thanon Maharat (for **Wat Pho** and the **Grand Palace**)–Sanam Luang (for **National Museum**)–Thanon Phra Arthit and Thanon Samsen (for **Banglamphu guest houses**)–Thewet.

#56 circular (also clockwise; ordinary, stops at 7pm): Thanon Phra Sumen–Wat Bowoniwes–Thanon Pracha Thipatai–Thanon Ratchasima (for **Vimanmek Palace**)–Thanon Rajwithi–Krung Thon Bridge–Thonburi–Phrapokklao Bridge–Thanon Chakraphet (for **Chinatown**)–Thanon Mahachai–Democracy Monument–Thanon Tanao (for **Khao San guest houses**)–Thanon Phra Sumen.

#124 (ordinary): Sanam Luang–Thanon Rajinee, near Information Centre (for **Banglamphu guest houses**)–Phra Pinklao Bridge–**Southern Bus Terminal**–Mahidol University.

run all day, every day are on the limited-stop **orange-flag** service (Nonthaburi to Wat Rajsingkorn in 1hr; roughly 6am–6.40pm, every 5–20min). Other limited-stop services run during rush hour, flying either a **yellow flag** (Nonthaburi to Tha Sathorn or Rajburana, far downriver beyond Krung Thep Bridge, in about 50min; Mon–Fri roughly 6–8.40am & 4–7pm), a **blue flag** (Nonthaburi to Tha Sathorn Mon–Fri 7–7.45am, Tha Sathorn to Nonthaburi Mon–Fri 5–6.25pm, stopping only at Wang Lang; 35min), or a **green-and-yellow flag** (Pakkred to Tha Sathorn Mon–Fri 6.15–8.05am, Tha Sathorn to Pakkred Mon–Fri 4.05–6.05pm; about 50min).

Tickets can be bought on board, and cost B9–13 on no-flag boats according to distance travelled, B14 flat rate on orange-flag boats, B19–28 on yellow-flag boats, B19–29 on blue-flag boats and B12–31 on green-and-yellow flag boats. Don't discard your ticket until you're off the boat, as the staff at some piers impose a B1 fine on anyone disembarking without one.

The Chao Phraya Express Boat Company also runs **tourist boats**, distinguished by their light-blue flags, between Sathorn (departs every 30min 9.30am–3pm on the hour and half-hour) and Phra Arthit piers (departs every 30min 10am–3.30pm on the hour and half-hour). In between (in both directions), these boats call in at Oriental, Si Phraya, Rachawongse, Saphan Phut, Thien, Maharat (near Wat Mahathat and the Grand Palace) and Wang Lang. On-board guides provide running commentaries, and a one-day ticket for unlimited trips, which also allows you to use other express boats within the same route on the same day, costs B150; one-way

#159 (ordinary): **Southern Bus Terminal**–Phra Pinklao Bridge–Democracy Monument–**Hualamphong Station**–MBK Shopping Centre–Thanon Ratchaprarop–Victory Monument–Chatuchak Weekend Market–**Northern Bus Terminal**.

#503 (air-con): Sanam Luang–Democracy Monument (for **Banglamphu guest houses**)–Thanon Rajdamnoen Nok (for **TAT** and **boxing stadium**)–Wat Benjamabophit–Thanon Sri Ayutthaya (for **Thewet guest houses**)–Victory Monument–**Chatuchak Weekend Market**–Rangsit. Note, however, that during rush hours, some #503 buses take the expressway, missing out Chatuchak Weekend Market.

#507 (air-con): **Southern Bus Terminal**–Phra Pinklao Bridge (for **Banglamphu guest houses**)–Sanam Luang–Thanon Charoen Krung (New Road)–Thanon Chakraphet–Thanon Yaowarat (for **Chinatown** and **Wat Traimit**)–**Hualamphong Station**–Thanon Rama IV–Bang Na Intersection–Pak Nam (for **Ancient City** buses).

#508 (air-con): Thanon Maharat–**Grand Palace**–Thanon Charoen Krung–Siam Square–Thanon Sukhumvit–**Eastern Bus Terminal**–Pak Nam (for **Ancient City** buses). Note, however, that during rush hours, some #508 buses take the expressway, missing out the Eastern Bus Terminal.

#509 (air-con): **Northern Bus Terminal**–Chatuchak Weekend Market–Victory Monument–Thanon Rajwithi–Thanon Sawankhalok–Thanon Phitsanulok–Thanon Rajdamnoen Nok (for **TAT** and **boxing stadium**)–Democracy Monument–Thanon Rajdamnoen Klang (for **Banglamphu guest houses**)–Phra Pinklao Bridge–Thonburi.

#511 (air-con, 24hr): **Southern Bus Terminal**–Phra Pinklao Bridge (for **Banglamphu guest houses**)–Democracy Monument–Thanon Lan Luang–Thanon Phetchaburi–Thanon Sukhumvit–**Eastern Bus Terminal**–Pak Nam (for **Ancient City** buses). Note, however, that between 4.30am and 8.30pm, some #511 buses take the expressway, missing out the Eastern Bus Terminal.

#512 (air-con): **Northern Bus Terminal**–Chatuchak Weekend Market–Thanon Phetchaburi–Thanon Lan Luang–Democracy Monument (for **Banglamphu guest houses**)–Sanam Luang–Tha Chang (for **Grand Palace**)–Pak Khlong Talat.

tickets are also available, costing, for example, B19 from Phra Arthit to Oriental.

Cross-river ferries

Smaller than express boats are the slow **cross-river ferries** (*reua kham fak*), which shuttle back and forth between the same two points. Found at or beside every express-boat stop and plenty of other piers in between, they are especially useful for exploring Thonburi. Fares are generally B3, payable at the entrance to the pier.

Canal boats

Longtail boats (*reua hang yao*) ply the **canals** of Thonburi like commuter buses, stopping at designated shelters (fares are in line with those of express boats), and are available for individual rental here and on the river (see box, p.95). On the Bangkok side, **Khlong Saen Saeb** is well served by passenger boats, which run at least every fifteen minutes during daylight hours from the Phan Fah pier at the Golden Mount (handy for Banglamphu, Ratanakosin and Chinatown), and head way out east to Wat Sribunruang, with useful stops at Thanon Phrayathai, aka Saphan Hua Chang (for Jim Thompson's House and Ratchathevi Skytrain stop); Pratunam (for the Erawan Shrine); Thanon Witthayu (Wireless Road); and Soi Nana Nua (Soi 3), Thanon Asok Montri (Soi 21, for TAT headquarters and Phetchaburi subway stop), Soi Thonglo (Soi 55) and Soi Ekamai (Soi 63), all off Thanon Sukhumvit. This is your quickest and most interesting way of getting between the west and east parts of town, if you can stand the stench of the canal.

Central stops for the Chao Phraya express boats

N15 Thewet (all boats except blue flag) – for Thewet guest houses.

N14 Rama VIII Bridge (no flag) – for Samsen Soi 5.

N13 Phra Arthit (no flag and orange flag) – for Thanon Phra Arthit, Thanon Khao San and Banglamphu guest houses.

N12 Phra Pinklao Bridge (all boats except blue flag) – for Royal Barge Museum and Thonburi shops.

N11 Thonburi Railway Station (or Bangkok Noi; no flag) – for trains to Kanchanaburi.

N10 Wang Lang (aka Siriraj or Prannok; all boats) – for Siriraj Hospital and hospital museums.

N9 Chang (no flag, orange flag and green-and-yellow flag) – for the Grand Palace, Sanam Luang and the National Museum.

N8 Thien (no flag and orange flag) – for Wat Pho, and the cross-river ferry to Wat Arun.

N7 Ratchini (aka Rajinee; no flag).

N6 Saphan Phut (Memorial Bridge; no flag and orange flag) – for Pahurat, Pak Khlong Talat and Wat Prayoon.

N5 Rachawongse (aka Rajawong; all boats except blue flag) – for Chinatown.

N4 Harbour (Marine) Department (no flag and orange flag).

N3 Si Phraya (all boats except blue flag) – walk north past the *Sheraton Royal Orchid Hotel* for River City shopping complex, head south for the GPO.

N2 Wat Muang Kae (no flag) – for the GPO.

N1 Oriental (no flag and orange flag) – for Thanon Silom.

Central Sathorn (all boats) – for the Skytrain (Saphan Taksin Station) and Thanon Sathorn.

You may have trouble actually locating the piers as few are signed in English and they all look very unassuming and rickety; see the Bangkok colour map at the back of the book for locations and keep your eyes peeled for a plain wooden jetty – most jetties serve boats running in both directions. Once on the boat, state your destination to the conductor when he collects your fare, which will be between B10 and B24. Due to the construction of some low bridges, all passengers change onto a different boat at Tha Pratunam – just follow the crowd.

The Skytrain

Although its network is limited, the **BTS Skytrain**, or *rot fai faa* (www.bts.co.th; see the colour map at the back of the book), provides a much faster alternative to the bus, and is clean, efficient and vigorously air-conditioned. There are only two Skytrain lines, which interconnect at Siam Square (**Central Station**). Both run every few minutes from around 6am to midnight, with **fares** of B15–40 per trip depending on

distance travelled. You buy tickets from machines that accept only coins, but you can change notes at staffed counters. You'd really have to be motoring to justify buying a day **pass** at B120, while the twenty-trip, thirty-trip and forty-trip cards, for B440, B600 and B800 respectively (valid for 30 days), are designed for long-distance commuters.

The **Sukhumvit Line** runs from Mo Chit (stop N8) in the northern part of the city to On Nut (Soi 77, Thanon Sukhumvit; E9) in around thirty minutes, though there are plans to extend the line eastward towards Samrong. The **Silom Line** runs from the National Stadium (W1), via Saphan Taksin (Taksin, or Sathorn, Bridge; S6), linking up with the full gamut of express boats on the Chao Phraya River, to Wongwian Yai (S8) in Thonburi (a continuation to Thanon Phetkasem is planned).

The subway

Bangkok's underground rail system, the **MRT subway** (or metro; in Thai, *rot fai tai din*; www.bangkokmetro.co.th; see the colour map at the back of the book), has similar advantages to the Skytrain, though its current single line connects few places of interest for visitors. It runs every few minutes between around 6am and midnight from Hualamphong train station, via Silom (near Sala Daeng Skytrain station), Sukhumvit (near Asoke Skytrain) and Chatuchak Park (near Mo Chit Skytrain), to Bang Sue train station in the north of the city. Plans are afoot to continue the line westwards from Hualam-phong along Thanon Charoen Krung, then across to Thonburi, finally completing a loop back to Bang Sue. Pay your **fare** of between B15 and B39 at a staffed counter or machine, where you'll receive a token to put through an entrance gate (the various day passes and stored-value cards available are unlikely to be worthwhile for visitors).

Taxis

Bangkok **taxis** come in three forms and are so plentiful that you rarely have to wait more than a couple of minutes before spotting an empty one of any description. Neither tuk-tuks nor motorbike taxis have meters, so you should agree on a price before setting off; expect to do a fair amount of haggling.

For nearly all journeys, the best and most comfortable option is to flag down one of Bangkok's metered, air-conditioned **taxi cabs**; look out for the "TAXI METER" sign on the roof, and a red light in the windscreen in front of the passenger seat, which means the cab is available for hire. Starting at B35, fares are displayed on a clearly visible meter that the driver should reset at the start of each trip (say "*poet meter, dai mai khrap/kha?*" to ask him to switch it on), and increase in stages on a combined distance/time formula; as an example, a medium-range journey from Thanon Ploenchit to Thanon Sathorn will cost around B50 at a quiet time of day. Try to have change with you as cabs tend not to carry a lot of money; tipping of up to ten percent is common, though occasionally a cabbie will round down the fare on the meter. If a driver tries to quote a flat fare rather than using the meter, let him go, and

avoid the now-rare unmetered cabs (denoted by a "TAXI" sign on the roof). Getting a metered taxi in the middle of the afternoon when the cars return to base for a change of drivers can sometimes be a problem; if you want to book a metered taxi (B20 surcharge), call Siam Taxi Co-operative on ☏1661 or Taxi Radio on ☏1681.

Somewhat less stable though typically Thai, **tuk-tuks** have very little to recommend them. These noisy, three-wheeled, open-sided buggies, which can carry three medium-sized passengers comfortably, fully expose you to the worst of Bangkok's pollution and weather. Locals might use tuk-tuks for short journeys – though you'll have to bargain hard to get a fare lower than the taxi-cab flagfall of B35 – while for a longer trip from Thanon Convent to Siam Square, for example, drivers will ask for as much as B200. Be aware, also, that tuk-tuk drivers tend to speak less English than taxi drivers – and there have been cases of robberies and attacks on women passengers late at night. During the day it's quite common for tuk-tuk drivers to try and **con** their passengers into visiting a jewellery, tailor's or expensive souvenir shop with them, for which they get a hefty commission; the usual tactic involves falsely informing tourists that the Grand Palace, or whatever their destination might be, is closed (see p.42), and offering instead a ridiculously cheap, even free, city tour.

Motorbike taxis generally congregate at the entrances to long sois – pick the riders out by their numbered, coloured vests – and charge around B10 for short trips down into the side streets. If you're short on time and have nerves of steel, it's also possible to charter them for hairy journeys out on the main roads (a trip from Thanon Convent to Siam Square will cost around B80). Crash helmets are compulsory on all main roads in the capital (traffic police fine non-wearers on the spot), though they're rarely worn on trips down the sois and the local press has reported complaints from people who've caught head-lice this way (they suggest wearing a headscarf under the helmet).

Information and maps

The efficient Tourism Authority of Thailand, or TAT (ⓦwww.tourismthailand.org), maintains offices in several cities abroad, where you can pick up a few glossy brochures and get fairly detailed answers to specific pre-trip questions. More comprehensive local information is given at the TAT offices in Bangkok and at booths run by the city's Bangkok Tourism Division.

The official source of information on the capital is the **Bangkok Tourism Division**, part of the Bangkok Metropolitan Administration (BMA), whose main office is next to Phra Pinklao Bridge at 17/1 Thanon Phra Arthit in Banglamphu (daily 9am–7pm; ☎02 225 7612–5, ⓦwww.bangkoktourist.com). This is supported by strategically placed satellite booths around the capital (daily 9am–5pm), including in front of the Grand Palace, at the Erawan Shrine, at River City and Mah Boon Krong shopping centres, in front of Robinson Department Store on Thanon Silom, and in front of Banglamphu's Wat Chana Songkhram.

The city's branches of the nationwide **Tourism Authority of Thailand** can also be useful. TAT maintains a booth in the airport arrivals concourse and runs a Tourist Service Centre at 4 Rajdamnoen Nok, Banglamphu (daily 8.30am–4.30pm; ☎02 283 1500 ext 1620; ⓦwww.tourismthailand.org; see colour map), a twenty-minute stroll from Thanon Khao San, or a short ride in air-conditioned bus #503. TAT's headquarters (daily 8.30am–4.30pm; ☎02 250 5500) are rather inconveniently located out at 1600 Thanon Phetchaburi Mai, 350m west of the junction with Sukhumvit Soi 21 and the Phetchaburi subway stop, or 150m east of the junction with Sukhumvit Soi 3 and Tha Nana Nua on the Khlong Saen Saeb canal boat service (see the Thanon Sukhumvit map on p.120). In addition, you can contact the **TAT Freephone Tourist Assistance Call Centre** from anywhere in the country on ☎1672 daily from 8am to 8pm.

Note, however, that the many other shops and offices across the capital displaying

signs announcing "TAT Tourist Information" or similar are **not official Tourism Authority of Thailand centres** and will not be dispensing impartial advice: the Tourism Authority of Thailand never uses the acronym "TAT" on its office-fronts or in its logo.

TAT offices abroad

Australia and New Zealand Suite 2002, Level 20, 56 Pitt St, Sydney, NSW 2000 ☎02/9247 7549, ⓦwww.thailand.net.au.
South Africa Contact the UK office.
UK and Ireland 1st Floor, 17–19 Cockspur St, London SW1Y 5BL ☎0870/900 2007, ⓦwww.tourismthailand.co.uk.
US and Canada 61 Broadway, Suite 2810, New York, NY 10006 ☎212/432-0433, ✉info@tatny.com; 611 North Larchmont Blvd, 1st Floor, Los Angeles, CA 90004 ☎323/461-9814, ✉tatla@tat.or.th.

Maps

To get around Bangkok on the cheap, you'll need to buy a **bus map**. Of the several available, the most useful and reliable is Bangkok Guide's *Bus Routes & Map*, which charts all major air-conditioned and non-air-conditioned bus routes. For a far more personal guide to Bangkok's most interesting shops, markets, restaurants and back streets, look for the famously idiosyncratic **hand-drawn maps** *Nancy Chandler's Map of Bangkok* and *Nancy Chandler's Map of Khao San and Old Bangkok*. Both carry a mass of annotated recommendations, are impressively accurate and frequently reissued; they're sold in most tourist areas and copies and interim updates are also available at ⓦwww.nancychandler.net.

Health

Although Thailand's climate, wildlife and cuisine present Western travellers with fewer health worries than in many Asian destinations, it's as well to know in advance what the risks might be, and what preventive or curative measures you should take.

For a start, there's no need to bring huge supplies of non-prescription medicines with you, as Thai **pharmacies** (*raan khai yaa*; typically open daily 8.30am–8pm) are well stocked with local and international branded medicaments, and of course they are generally much less expensive than at home. Nearly all pharmacies – including the city-wide branches of the British chain, Boots (see p.203) – are run by trained English-speaking pharmacists, who are usually the best people to talk to if your symptoms aren't acute enough to warrant seeing a doctor.

Medical resources for travellers

UK and Ireland

Hospital for Tropical Diseases Travel Clinic London ☎ 0845/155 5000 or 020/7387 4411, ⍟ www.thehtd.org.
MASTA (Medical Advisory Service for Travellers Abroad) UK ☎ 0870/606 2782 or ⍟ www.masta.org for the nearest clinic.
NHS Travel Health Website ⍟ www.fitfortravel.scot.nhs.uk.
Travel Medicine Services Belfast ☎ 028/9031 5220.
Tropical Medical Bureau Dublin ☎ 1850/487674, ⍟ www.tmb.ie.

US and Canada

Canadian Society for International Health ☎ 613/241-5785, ⍟ www.csih.org. Extensive list of travel health centres.
CDC ⍟ wwwn.cdc.gov/travel. Official US government travel health site.
International Society for Travel Medicine ☎ 1-770/736-7060, ⍟ www.istm.org. Has a full list of travel health clinics.

Australia, New Zealand and South Africa

Travellers' Medical and Vaccination Centre ⍟ www.tmvc.com.au. in Australia ☎ 1300/658 844. Travel clinics in Australia, New Zealand and South Africa.

Inoculations

There are no compulsory **inoculation** requirements for people travelling to Thailand from the West, but you should consult a doctor or other health professional, preferably at least four weeks in advance of your trip, for the latest information on recommended immunizations. Most doctors strongly advise vaccinations or boosters against polio, tetanus, diphtheria, hepatitis A and, in many cases, typhoid, and sometimes they might also recommend protecting yourself against rabies, hepatitis B and other diseases. If you forget to have all your inoculations before leaving home, or don't leave yourself sufficient time, you can get them in Bangkok at, for example, the Thai Red Cross Society's Queen Saovabha Memorial Institute (QSMI) and Snake Farm on the corner of Thanon Rama IV and Thanon Henri Dunant (Mon–Fri 8.30am–noon & 1–4pm, Sat 8.30am–noon; ☎ 02 252 0161–4, ⍟ www.redcross.or.th; see also p.115) or Global Doctor (see p.39).

Mosquito-borne diseases

Only certain regions of Thailand are now considered malarial, and **Bangkok is malaria-free**, so if you are restricting yourself to the capital you do not have to take malaria prophylactics. Bangkok does however have its fair share of **mosquitoes**; though nearly all the city's hotels and guest houses have screened windows, you will probably need to have mosquito repellent containing the chemical compound DEET. Supermarkets and pharmacies in Bangkok stock it, but if you want the highest-strength repellent, or convenient roll-ons or sprays, it's probably best to do your shopping before you leave home. DEET is strong stuff, and if you have sensitive skin, a natural alternative is citronella (available in the UK as Mosi-guard), made from a blend of eucalyptus oils; the Thai version is made with lemon grass.

A further reason to protect yourself is the possibility of contracting **dengue fever**, a viral disease spread by mosquitoes that's on the increase throughout tropical Asia, particularly during and just after the rainy season. There's no inoculation against it, though it's rarely fatal; symptoms usually develop between five and eight days after being bitten and may include fever, headaches, severe joint and muscle pain ("breakbone fever" is another name for dengue), and possibly a rash. The only treatment is bed rest, liquids and paracetamol or other non-aspirin-based painkillers, though more serious cases may require hospitalization.

Digestive problems

By far the most common travellers' complaint in Thailand, **digestive troubles** are often caused by contaminated food and water, or sometimes just by an overdose of unfamiliar foodstuffs. For advice on food and water hygiene, see p.174.

Stomach trouble usually manifests itself as simple **diarrhoea**, which should clear up without medical treatment within three to seven days and is best combated by drinking lots of fluids. If this doesn't work, you're in danger of getting **dehydrated** and should take some kind of rehydration solution, either a commercial sachet of ORS (oral rehydration solution), sold in all Thai pharmacies, or a do-it-yourself version, which can be made by adding a handful of sugar and a pinch of salt to every litre of boiled or bottled water (soft drinks are not a viable alternative). If you can eat, avoid fatty foods.

Anti-diarrhoeal agents such as Imodium are useful for blocking you up, but only attack the symptoms and may prolong infections; an antibiotic such as ciprofloxacin, however, can often reduce a typical attack of traveller's diarrhoea to one day. If the diarrhoea persists for a week or more, or if you have blood or mucus in your stools, or an accompanying fever, go to a doctor or hospital.

Other diseases

Rabies is endemic in Thailand, mainly carried by dogs (between four and seven percent of stray dogs in Bangkok are reported to be rabid), but also cats and monkeys. It is transmitted by bites, scratches or even occasionally licks. Rabies is invariably fatal if the patient waits until symptoms begin, though modern vaccines and treatments are very effective and deaths are rare. The important thing is, if you are bitten, licked or scratched by an animal, to vigorously clean the wound with soap and disinfect it, preferably with something containing iodine, and to seek medical advice regarding treatment (at the Thai Red Cross Society, for example; see p.37) right away.

AIDS is widespread in Thailand, primarily because of the sex trade. **Condoms** (*meechai*) are sold in pharmacies, convenience stores, department stores, hairdressers and even street markets. Due to rigorous screening methods, Thailand's medical blood supply is now considered safe.

There have been outbreaks of **Avian Influenza** (**bird flu**) in domestic poultry and wild birds in Thailand which have led to a small number of human fatalities, believed to have arisen through close contact with infected poultry. There has been no evidence of human-to-human transmission in Thailand, and the risk to humans is believed to be very low. However, as a precaution, you should avoid visiting live animal markets and other places where you may come into close contact with birds, and ensure that poultry and egg dishes are thoroughly cooked.

Hospitals, clinics and dentists

Hospital (*rong phayaabahn*) cleanliness and efficiency vary, but generally hygiene and healthcare standards are good, the ratio of medical staff to patients is considerably higher than in most parts of the West, and the doctors speak English. In the event of a major health crisis, get someone to contact your embassy (see p.49) and insurance company. Most expats rate the private Bumrungrad

International Hospital, 33 Sukhumvit Soi 3 (☎02 667 1000, emergency ☎02 667 2999, ⓦwww.bumrungrad.com), with its famously five-star accommodation, as the best and most comfortable in the city, followed by the BNH (Bangkok Nursing Home) Hospital, 9 Thanon Convent (☎02 686 2700, emergency ☎02 632 1000, ⓦwww.bnhhospital.com), the Bangkok Hospital Medical Centre, 2 Soi Soonvijai 7, Thanon Phetchaburi Mai (☎02 310 3000, emergency ☎17192, ⓦwww.bangkokhospital.com) and the Samitivej Sukhumvit Hospital, 133 Sukhumvit Soi 49 (☎02 711 8000, ⓦwww.samitivej.co.th). Other recommended private hospitals include Bangkok Mission Hospital, 430 Thanon Phitsanulok, cnr Thanon Lan Luang, just east of Banglamphu (☎02 282 1100, ⓦwww.tagnet.org/mission-net), and Bangkok

Christian Hospital, 124 Thanon Silom (☎02 233 6981–9, ⓦwww.bkkchristianhosp.th.com).

Among **general clinics**, there's one on Soi Rambuttri in Banglamphu run by the Bangkok Hospital (☎02 629 5260; daily 8am–7pm); and Global Doctor, on the ground floor of the Holiday Inn Hotel, 981 Thanon Silom (cnr Thanon Surasak; ☎02 236 8442–4, ⓦwww.globaldoctorclinic.com), is recommended.

For **dental problems**, try the Bumrungrad Hospital's dental department on ☎02 667 2300, or the following dental clinics (not 24hr): Dental Hospital, 88/88 Sukhumvit Soi 49 (☎02 260 5000–15, ⓦwww.dentalhospitalbangkok.com); and Siam Family Dental Clinic, 292/6 Soi 4, Siam Square (☎02 255 6664–5, ⓦwww.siamfamilydental.com).

The media

To keep you abreast of world affairs, there are several English-language newspapers in Thailand, though a mild form of censorship affects the predominantly state-controlled media, even muting the English-language branches on occasion.

Newspapers and magazines

Of the hundreds of **Thai-language newspapers and magazines** published every week, the sensationalist daily tabloid *Thai Rath* attracts the widest readership, with circulation of around a million, while the moderately progressive *Matichon* is the leading quality daily, with an estimated circulation of 600,000.

Alongside these, two daily **English-language papers** – the *Bangkok Post* (ⓦwww.bangkokpost.com) and the *Nation* (ⓦwww.nationmultimedia.com) – are capable of adopting a fairly critical attitude to governmental goings-on and cover major domestic and international stories as well as tourist-related issues. The *Nation* has recently adopted a split personality, covering mostly business news on its main pages while carrying a lively, poppy tabloid, the

Xpress, inside. The *Post's Spectrum* supplement, which comes inside the Sunday edition, stands out for its investigative journalism. Both the *Post* and *Nation* are sold at most newsstands in the capital.

You can also pick up **foreign publications** such as *Newsweek*, *Time* and the *International Herald Tribune* in Bangkok; from Monday to Saturday, the *IHT* now publishes a special Thai edition, though it's short on Thai news. English-language bookstores such as Bookazine and some expensive hotels carry air-freighted, or sometimes locally printed and stapled, copies of foreign national newspapers for at least B50 a copy.

Television

There are six government-controlled, terrestrial **TV channels** in Thailand: channels 3, 5 (owned and operated by the army), 7 and 9 transmit a blend of news, documentaries, soaps, sports, talk and quiz shows, while the more serious-minded PBS (formerly Thaksin Shinawatra's ITV) and NBT are public-service channels, owned and operated by the government's public relations department. **Cable** networks – available in many mid-range and most upmarket hotel rooms – carry channels from all around the world, including CNN from the US, BBC World from the UK and sometimes ABC from Australia, as well as English-language movie channels, MTV and various sports and documentary channels. Both the *Bangkok Post* and the *Nation* print the daily TV and cable **schedule**.

Radio

Thailand boasts over five hundred **radio stations**, mostly music-oriented, ranging from Virgin Radio's Eazy (105.5 FM), which serves up Western pop, to Fat Radio, which plays Thai indie sounds (104.5 FM). Chulalongkorn University Radio (101.5 FM) plays classical music from 9.30pm to midnight every night. Net 107 on 107 FM is one of several stations that include English-language news bulletins.

With a **shortwave radio** – or by going **online** – you can pick up the BBC World Service (Ⓦ www.bbc.co.uk/worldservice), Radio Australia (Ⓦ www.radioaustralia.net .au), Voice of America (Ⓦ www.voanews .com), Radio Canada (Ⓦ www.rcinet.ca) and other international stations. Times and wavelengths change regularly, so get hold of a recent schedule just before you travel or consult the websites for frequency and programme guides.

Festivals

Nearly all Thai festivals have a religious aspect. The most theatrical are generally Brahmin (Hindu) in origin, honouring elemental spirits with ancient rites and ceremonial costumed parades. In Buddhist celebrations, merit-making plays an important role and events are usually staged at the local temple, but a light-hearted atmosphere prevails, as the wat grounds are swamped with food- and trinket-vendors and makeshift stages are set up to show *likay* folk theatre, singing stars and beauty contests; there may even be funfair rides as well.

Few of the dates for religious festivals are fixed, so check with TAT for specifics (Ⓦ www.tourismthailand.org). Some of the festivals below are designated as national holidays – see p.52.

January/February Chinese New Year (new moon of the first lunar month: some time between mid-Jan and late Feb; Thanon Yaowarat and Charoen Krung). Even more foodstalls than usual in Chinatown and plenty to feast your eyes on too, including Chinese opera shows and jaunty parades led by traditional Chinese dragons and lions.

February Maha Puja (on the day of full moon). A day of merit-making marks the occasion when 1250 disciples gathered spontaneously to hear the Buddha preach. Best experienced at Wat Benjamabophit,

where the festival culminates with a candlelit procession round the temple.

Late February to mid-April Kite fights and flying contests (Sanam Luang, Ratanakosin). Sanam Luang next to the Grand Palace is the venue for demonstrations and competitions of kite-flying and fighting (see p.68).

April 13–15 Songkhran: Thai New Year. The Thai New Year is welcomed in with massive waterfights and no one, least of all foreign tourists, escapes a good-natured soaking. Trucks roam the streets spraying passers-by with hosepipes and half the population cary huge water pistols for the duration. Don't wear your favourite outfit as water is sometimes laced with dye. Celebrated throughout the city but famously raucous on Thanon Silom and, especially, on

Thanon Khao San, which also stages special organized entertainments.

May Raek Na, Royal Ploughing Ceremony (early in the month; Sanam Luang). To mark the beginning of the rice-planting season, ceremonially clad Brahmin leaders parade sacred oxen and the royal plough across Sanam Luang, interpreting omens to forecast the year's rice yield (see also p.69).

May/June Visakha Puja (on the day of full moon of the sixth lunar month). Temples across the city are the focus of this holiest day of the Buddhist calendar, which commemorates the birth, enlightenment and death of the Buddha. The most photogenic event is the candlelit evening procession around the wat, particularly at Wat Benjamabophit in Dusit.

September Bangkok International Film Festival (most recently held over a week in September, but has also been staged in January and July; ⓦ www .bangkokfilm.org). An annual chance to preview new and unusual Thai films alongside features and documentaries from Southeast Asia and beyond.

October 23 Chulalongkorn Day The city marks the anniversary of the death of the widely loved Rama V, King Chulalongkorn (1868–1910), by laying offerings around the famous equestrian statue of the king, at the Thanon U-Thong-Thanon Sri Ayutthaya crossroads in Dusit (see p.100).

October Awk Pansa (on the day of full moon). Devotees at temples across the city make offerings to monks and there's general merrymaking to celebrate the Buddha's descent to earth from Tavatimsa heaven and the end of the Khao Pansa retreat.

October/November Loy Krathong (on the full moon day of the twelfth lunar month, between late Oct and early Nov). Wishes and prayers wrapped up in banana-leaf baskets full of flowers and lighted candles are released on to the Chao Phraya River and

Thonburi canals in this charming festival that both honours the water spirits and celebrates the end of the rainy season.

October/November Vegetarian Festival (Ngan Kin Jeh) (held over nine days during the ninth lunar month in the Chinese calendar; Chinatown). Many Chinese people become vegetarian for this annual nine-day Taoist detox, so most food vendors and restaurants in Chinatown, and many outlets in other parts of the city, turn veggie too, displaying a yellow pennant to alert their customers (see p.178).

November Ngan Wat Saket (first week; Wat Saket, near Democracy Monument). Probably Thailand's biggest temple fair, held around Wat Saket and the Golden Mount, with funfairs, folk theatre, music and tons of food.

November Bangkok Pride (usually mid-month; Thanon Silom and Lumphini Park). The capital's gay community stages parades, cabarets, fancy-dress shows and sports contests. See ⓦ www .bangkokpride.org.

December 2 Trooping the Colour (Suan Amporn, Dusit). An extraordinary array of sumptuous uniforms makes this annual marshalling of the Royal Guards a sight worth stopping for.

December 5 King's Birthday (Sanam Luang, Ratanakosin). In the evening thousands of people gather in Sanam Luang to light candles and sing the king's anthem, after which there's free entertainment into the night from pop stars and folk theatre troupes, capped by a huge fireworks display. Nearby Rajadamnoen Klang is prettily decorated with special lights and portraits of the king.

December 31 Western New Year's Eve. The new year is greeted with fireworks along the river and at Sanam Luang, and huge crowds gather for a mass countdown around the Central World Plaza and Siam Square area, which is usually pedestrianized for the night.

Crime, safety and the law

As long as you keep your wits about you, you shouldn't encounter much trouble in Bangkok. Theft and pickpocketing are two of the main problems, but the most common cause for concern is the number of con-artists who dupe tourists into parting with their cash. There are also various Thai laws that tourists need to be aware of, particularly regarding passports, the age of consent and smoking in public.

Theft

To **prevent theft**, most travellers prefer to carry their valuables with them at all times, but it's sometimes possible to leave your valuables in a hotel or guest-house locker – the safest lockers are those that require your own padlock, as there are occasional reports of valuables being stolen by hotel staff. **Padlock your luggage** when leaving it in hotel or guest-house rooms, as well as when consigning it to storage or taking it on public transport. Padlocks also come in handy as extra security on your room.

Personal safety

Be wary of accepting food and drink from strangers as it may be drugged. This might sound paranoid, but there have been enough **drug-muggings** for TAT to publish a specific warning about the problem. Drinks are sometimes spiked in bars and clubs, especially by sex-workers who later steal from their victim's room.

Violent crime against tourists is not common, but it does occur, and there have been several serious attacks on women travellers in the last few years. However, bearing in mind that over fourteen million foreigners visit Thailand every year, the statistical likelihood of becoming a victim is extremely small. **Obvious precautions** for travellers of either sex include locking accessible windows and doors at night (with your own padlock in the simpler guest houses), and not travelling alone at night in a taxi or tuk-tuk. Nor should you risk jumping into an unlicensed taxi at the airport in Bangkok at any time of day: there have been some very violent robberies in these, so take the well-marked licensed, metered taxis instead, or one of the airport buses.

Unfortunately, it is also necessary for female tourists to think twice about spending time alone with a **monk**, as not all men of the cloth uphold the Buddhist precepts and there have been rapes and murders committed by men wearing the saffron robes of the monkhood. See p.230 for more about the changing Thai attitudes towards the monkhood.

Though unpalatable and distressing, Thailand's high-profile **sex industry** is relatively unthreatening for Western women, with its energy focused exclusively on farang men; it's also quite easily avoided, being contained within certain pockets of the capital. As for **harassment** from men, it's hard to generalize, but most Western women find it less of a problem in Thailand than they do back home.

For advice on safe travelling in Thailand, consult your government's travel advisory.

Scams

Despite the best efforts of guidebook writers, TAT and the Thai tourist police, countless travellers to Thailand get scammed every year. Nearly all **scams** are easily avoided if you're on your guard against anyone who makes an unnatural effort to befriend you. We have outlined the main scams in the relevant sections of this guide, but con-artists are nothing if not creative, so if in doubt walk away at the earliest opportunity.

Many Bangkok **tuk-tuk drivers** earn most of their living through securing **commissions** from tourist-oriented shops and will do their damnedest to get you to go to a gem shop (see p.211). The most common tactic is for drivers to pretend that the Grand Palace or other major sight you intended to visit is closed for the day (they usually invent a plausible reason, such as a festival or royal

Reporting a crime or emergency

For all emergencies, contact the English-speaking **tourist police**, who maintain a 24-hour toll-free nationwide line (☏1155) and have their headquarters on the eastern edge of town at 2107 Bangkok Tower, Thanon Phetchaburi Mai (east of Phetchaburi subway station and the Wat Mai Chong Lom stop on the Saen Saeb canal-boat service; ☏02 308 0333). In the evenings, you'll also find tourist police in Suan Lum Night Bazaar and at the Silom end of Patpong 1. Alternatively, drop in at the more convenient Chana Songkhram Police Station at the west end of Thanon Khao San in Banglamphu (☏02 282 2323).

Getting in touch with the tourist police first is invariably more efficient than directly contacting the local police, ambulance or fire service. The tourist police's job is to offer advice and tell you what to do next, but they do not file crime reports, which must be done at the nearest police station.

TAT has a special department for mediating between tourists, police and accused persons (particularly shopkeepers and tour agents) called the Tourist Assistance Center, or **TAC**; it's based in the TAT office on Thanon Rajdamnoen Nok in Banglamphu (daily 8.30am– 4.30pm; ☏02 281 5051).

The **British Embassy** in Bangkok provides advice for British victims of crime in Thailand and also posts practical tips and a list of useful contacts on its website (☏02 305 8333 ext. 2334, 2318, ⓦukinthailand.fco.gov.uk/en/help-for-british-nationals).

occasion; see p.59), and to then offer to take you on a round-city tour instead, perhaps even for free. The tour will invariably include a visit to a gem shop. The easiest way to avoid all this is to take a **metered taxi**; if you're fixed on taking a tuk-tuk, ignore any tuk-tuk that is parked up or loitering and be firm about where you want to go.

Self-styled **tourist guides**, **touts** and anyone else who might introduce themselves as **students** or **businesspeople** and offer to take you somewhere of interest, or invite you to meet their family, are often the first piece of bait in a well-honed chain of con-artists. If you bite, chances are you'll end up either at a gem shop or in a gambling den, or, at best, at a tour operator or hotel that you had not planned to patronize. This is not to say that you should never accept an invitation from a local person, but be extremely wary of doing so following a street encounter in Bangkok or the resorts. Tourist guides' ID cards are easily faked.

For many of these characters the goal is to get you inside a dodgy **gem shop**. There is a full run-down of advice on how to avoid falling for the notorious low-grade gems scam on p.211, but the bottom line is that if you are not experienced at buying and trading in valuable gems you will definitely be ripped off,

possibly even to the tune of several thousand pounds or dollars. Check the 2Bangkok website's account of a **typical gem scam** (ⓦ www.2bangkok.com/2bangkok/Scams /Sapphire.shtml) before you shell out any cash at all.

A less common but potentially more frightening scam involves a similar cast of warm-up artists leading tourists into a **gambling** game. The scammers invite their victim home on an innocent-sounding pretext, get out a pack of cards, and then set about fleecing the incomer in any number of subtle ways. Often this can be especially scary as the venue is likely to be far from hotels or recognizable landmarks. You're unlikely to get any sympathy from police, as gambling is **illegal** in Thailand.

Age restrictions and other laws

Thai law requires that tourists **carry their original passports** at all times, though sometimes it's more practical to carry a photocopy and keep the original locked in a safety deposit. The **age of consent** is 15, but the law allows anyone under the age of 18, or their parents, to file charges in retrospect even if they consented to sex at the time. It is against the law to have sex with a prostitute who is under 18. It is illegal for under-18s to

Governmental travel advisories

Australian Department of Foreign Affairs ⓦ www.dfat.gov.au,
ⓦ www.smartraveller.gov.au
British Foreign & Commonwealth Office ⓦ www.fco.gov.uk
Canadian Department of Foreign Affairs ⓦ www.international.gc.ca
Irish Department of Foreign Affairs ⓦ www.foreignaffairs.gov.ie
New Zealand Ministry of Foreign Affairs ⓦ www.mft.govt.nz
US State Department ⓦ www.travel.state.gov
South African Department of Foreign Affairs ⓦ www.dfa.gov.za

buy cigarettes or **to drive** and you must be 20 or over to **buy alcohol** or be allowed into a **bar or club** (ID checks are often enforced in Bangkok). It is illegal for anyone to **gamble** in Thailand (though many do).

Smoking in public is widely prohibited. The ban covers all air-conditioned public buildings (including restaurants but usually excluding bars and clubs) and air-conditioned trains, buses and planes and even extends to parks and the street; violators are subject to a B2000 fine. Dropping cigarette butts, **littering** and spitting in public places can also earn you a B2000 fine, and jaywalking instead of using a footbridge or road crossing could get you done for B200. There are fines for **overstaying your visa** (see p.24), **working without a permit**, and **not wearing a motorcycle helmet** and violating other **traffic laws**.

Drugs

Drug-smuggling carries a maximum penalty in Thailand of death and **dealing drugs** will get you anything from four years to life in a Thai prison; penalties depend on the drug and the amount involved. Travellers caught with even the smallest amount of drugs at airports and international borders are prosecuted for trafficking, and no one charged with trafficking offences gets bail. Heroin, amphetamines, LSD and ecstasy are classed as Category 1 drugs and carry the most severe penalties: even **possession** of Category 1 drugs for personal use can result in a **life sentence**. Away from international borders, most foreigners arrested in possession of small amounts of cannabis are released on bail, then fined and deported,

but the law is complex and prison sentences are possible.

Despite occasional royal pardons, don't expect special treatment as a farang: you only need to read one of the first-hand accounts by foreign former **prisoners** (reviewed on p.240) or read the blogs at ⓦ www.thaiprisonlife.com to get the picture. The **police** actively look for tourists doing drugs, reportedly searching people regularly and randomly on Thanon Khao San, for example. They have the power to order a urine test if they have reasonable grounds for suspicion, and even a positive result for marijuana consumption could lead to a year's imprisonment. Be wary also of **being shopped** by a farang or local dealer keen to earn a financial reward for a successful bust, or having substances slipped into your luggage (simple enough to perpetrate unless all fastenings are secured with padlocks).

If you are arrested, ask for your embassy to be contacted immediately, which is your right under Thai law (see p.49 for phone numbers), and embassy staff will talk you through procedures; the website of the British Embassy in Thailand also posts useful information, including a list of English-speaking lawyers, at ⓦ ukinthailand.fco.gov.uk/en/help-for-british-nationals. The British charity Prisoners Abroad (ⓦ www.prisonersabroad .org.uk) carries a detailed survival guide on its website, which outlines what to expect if arrested in Thailand, from the point of arrest through trial and conviction to life in a Thai jail; if contacted, the charity may also be able to offer direct support to a British citizen facing imprisonment in a Thai jail.

Culture and etiquette

Tourist literature has marketed Thailand as the "Land of Smiles" so successfully that a lot of farangs arrive in Bangkok expecting to be forgiven any outrageous behaviour. This is just not the case: there are some things so universally sacred in Thailand that even a hint of disrespect will cause deep offence. TAT publishes a special leaflet on the subject, entitled *Dos and Don'ts in Thailand*, reproduced at Ⓦ www.tourismthailand.org.

The monarchy

It is both socially unacceptable and a criminal offence to make critical or defamatory remarks about the **royal family**. Thailand's monarchy might be a constitutional one, but almost every household displays a picture of King Bhumibol and Queen Sirikit in a prominent position, and respectful crowds mass whenever either of them makes a public appearance. The second of their four children, Crown Prince Vajiralongkorn, is the heir to the throne; his younger sister, Princess Royal Maha Chakri Sirindhorn, is often on TV and in the English newspapers as she is involved in many charitable projects. When addressing or speaking about royalty, Thais use a special language full of deference, called *rajasap* (literally "royal language").

Thailand's **lese-majesty laws** are among the most strictly applied in the world, increasingly invoked as the Thai establishment becomes ever more uneasy over the erosion of traditional monarchist sentiments and the rise of critical voices, particularly on the internet (though these are generally quickly censored). Accusations of lese-majesty can be levelled by and against anyone, Thai national or farang, and must be investigated by the police. As a few high-profile cases involving foreigners have demonstrated, they can be raised for seemingly minor infractions, such as defacing a poster or being less than respectful in a work of fiction. Transgressions are met with jail sentences of up to 75 years.

Aside from keeping any anti-monarchy sentiments to yourself, you should be prepared to stand when the **king's anthem** is played at the beginning of every cinema programme, and to stop in your tracks if the neighbourhood or public building you're in follows tradition and plays the **national anthem** over its public address system at 8am and 6pm. A less obvious point: as the king's head features on all Thai currency, you should never step on a coin or banknote, which is tantamount to kicking the king in the face.

Religion

Almost equally insensitive would be to disregard certain **religious** precepts. **Buddhism** plays an essential part in the lives of most Thais, and Buddhist monuments should be treated with respect – which basically means wearing long trousers or knee-length skirts, covering your arms and removing your shoes whenever you visit one.

All **Buddha images** are sacred, however small, tacky or ruined, and should never be used as a backdrop for a portrait photo, clambered over, placed in a position of inferiority or treated in any manner that could be construed as disrespectful. In an attempt to prevent foreigners from committing any kind of transgression the government requires a special licence for all Buddha statues exported from the country.

Monks come only just beneath the monarchy in the social hierarchy, and they too are addressed and discussed in a special language. If there's a monk around, he'll always get a seat on the bus, usually right at the back. Theoretically, monks are forbidden to have any close contact with women, which means, as a female, you mustn't sit or stand next to a monk, or even brush against his robes; if it's essential to pass him something, put the object down so that he can then pick it up – never hand it over directly. Nuns, however, get treated like ordinary women.

See Contexts p.227 for more on religious practices in Thailand.

The body

The Western liberalism embraced by the Thai sex industry is very unrepresentative of the majority Thai attitude to the body. **Clothing** – or the lack of it – is what bothers Thais most about tourist behaviour. As mentioned above, you need to dress modestly when entering temples, but the same also applies to other important buildings and all public places. Stuffy and sweaty as it sounds, you should keep short shorts and vests for the beach.

According to ancient Hindu belief, the **head** is the most sacred part of the body and the **feet** are the most unclean. This belief, imported into Thailand, means that it's very rude to touch another person's head or to point your feet either at a human being or at a sacred image – when sitting on a temple floor, for example, you should **tuck your legs beneath you** rather than stretch them out towards the Buddha. These hierarchies also forbid people from wearing **shoes** (which are even more unclean than feet) inside temples and most private homes, and – by extension – Thais take offence when they see someone sitting on the "head", or prow, of a boat. **Putting your feet up** on a table, a chair or a pillow is also considered very uncouth, and Thais will always take their shoes off if they need to stand on a train or bus seat to get to the luggage rack, for example. On a more practical note, the **left hand** is used for washing after going to the toilet, so Thais never use it to put food in their mouth, pass things or shake hands – as a farang though, you'll be assumed to have different customs, so left-handers shouldn't worry unduly.

Social conventions

Thais very rarely shake hands, instead using the **wai** to greet and say goodbye and to acknowledge respect, gratitude or apology. A prayer-like gesture made with raised hands, the *wai* changes according to the relative status of the two people involved: Thais can instantaneously assess which *wai* to use, but as a farang your safest bet is to go for the "stranger's" *wai*, which requires that your hands be raised close to your chest and your fingertips placed just below your chin. If someone makes a *wai* at you, you should generally *wai* back, but it's safer not to initiate.

Public displays of **physical affection** in Thailand are more common between friends of the same sex than between lovers, whether hetero- or homosexual. Holding hands and hugging is as common among male friends as with females, so if you're caressed by a Thai acquaintance of the same sex, don't assume you're being propositioned.

Finally, there are three specifically Thai **concepts** you're bound to come across, which may help you comprehend a sometimes laissez-faire attitude to delayed buses and other inconveniences. The first, **jai yen**, translates literally as "cool heart" and is something everyone tries to maintain – most Thais hate raised voices, visible irritation and confrontations of any kind, so losing one's cool can have a much more inflammatory effect than in more combative cultures. Related to this is the oft-quoted response to a difficulty, **mai pen rai** – "never mind", "no problem" or "it can't be helped" – the verbal equivalent of an open-handed shoulder shrug, which has its basis in the Buddhist notion of karma. And then there's **sanuk**, the wide-reaching philosophy of "fun", which, crass as it sounds, Thais do their best to inject into any situation, even work. Hence the crowds of inebriated Thais who congregate at beauty spots on public holidays (travelling solo is definitely not *sanuk*), the inability to do almost anything without high-volume musical accompaniment, and the national waterfight which takes place every April.

Thai names

Although all Thais have a first **name** and a family name, everyone is addressed by their first name – even when meeting strangers – prefixed by the title **"Khun"** (Mr/Ms); no one is ever addressed as Khun Surname. Among friends and relatives, **Phii** ("older brother/sister") is often used instead of Khun when addressing older familiars (though as a tourist you're on surer ground with Khun), and **Nong** ("younger brother/sister") is used for younger ones.

Thais of all ages are commonly known by the **nickname** given them soon after birth rather than by their official first name. This

tradition arises out of a deep-rooted superstition that once a child has been officially named the spirits will begin to take an unhealthy interest in them, so a nickname is used instead to confuse the spirits. Common nicknames – which often bear no resemblance to the adult's personality or physique – include Yai (Big), Oun (Fat) and Muu (Pig); Lek or Noi (Little), Nok (Bird), Noo (Mouse)

and Kung (Shrimp); and English nicknames like Apple, Joy or even Pepsi.

Family names were only introduced in 1913 (by Rama VI, who invented many of the aristocracy's surnames himself), and are used only in very formal situations, always in conjunction with the first name. It's quite usual for good friends never to know each other's surname.

Travel essentials

Car rental

Theoretically, foreigners need an international driver's licence to rent a car, but most companies accept national licences. Prices for a small car start at about B1200 per day; petrol currently costs around B28 a litre. Thais drive on the left, and the speed limit is 60km per hour within built-up areas and 90km per hour outside them.

Avis ☎02 251 1131–2; ⊛www.avisthailand.com 2/12 Thanon Witthayu (Wireless Rd), Suvarnabhumi and Don Muang airports.

Budget ☎02 203 0250; ⊛www.budget.co.th: 19/23 Building A, Royal City Ave, Thanon Phetchaburi Mai and Suvarnabhumi Airport.

National (SMT Rent-A-Car) ☎02 722 8487, ⊛www.nationalcarrental.co.th: 727 Thanon Srinakharin and Suvarnabhumi Airport.

Charities and volunteer projects

Reassured by the plethora of well-stocked shopping plazas, efficient services and abundance of bars and restaurants, it is easy to forget that life is extremely hard for many people in Bangkok. Countless **charities** work with Thailand's many poor and disadvantaged communities: listed below are a few that would welcome help in some way from visitors.

Human Development Foundation 100/11 Kae Ha Klong Toey 4, Thanon Damrongrathhaphipat, Klong Toey, Bangkok ☎02 671 5313, ⊛www .mercycentre.org. Since 1972, this organization

has been providing education and support for Bangkok's street kids and slum-dwellers as well as caring for those with HIV/AIDS. It now runs more than thirty kindergartens in the slums. Contact the centre for information about volunteering, or visit it to purchase gifts. *The Slaughterhouse: Stories from Bangkok's Klong Toey Slum* (see p.240) gives an eye-opening insight into this often invisible side of Thai life.

Students' Education Trust (SET) ⊛www .thaistudentcharity.org. High-school and further education in Thailand is a luxury that the poorest kids cannot afford so many are sent to live in temples instead. The SET helps such kids pursue their education and escape from the poverty trap. Some of their stories are told in *Little Angels: The Real-Life Stories of Twelve Thai Novice Monks* (see p.241). SET welcomes donations and sponsorship.

We-Train International House ☎02 967 8550–4, ⊛www.we-train.co.th. Run by the Association for the Promotion of the Status of Women (APSW), this is a comfortable, a/c hotel (❸; dorms from B100) set beside a lake close to Don Muang Airport, whose profits go towards helping APSW support, house and train disadvantaged women and children. Contact the hotel for help with transport.

Cookery classes

Nearly all the five-star hotels will arrange Thai cookery classes for guests if requested.

Baipai 150/12 Soi Naksuwan, Thanon Nonsee, off Thanon Rama III ☎02 294 9029, ⊛www.baipai .com. Thorough, morning classes in a quiet, suburban house in southern downtown. B1600, including transfers from central hotels. Closed Mon.

Bangkok Marriott (see p.169). Morning classes Mon–Fri aboard a converted rice barge, the *Manohra* (☎02 476 0022, ext 1416, ⊛www.manohracruises .com), including a market tour. B2600.

Blue Elephant 233 Thanon Sathorn Tai ☎02 673 9353–4, ⊛www.blueelephant.com. Held in a grand, century-old building, the courses here range from B2800 for half a day to a five-day private course for professional chefs for B68,000.

May Kaidee 33 Thanon Samsen, Banglamphu ☎089 137 3173, ⊛www.maykaidee.com. Banglamphu's famous veggie cook shares her culinary expertise at one of her restaurants (see p.176) for B1200 per day.

Saovapa On the connecting soi between Sois 21 and 23, Thanon Sukhumvit ☎02 204 1143, ⊛www.saovapaschool.com. Ministry of Education-approved courses in Thai cooking and fruit and veg carving; from B1600 for four classes.

Thai House ☎02 903 9611 or 02 997 5161, ⊛www.thaihouse.co.th. Set in an orchard in a rural part of Nonthaburi, this place runs one- (B3500) to three-day (B16,650) cooking courses, all including transfers from downtown, the latter including vegetable- and fruit-carving and homestay accommodation in traditional wooden houses.

Costs

Bangkok can be a very cheap place to visit. At the bottom of the scale, you can just about manage on a **daily budget** of around B650 (£13/US$19) if you're willing to opt for basic accommodation and eat, drink and travel as the locals do. With extras like air conditioning, taxis and a meal and beer in a more touristy restaurant, a day's outlay would look more like B1000 (£20/US$30). Staying in well-equipped, mid-range hotels and eating in the more exclusive restaurants, you should be able to live very comfortably for around B2000 a day (£40/US$60).

Bargaining is expected practice for a lot of commercial transactions, particularly at markets and when hiring tuk-tuks and motorbike taxis (though not in supermarkets or department stores). It's a delicate art that requires humour, tact and patience. If your price is way out of line, the vendor's vehement refusal should be enough to make you increase your offer: never forget that the few pennies or cents you're making such a fuss over will go a lot further in a Thai person's hands than in your own.

Customs regulations

The **duty-free** allowance on entry to Thailand is 200 cigarettes (or 250g of tobacco) and a litre of spirits or wine.

To **export antiques** or newly cast **Buddha images** from Thailand, you need to have a licence granted by the Fine Arts Department (the export of antique Buddhas is forbidden). Licences can be obtained through the Office of Archeology and National Museums, 81/1 Thanon Si Ayutthaya (near the National Library), Bangkok (☎02 628 5032). Applications take at least three working days, and need to be accompanied by the object itself, some evidence of its rightful possession, two postcard-sized colour photos of it, taken face-on and against a white background, and photocopies of the applicant's passport; furthermore, if the object is a Buddha image, the passport photocopies need to be certified by your embassy in Bangkok. Some antiques shops can organize all this for you.

Departure taxes

Domestic and international departure taxes are included in the price of the air ticket.

Electricity

Mains **electricity** is supplied at 220 volts AC. If you're packing phone and camera chargers, a laptop or other appliance, you'll need to take a set of travel-plug adaptors as several plug types are commonly in use, most usually with two round pins, but also with two flat-blade pins, and sometimes with both options.

Embassies and consulates

See ⊛www.mfa.go.th/web/2694.php for a full list with links.

Australia 37 Thanon Sathorn Tai ☎02 344 6300, ⊛www.austembassy.or.th; **Burma** (Myanmar) 132 Thanon Sathorn Nua ☎02 234 4789; **Cambodia** 518/4 Thanon Pracha Uthit (Soi Ramkamhaeng 39) ☎02 957 5851–2; **Canada** 15th floor, Abdulrahim Place, 990 Thanon Rama IV ☎02 636 0540, ⊛www .international.gc.ca/bangkok; **China** 57 Thanon Rajadapisek ☎02 245 7033 or 02 245 7036; **India** 46, Sukhumvit Soi 23 ☎02 258 0300–5, ⊛indianembassy.gov.in/bangkok; **Indonesia** 600–602 Thanon Phetchaburi ☎02 252 3135–9, ⊛www.kbri-bangkok.com; **Ireland** (honorary consul) 28th Floor, Q House Lumpini Building, 1 Thanon Sathorn Tai ☏02 677 7500, ⓦwww .irelandinthailand.com; **Laos** 502/1–3 Soi Sahakarnpramoon, Thanon Pracha Uthit ☏02 539 6667–8, ext 106, ⓦwww.bkklaoembassy.com; **Malaysia** 35 Thanon Sathorn Tai ☏02 629 6800; **New Zealand** 14th Floor, M Thai Tower, All Seasons Place, 87 Thanon Witthayu ☏02 254 2530; **Singapore** 129 Thanon Sathorn Tai ☏02 286 2111; **South Africa** Floor 12A, M Thai Tower, All Seasons Place, 87 Thanon Witthayu ☏02 659 2900, ⓦwww .saembbangkok.com; **UK** 14 Thanon Witthayu ☏02 305 8333; **US** 120 Thanon Witthayu ☏02 205 4000; **Vietnam** 83/1 Thanon Witthayu ☏02 650 8979.

Insurance

Most visitors to Thailand will need to take out **specialist travel insurance**, though you should check exactly what's covered.

Internet

An increasing number of hotels, guest houses and a few restaurants and bars in Bangkok offer **wi-fi**, occasionally for free, more usually for a minimal fee; True provide free wi-fi to the whole Siam Square area. For a list of other hotspots, try ⓦwww.jiwire.com. Banglamphu is packed with places offering **internet access**, in particular along Thanon Khao San. To surf in style, head for *True*, housed in a beautiful early twentieth-century villa at the back of *Tom Yam Kung* restaurant where you also can sip coffee, recline on retro sofas and browse lifestyle mags. The Ratchadamnoen Post Office on Banglamphu's Soi Damnoen Klang Neua (Mon–Fri 8.30am–4.30pm) has very cheap public **Catnet** internet booths; to use the service, you need to buy a B100 card with a Catnet PIN, which should give you

around three hours of internet time. On Thanon Sukhumvit the Time Internet Centre on the second floor of Times Square, between sois 12 and 14 (daily 9am–midnight), is reliable. The TOT office on the north side of Thanon Ploenchit near Central Chidlom offers cheap surfing in quite a civilized atmosphere, with refreshments available, and there's a branch of *True* (see above) on Soi 3, Siam Square, that's only a little more expensive. Elsewhere in the downtown area, during the day, there are several rather noisy places on Floor 7 of the MBK Shopping Centre (Zone D, towards the *Pathumwan Princess Hotel*), while *Chart Gallery Café* on the ground floor of River City shopping centre offers a bit more style and tranquillity, as well as food and drink while you're online. There's a Catnet centre in the GPO's public telephone office on Thanon Charoen Krung (see p.53).

Language classes

The most popular place to **study Thai** is at the AUA (American University Alumni; ⓦwww.auathailand.org). Other language schools include Jentana and Associates (ⓦwww.thai-lessons.com), and Nisa Thai Language School (ⓦwww.nisathailanguage school.com). For more information and directories of language schools, see ⓦwww .learningthai.com.

Laundry

Guest houses and hotels all over the city run low-cost, same-day **laundry** services. In some places you pay per item, in others you're charged by the kilo (about B35 per kg). There are several self-service laundries on and around Thanon Khao San, including Wearever on Thanon Samsen, between sois 1 and 3, which has sofas, coffee and free wi-fi.

Left luggage

At Suvarnabhumi Airport (B100 per day); Don Muang Airport (B75 per day); Southern Bus Terminal (B20–60 per day); Hualamphong train station (B30–80 per day); and most hotels and guest houses.

Living in Bangkok

The most common source of **employment** in Bangkok is **teaching English** and a good place to search for openings is Ⓦwww.ajarn.com; the website also features extensive advice on all sorts of issues to do with teaching and living in Thailand. Another useful resource is the excellent Ⓦwww.thaivisa.com, whose scores of well-used forums focus on specific topics that range from employment in Thailand to legal issues and cultural and practical topics. Guest house noticeboards occasionally carry adverts for more unusual jobs, such as playing extras in Thai movies.

A tourist visa does not entitle you to work in Thailand, so, legally, you'll need to apply for a **work permit**.

Mail

Overseas airmail usually takes around seven days from Bangkok. **Post offices**, which generally offer poste restante and money-wiring facilities (in association with Western Union), are the best places to buy **stamps**. An airmail letter of under 10g costs B17 to send to Europe or Australia and B19 to North America; standard-sized postcards cost B12, larger ones and aerogrammes B15, regardless of where they're going. The **surface** rate for parcels to the UK is B950 for the first kg, then B175 per kg; to the US B550 for the first kg, then B140 per kg; and to Australia B650 for the first kg, then B110 per kg; the package should reach its destination in three months. The **airmail** rate for parcels to the UK is B900 for the first kg, then B380 per kg; to the US B950 for the first kg, then B500 per kg; and to Australia B750 for the first kg, then B350 per kg; the package should reach its destination in one or two weeks.

The GPO is at 1160 Thanon Charoen Krung (postcode 10501), near Wat Muang Kae express-boat pier and walkable from Si Phraya pier. Poste restante, which is kept for two months, can be collected here. This and most other services at the GPO are open Mon–Fri 8am–8pm, Sat & Sun 8am–1pm; the parcel-packing service, however, operates Mon–Fri 8am–5pm, Sat 9am–noon. If you're staying on or near Thanon Khao San in Banglamphu, it's more convenient to use the local postal, packing and poste restante services at either Ratchadamnoen Post Office, Soi Damnoen Klang Neua, Bangkok 10200 (Mon–Fri 8am–5pm, Sat 9am–1pm); or Banglamphubon PO, Soi Sibsam Hang, Bangkok 10203 (daily 8am–5pm). On Thanon Sukhumvit use Nana PO, between sois 4 and 6, Thanon Sukhumvit, Bangkok 10112 (Mon–Fri 8.30am–8pm, Sat, Sun & hols 9am–5pm).

Money and exchange

Thailand's unit of currency is the **baht** (abbreviated to "B"), divided into 100 satang – which are rarely seen these days. Silver coins come in B1, B2 (also available as gold coins), B5 and B10 (with a small brass centre encircled by a silver ring) denominations, notes in B20, B50, B100, B500 and B1000 denominations, inscribed with Western as well as Thai numerals, and generally increasing in size according to value.

At the time of writing, **exchange rates** were around B35 to US$1, B45 to €1 and B50 to £1. A good site for current exchange rates is Ⓦwww.xe.com. Because of severe currency fluctuations in the late 1990s, a few tourist-oriented businesses now quote their prices in **US dollars**, particularly luxury hotels.

Banking hours are Monday to Friday from 8.30am to 3.30/4.30pm. The Suvarnabhumi Airport exchange desks and those in the upmarket hotels are open 24 hour, while many other exchange booths stay open till 8pm or later, especially along Khao San, Sukhumvit and Silom roads and in the major malls.

Sterling and US dollar **traveller's cheques** are accepted by banks, exchange booths and upmarket hotels, and most places also deal in a variety of other currencies; everyone offers better rates for cheques than for straight cash. Generally, a total of B33 in commission and duty is charged per cheque, so you'll save money if you deal in larger cheque denominations.

American Express, Visa and MasterCard **credit and debit cards** are accepted at top hotels as well as in some posh restaurants, department stores, tourist shops and travel agents, but surcharging of up to seven percent is rife, and theft and forgery are major industries – try not to let the card out of your sight, always demand any carbon copies, and never leave cards in baggage storage. With a debit or credit card and personal identification number (PIN), you can also withdraw cash from hundreds of 24-hour **ATMs** around the city, including a growing number of stand-alone ATMs in supermarkets.

Opening hours and public holidays

Most **shops** open at least Monday to Saturday from about 8am to 8pm, while department stores operate daily from around

National holidays

Jan 1 Western New Year's Day
Feb (day of full moon) Maha Puja: commemorates the Buddha preaching to a spontaneously assembled crowd of 1250.
April 6 Chakri Day: the founding of the Chakri dynasty.
April (usually 13–15) Songkhran: Thai New Year.
May 1 National Labour Day
May 5 Coronation Day
May (early in the month) Royal Ploughing Ceremony: marks start of rice-planting season.
May (day of full moon) Visakha Puja: the holiest of all Buddhist holidays, which celebrates the birth, enlightenment and death of the Buddha.
July (day of full moon) Khao Pansa: the start of the annual three-month Buddhist rains retreat, when new monks are ordained.
Aug 12 Queen's birthday
Oct 23 Chulalongkorn Day: the anniversary of Rama V's death.
Dec 5 King's birthday: also celebrated as national Fathers' Day.
Dec 10 Constitution Day
Dec 31 Western New Year's Eve

10am to 9pm. Private office hours are generally Monday to Friday 8am to 5pm and Saturday 8am to noon, though in tourist areas these hours are longer, with weekends worked like any other day. Government offices work Monday to Friday 8.30am to noon and 1 to 4.30pm, and national museums tend to stick to these hours too, but some close on Mondays and Tuesdays rather than at weekends.

Many tourists only register **national holidays** because trains and buses suddenly get extraordinarily crowded: although banks and government offices shut on these days, most shops and tourist-oriented businesses carry on regardless, and TAT branches continue to dispense information. The only time an inconvenient number of shops, restaurants and hotels do close is during **Chinese New Year**, which, though not marked as an official national holiday, brings many businesses to a standstill for several days in late January or February.

Thais use both the Western Gregorian **calendar** and a Buddhist calendar – the Buddha is said to have died (or entered Nirvana) in the year 543 BC, so Thai dates start from that point: thus 2010 AD becomes 2553 BE (Buddhist Era).

Phones

Local **calls in Bangkok** are very cheap (as little as B1 for 3min from a coin payphone), though inter-provincial rates cost B3–12 per minutes. Deregulation of the Thai telecommunications industry has made **calling internationally** from Thailand a convoluted, though cheaper, business, with the state-owned companies, CAT (contact centre ☎1322, ⓦ www.cattelecom.com) and TOT (☎1100, ⓦ www.tot.co.th), competing for business: each now offers a premium-rate service with its own **prefix** (CAT's ☎001 and TOT's ☎007), as well as a cheaper, generally lower-quality, VOIP (voice-over-internet protocol) prefix (CAT's ☎009 and TOT's ☎008). Visitors can access these prefixes on mobile phones or via phone cards, while many private **international call offices** (where your call is timed and you pay at the end) in tourist areas such as Khao San now use ☎009 or 008 to access the lower VOIP rates – plus a service charge to the customer, of course.

When **dialling** any number in Thailand, you must now always preface it with what used to be the area code (02 in Bangkok), even when dialling from the same area. Where we've given several line numbers – eg ☎02 431 1802–9 – you can substitute the last digit, 2, with any digit between 3 and 9. For **directory enquiries** within Thailand, call ☎1133.

All mobile phone numbers in Thailand have recently been changed from nine to ten digits, by adding the number "8" after the initial zero (you may still come across cards and brochures giving the old nine-digit number). Note also, however, that Thais tend to change mobile-phone providers – and therefore numbers – comparatively frequently, in search of a better deal. One final local idiosyncrasy: Thai phone books list people by their first name, not their family name.

International cardphones are dotted all over the city, so there's now little call for the **public telephone offices** in or adjacent to post offices, though their booths do at least guarantee some peace and quiet. The largest and most convenient is the CAT office in the compound of the GPO on Thanon Charoen Krung (Mon–Fri 8am–8pm, Sat & Sun 8am–4pm) which, as well as cardphones, offers a fax and internet service, a free collect-call service and even video-conferencing (see p.51 for location details). The Ratchadamnoen post office in Banglamphu (see p.51) also has international telephone offices attached, but these close at 5pm.

Phone cards

The most flexible **phone card** available is TOT's **Pin Phone 108** Card, which allows both domestic and international calls. Equipped with a pin number, it can be used from any payphone or fixed landline. Offering the same services, the **TOT Card** has no PIN number but can only be used in special TOT green and yellow payphones, not in the more commonly found stainless steel payphones. With either of these cards, which are available in B50–500 denominations from 7–Eleven and Family Mart supermarkets, for example, calls to the UK and Australia cost B9 (☎007) or B7 (☎008) per minute, US and Canada B9 (☎007) or B5 (☎008), New Zealand B17 (☎007) or B15 (☎008) and South Africa B32 (☎007) or B7

(☎008); calls to Ireland currently cost B24 per minute with either prefix.

CAT's cards are available from post offices and supermarkets, but can only be used for international calls. Their Thaicard, available in B100–1000 denominations, can be used in designated purple cardphones – if you can't happen to find one, head for the nearest public telephone office (see above). With a Thaicard, you use the ☎001 prefix, at rates roughly comparable with TOT's ☎007 phone-card charges. CAT's **Phone Net** cards, which use the ☎009 prefix and come in B200–500 denominations, can be used, in conjunction with a PIN number, from any payphone or fixed landline or from a mobile with international roaming. Rates are roughly comparable with TOT's ☎008 phone-card charges, though there's currently a long-term special promotion of B2 per minute to landlines in the UK, US and Canada, B2.5 Ireland, Australia and New Zealand and B4 South Africa.

There's also a **private cardphone system** called **Lenso** (Ⓦwww.lensophonecard.com). To use Lenso's yellow phones, you either need a special Lenso phone card (available from shops such as 7-Eleven and Family Mart in B200, B300 and B500 denominations), or you can use a credit card. Rates, however, are generally higher than TOT's phone card rates. If you're really hunting for a telephonic bargain, keep your eyes peeled for new, smaller **private phone cards**, such as Dee (Ⓦwww.thookdee.com) and Hello by Hatari (Ⓦwww.hatari.net), which use call-back and/or PIN number systems, and offer international calls to the most popular destinations for as little as B1 per minute.

Mobile phones

An increasing number of tourists are taking their **mobile phones** (*meu teu*) to Thailand. Visitors from the US may well need to have a dual- or tri-band phone, but GSM 900Hz and 1800Hz, and 3G, the systems most commonly found in other parts of the world, are all available in Thailand. Most foreign networks have links with Thai networks, but it's worth checking with your phone provider before you travel. For a list of network types and providers in Thailand, along with coverage maps and roaming partners, go to Ⓦwww.gsmworld.com/roaming.

International dialling codes

Calling from abroad, the international **country code** for Thailand is **66**, after which you leave off the initial zero of the Thai number.

Calling from Thailand, you'll need the relevant country code (see p.52 for information on prefixes):

Australia ☎61	**Canada** ☎1	**Ireland** ☎353
New Zealand ☎64	**South Africa** ☎27	**UK** ☎44
US ☎1		

For **international directory enquiries** and operator services, call ☎100.

If you want to use your mobile a lot in Thailand, it may well be worth getting hold of a rechargeable **Thai SIM card** with a local phone number. An AIS 1-2-Call card (ⓦ www.one-2-call.ais.co.th) will give you the widest coverage in Thailand, and top-up cards are available at 7-Eleven stores across the country. Their call rates start at B0.75 per minute within Thailand; international call rates depend on the prefix used (see p.52), ranging from B7 per minute to the UK, for example, on ☎008 or 009, through B9 on ☎007, to B18 on ☎001. Texts cost B2 domestic, B9 to the UK, for example.

Your own network operator may be able to give you useful advice before you leave home about **exchanging SIM cards**, including any unlocking codes that may be necessary. Thai SIM cards are available at mobile phone outlets all over Bangkok, but the best place to buy a card and have any necessary technical adjustments made, including setting up voicemail, is the Mah Boon Krong Centre (see p.203); an AIS 1-2-Call SIM card, for example, will cost you around B300, including your first B50 worth of calls, though look out for periodic special offers that include substantial credit bonuses.

Time

Thailand is in the same time zone year-round, with no daylight savings period. Bangkok is five hours ahead of South Africa, seven hours ahead of GMT, twelve hours ahead of US Eastern Standard Time, three hours behind Australian Eastern Standard Time and five hours behind New Zealand Standard Time.

Tipping

It is usual to **tip** hotel bellboys and porters B20 and to round up taxi fares to the nearest B10. Most guides, drivers, masseurs, waiters and maids also depend on tips, and although some upmarket hotels and restaurants will add an automatic ten percent service charge to your bill, this is not always shared out.

Travellers with disabilities

Thailand makes few provisions for its disabled citizens and this obviously affects **travellers with disabilities**, though taxis, comfortable hotels and personal tour guides are all more affordable than in the West and most travellers with disabilities find Thais only too happy to offer assistance where they can. Hiring a local tour guide to accompany you on a day's sightseeing is particularly recommended: government tour guides can be arranged through any TAT office.

Most **wheelchair users** end up driving on Bangkok's roads because it's too hard to negotiate the uneven pavements, which are high to allow for flooding and invariably lack dropped kerbs. Crossing the road can be a trial, as it's usually a question of climbing steps up to a bridge rather than taking a ramped underpass. Few buses and trains have ramps but some Skytrain stations and all subway stations have lifts.

Several **tour companies** in Thailand specialize in organizing trips featuring adapted facilities, accessible transport and escorts. Help and Care Travel Company (☎081 375 0792, ⓦ www.wheelchairtours.com) designs **accessible holidays** in Thailand for slow walkers and wheelchair users and its website carries a (short) list of wheelchair-accessible hotels in the main tourist centres. Thai Focus (ⓦ www.thaifocus.com) can also tailor-make trips for disabled travellers and provides carers where appropriate.

The City

The City

www.roughguides.com

Ratanakosin

T he only place to start your exploration of Bangkok is **Ratanakosin**, the royal island on the east bank of the Chao Phraya River, where the city's most important and extravagant sights are. When Rama I developed Ratanakosin for his new capital in 1782, after the sacking of Ayutthaya and a temporary stay across the river in Thonburi, he paid tribute to its precursor by imitating Ayutthaya's layout and architecture – he even shipped the building materials downstream from the ruins of the old city. Like Ayutthaya, the new capital was sited for protection beside a river and turned into an artificial island by the construction of defensive canals, with a central **Grand Palace** and adjoining royal temple, **Wat Phra Kaeo**, fronted by an open cremation field, **Sanam Luang**; the Wang Na (Palace of the Second King), now the **National Museum**, was also built at this time. **Wat Pho**, which predates the capital's founding, was further embellished by Rama I's successors, who have consolidated Ratanakosin's pre-eminence by building several grand European-style palaces (now housing government institutions); Wat Mahathat, the most important centre of Buddhist learning in southeast Asia; the National Theatre; the National Gallery; and Thammasat and Silpakorn universities.

Bangkok has expanded eastwards away from the river, leaving the Grand Palace a good 5km from the city's commercial heart, and the royal family have long since moved their residence to Dusit, but Ratanakosin remains the ceremonial centre of the whole kingdom – so much so that it feels as if it might sink into the boggy ground under the weight of its own mighty edifices. The heavy, stately feel is lightened by traditional shophouses selling herbal medicines,

Getting to and from Ratanakosin

Ratanakosin is within easy walking distance of Banglamphu, but is best approached from the river, via the **express-boat** piers of Tha Chang (the former bathing place of the royal elephants, which gives access to the Grand Palace and Sanam Luang), Tha Thien (for Wat Pho) or Tha Ratchini (for the Museum of Siam, weekday rush hours only). Coming from the downtown area or Thanon Sukhumvit, the most comfortable and scenic approach is to catch a Skytrain to Saphan Taksin station, then an express boat from Central Pier (Sathorn). From Soi Kasemsan 1 (Tha Saphan Hua Chang) and from several piers near Thanon Sukhumvit, you might also consider the regular **longtails** along Khlong Saen Saeb and a walk from their Golden Mount terminus, which make up in speed for their lack of comfort and scenery. Otherwise take your pick from the scores of **buses** that stop or terminate on Sanam Luang and the surrounding streets – many of them after a slow crawl through congested Chinatown streets.

RATANAKOSIN

N8 Express-boat pier

N11 *Tha Bangkok Noi*

Banglamphu ▶

THONBURI

Bangkok Tourism Division

National Theatre

National Gallery

National Museum

Tha Prachan

Thammasat University

THANON PHRA ARTHIT

THANON CHAO FA

PHRAPINKLAO BRIDGE

THANON CHAKRABONGSE

RAJDAMNOEN KLANG

Royal Hotel

N10 *Tha Wang Lang (Siriraj)*

Tha Maharat

Chao Phraya River

THANON PHRA CHAN

THANON NA PHRA THAT

Wat Mahathat

Sanam Luang

THANON RAJDAMNOEN NAI

Mae Toranee Statue

THANON RACHINI

THANON ATSADANG

Silpakorn University

Tha Chang

N9

THANON NA PHRA LAN

1 ✉

Lak Muang

THANON LAKMUANG

THANON MAHARAT

Wat Phra Kaeo

Grand Palace

THANON BAMRUNG MUANG

THANON SANAM CHAI

THANON SARANROM

THANON RACHINI

THANON ATSADANG

Wat Rajapradit

Wat Rajabophit

THANON FUANG NAKHON

Inner Palace

Khlong Lot

Pahurat & Chinatown ▶

N ✦

Tha Thien

2

N8

3

THANON THAI WANG

THANON CHAROEN KRUNG (NEW ROAD)

SOI PEN PHAT

A Wat Pho Massage School

Wat Pho

SOI CHETUPHON

B

SOI SATTHAKAN

Museum of Siam

C

Wat Arun

EATING & DRINKING	
Na Pralan Café	1
Po	2
Rub Ar Roon	3

ACCOMMODATION	
Arun Residence	A
Aurum: The River Place	B
Chakrabongse Villas	C

0   200 m

N7 *Tha Ratchini*

pavement amulet sellers and studenty canteens along the riverside road, **Thanon Maharat**; and by **Sanam Luang**, still used for cremations and royal ceremonies, but also functioning as a popular open park and the hub of the modern city's bus system. Despite containing several of the country's main sights, the area is busy enough in its own right not to have become a swarming tourist zone and strikes a neat balance between liveliness and grandeur.

A **word of warning**: when you're heading for the Grand Palace or Wat Pho, you may be approached by someone, possibly pretending to be a student or an official, who will tell you the sight is closed when it's not, or some other lies to try to lead you away from the entrance, because they want to lead you on a shopping trip for souvenirs, tailored clothes or, if you seem really gullible, gems (see p.211). The opening hours of the Grand Palace – but not Wat Pho – are indeed sometimes erratic because of state occasions, but you can check the details on its website, ⓦ www.palaces.thai.net – and even if it's closed on the day you want to visit, that's no reason to throw yourself at the mercy of these shysters.

Wat Phra Kaeo and the Grand Palace

Hanging together in a precarious harmony of strangely beautiful colours and shapes, **Wat Phra Kaeo** is the apogee of Thai religious art and the holiest Buddhist site in the country, housing the most important image, the **Emerald Buddha**. Built as the private royal temple, Wat Phra Kaeo occupies the northeast corner of the huge **Grand Palace**, whose official opening in 1785 marked the founding of the new capital and the rebirth of the Thai nation after the Burmese invasion. Successive kings have all left their mark here, and the palace complex now covers 25 hectares, though very little apart from the wat is open to tourists.

The only **entrance** to the complex in 2km of crenellated walls is the Gate of Glorious Victory in the middle of the north side, on Thanon Na Phra Lan. This brings you onto a driveway with a tantalizing view of the temple's glittering spires on the left and the dowdy buildings of the Offices of the Royal Household on the right: this is the powerhouse of the kingdom's ceremonial life, providing everything down to chairs and catering, even lending an urn when someone of rank dies. A textile museum under the auspices of the queen is scheduled to open among these buildings, perhaps in 2010, but for now you'll have to content yourself with some crafts shopping at the Queen's Support Foundation (see p.205).

Admission to Wat Phra Kaeo and the palace is B300 (daily 8.30am–4pm, last admission 3.30pm, weapons museum, Phra Thinang Amarin Winichai and Dusit Maha Prasat interiors closed Sat & Sun; 2hr personal audioguide B200, with passport or credit card as deposit). This includes a free brochure with a map (dispensed at the entrance turnstiles) and admission to Dusit Park (within 7 days; see p.101), plus either the missable Ananta Samakhom Throne Hall in Dusit or Sanam Chandra Palace in Nakhon Pathom (see p.143). As this is Thailand's most sacred site, you have to **dress in smart clothes**: no vests or see-through clothes; men must wear full-length trousers, women trousers or below-the-knee skirts. Suitable garments can be borrowed from the office to the right just inside the Gate of Glorious Victory (same building as the Queen's Support Foundation shop; free, deposit of B100 per item).

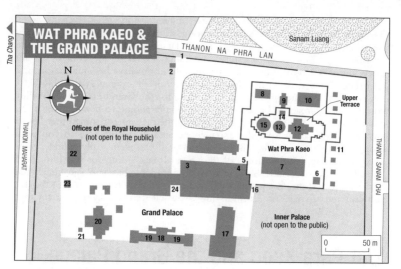

Gate of Glorious Victory	1	Porcelain viharn	9	Phra Thinang Amarin Winichai	17
Queen's Support Foundation Shop	2	Supplementary library	10	Chakri Maha Prasat	18
Ticket office	3	Prangs	11	Weapons museum	19
Royal Decorations & Coins Pavilion	4	Royal Pantheon	12	Dusit Maha Prasat	20
Entrance turnstiles to Wat Phra Kaeo	5	Phra Mondop	13	Mount Krailas model	21
Chapel of the Gandhara Buddha	6	Angkor Wat model	14	Wat Phra Kaeo museum	22
The bot and Emerald Buddha	7	Phra Si Ratana Chedi	15	Café	23
Royal mausoleum	8	Exit from Wat Phra Kaeo	16	Exit from Grand Palace	24

Wat Phra Kaeo

It makes you laugh with delight to think that anything so fantastic could exist on this sombre earth.

W. Somerset Maugham, *The Gentlemen in the Parlour*

Entering the temple is like stepping onto a lavishly detailed stage set, from the immaculate flagstones right up to the gaudy roofs. Reinforcing the sense of unreality, the whole compound is surrounded by arcaded walls, decorated with extraordinary murals of scenes from the *Ramayana*. Although it receives hundreds of foreign sightseers and at least as many Thai pilgrims every day, the temple, which has no monks in residence, maintains an unnervingly sanitized look, as if it were built only yesterday.

The approach to the bot

Inside the entrance turnstiles, you're confronted by six-metre tall **yaksha**, gaudy demons from the *Ramayana*, who watch over the Emerald Buddha from every gate of the temple and ward off evil spirits; the king of the demons, green, ten-faced Totsagan (labelled "Tosakanth"), stands to the left of the entrance by the southwest corner of the golden Phra Si Ratana Chedi. Less threatening is the toothless old codger, cast in bronze and sitting on a plinth immediately inside the turnstiles by the back wall of the bot, who represents a Hindu **hermit** credited with inventing yoga and herbal medicine. In front of him is a large grinding stone where previously herbal practitioners could come to grind their ingredients – with enhanced powers, of course. Skirting around the bot, you'll reach its **main entrance** on the eastern side, in front of which stands a cluster of grey **statues**, which have a strong Chinese feel: next to Kuan Im, the Chinese *bodhisattva* of mercy shown holding a bottle of *amritsa* (sacred elixir), are a sturdy pillar topped by a lotus flower, which Bangkok's Chinese community presented to Rama IV during his 27 years as a monk, and two handsome cows which commemorate Rama I's birth in the Year of the Cow. Worshippers make their offerings to the Emerald Buddha at two small, stand-in Buddhas here, where they can look at the main image through the open doors of the bot without messing up its pristine interior with candle wax and joss-stick ash.

Nearby, in the southeastern corner of the temple precinct, look out for the exquisite scenes of rice sheaves, fish and turtles painted in gold on blue glass on the doors and windows of the **Chapel of the Gandhara Buddha** (labelled "Hor Phra Kanthara Rat"). The decorations allude to the fertility of the ricefields, as this building was crucial to the old royal rainmaking ritual and is still used during the Royal Ploughing Ceremony (see p.69). Adorning the roof are thousands of nagas (serpents), symbolizing water; inside the locked chapel, among the paraphernalia used in the ritual, is kept the Gandhara Buddha, a bronze image in the gesture of calling down the rain with its right hand, while cupping the left to catch it. In times of drought the king would order a week-long rainmaking ceremony to be conducted, during which he was bathed regularly and kept away from the opposite sex while Buddhist monks and Hindu Brahmins chanted continuously.

The bot and the Emerald Buddha

The **bot**, the largest building of the temple, is one of the few original structures left at Wat Phra Kaeo, though it has been augmented so often it looks like the work of a wildly inspired child. Eight *sema* stones mark the boundary of the consecrated area around the bot, each sheltering in a psychedelic fairy castle, joined by a low wall decorated with Chinese porcelain tiles, which depict

▲ Mural in the Grand Palace

delicate landscapes. The walls of the bot itself, sparkling with gilt and coloured glass, are supported by 112 golden garudas (birdmen) holding nagas, representing the god Indra saving the world by slaying the serpent-cloud that had swallowed up all the water. The symbolism again reflects the king's traditional role as a rain maker.

Of the bot's three doorways, the largest, in the middle, is reserved for the king himself. Inside, a nine-metre-high pedestal supports the tiny **Emerald Buddha**, a figure whose mystique draws pilgrims from all over Thailand – as well as politicians accused of corruption, who traditionally come here to publicly swear their innocence. Here especially you must act with respect, sitting with your feet pointing away from the Buddha. The spiritual power of the sixty-centimetre jadeite image derives from its legendary past. Reputed to have been sculpted by the gods in Patna, India in 234 BC, it was revealed when lightning cracked open an ancient chedi in Chiang Rai in the early fifteenth century. The image was then moved around the north, dispensing miracles wherever it went, before being taken to Laos for two hundred years. As it was believed to bring great fortune to its possessor, the future Rama I snatched it back when he captured Vientiane in 1779, installing it at the heart of his new capital as a talisman for king and country.

Seated in the *Dhyana Mudra* (meditation), the Emerald Buddha has three **costumes**, one for each season: the crown and ornaments of an Ayutthayan king for the hot season; a gilt monastic robe for the rainy season, when the monks retreat into the temples; this is augmented with a full-length gold shawl in the cool season. To this day it's the job of the king himself to ceremonially change the Buddha's costumes – though in recent years, due to the present king's age, the Crown Prince has conducted proceedings. The Buddha was granted a new set of these three costumes in 1997: the old set is now in the Wat Phra Kaeo Museum – see p.65 – while the two costumes of the new set that are not in use are on display among the blinding glitter of crowns and jewels in the Royal Decorations and Coins Pavilion, which lies between the ticket office and the entrance to Wat Phra Kaeo.

Among the paraphernalia in front of the pedestal sits the tiny, silver Phra Chai Lang Chang (Victory Buddha), which Rama I always carried into battle on the back of his elephant for luck and which still plays an important part in coronation ceremonies. Recently covered in gold, it occupies a prestigious spot dead centre, but is modestly obscured by a fan and by the umbrella of a larger gold Buddha in front. The tallest pair of a dozen standing Buddha images, all made of bronze but encased in gold and raising both hands to dispel fear, are at the front: Rama III dedicated the one on the Emerald Buddha's left to Rama I, the one on his right to Rama II, and Rama IV enshrined relics of the Buddha in their crowns.

The upper terrace

The eastern end of the **upper terrace** is taken up with the **Prasat Phra Thep Bidorn**, known as the **Royal Pantheon**, a splendid hash of styles. The pantheon has its roots in the Khmer concept of *devaraja*, or the divinity of kings: inside are bronze and gold statues, precisely life-size, of all the kings since Bangkok became the Thai capital. Constructed by Rama IV, the building is open only on special occasions, such as Chakri Day (April 6), when the dynasty is commemorated, and Coronation Day (May 5).

From here you get the best view of the **royal mausoleum**, the **porcelain viharn** and the **supplementary library** to the north (all of which are closed to tourists, though you can sometimes glimpse Thai Buddhists worshipping in the library), and, running along the east side of the temple, a row of eight bullet-like **prangs**, each of which has a different nasty ceramic colour. Described as "monstrous vegetables" by Somerset Maugham, they represent, from north to south, the Buddha, Buddhist scripture, the monkhood, the nunhood, the Buddhas who attained enlightenment but did not preach, previous emperors, the Buddha in his previous lives and the future Buddha.

In the middle of the terrace, dressed in deep-green glass mosaics, the **Phra Mondop** was built by Rama I to house the *Tripitaka*, or Buddhist scripture, which the king had revised at Wat Mahathat in 1788, the previous version having been lost in the sack of Ayutthaya. It's famous for the mother-of-pearl cabinet and solid-silver mats inside, but is never open. Four tiny **memorials** at each corner of the mondop show the symbols of each of the nine Chakri kings, from the ancient crown representing Rama I to the present king's discus, while the bronze statues surrounding the memorials portray each king's lucky white elephants, labelled by name and pedigree. A contribution of Rama IV, on the north side of the mondop, is a **scale model of Angkor Wat**, the prodigious Cambodian temple, which during his reign (1851–68) was under Thai rule (apparently, the king had wanted to shift a whole Khmer temple to Bangkok but his officials dissuaded him). At the western end of the terrace, you can't miss

The Ramayana/Ramakien

The **Ramayana** is generally thought to have originated as an oral epic in India, where it appears in numerous dialects. The most famous version is that of the sage Valmiki, who is said to have drawn together the collection of stories as a tribute to his king over two thousand years ago. From India, the *Ramayana* spread to all the Hindu-influenced countries of South Asia and was passed down through the Khmers to Thailand, where as the **Ramakien** it has become the national epic, acting as an affirmation of the Thai monarchy and its divine Hindu links. As a source of inspiration for literature, painting, sculpture and dance-drama, it has acquired the authority of holy writ, providing Thais with moral and practical lessons, while its appearance in the form of films and comic strips shows its huge popular appeal. The version current in Thailand was composed by a committee of poets sponsored by Rama I (all previous Thai texts were lost in the sack of Ayutthaya in 1767), and runs to three thousand pages (see p.242).

The central story of the *Ramayana* concerns **Rama** (in Thai, Phra Ram), son of the king of Ayodhya, and his beautiful wife **Sita**, whose hand he wins by lifting, stringing – and breaking – a magic bow. The couple's adventures begin when they are exiled to the forest, along with Rama's good brother, **Lakshaman** (Phra Lak), by the hero's father under the influence of his evil stepmother. Meanwhile, in the city of Lanka (Longka), the demon king **Ravana** (Totsagan) has conceived a passionate desire for Sita and, disguised as a hermit, sets out to kidnap her. By transforming one of his demon subjects into a beautiful deer, which Rama and Lakshaman go off to hunt, Ravana catches Sita alone and takes her back to Lanka. Rama then wages a long war against the demons of Lanka (into which are woven many battles, spy scenes and diversionary episodes), eventually kills Ravana and rescues Sita.

The Thai version shows some characteristic differences from the Indian, emphasizing the typically Buddhist virtues of filial obedience and willing renunciation. In addition, Hanuman, the loyal monkey general, is given a much more playful role in the *Ramakien*, with the addition of many episodes which display his cunning, talent for mischief and promiscuity. The major alteration comes at the end of the story, when Phra Ram doubts Sita's faithfulness after rescuing her from Totsagan. In the Indian story, this ends with Sita being swallowed up by the earth so that she doesn't have to suffer Rama's doubts any more; in the *Ramakien* the ending is a happy one, with Phra Ram and Sita living together happily ever after.

the golden dazzle of the **Phra Si Ratana Chedi**, which Rama IV erected, in imitation of the famous bell-shaped chedis at Ayutthaya's Wat Phra Si Sanphet, to enshrine a piece of the Buddha's breastbone.

The murals

Extending for about a kilometre in the arcades that run inside the wat walls, the **murals of the Ramayana** (see box, p.63) depict every blow of this ancient story of the triumph of good over evil, using the vibrant buildings of the temple itself as backdrops, and setting them off against the subdued colours of richly detailed landscapes. Because of the damaging humidity, none of the original work of Rama I's time survives: maintenance is a never-ending process, so you'll always find an artist working on one of the scenes. The story is told in 178 panels, labelled and numbered in Thai only, starting in the middle of the northern side opposite the porcelain viharn: in the first episode, a hermit, while out ploughing, finds the baby Sita, the heroine, floating in a gold urn on a lotus leaf and brings her to the city. Panel 109, near the gate leading to the palace buildings, shows the climax of the story, when Rama, the hero, kills the ten-headed demon Totsagan (Ravana), and the ladies of the enemy city weep at the demon's death. Panel 110 depicts his elaborate funeral procession, and 113 shows the funeral fair, with acrobats, sword-jugglers and tightrope-walkers. In between, Sita – Rama's wife – has to walk on fire to prove that she has been faithful during her fourteen years of imprisonment by Totsagan. If you haven't the stamina for the long walk round, you could sneak a look at the end of the story, to the left of the first panel, where Rama holds a victory parade and distributes thank-you gifts.

The palace buildings

The exit in the southwest corner of Wat Phra Kaeo brings you to the palace proper, a vast area of buildings and gardens, of which only the northern edge is on show to the public. Though the king now lives in the Chitrlada Palace in Dusit, the Grand Palace is still used for state receptions and official ceremonies, during which there is no public access to any part of the palace.

Phra Maha Monthien

Coming out of the temple compound, you'll first of all see to your right a beautiful Chinese gate covered in innumerable tiny porcelain tiles. Extending in a straight line behind the gate is the **Phra Maha Monthien**, which was the grand residential complex of earlier kings.

Only the **Phra Thinang Amarin Winichai**, the main audience hall at the front of the complex, is open to the public. The supreme court in the era of the absolute monarchy, it currently serves as the venue for ceremonies such as the king's birthday speech. Dominating the hall are two gleaming, intricately carved thrones that date from the reign of Rama I: a white umbrella with the full nine tiers owing to a king shelters the front seat, while the unusual *busbok* behind is topped with a spired roof and floats on a boat-shaped base. The rear buildings are still used for the most important part of the elaborate coronation ceremony, and each new king is supposed to spend a night there to show solidarity with his forefathers.

Chakri Maha Prasat and the Inner Palace

Next door you can admire the facade of the "farang with a Thai hat", as the **Chakri Maha Prasat** is nicknamed. Rama V, whose portrait you can see over its entrance, employed an English architect to design a purely Neoclassical residence, but other members of the royal family prevailed on the king to add the three Thai spires. This used to be the site of the elephant stables: the large red tethering posts are still there and the bronze elephants were installed as a reminder. The building displays the emblem of the Chakri dynasty on its gable, which has a trident (*ri*) coming out of a *chak*, a discus with a sharpened rim. The only part of the Chakri Maha Prasat open to the public is the ground-floor **weapons museum**, which houses a forgettable display of hooks, pikes and guns.

The **Inner Palace** (closed to the public), which used to be the king's harem, lies behind the gate on the left-hand side of the Chakri Maha Prasat. Vividly described in M.R. Kukrit Pramoj's *Si Phaendin* (see p.243), the harem was a town in itself, with shops, law courts and an all-female police force for the huge population: as well as the current queens, the minor wives and their children (including pre-pubescent boys) and servants, this was home to the daughters and consorts of former kings, and the daughters of the aristocracy who attended the harem's finishing school. Today, the Inner Palace houses a school of cooking, fruit-carving and other domestic sciences for well-bred young Thais.

Dusit Maha Prasat

On the western side of the courtyard, the delicately proportioned **Dusit Maha Prasat**, an audience hall built by Rama I, epitomizes traditional Thai architecture. Outside, the soaring tiers of its red, gold and green roof culminate in a gilded *mongkut*, a spire shaped like the king's crown, which symbolizes the 33 Buddhist levels of perfection. Each tier of the roof bears a typical *chofa*, a slender, stylized bird's-head finial, and several *hang hong* (swans' tails), which represent three-headed nagas. Inside, you can still see the original throne, the **Phra Ratcha Banlang Pradap Muk**, a masterpiece of mother-of-pearl inlaid work. When a senior member of the royal family dies, the hall is used for the lying-in-state: the body, embalmed and seated in a huge sealed urn, is placed in the west transept, waiting up to two years for an auspicious day to be cremated.

The Wat Phra Kaeo Museum

In the nineteenth-century Royal Mint in front of the Dusit Maha Prasat – next to a small, basic **café** and an incongruous hair salon – the **Wat Phra Kaeo Museum** houses a mildly interesting collection of artefacts donated to the Emerald Buddha, along with architectural elements rescued from the Grand Palace grounds during restoration in the 1980s. Highlights include the bones of

---

The royal tonsure ceremony

To the right and behind the Dusit Maha Prasat rises a strange model mountain, decorated with fabulous animals and topped by a castle and prang. It represents **Mount Krailas**, the Himalayan home of the Hindu god Shiva (Phra Isuan in Thai), and was built by Rama IV as the site of the **royal tonsure ceremony**, last held here in 1932, just three months before the end of the absolute monarchy. In former times, Thai children generally had shaved heads, except for a tuft or topknot on the crown, which, between the age of eleven and thirteen, was cut in a Hindu initiation rite to welcome adolescence. For the royal children, the rite was an elaborate ceremony that sometimes lasted seven days, culminating with the king's cutting of the hair knot, which was then floated away on the Chao Phraya River. The child was then bathed at the model Krailas, in water representing the original river of the universe flowing down the central mountain.

various kings' white elephants, and upstairs, the Emerald Buddha's original costumes and two useful scale models of the Grand Palace, one as it is now, the other as it was when first built. Also on the first floor stands the grey stone slab of the Manangasila Seat, where Ramkhamhaeng, the great thirteenth-century king of Sukhothai, is said to have sat and taught his subjects. It was discovered in 1833 by Rama IV during his monkhood and brought to Bangkok, where Rama VI used it as the throne for his coronation.

Wat Pho (Wat Phra Chetuphon)

Where Wat Phra Kaeo may seem too perfect and shrink-wrapped for some, **Wat Pho** (daily 8am–6pm; B50; ⓦ www.watpho.com), to the south of the Grand Palace, is lively and shambolic, a complex arrangement of lavish structures which jostle with classrooms, basketball courts and a turtle pond. Busloads of tourists shuffle in and out of the **north entrance**, stopping only to gawp at the colossal Reclining Buddha, but you can avoid the worst of the crowds by using the **main entrance** on Soi Chetuphon to explore the huge compound.

Wat Pho is the oldest temple in Bangkok and older than the city itself, having been founded in the seventeenth century under the name Wat Photaram. Foreigners have stuck to the contraction of this old name, even though Rama I, after enlarging the temple, changed the name in 1801 to **Wat Phra Chetuphon**, which is how it is generally known to Thais. The temple had another major overhaul in 1832, when Rama III built the chapel of the Reclining Buddha, and turned the temple into a public centre of learning by decorating the walls and pillars with inscriptions and diagrams on subjects such as history, literature, animal husbandry and astrology. Dubbed Thailand's first university, the wat is still an important centre for traditional medicine, notably **Thai massage**, which is used against all kinds of illnesses, from backaches to viruses. Excellent massages

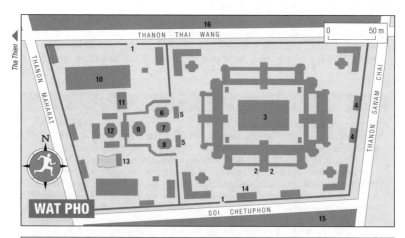

Visitors' entrances	1	Traditional Medicine Pavilions	5	Rama IV Chedi		European Pavilion	13
Entrances to Bot	2	Rama II Chedi	6	Chapel of the Reclining Buddha	10	Café	14
Bot	3	Phra Si Sanphet Chedi	7	Chinese Pavilion	11	Monks' Quarters	15
Massage Pavilions	4	Rama III Chedi	8	Library	12	Grand Palace	16

are available in the air-conditioned buildings on the east side of the main compound; allow two hours for the full works (B360 per hr; foot reflexology massage B360 per 45min). There are often long queues though, so you might be better off going to the massage centre's head office just outside the temple, at 392/25–28 Soi Pen Phat 1, Thanon Maharat (℡02 622 3533 or 02 622 3551, ⓦwww.watpomassage.com). Here, you can also enrol on a thirty-hour **massage training course** in English, over five days (B8500), and foot-massage courses for B6500.

The eastern courtyard

The main entrance on Soi Chetuphon is one of a series of sixteen monumental gates around the main compound, each guarded by stone **giants**, many of them comic Westerners in wide-brimmed hats – ships which exported rice to China would bring these statues back as ballast.

The entrance brings you into the eastern half of the main complex, where a courtyard of structures radiates from the bot in a disorientating symmetry. To get to the **bot**, the principal congregation and ordination hall, turn right and cut through the two surrounding cloisters, which are lined with hundreds of Buddha images. The elegant bot has beautiful teak doors decorated with mother-of-pearl, showing stories from the *Ramayana* (see p.63) in minute detail. Look out also for the stone bas-reliefs around the base of the bot, which narrate the story of the capture and rescue of Sita from the *Ramayana* in 152 action-packed panels. The plush interior has a well-proportioned altar on which ten statues of disciples frame a graceful, Ayutthayan Buddha image containing the remains of Rama I, the founder of Bangkok (Rama IV placed them there so that the public could worship him at the same time as the Buddha).

Back outside the entrance to the double cloister, keep your eyes open for a miniature mountain covered in statues of naked men in tall hats who appear to be gesturing rudely: they are *rishis* (hermits), demonstrating various positions of healing massage. Skirting the southwestern corner of the cloisters, you'll come to two pavilions between the eastern and western courtyards, which display plaques inscribed with the precepts of traditional medicine, as well as anatomical pictures showing the different pressure points and the illnesses that can be cured by massaging them.

The western courtyard

Among the 99 chedis strewn about the grounds, the four **great chedis** in the western courtyard stand out as much for their covering of garish tiles as for their size. The central chedi is the oldest, erected by Rama I to hold the remains of the most sacred Buddha image of Ayutthaya, the Phra Si Sanphet. Later, Rama III built the chedi to the north for the ashes of Rama II and the chedi to the south to hold his own remains; Rama IV built the fourth, with bright blue tiles, though its purpose is uncertain.

In the northwest corner of the courtyard stands the chapel of the **Reclining Buddha**, a 45-metre-long gilded statue of plaster-covered brick which depicts the Buddha entering Nirvana, a common motif in Buddhist iconography. The chapel is only slightly bigger than the statue – you can't get far enough away to take in anything but a surreal close-up view of the beaming five-metre smile. The vast black soles of the statue's feet are beautifully inlaid with delicate mother-of-pearl showing the 108 *lakshanas*, or auspicious signs, which distinguish the true Buddha. Along one side of the statue are 108 bowls: putting a coin in each will bring you good luck and a long life.

Museum of Siam (National Discovery Museum)

The hi-tech and mostly bilingual **Museum of Siam** is an excellent, new attraction that occupies the century-old, European-style, former Ministry of Commerce (Tues–Sun 10am–6pm; free; ⓦ www.ndmi.or.th). Approached from either Thanon Maharat or Thanon Sanam Chai to the south of Wat Pho (and handy also for Ratchini express-boat pier during weekday rush hours), it looks at what it is to be Thai, with lots of humorous short films and imaginative touches such as shadow-puppet cartoons and war video games. Generally, it's great fun for adults and kids, and there's a nice little indoor-outdoor **café-restaurant** in the grounds run by the Black Canyon chain.

It all starts with the prehistory of Southeast Asia, or Suvarnabhumi (Land of Gold) as the Thais call it, and the arrival of Buddhism via missionaries sent by the great Indian emperor, Ashoka (Asoke). Much space is devoted to Ayutthaya, including the twenty outbreaks of war with the Burmese states before the final annihilation in 1767, but beyond this, look out for a fascinating map of one-time capital Thonburi (1768–82) as drawn by a Burmese spy. There's coverage of the Chinese in Thailand and of early twentieth-century racialism, but next to nothing on the country's Muslims. Towards the end, under the banner of Westernization, visitors can wind up cartoon peep shows and dress up in "colonial" pith helmets.

Sanam Luang and around

Sprawling across twelve hectares north of the Grand Palace, **Sanam Luang** is one of the last open spaces left in Bangkok, a bare field where residents of the capital gather in the early evening to meet, eat and play. The nearby

Kite-flying

Flying intricate and colourful **kites** is now done mostly for fun in Thailand, but it has its roots in more serious activities. Filled with gunpowder and fitted with long fuses, kites were deployed in the first Thai kingdom at Sukhothai (1240–1438) as machines of war. In the same era, special *ngao* kites, with heads in the shape of bamboo bows, were used in Brahmin rituals: the string of the bow would vibrate in the wind and make a noise to frighten away evil spirits (nowadays noisy kites are still used, though only by farmers, to scare the birds). By the height of the Ayutthayan period (1351–1767) kites had become largely decorative: royal ceremonies were enhanced by fantastically shaped kites, adorned with jingling bells and ornamental lamps.

In the nineteenth century, Rama V, by his enthusiastic lead, popularized kite-flying as a wholesome and fashionable recreation. **Contests** are now held all over the country between February and April, when winds are strong enough and farmers traditionally have free time after harvesting the rice. These contests fall into two broad categories: those involving manoeuvrable flat kites, often in the shapes of animals; and those in which the beauty of static display kites is judged. The most popular contest of all, which comes under the first category, matches two teams, one flying star-shaped *chulas*, two-metre-high "male" kites, the other flying the smaller, more agile *pakpaos*, diamond-shaped "females". Each team uses its skill and teamwork to ensnare the other's kites and drag them back across a dividing line.

▲ Flying kites, Sanam Luang

pavements are the marketplace for some exotic spiritual salesmen: on the eastern side sit astrologers, palm-readers and sellers of bizarre virility potions and contraptions; on the western side and spreading around Thammasat University and Wat Mahathat, scores of small-time hawkers sell amulets (see p.83), taking advantage of the spiritually auspicious location. In the early part of the year, especially in March, the sky is filled with kite-fighting contests.

The field is also the venue for national ceremonies, such as **royal cremations**, when huge, intricate, wooden *meru* or *phra mane* (funeral pyres) are constructed, representing Mount Meru, the Himalayan centre of the Hindu-Buddhist universe; and the **Ploughing Ceremony**, held in May at a time selected by astrologers to bring good fortune and rain to the coming rice harvest. The elaborate Brahmin ceremony is led by an official from the Ministry of Agriculture, who stands in for the king in case the royal power were to be reduced by any failure in the ritual. At the designated time, the official cuts a series of circular furrows with a plough drawn by two white oxen, and scatters rice (sprinkled with lustral water by the Brahmin priests of the court) from the king's experimental crop station at Chitrlada Palace. When the ritual is over, spectators rush in to grab handfuls of the rice, which they then plant in their own paddies for good luck.

Wat Mahathat

On Sanam Luang's western side, with its main entrance on Thanon Maharat, eighteenth-century **Wat Mahathat** provides a welcome respite from the surrounding tourist hype and a chance to engage with the eager monks studying at **Mahachulalongkorn Buddhist University** here. As the nation's centre for the Mahanikai monastic sect (where Rama IV spent 24 years as a monk before becoming king in 1851) and housing one of the two Buddhist universities in Bangkok, the wat buzzes with purpose. It's this activity, and the chance of interaction and participation, rather than any special architectural features, which make a visit so rewarding. The monks at the wat are friendly and keen to practise their English, and are more than likely to approach you: diverting topics might range from the poetry of Dylan Thomas to English football results.

Situated in Section Five of the wat is its **Vipassana Meditation Centre**, where sitting and walking meditation practice is available in English (daily 7–10am, 1–4pm & 6–8pm; ☎02 222 6011 or 02 222 4981). Participants generally stay in the simple surroundings of the meditation building itself (donation requested), and must wear white clothes (available to rent at the centre) and observe the eight main Buddhist precepts (see p.229). Talks in English on meditation and Buddhism are held here every evening (8–9pm), as well as at the International Buddhist Meditation Centre (Room 106; ☎02 623 6326 or 089 220 1754, ⓦwww .sirimangalo.org) in the Mahachulalongkorn University building on the second and fourth Saturdays of every month (3–5pm).

The National Museum

At the northwest corner of Sanam Luang, the **National Museum** (Wed–Sun 9am–4pm, some rooms may close at lunchtime; B200 including leaflet with map; ⓦwww.thailandmuseum.com) houses a colossal hoard of Thailand's chief artistic riches, ranging from sculptural treasures in the north and south wings, through bizarre decorative objects in the older buildings, to outlandish funeral chariots and the exquisite Buddhaisawan Chapel, as well as sometimes staging worthwhile temporary exhibitions. It's worth making time for the free **guided tours in English** on Wednesday and Thursday at 9.30am by the National Museum Volunteers (who also organize interesting lectures and excursions; ⓦwww.museumvolunteersbkk.net): they're generally entertaining and their explication of the choicest exhibits provides a good introduction to Thai religion and culture. By the ticket office are a bookshop and a pleasant, air-conditioned **café**, while the **restaurant** inside the museum grounds, by the funeral chariots building, dishes up decent, inexpensive Thai food.

The first building you'll come to near the ticket office houses an overview of the history of Thailand, including a small archeological gem: a black stone **inscription**, credited to King Ramkhamhaeng of Sukhothai, which became the first capital of the Thai nation (c.1278–99) under his rule. Discovered in 1833 by the future Rama IV, it's the oldest extant inscription using the Thai alphabet. This, combined with the description it records of prosperity and piety in Sukhothai's Golden Age, has made the stone a symbol of Thai nationhood.

The main collection: southern building

At the back of the compound, two large modern buildings, flanking an old converted palace, house the museum's **main collection**, kicking off on the ground floor of the **southern building**. Look out here for some historic sculptures from the rest of Asia, including one of the earliest representations of the Buddha, from Gandhara in northwest India. Alexander the Great left a garrison at Gandhara, which explains why the image is in the style of Classical Greek sculpture: for example, the *ushnisha*, the supernatural bump on the top of the head, which symbolizes the Buddha's intellectual and spiritual power, is rationalized into a bun of thick, wavy hair.

Upstairs, the **prehistory** room displays axe heads and spear points from Ban Chiang in the northeast of Thailand, one of the earliest Bronze Age cultures ever discovered. Alongside are many roughly contemporaneous metal artefacts from Kanchanaburi province, as well as some excellent examples of the developments of Ban Chiang's famous pottery. In the adjacent **Dvaravati** room (S7; sixth to eleventh centuries), the pick of the stone and terracotta Buddhas is a small head in smooth, pink clay, whose downcast eyes and faintly smiling full lips typify the serene look of this era. At the far end of the first floor, you can't miss a voluptuous Javanese statue of elephant-headed Ganesh, Hindu god of wisdom and the arts, which, being the symbol of Thailand's Fine Arts, is always freshly garlanded.

Room S9 next door contains the most famous piece of **Srivijaya** art (seventh to thirteenth centuries), a bronze Bodhisattva Avalokitesvara found at Chaiya (according to Mahayana Buddhism, a *bodhisattva* is a saint who has postponed his passage into Nirvana to help ordinary believers gain enlightenment). With its pouting face and sinuous torso, this image has become the ubiquitous emblem of southern Thailand. The rough chronological order of the collection continues back downstairs with an exhibition of **Khmer** and **Lopburi** sculpture (seventh to fourteenth centuries), most notably some dynamic bronze statuettes and stone lintels. Look out for an elaborate lintel that depicts Vishnu reclining on a dragon in the sea of eternity, dreaming up a new universe after the old one has been annihilated in the Hindu cycle of creation and destruction. Out of his navel comes a lotus, and out of this emerges four-headed Brahma, who will put the dream into practice.

The main collection: northern building

The second half of the survey, in the northern building, begins upstairs with the **Sukhothai** collection (thirteenth to fifteenth centuries), which features some typically elegant and sinuous Buddha images, as well as chunky bronzes of Hindu gods and a wide range of ceramics. The **Lanna** rooms (covering the north of Thailand from roughly the thirteenth to sixteenth centuries) include a miniature set of golden regalia, among them tiny umbrellas and a pair of filigree flip-flops, which would have been enshrined in a chedi. An ungainly but serene Buddha head, carved from grainy, pink sandstone, represents the **Ayutthaya** style of sculpture (fourteenth to eighteenth centuries): the faintest incision of a moustache above the lips betrays the Khmer influences that came to Ayutthaya after its conquest of Angkor. A sumptuous scripture cabinet, showing a cityscape of old Ayutthaya, is a more unusual piece, one of a surviving handful of such carved and painted items of furniture.

Downstairs in the section on **Bangkok** or **Ratanakosin** art (eighteenth century onwards), a stiffly realistic standing bronze Buddha brings you full circle. In his zeal for Western naturalism, Rama V had the statue made in the Gandhara style of the earliest Buddha image displayed in the first room of the museum.

The funeral chariots

To the east of the northern building, beyond the café on the left, stands a large garage where the fantastically elaborate **funeral chariots** of the royal family are stored. Pre-eminent among these is the Vejayant Rajarot, built by Rama I in 1785 for carrying the urn at his own funeral. The thirteen-metre-high structure symbolizes heaven on Mount Meru, while the dragons and divinities around the sides – piled in five golden tiers to suggest the flames of the cremation – represent the mythological inhabitants of the mountain's forests. Each weighing around forty tonnes and requiring the pulling power of three hundred men, the teak chariots last had an outing in 2008, for the funeral of the present king's much-revered elder sister, Princess Galyani.

Wang Na (Palace of the Second King)

The sprawling central building of the compound was originally part of the **Wang Na**, a huge palace stretching across Sanam Luang to Khlong Lod, which housed the "second king", appointed by the reigning monarch as his heir and deputy. When Rama V did away with the office in 1887, he turned the palace into a museum, which now contains a fascinating array of Thai *objets d'art*. As you enter (room 5), the display of sumptuous rare gold pieces behind heavy iron bars includes a well-preserved armlet taken from the ruined prang of fifteenth-century Wat Ratburana in Ayutthaya. In adjacent room 6, an intricately carved ivory seat turns out, with gruesome irony, to be a *howdah*, for use on an elephant's back. Among the masks worn by *khon* actors next door (room 7), look out especially for a fierce Hanuman, the white monkey-warrior in the *Ramayana* epic, gleaming with mother-of-pearl.

The huge and varied ceramic collection in room 8 includes some sophisticated pieces from Sukhothai, while the room behind (9) holds a riot of mother-of-pearl items, whose flaming rainbow of colours comes from the shell of the turbo snail from the Gulf of Thailand. It's also worth seeking out the display of richly decorated musical instruments in room 15.

The Buddhaisawan chapel

The second holiest image in Thailand, after the Emerald Buddha, is housed in the **Buddhaisawan chapel**, the vast hall in front of the Wang Na's eastern entrance. The fine proportions of the hall's interior, with its ornate coffered ceiling and lacquered window shutters, are enhanced by painted rows of divinities and converted demons, all turned to face the chubby, glowing **Phra Sihing Buddha**, which according to legend was magically created in Sri Lanka and sent to Sukhothai in the thirteenth century. Like the Emerald Buddha, the image was believed to bring good luck to its owner and was frequently snatched from one northern town to another, until Rama I brought it down from Chiang Mai in 1795 and installed it here in the second king's private chapel. Two other images (in Nakhon Si Thammarat and Chiang Mai) now claim to be the authentic Phra Sihing Buddha, but all three are actually derived from a lost original – this one is in a fifteenth-century Sukhothai style. It's still much loved by ordinary people and at Thai New Year is carried out onto Sanam Luang, where worshippers sprinkle it with water as a merit-making gesture.

The careful detail and rich, soothing colours of the surrounding two-hundred-year-old **murals** are surprisingly well preserved; the bottom row between the windows narrates the life of the Buddha, beginning in the far right-hand corner with his parents' wedding.

Tamnak Daeng

On the south side of the Buddhaisawan chapel, the sumptuous **Tamnak Daeng** (Red House) stands out, a large, airy Ayutthaya-style house made of rare golden teak, surmounted by a multi-tiered roof decorated with carved foliage and swan's-tail finials. Originally part of the private quarters of Princess Sri Sudarak, elder sister of Rama I, it was moved from the Grand Palace to the old palace in Thonburi for Queen Sri Suriyen, wife of Rama II; when her son became second king to Rama IV, he dismantled the edifice again and shipped it to the Wang Na compound. Inside, it's furnished in the style of the early Bangkok period, with some of the beautiful objects that once belonged to Sri Suriyen, a huge, ornately carved box bed, and the uncommon luxury of an indoor toilet and bathroom.

The National Gallery and Silpakorn University Art Centre

If the National Museum hasn't finished you off, two other lesser galleries nearby might. The **National Gallery**, across from the National Theatre on the north side of Sanam Luang at 4 Thanon Chao Fa (Wed–Sun 9am–4pm; B30; T 02 282 0637 or 02 282 2639–40, W www.thailandmuseum.com), displays in its upstairs gallery some rather beautiful early twentieth-century temple banners depicting Buddhist subjects, but houses a permanent collection of largely uninspiring and derivative twentieth-century Thai art downstairs. Its temporary exhibitions can be pretty good however. The fine old wooden building that houses the gallery is also worth more than a cursory glance – it used to be the Royal Mint, and is constructed in typical early twentieth-century style, around a central courtyard.

The **Silpakorn University Art Centre** (T 02 623 6115 ext 1422, W www .art-centre.su.ac.th) on Thanon Na Phra Lan, directly across the road from the entrance to the Grand Palace, also stages regular exhibitions, by students, teachers, artists-in-residence and national artists. The country's first art school, the university was founded in 1943 (in a palace built during the reign of Rama I) by Professor Silpa Bhirasri, the much-revered, naturalized Italian sculptor Corrado Feroci (see p.237); a charming, shady garden along the east wall of the art centre is dotted with his sculptures.

The lak muang

At 6.54am on April 21, 1782 – the astrologically determined time for the auspicious founding of Bangkok – a pillar containing the city's horoscope was ceremonially driven into the ground opposite the northeast corner of the Grand Palace. This phallic pillar, the **lak muang** – all Thai cities have one, to provide a home for their guardian spirits – was made from a four-metre tree trunk carved with a lotus-shaped crown, and is now sheltered in an elegant shrine surrounded by immaculate gardens. It shares the shrine with the taller *lak muang* of Thonburi, which was recently incorporated into Greater Bangkok. From here, mileages are calculated to the *lak muang* of every city in Thailand.

Hundreds of worshippers come every day to pray and offer flowers, particularly childless couples seeking the gift of fertility. In one corner of the gardens you can often see short performances of **classical dancing** (see p.195), paid for by well-off families when they have a piece of good fortune to celebrate.

Banglamphu and the Democracy Monument area

Best known as the site of the travellers' hub Thanon Khao San, the **Banglamphu** district, immediately north of Ratanakosin, has some noteworthy temples and still boasts a number of wooden shophouses and narrow alleyways alongside the purpose-built guest houses, travel agents and jewellery shops. But the most interesting sights in this part of the city are found in the charmingly old-fashioned neighbourhoods to the south and east of the huge stone **Democracy Monument**, which forms the centrepiece of an enormous roundabout that siphons traffic from the Rajdamnoen Klang artery. Most of these areas are within walking distance of the Khao San guest houses and equally accessible from the Grand Palace; their proximity to the royal district means they retain a traditional flavour, unsullied by high-rise architecture. The string of temple-supply shops around Wat Suthat and Sao Ching Cha make Thanon Bamrung Muang a rewarding area to explore, there are some great traditional food shops along Thanon Tanao, and the amulet market in the grounds of Wat Rajnadda is also worth seeking out.

Banglamphu

Banglamphu's primary attraction is the legendary **Thanon Khao San** (Ⓦ www.khaosanroad.com), a narrow road no more than four hundred metres long that is well established as *the* backpackers' hub of Southeast Asia. Crammed with internet cafés, guest houses and restaurants serving yoghurt shakes and muesli, its sidewalks lined with tattooists, hair-braiders and stalls piled high with bootleg PlayStation games, it's a lively, high-energy place that's fun to visit even if you're not staying in the area. Cheap clothes, jewellery and handicrafts are all good buys here (little is top quality on Khao San, but vendors are quick to pick up on global trends) and it's also a good spot to organize onward travel – bearing in mind the innumerable Khao San scams (see p.42).

▲ Thanon Khao San

Though ultra budget-conscious world travellers are still Khao San's main customers, Banglamphu attracts higher-spending sophisticates to its growing number of **stylish restaurants** and **lively bars and clubs**. At night, young Thais from all over the city gather here to browse the fashion stalls and pavement displays set up by local art students, mingling with the crowds of foreigners and squashing into the trendy bars and clubs that have made Khao San the city's most happening place to party (see p.187 for recommendations). Banglamphu boasts a surprising range of eating places too, from guest-house cafés on Thanon Khao San to bohemian Thai restaurants on Thanon Phra Athit; the best are listed on p.174. For accommodation on Khao San and elsewhere in Banglamphu, see p.160.

Wat Chana Songkhram

Sandwiched between Thanon Khao San and the Chao Phraya River, at the heart of the Banglamphu backpackers' ghetto, stands the lusciously renovated eighteenth-century **Wat Chana Songkhram**. As with temples throughout the country, the compound doubles as general-purpose neighbourhood yard; beside a knot of stalls selling secondhand books and travellers' clothes, a stream of tourists cuts through the wat en route between the river and Khao San. It's worth slowing down for a closer look though: the bot's roof gables are beautifully ornate, embossed with a golden relief of Vishnu astride Garuda, enmeshed in an intricate design of red and blue glass mosaics, and the golden finials are shaped like nagas. Peeking over the compound walls onto the guest houses and bars of Soi Ram Bhuttri are a row of *kuti*, or monks' quarters: simple, elegant wooden cabins on stilts with steeply pitched roofs.

Phra Athit and the riverside walkway

Thanon **Phra Athit**, the Banglamphu road that runs alongside the (mostly obscured) Chao Phraya River, is known for its arty atmosphere and numerous

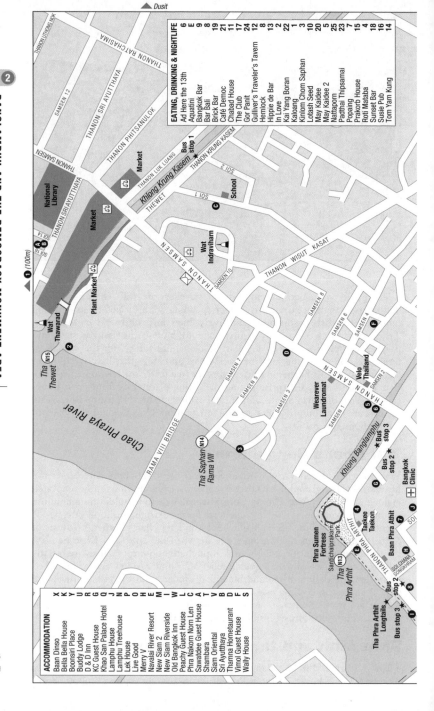

ACCOMMODATION

Baan Dinso	X
Bella Bella House	K
Boonsiri Place	Y
Buddy Lodge	U
D & D Inn	R
KC Guest House	G
Khao San Palace Hotel	Q
Lamphu House	J
Lamphu Treehouse	N
Lek House	P
Live Good	O
Merry V	H
Navalai River Resort	E
New Siam 2	M
New Siam Riverside	I
Old Bangkok Inn	W
Peachy Guest House	L
Phra Nakorn Norn Len	C
Sawatdee Guest House	A
Shambara	T
Siam Oriental	V
Sri Ayutthaya	B
Thanna Hometaurant	D
Vimol Guest House	F
Wally House	S

EATING, DRINKING & NIGHTLIFE

Ad Here the 13th	6
Aquatini	E
Bangkok Bar	9
Bar Bali	8
Brick Bar	19
Café Democ	21
Chabad House	11
The Club	17
Gor Panit	24
Gulliver's Traveler's Tavern	12
Hemlock	8
Hippie de Bar	13
In Love	2
Kai Yang Boran	22
Kaloang	1
Kinlom Chom Saphan	3
Lotash Seed	10
May Kaidee	20
May Kaidee 2	5
Nattaporn	25
Padthai Thipsamai	7
Popaing	15
Prakorb House	23
Roti Mataba	4
Sunset Bar	18
Susie Pub	16
Tom Yam Kung	14

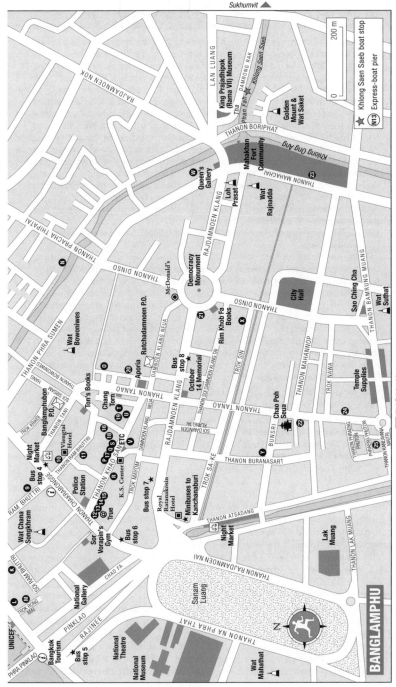

Sukhumvit ▲

King Prajadhipok
(Rama VII) Museum

Golden
Mount &
Wat Saket

★ Khlong Saen Saeb boat stop
M13 Express-boat pier

0   200 m

LAN LUANG

Tha
Damrong
Rak

Khlong Saen Saeb

THANON BORIPHAT

Mahakhan
Fort
Community

Queen's
Gallery

Loh
Prasat

Wat
Rajanadda

Khlong Ong Ang

THANON MAHACHAI

23

RAJDAMNOEN KLANG

Democracy
Monument

McDonald's

THANON DINSO

City
Hall

Sao Ching Cha

Wat
Suthat

THANON BAMRUNG MUANG

THANON PRACHA THIPATAI

Wat
Bowoniwes

Rim Khob Fa
Books

21

October
14 Memorial

Bus
stop 8

THANON DINSO

TRIK SIN

THANON MAHANNOP

Temple
Supplies

THANON PHRA SUMEN

THANON BOWONIWES

HANG

Ton's Books

Aporia

Ratchadamnoen P.O.

O

20

DAMROEN KLANG NEUA

THANON TANAO

THANON SRI DAMNOEN KLANG TAI

TRIK NAWA

▶ Wat Rajabophit

THANON TANI

Banglamphubon
P.O.

Night
Market

Bus
stop 4

9

SOI SIRI SIS

TROK KHAO

Chang
Toom

19

0

10

Viengtai
Hotel

16

18

THANON RAM BHUTTRI

11

P

0

ETC

V

K.S. Center

17

THANON KHAO SAN

13 12

15

14

True

@

R

RAJDAMNOEN KLANG

THANON SRI DAMNOEN KLANG NEUA

THANON SRI DAMNOEN KLANG TAI

SOI DAMNOEN
KLANG TAI

BUNSRI

Chao Poh
Seua

22

THANON PHRAENG
PHUTON

PHRAENG PHUTON

THANON WANGLAYONG
MAITRI

24

Y

THANON RAM BHUTTRI

Wat Chana
Songkhram

RAM BHUTTRI

THANON CHAKRABONGSE

i

Police
Station

Sor
Vorapin's
Gym

Bus
stop 7

Bus
stop 6

Royal
Ratanakosin
Hotel

Minibuses to
Kanchanaburi

THANON BURANASART

TRIK SA-KE

TROK MAYOM

K

SOI RAM BHUTTRI

National
Gallery

L

TROK RONG
MAI

M

CHAD FA

PINKLAO

RAJINEE

UNICEF ▲

i

Bangkok
Tourism

Bus
stop 5

PHRA PINKLAO

National
Theatre

National
Museum

THANON RAJADAMNOEN NAI

Sanam
Luang

THANON NA PHRA THAT

Wat
Mahathat

THANON ATSADANG

Night
Market

Lak
Muang

THANON LAK MUANG

THANON RAJDAMNOEN NAI

BANGLAMPHU

N

RAJDAMNOEN NOK

RAJDAMNOEN NOK

THANON

Getting to and from Banglamphu

The fastest and least stressful way of getting to the Banglamphu area is by boat. **Public longtail boats** run along Khlong Saen Saeb to the Tha Phan Fah terminus close by the Golden Mount compound from various spots in downtown Bangkok (see p.33), including to and from Tha Saphan Hua Chang, which is a few minutes' walk from both the Ratchathewi and Siam Skytrain stops. (The other fast way to get on to the Skytrain system is to take a taxi from Banglamphu to the National Stadium Skytrain stop.) The Chao Phraya **express boats** (see p.31) operate an equally efficient service to three different piers in the Banglamphu area: Tha Phra Athit (stop N13), a few hundred metres west of Thanon Khao San; Tha Saphan Rama VIII (Rama VIII Bridge; N14) at the western end of Samsen Soi 5; and Tha Thewet (N15) at the west end of Thanon Krung Kasem. If you're simply crossing the river, there's no need to wait for the Chao Phraya Express as a **cross-river shuttle boat** runs continually during daylight hours from under Pinklao bridge, beside the tourist information centre on Thanon Phra Athit, to Tha Phra Pinklao on the Thonburi bank.

Airport express bus AE2 runs to Banglamphu from **Suvarnabhumi Airport** (see p.27) and has many drop-offs in the area but only one pick-up point, outside the *Mayompuri Restaurant* on Thanon Chakrabongse, about 50m from the west end of Thanon Khao San.

For access from anywhere else you'll need to make use of the city **bus** network: Democracy Monument is served by buses from all parts of the city and is a landmark hard to miss; if you're coming from eastern or northern parts of the city (such as Hualamphong Station, Siam Square or Sukhumvit), get off the bus as soon as you see it rather than waiting for Rajdamnoen Klang's more westerly stop outside the *Royal Ratanakosin Hotel*, where it's almost impossible to cross the multiple lanes of traffic. Buses running out of Banglamphu have many different pick-up points in the area: to make things simpler, we've assigned numbers to these **bus stops**, though they are not numbered on the ground. Where there are two bus stops on the same route they share a number. Bus stops are marked on the Banglamphu map on p.76. For a more detailed breakdown of Bangkok's bus routes see p.32.

Bus stop 1: Thanon Krung Kasem, north side
#53 to Hualamphong train station (buses start from here)

Bus stop 2: Thanon Phra Arthit, south side, near Hemlock; and Thanon Phra Sumen, south side, near Banglumpoo Place hotel
#3 to the Museum of Siam, Pak Khlong Talat and Wongwian Yai train station
#9 to Wat Pho, Pak Khlong Talat
#53 to the Grand Palace and Chinatown

little bar-restaurants that draw crowds of students from nearby Thammasat University. Many of these places open only at night, but some serve passing tourists during the day. There are also a few shops selling unusual Thai crafts and art-photocards towards the northern end of the road.

This northern stretch of Thanon Phra Athit is dominated by the crenellated whitewashed tower of **Phra Sumen Fortress** (aka Phra Sumeru), a renovated corner of the original eighteenth-century city walls that stands beside the river and its juncture with Khlong Banglamphu. The fortress was the northernmost of fourteen octagonal towers built by Rama I in 1783 to protect the royal island of Ratanakosin and originally contained 38 rooms for storing ammunition. (The only other surviving tower, also renovated, is Phra Mahakhan Fortress, next to the Golden Mount; see p.83.) There's nothing to see inside the Phra Sumen tower, but it makes a striking landmark and the area around it has been turned into a pleasant grassy riverside recreation area, **Santichaiprakarn Park**,

Bus stop 3: Thanon Phra Arthit, north side, near New Siam Riverside; and Thanon Phra Sumen, north side, opposite Banglumpoo Place hotel

#3 to Chatuchak Weekend Market and Mo Chit Northern Bus Terminal
#53 to Hualamphong train station (change at Bus Stop 1, but same ticket)
#56 (from Phra Sumen stop only) to Thanon Ratchasima for Vimanmek Palace and Dusit

Bus stop 4: Thanon Chakrabongse, near the 7–Eleven

#15 to Jim Thompson's House, Siam Square, Thanon Silom and Patpong
#30 to the Southern Bus Terminal
#32 to Wat Pho

Bus Stop 5: Thanon Rajinee (Rachini), near Bangok Tourism Information Centre

#124 (non-air-con) to Southern Bus Terminal

Bus stop 6: Thanon Chakrabongse, outside the Mayompuri Restaurant

AE2 Airport Express to Suvarnabhumi Airport

Bus stop 7: Thanon Rajdamnoen Klang, north side, outside Lottery Building

#2 to Ekamai Eastern Bus Terminal
#47 to Jim Thompson's House, Thanon Silom and Patpong
#47, #79 to Siam Square
#59, #503 (air-con; non-expressway), #509 to Chatuchak Weekend Market
#47 to Lumphini boxing stadium
#59 to Don Muang Airport
#70, #201, #503, #509 to TAT and Ratchadamnoen boxing stadium
#70 (non-expressway) to Dusit
#157 (air-con) to Mo Chit Northern Bus Terminal
#159 (non-air-con) to Hualamphong train station
#511 to Ekamai Eastern Bus Terminal and Pak Nam (for Ancient City buses)

Bus stop 8: Thanon Rajdamnoen Klang, south side

#44, #512 to Sanam Luang, the Grand Palace and Wat Pho
#60, #512 to Pak Khlong Talat
#79 to Taling Chan weekend floating market
#159 (non-air-con), # 511 and #516 to Southern Bus Terminal

with English-language signs describing the history of the fortifications. A park sign also highlights one of the area's last remaining lamphu trees (*duabanga grandiflora*), which continues to grow in a muddy pool on the edge of the river to the left of the royal *sala*. Lamphu trees were once so common in this neighbourhood that they gave the area its name – Banglamphu means "the place with lamphu trees" – though they've all but disappeared now.

The fort marks the northernmost limit of a **riverside walkway** that runs down to the Bangkok Tourism Division's information centre beside Phra Pinklao Bridge. The walkway provides a good view of the boats and barges on the Chao Phraya and takes you past the front entrances of two very grand and beautifully restored buildings, both currently occupied by international organizations. The United Nations' Food and Agriculture Organization (FAO) uses the early-twentieth-century mansion known as **Baan Maliwan** as its library (closed to casual visitors), while the nearby UNICEF office is housed in the late-nineteenth-century palace of one of the wives of Rama IV, which also served as the headquarters of the clandestine Seri Thai resistance movement (see p.222) during World War II. Both mansions show their most elegant faces to the river as visitors would have arrived by boat. On the eastern side of Thanon Phra Athit, there's another fine early-twentieth-century mansion, **Baan Phra Athit**, at #201/1.

Wat Indraviharn

Though it can't match the graceful serenity of Ratanakosin's enormous Reclining Buddha, Banglamphu has its own super-sized Standing Buddha at **Wat Indraviharn** (also spelt Wat Intharawihan or Wat In), a glittering 32-metre-high mirror-plated statue of the Buddha bearing an alms bowl. Commissioned by Rama IV in the mid-nineteenth century to enshrine a Buddha relic from Sri Lanka (in the topknot), it's hardly the most elegant of images, but the foot-long toenails peep out prettily beneath garlands of fragrant jasmine left as offerings, and you can get reasonable views of the neighbour-hood by climbing the stairways of the supporting tower; when unlocked, the doorways in the upper tower give access to the statue's hollow interior, affording vistas from shoulder level. The rest of the temple compound features the usual amalgam of architectural and spiritual styles, including a Chinese shrine and statues of Ramas IV and V.

Wat In is about twenty minutes' walk north of Khao San, off Thanon Wisut Kasat. Unfortunately, it's an established hangout for **con-artists** (see p.42) offering tourists a tuk-tuk tour of Bangkok for a bargain B20, which invariably features a hard-sell visit to a jewellery shop (see p.211). Avoid all these hassles by hailing a passing metered taxi, or use **public transport**: Chao Phraya express boat stops N14 and N15 are within reach, and bus #3 runs from Thanon Samsen to Thanon Phra Arthit.

Democracy Monument and around

The megalithic, yellowy wings of **Democracy Monument** (*Anu Sawari Pracha Tippatai*) loom provocatively over Rajdamnoen Klang, the avenue that links the Grand Palace with the new royal district of Dusit, and have since their erection in 1939 acted as a focus for pro-democracy rallies. Conceived as a testimony to the ideals that fuelled the 1932 revolution and the move to a constitutional monarchy, the monument's positioning between the royal residences is significant, as are its dimensions, which allude to June 24, 2475 BE (1932 AD), the date the system was changed. Since then, Thailand's leaders have promulgated numerous interim charters and constitutions, the more repressive and regressive of which have been vigorously challenged in demon-strations on these very streets.

One of the biggest and most notorious demonstrations was the fateful student-led protest of October 14, 1973, when half a million people gathered on Rajdamnoen Klang to demand an end to the autocratic regime of the so-called "Three Tyrants". It was savagely quashed and turned into a bloody riot that culminated in the death of several hundred protesters at the hands of the police and the military. After three decades of procrastination, the events of this catastrophic day were finally commemorated with the erection of the

Bangkok by boat

With traffic on the roads frequently gridlocked, Bangkok's waterways are often the fastest way of getting around – and they boast all the best views too. The city was founded on the east bank of the Chao Phraya – the "River of Kings" – and designed to be negotiated by water, so many of its finest monuments and temples, not least the Grand Palace and Wat Arun, have handsome river profiles. The network of *khlong* (canals) are fun to explore too, especially in the traditional neighbourhoods of the west-bank Thonburi district.

Public canal-boat service, Khlong Saen Saeb ▲

Canal-side homes ▼

The Chao Phraya River

The easiest and most economical way to enjoy sights along the Chao Phraya is to leap aboard the **express-boat service** that transports commuters and visitors some 21km from near Krung Thep Bridge in the south to **Nonthaburi** in the north. The full ride takes an hour and a half and costs B13. There's always plenty to look at: longtail taxis and sightseeing boats roar up and down, cross-river ferries beetle between the two banks and tugboats lug convoys of barges heavy with rice, sugar and tapioca grown in the fertile central plains and destined for Bangkok's cargo port at Khlong Toey. Pastel-painted colonial-style facades, obtruding skyscrapers and glittering temple rooftops dominate downriver vistas, while upstream frontages include the Bangyikan distillery, home of Thailand's fiery Mekong whisky.

Of the dozen bridges across the Chao Phraya, the modern, cable-stayed **Rama VIII Bridge** stands out, hanging asymmetrically from a single pylon erected on the Thonburi bank to comply with a law prohibiting tall structures within sight of the Grand Palace.

Exploring the canals

Public boats also ply some of the **canals**, most usefully Khlong Saen Saeb, which zips eastwards from Banglamphu to Sukhumvit and beyond. For a glimpse of the more scenic khlong-side neighbourhoods you're best off chartering your own longtail taxi for a tour around the much-visited but undeniably atmospheric backwaters of **Thonburi**. Homes here range from rickety wooden shacks to plush villas with waterside lawns, and though the once-photogenic floating markets are now undisguised tourist traps, individual vendors do still paddle up and down flogging everything from plastic buckets to hot noodle soup; banking services and mail delivery are still waterborne in some corners, monks do their early-morning alms rounds by canoe and some residents brave the murky waters for an evening bathe. For details of tours and charters around the Thonburi canals, see p.95.

The longtail boat

Like its road-bound counterpart the tuk-tuk, the **longtail boat** (*reua hang yao*) is a Bangkok icon: fast, colourful, ubiquitous – and excessively noisy and polluting. The nerve-wearying roar is produced by the boat's diesel-powered Isuzu engine, appropriated from pick-up trucks and operated by an elongated propeller shaft, the eponymous longtail. But much else about the design is graceful, not least the streamlined wooden hulls whose improbably steep prows enable the longtails to shoot across the water, and their rainbow-hued livery, often with matching multi-coloured canopies. The look barely varies, whether it's a taxi-style longtail seating eight, or one that plies scheduled routes and crams in fifty passengers or more. Most longtail drivers festoon the prow, which is considered sacred, like the human head, with garlands of plastic flowers to both honour and ask protection from the spirits; this special status also means that it's offensive to sit on or astride the prow. Plastic sheets rigged along the sides of the boats provide more pragmatic protection – from health-endangering contact with the foetid canal water, at its vilest inky-black along the east–west artery, Khlong Saen Saeb.

▲ Doing the dishes in a Thonburi canal

▼ Floating Vendor, Thonburi

Rama VIII Bridge ▲

The Chao Phraya at night ▼

River views

Many of Bangkok's finest **hotels** are built along the banks of the Chao Phraya. The *grande dame* of the river has long been the *Oriental Hotel* (see p.170), constructed here in 1876 and renowned for its roster of famous guests. Among these was the author Somerset Maugham, who first stayed in the 1920s; convalescing from malaria, he appreciated having "nothing to do except look at the river". Across on the Thonburi bank, the swanky 21st-century *Peninsula Bangkok* (see p.170) is an even more luxurious alternative, with sweeping river vistas enjoyed from every room.

Further upriver, across the Chao Phraya from the Grand Palace, the tiny, three-room *Ibrik Resort on the River* (see p.165) is a far more intimate experience: buried in a lively Thonburi neighbourhood you are literally at the water's edge, close enough to dip your toe in. In the vicinity of the Grand Palace itself, the charmingly sophisticated *Chakrabongse Villas* (see p.163) occupies the former riverside home of a member of the Thai royal family, or there's more affordable river-view accommodation at *New Siam Riverside* (see p.162) in the nearby travellers' centre of Banglamphu.

Dining beside the river – and even on it – is another good way of absorbing riverine life: once the sun sets and the river traffic quietens, locals flock to *Aquatini* in Banglamphu for the seafood and river breezes (see p.176), and to nearby *Kinlom Chom Saphan* (see p.176) for its fine outlook on the elegant Rama VIII Bridge. Dinner cruises along the Chao Phraya, some of them on converted teakwood barges, also offer a memorable perspective on the floodlit riverside sights: see p.182 for details.

October 14 Memorial, a small granite amphitheatre encircling an elegant modern chedi bearing the names of some of the dead; photographs and a bilingual account of the ten-day protest fill the back wall. The memorial stands in front of the former headquarters of Colonel Narong Kittikachorn, one of the Three Tyrants, 200m west of Democracy Monument, at the corner of Rajdamnoen Klang and Thanon Tanao.

Thanon Tanao

A stroll down **Thanon Tanao** brings much-needed light relief, drawing you into some engagingly old-fashioned neighbourhoods where traditional shops still dominate. The first point of interest is **Chao Poh Seua** (Jao Paw Sua), the **Tiger God Shrine** (daily 6am–5pm), an atmospheric incense-filled Taoist shrine honouring the Chinese tiger guardian spirit and the God of the North Stars, whose image graces the centre of the main altar. It's a favourite with Chinese-Thais who come here to pray for power, prestige and successful pregnancy and offer in return pork rashers, fresh eggs, sticky rice, bottles of oil and sugar tigers.

South of the shrine, Thanon Tanao and its arterial alleys, especially the attractive Soi Phraeng Phuton, are known for their nineteenth-century wooden shophouses selling outstanding specialist **traditional Thai foods**. Many of these places have been making their specialities for generations, and it's fun to browse here, even if you're not inclined to taste, from beef noodles to pigs' brain soup, home-made ice cream to sticky rice with mango. See p.177 for some recommendations, but for an exhaustive survey consult the *Good Eats Ratanakosin* map (published by Pan Siam Publishing and available in major bookstores), which is especially handy given that few of these places have English-language signs or shop numbers.

This area is also sometimes referred to as Sao Ching Cha, after the Giant Swing, which is easily reached either by following any of the east-bound lanes off Thanon Tanao to Thanon Dinso, or via Thanon Bamrung Muang, which is lined with interesting shops selling Buddhist paraphernalia. Alternatively, if you continue one block south along Tanao you'll reach the lovely little temple of Wat Rajabophit.

Wat Rajabophit

One of Bangkok's prettiest temples, **Wat Rajabophit**, is another example of the Chinese influence in this neighbourhood. Built by Rama V, it's unusual in its design, with a circular cloister enclosing a chedi and linking the rectangular bot and viharn. Every external wall in the compound is covered in the pastel shades of Chinese *bencharong* ceramic tiles, creating a stunning overall effect, while the bot interior looks like a tiny banqueting hall, with gilded Gothic vaults and intricate mother-of-pearl doors. The wat is on Thanon Rajabophit, one block south of the Tanao/Bamrung Muang intersection, just to the east of Khlong Lod and the back of the Grand Palace compound.

Crossing the bridge over Khlong Lod en route to or from the Grand Palace, you'll pass a gold **statue of a pig**, erected in tribute to one of Rama V's wives, born in the Chinese Year of the Pig. Alternatively, walking in a southerly direction down Thanon Fuang Nakhon to its continuation, Thanon Banmo, will lead you all the way down to the Chao Phraya River and Memorial Bridge, taking in some fine old Chinese shophouses and the sprawling flower and vegetable market, Pak Khlong Talat, along the way (see p.90).

Thanon Bamrung Muang, Sao Ching Cha and Wat Suthat

Thanon Bamrung Muang, which runs east from Thanon Thanao to Sao Ching Cha and Wat Suthat, is famous as the best place in Thailand to buy **Buddhist paraphernalia**, or *sanghapan*, and is well worth a browse even for tourists. The road is lined with shops selling everything a good Buddhist might need, from household offerings tables to temple umbrellas and cellophane-wrapped Buddha images up to two metres high. They also sell special alms packs for donating to monks, which typically come in saffron-coloured plastic buckets (used by monks for washing their robes, or themselves), and include such necessities as soap, toothpaste, soap powder, toilet roll, candles and incense.

Midway along Thanon Bamrung Muang, just in front of Wat Suthat, about 700m south of Democracy Monument, you can't miss the towering, red-painted teak posts of **Sao Ching Cha**, otherwise known as the **Giant Swing**. This strange contraption was once the focal point of a Brahmin ceremony to honour the Hindu god Shiva's annual visit to earth, in which teams of young men competed to swing up to a height of 25m and grab a suspended bag of gold with their teeth. The act of swinging probably symbolized the rising and setting of the sun, though legend also has it that Shiva and his consort Uma were banned from swinging in heaven because doing so caused cataclysmic floods on earth – prompting Shiva to demand the practice be continued on earth to ensure moderate rains and bountiful harvests. Accidents were so common with the terrestrial version that it was outlawed in the 1930s.

Were the swing still in operation, you'd get a fine view over adjacent **Wat Suthat** (daily 9am–5pm; B20) and its towering central viharn, Bangkok's tallest. This is one of Thailand's six most important temples, built in the early nineteenth century to house the eight-metre-high statue of the meditating **Phra Sri Sakyamuni Buddha**. It now sits on a glittering mosaic dais surrounded with surreal murals that depict the last 24 lives of the Buddha rather than the more usual ten. The encircling galleries contain 156 serenely posed Buddha images, making a nice contrast to the **Chinese statues** dotted around the temple courtyards, most of which were brought over from China during Rama I's reign, as ballast in rice boats; there are some fun character studies among them, including gormless Western sailors and pompous Chinese scholars.

Wat Rajnadda and the amulet market

Five minutes' walk east of Democracy Monument, at the point where Rajdamnoen Klang meets Thanon Mahachai, stands the assortment of religious buildings known collectively as **Wat Rajnadda** (daily 9am–5pm; free). Its most striking feature is the multi-tiered, castle-like **Loh Prasat**, or "Iron Monastery", whose 37 forbidding metal spires represent the 37 virtues necessary for attaining enlightenment. Modelled on a Sri Lankan monastery, its tiers are pierced by passageways running north–south and east–west – fifteen in each direction at ground level – with small meditation cells at each point of intersection.

In the southeast (Thanon Mahachai) corner of the temple compound, Bangkok's biggest **amulet market**, the **Wat Rajnadda Buddha Center**, comprises at least a hundred stalls selling tiny Buddha images of all designs (see box opposite). Alongside these miniature charms are statues of Hindu deities, dolls and carved wooden phalluses, also bought to placate or ward off disgruntled spirits, as well as love potions and CDs of sacred music.

To invite good fortune, ward off malevolent spirits and gain protection from physical harm, Thais wear or carry at least one **amulet** at all times. The most popular **images** are copies of sacred statues from famous wats, while others show revered monks, kings (Rama V is a favourite) or healers. On the reverse side a *yantra* is often inscribed, a combination of letters and figures also designed to deflect evil, sometimes of a very specific nature: protecting your durian orchards from gales, for example, or your tuk-tuk from oncoming traffic. Individually hand-crafted or mass-produced, amulets can be made from bronze, clay, plaster or gold, and some even have **sacred ingredients** added, such as special herbs, or the ashes of burnt holy texts. But what really determines an amulet's efficacy is its **history**: where and by whom it was made, who or what it represents and who consecrated it. Stories of miracle cures and lucky escapes also prompt a rush on whatever amulet the survivor was wearing. Monks are often involved in the making of the images and are always called upon to consecrate them – the more charismatic the monk, the more powerful the amulet. Religious authorities take a relaxed view of the amulet industry, despite its anomalous and commercial functions, and proceeds contribute to wat funds and good causes.

The **belief in amulets** is thought to have originated in India, where tiny images were sold to pilgrims who visited the four holy sites associated with the Buddha's life. But not all amulets are Buddhist-related; there's a whole range of other enchanted objects to wear for protection, including tigers' teeth, rose quartz, tamarind seeds, coloured threads and miniature phalluses. Worn around the waist rather than the neck, the phallus amulets provide protection for the genitals as well as being associated with fertility, and are of Hindu origin.

For some people, amulets are not only a vital form of spiritual protection, but valuable **collectors' items** as well. Amulet-collecting mania is something akin to stamp collecting and there are at least half a dozen Thai magazines for collectors, which give histories of certain types, tips on distinguishing between genuine items and fakes, and personal accounts of particularly powerful amulet experiences. The most rewarding places to watch the collectors and browse the wares yourself are at Wat Rajnadda Buddha Center, probably the best place in Bangkok (see opposite); along "Amulet Alley" on Trok Mahathat, between Wat Mahathat (see p.69) and the river, where streetside vendors will have cheaper examples; and at Chatuchak Weekend Market (see p.122). Prices start as low as B50 and rise into the thousands.

Phra Mahakhan

Across the road from Wat Rajnadda, the **Phra Mahakhan Fortress Community** occupies the land between the whitewashed crenellations of the renovated eighteenth-century city walls and Khlong Ong Ang. It's a historic neighbourhood and welcomes visitors with informative signboards describing some of its traditions, including massage therapy, fish bladder soup and *likay* popular theatre. Immediately south of the crenellations is a block of shops specializing in Thai and Chinese antiques.

Wat Saket and the Golden Mount

Beautifully illuminated at night, when it seems to float unsupported above the neighbourhood, the gleaming gold chedi east of Wat Rajnadda actually sits atop a structure known as the Golden Mount, within the compound of the late eighteenth-century **Wat Saket**. Being outside the capital's city walls, the wat initially served as a crematorium and then a dumping ground for sixty thousand plague victims left to the vultures because they couldn't afford funeral pyres.

There's no sign of this grim episode at modern-day Wat Saket of course, which is today a smart, buzzing hive of religious activity at the base of the golden hilltop chedi.

The **Golden Mount**, or **Phu Khao Tong** (daily 7.30am–5.30pm; B10), dates back to the early nineteenth century, when Rama III commissioned a huge chedi to be constructed here on ground that proved too soft to support it. The whole thing collapsed into a hill of rubble, but as Buddhist law states that a religious building can never be destroyed, however tumbledown, fifty years later Rama V simply crowned it with the more sensibly sized chedi we see today, in which he placed some relics, believed by some to be the Buddha's teeth. These days the old rubbly base is picturesquely planted with shrubs and shady trees and dotted with gravestones and memorials. Winding stairways take you up to the chedi terrace and a fine view over Banglamphu and Ratanakosin landmarks, including the golden spires of the Grand Palace, the finely proportioned prangs of Wat Arun across the river beyond and, further upriver, the striking super-structure of the Rama VIII Bridge.

Wat Saket hosts an enormous annual **temple fair** in the first week of November, when the mount is illuminated with lanterns and the compound seethes with funfair rides and travelling theatre shows. Easiest **access** to the Golden Mount is along Thanon Boriphat (the specialist street for custom-carved wooden doors), five minutes' walk south from the khlong bridge and Phan Fah canal boat stop at the eastern end of Rajdamnoen Klang.

King Prajadhipok (Rama VII) Museum

Appropriately located just 400m east of Democracy Monument, the **King Praja-dhipok Museum** (Tues–Sun 9am–4pm; B40; ⓦwww.kpi.ac.th/museum) on Thanon Lan Luang charts the life and achievements of **Rama VII**, the king whose ten-year reign embraced Thailand's 1932 transition from rule by absolute monarchy to rule by democratic constitutional monarchy. Situated within the elegant European-style walls of an early-twentieth-century former shop, the museum is hardly an unmissable attraction, though its displays are accessible and easy to digest, and offer expansive English-language captions. The section explaining the background to the 1932 revolution is the most important, featuring browsable copies of early drafts of the Constitution and some insight into the exchanges between the king and the committed group of intellectuals behind this radical political change. When this group finally seized power in 1932, Rama VII agreed to take the compromise option, later presiding at a ceremony in which the Constitution was officially conferred. It wasn't long however, before relations between Rama VII and Thailand's new leaders soured, leading to his abdication in 1935. Rama VII was a keen amateur film-maker and he commis-sioned the building of Thailand's first cinema, the Sala Chalermkrung Theatre (see p.197) in 1933; the museum contains a miniature replica of this movie theatre, where old films from the Rama VII era are screened twice daily, at 10am and 2pm.

The Queen's Gallery

North across Rajdamnoen Klang from Wat Rajnadda, on the corner of Thanon Phra Sumen, is the privately funded, five-storey **The Queen's Gallery** (Thurs–Tues 10am–7pm; B20; ⓦwww.queengallery.org). It hosts temporary shows of contemporary Thai art, plus the occasional exhibition by foreign artists, and makes a more stimulating alternative to the rather staid National Gallery down the other end of Rajdamnoen Klang. Its bookshop sells hard-to-find Thai art books.

Chinatown and Pahurat

W hen the newly crowned Rama I decided to move his capital across to the east bank of the river in 1782, the Chinese community living on the proposed site of his palace was given no choice but to relocate downriver, to the **Sampeng** area. Two centuries on, **Chinatown** has grown into the country's largest Chinese district, a sprawl of narrow, relentlessly crowded alleyways, temples and shophouses that's chiefly of interest for its markets and its colonial-style architecture, though you'll also find a couple of enticing temples here as well as some rewarding eating experiences (see p.177). It's all packed in between Thanon Charoen Krung (New Road) and the river, separated from Ratanakosin by the Indian area of **Pahurat** – famous for its cloth and dressmakers' trimmings – and bordered to the east by Hualamphong train station.

The **Chinese influence** on Thai culture and commerce has been significant ever since the first Chinese merchants gained a toehold in Ayutthaya in the

Getting to and from Chinatown and Pahurat

The easiest access to Chinatown is either by **subway** to Hualamphong Station, or by Chao Phraya **express boat** to Tha Rachawongse (Rajawong; N5) at the southern end of Thanon Rajawong, which runs through the centre of Chinatown. The express boat service also stops just a few metres from Pak Khlong Talat market and the southern end of Thanon Triphet, at Tha Saphan Phut (Memorial Bridge; N6).

This part of the city is also well served by **buses** from downtown Bangkok, as well as from Banglamphu and Ratanakosin (see boxes, p.78 & p.32); from Banglamphu either take any Hualamphong-bound bus and then walk from the train station, or catch the non-air-conditioned bus #56, which runs along Thanon Tanao at the end of Thanon Khao San and then goes all the way down Mahachai and Chakraphet roads in Chinatown – get off just after the Merry King department store for Sampeng Lane. Coming from downtown Bangkok and/or the Skytrain network, either switch to the subway, or jump on a #25 bus, which runs from Thanon Sukhumvit, via Siam Square to Hualamphong, then Thanon Yaowarat and on to Pahurat. Travelling out of Chinatown, westbound #25, #53 and #507 all go to Sanam Luang (for Wat Pho and the Grand Palace).

Be warned that buses and taxis may take an unexpectedly circuitous route due to the many and complex **one-way systems** in Chinatown.

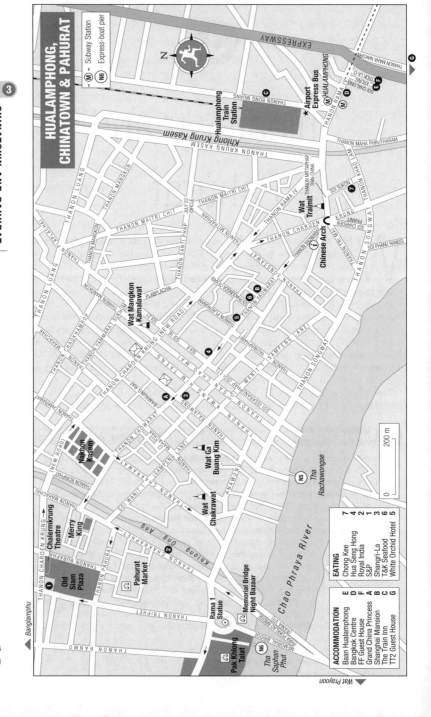

HUALAMPHONG, CHINATOWN & PAHURAT

Ⓜ – Subway Station
Ⓝ6 – Express-boat pier

N

EXPRESSWAY

THANON RAMA IV

THANON MAHA NAKHON

Airport
Express Bus

★ Hualamphong

Ⓜ HUALAMPHONG

Ⓜ IV

Ⓓ

SOI CHALONG
KRUNG

SOI
TUEK-LA-O

Ⓔ Ⓕ

Ⓖ

THANON MAHA PHRUTHARAM

Hualamphong
Train Station

THANON HONG MUANG

Khlong Krung Kasem

THANON KRUNG KASEM

Wat
Traimit

THANON RAMA IV

THANON MITTAPHAP
THAI-CHINA

SOI SUKON 1

Ⓖ

THANON KHAO LAM

Ⓘ
Chinese Arch

THANON CHAROEN
KRUNG

SOI CHAROEN
PHANIT

THANON TRI MIT

SOI PHANU RANGSI

THANON SONGWAT

Ⓑ

Ⓗ JULY 22
CIRCLE

THANON MAITRI CHIT

THANON SANTI PHAP

THANON MAITRI CHIT

THANON MANGKON

THANON LUANG

THANON MANGKON

THANON CHAROEN KRUNG (NEW ROAD)

PLABPLACHAI

Wat Mangkon
Kamalawat

SOI 26

SOI 16

THANON PLAENG NAAM

Ⓕ

THANON YAOWARAT

THANON PHADUNG DAO

THANON YAOWAPHANIT

SOI ISSARANUPHAP (SOI 16)

Ⓕ

SAMPENG LANE

THANON SONGWAT

Tha
Rachawongse

Ⓝ5

THANON LUANG

THANON CHAO KHAM OP

THANON MANGKON

THANON CHAKRAWAT

THANON YAMMARAI SUKHUM

BAMRUNG RAT

THANON CHAROEN KRUNG (NEW ROAD)

Ⓗ

Ⓓ

Ⓒ

SOI ISSARANUPHAP (SOI 11)

SAMPENG LANE

THANON ANUWONG

THANON RATCHAWONG

THANON MAHACHAK

THANON CHAKRAWAT

THANON CHAO KHAM OP

THANON CHAKKRAPHET

Wat Ga
Buang Kim

THANON BORIPHAT

SOI WANIT 1 (SAMPENG LANE)

KHLONG ONG ANG

Wat
Chakrawat

200 m

THANON MAHACHAI

Nakhon
Kasem

THANON YAOWARAI

Chao Phraya River

THANON CHAROEN KRUNG ←
Chalermkrung
Theatre

Merry
King

THANON BURAPHA

THANON PAHURAT

THANON CHAKKRAPHET

Pahurat
Market

KHLONG ONG ANG

Ⓐ

Memorial
Bridge
Night Bazaar

MEMORIAL BRIDGE

SAPHAN PHUT (MEMORIAL) BRIDGE

Banglamphu →

Old
Siam
Plaza

Ⓘ

THANON TRIPHET

Rama 1
Statue

Pak Khlong
Talat

THANON BANMO

THANON MAHARAT

Tha
Saphan Phut

Ⓝ6

Wat Prayoon →

ACCOMMODATION

Baan Hualamphong	E
Bangkok Centre	D
FF Guest House	F
Grand China Princess	A
Shanghai Mansion	B
The Train Inn	C
TT2 Guest House	G

EATING

Chong Kee	7
Hua Seng Hong	4
Royal India	2
S&P	1
Shangri-La	3
T&K Seafood	6
White Orchid Hotel	5

fourteenth century. Following centuries of immigration and intermarriage, there is now some Chinese blood in almost every Thai citizen, including the king, and Chinese-Thai business interests play an enormous role in the Thai economy. This is played out at its most frantic in Sampeng, whose real estate is said to be amongst the most valuable in the country; there are over a hundred gold and jewellery shops along Thanon Yaowarat – Chinatown's nerve centre – alone.

Nearly all Chinatown's shops and restaurants shut down for the annual three-day holiday held to celebrate **Chinese New Year** (on the new moon of the first lunar month, sometime between late January and mid-February), but throughout this period Sampeng's main roads throng with foodstalls and the streets are enlivened by Chinese dragon parades and Chinese opera shows. During the nine-day **Vegetarian Festival** in October or November (see p.178) most of the city's Chinese restaurants stop serving meat, flying special yellow flags to show that they're upholding the community's tradition.

Sampeng

The following fairly lengthy route takes you through **Sampeng**'s most interesting neighbourhoods and could easily easily soak up a whole day, allowing for frequent breaks from the thundering traffic and choking fumes. For the most authentic Chinatown experience it's best to come during the week, as some shops and stalls shut at weekends; on weekdays they begin closing around 5pm after which time the neighbourhood's other big draw – its **food** – takes centre stage. Orientation in Chinatown can be quite tricky: the alleys (known as *trok* rather than the more usual soi) are extremely narrow, their turn-offs often obscured by mounds of merchandise and thronging crowds. One other point to bear in mind: Chinatown's two main arteries are one-way streets, with traffic running west along the entire length of Thanon Yaowarat, and east along Thanon Charoen Krung as far as Thanon Songsawat. For a detailed tour of the alleys and markets, use *Nancy Chandler's Map of Bangkok*; alternatively, ask for help at the BMA **tourist information** booth (Mon–Sat 9am–5pm) just northwest of the Chinese Arch on Thanon Yaowarat, beside Soi 5.

Wat Traimit and the Golden Buddha

The obvious place to start a Chinatown tour is on its eastern perimeter, just west of Hualamphong train and subway stations (exit 1), with **Wat Traimit** (daily 9am–5pm) and its famous Golden Buddha, on Thanon Mittaphap Thai-China. You can see the temple mondop's golden spire from quite a distance, a fitting beacon for its gleaming treasure, the world's largest solid-gold Buddha. It's an apt attraction for a community so closely linked with the gold trade, even if the image has nothing to do with China's spiritual heritage. Over 3m tall and weighing five tonnes, the **Golden Buddha** gleams as if coated in liquid metal, seated amid candles and surrounded with offerings of lotus buds and incense. It's a fine example of the curvaceous grace of Sukhothai art, slim-waisted and beautifully proportioned.

Cast in the thirteenth century, the image was brought to Bangkok by Rama III, completely encased in stucco – a common ruse to conceal valuable statues from would-be thieves. The disguise was so good that no one guessed what was underneath until 1955 when the image was accidentally knocked in the process of being moved to Wat Traimit, and the stucco cracked to reveal a patch of gold. The discovery launched a country-wide craze for tapping away at plaster Buddhas in search of hidden precious metals, but Wat Traimit's is still the most valuable – it's valued, by weight alone, at over US$10 million.

Sampeng Lane

Sampeng Lane is one of Chinatown's most enjoyable shopping alleys. To reach it from Wat Traimit, walk northwest along Thanon Yaowarat from the big, ceremonial, Chinese Arch roundabout (*Soom Pratu Chalerm Prakiat*, also referred to as Odeon Circle), make a left turn onto Thanon Songsawat, then a right on to Sampeng Lane (also signposted as Soi Wanit 1). Stretching southeast–northwest for about 1km, it's a great place to browse, unfurling like a serpentine department store selling everything from Chinese silk pyjama pants to computer games at bargain-basement rates. Similar goods are more or less gathered in sections, so at the eastern end you'll find mostly cheap jewellery and hair accessories, for example, before passing through stalls specializing in ceramics, Chinese lanterns, then shoes, clothes (west of Thanon Rajawong) and, as you near Pahurat, fabrics, haberdashery and irresistibly girlie accessories. See *Nancy Chandler's Map of Bangkok* for a detailed breakdown of what's sold where. To complete the shopping experience, there are food outlets every few steps to help sustain your energy.

Soi Issaranuphap

For a rather more sensual experience, take a right about halfway down Sampeng Lane, into **Soi Issaranuphap** (also signed along its course as Yaowarat Soi 11 then Soi 6, and later Charoen Krung sois 16 and 21). Packed with people from dawn till dusk, this long, dark alleyway, which also traverses Charoen Krung, is where you come in search of ginseng roots (essential for good health), quivering fish heads, cubes of cockroach-killer chalk and a

▲ Chinatown tea shop

gastronome's choice of dried mushrooms and brine-pickled vegetables. Alleys branch off to florid Chinese temples and tiny squares before Soi Issaranuphap finally ends at the Thanon Plaplachai intersection amid a flurry of shops specializing in paper **funeral art**. Believing that the deceased should be well provided for in their afterlife, Chinese people buy miniature paper replicas of necessities to be burned with the body: especially popular are houses, cars, suits of clothing and, of course, money.

Wat Mangkon Kamalawat

If Soi Issaranuphap epitomizes age-old Chinatown commerce, then **Wat Mangkon Kamalawat** (also known as **Wat Leng Nee Yee** or, in English, "Dragon Flower Temple") stands as a fine example of the community's spiritual practices. Best approached via its dramatic multi-tiered gateway 10m up Thanon Charoen Krung from the Soi Issaranuphap junction, Wat Mangkon receives a constant stream of devotees, who come to leave offerings at the altars inside this important Mahayana Buddhist temple. As with the Theravada Buddhism espoused by the Thais, Mahayana Buddhism (see Contexts, p.228) fuses with other ancient religious beliefs, notably Confucianism and Taoism, and the statues and shrines within Wat Mangkon cover the spectrum. As you pass through the secondary gateway, under the glazed ceramic gables topped with undulating Chinese dragons, you're greeted by a set of four outsize statues of bearded and rather forbidding sages, each symbolically clasping either a parasol, a pagoda, a snake's head or a mandolin. Beyond them, a series of Buddha images swathed in saffron netting occupies the next chamber, a lovely open-sided room of gold paintwork, red-lacquered wood, lattice lanterns and pictorial wall panels inlaid with mother-of-pearl. Elsewhere in the compound are booths selling devotional paraphernalia, a Chinese medicine stall and a fortune-teller.

Wat Ga Buang Kim

Less than 100m up Thanon Charoen Krung (New Rd) from Wat Mangkon, a left turn into Thanon Rajawong, followed by a right turn into Thanon Anawong and a further right turn into the narrow, two-pronged Soi Krai brings you to the atmospheric neighbourhood temple of **Wat Ga Buang Kim**. Here, as at more typically Thai temples upcountry, local residents socialize in the shade of the tiny, enclosed courtyard and the occasional worshipper drops by to make offerings at the altar. This particular wat is remarkable for its exquisitely ornamented Chinese-style "vegetarian hall", a one-room shrine with altar centrepiece framed by intricately carved wooden tableaux – gold-painted miniatures arranged as if in sequence, with recognizable characters reappearing in new positions and in different moods. The hall's outer wall is adorned with small tableaux, too, the area around the doorway at the top of the stairs peopled with finely crafted ceramic figurines drawn from Chinese opera stories. The other building in the wat compound is a stage used for Chinese opera performances.

Wat Chakrawat

Back on Anawong, a right turn down Thanon Chakrawat leads to the quite dissimilar **Wat Chakrawat**, home to several long-suffering crocodiles, not to mention monkeys, dogs and chess-playing local residents. **Crocodiles** have lived in the tiny pond behind the bot for about fifty years, ever since one was brought here after being hauled out of the Chao Phraya River, where it had been endangering the limbs of bathers. The original crocodile – stuffed – sits in a glass case overlooking the current generation in the pond.

Across the other side of the wat compound is a grotto housing two unusual Buddhist relics. The first is a black silhouette on the wall, decorated with squares of gold leaf and believed to be the Buddha's shadow. Nearby, the statue of a fat monk looks on. The story goes that this monk was so good-looking that he was forever being tempted by the attentions of women; the only way he could deter them was to make himself ugly – which he did by gorging himself into obesity.

Nakhon Kasem

Further along Thanon Chakrawat, away from the river, is the western limit of Chinatown and an odd assortment of shops in the grid of lanes known as **Nakhon Kasem** (Thieves' Market), bordered by Thanon Charoen Krung and Thanon Yaowarat to the north and south and Chakrawat and Boriphat roads to the east and west. In the sois that crisscross Nakhon Kasem, outlets once full of illicitly acquired goods now stock a vast range of metal wares, from antique gongs to modern musical instruments and machine parts.

Pahurat and Pak Khlong Talat

The ethnic emphasis changes west of Nakhon Kasem. Cross Khlong Ong Ang and you're in **Pahurat** – here, in the small square south of the intersection of Chakraphet and Pahurat roads, is where the capital's sizeable Indian community congregates. Unless you're looking for *beedi* cigarettes or Bollywood VCDs, curiosity-shopping is not as rewarding here as in Chinatown, but if you're interested in buying **fabrics** this is definitely the place: Thanon Pahurat is chock-a-block with cloth merchants specializing in everything from curtain materials through sari lengths to *lakhon* dance costumes complete with accessories. Pahurat is also renowned for its Indian restaurants, and a short stroll along Thanon Chakraphet takes you past a choice selection of curry houses and street vendors.

The Old Siam Plaza

With its mint-green and cream exterior, resplendent with shutters and balustraded balconies, the **Old Siam Plaza**, at the Charoen Krung (New Rd)/Thanon Triphet intersection, is redolent of a colonial summer palace. It's the consumer that's king here however: the three-storey interior is filled with a strange combination of shops selling either upmarket gifts or hi-tech consumer goods. Much more interesting is its permanent food festival that dominates the ground floor, packed with stalls selling traditional Thai sweets and sticky desserts, some beautifully packaged, others made on the spot. The adjacent Sala Chalermkrung Theatre sometimes stages classical Thai drama for non-Thai speakers (see p.197).

Pak Khlong Talat

A stroll through the 24-hour flower and vegetable market **Pak Khlong Talat** is a fine and fitting way to round off a day in Chinatown, though if you're an early riser it's also a great place to come before dawn, when market gardeners from Thonburi boat and truck their freshly picked produce across the Chao Phraya River ready for sale to the shopkeepers, restaurateurs and hoteliers. Occupying an ideal position close to the river, the market has been operating from covered halls between the southern ends of Khlong Lod, Thanon Banmo, Thanon Chakraphet and the river bank since the nineteenth century and is the biggest wholesale market in the capital. The flower stalls, selling twenty different varieties of cut orchids and myriad other tropical blooms, spill onto the streets along the riverfront as well and, though prices are lowest in the early morning, you can still get some good bargains here in the afternoon.

For the most interesting **approach** to the flower market from the Old Siam Plaza, turn west across Thanon Triphet to reach Thanon Banmo, and then follow this road south down towards the Chao Phraya River. As you near the river, notice the facing rows of traditional Chinese shophouses, still in use today, which retain their characteristic (peeling) pastel-painted facades, shutters and stucco curlicues. There's an entrance into the market on your right and just after sundown this southernmost stretch of Thanon Banmo fills with handcarts and vans unloading the most amazing quantities of fresh blooms. The Chao Phraya express boat service stops just a few metres from the market at Tha Saphan Phut (N6).

Memorial Bridge and night bazaar

The riverside end of Thanon Triphet and the area around the base of Memorial Bridge host a huge **night bazaar** (Tues–Sun 8pm–midnight) that's dominated by cheap and unusual fashions – and by throngs of teenage fashion victims.

Memorial Bridge itself (aka **Saphan Phut**) was built in 1932 to commemorate the 150th anniversary of the foundation of the Chakri dynasty and of Bangkok, and is dedicated to Rama I (or Phra Buddha Yodfa, to give him his official title), whose bronze statue sits at the approach. The bridge carries traffic across to Thonburi and has since been supplemented by the adjacent twin-track Saphan Phra Pokklao.

Thonburi

Bangkok really began across the river from Ratanakosin in **Thonburi**, and though you won't find any portentous ruins on this side of the Chao Phraya River you will get a glimpse of an age-old way of life that has all but disappeared from Bangkok proper. For Thonburi is still crisscrossed by **canals**, or khlongs, and life here continues to revolve around the waterways. The main arteries of Khlong Bangkok Noi and Khlong Bangkok Yai are particularly important: vendors of food and household goods paddle their boats along the subsidiary canals that weave through the residential areas, and canalside factories use them to transport their wares to the Chao Phraya River. The **architecture** along the canals ranges from ramshackle, makeshift homes balanced just above the water – and prone to flooding during the monsoon season – to villa-style residences fronted by lawns and waterside verandas. Venture on to the Thonburi backroads just 3 or 4km west of the river and you find yourself surrounded by market gardens and rural homes, with no hint of the throbbing metropolis across on the other bank. Modern Thonburi, on the other hand, sprawling to each side of Thanon Phra Pinklao, consists of the prosaic line-up of department stores, cinemas, restaurants and markets found all over urbanized Thailand.

Devoid of grand ruins and isolated from central Bangkok, it's hard to imagine Thonburi as a former capital of Thailand, but so it was for fifteen years, between the fall of Ayutthaya in 1767 and the establishment of Bangkok in 1782. General Phraya Taksin set up his capital here, strategically near the sea

Getting to and from Thonburi

Getting to Thonburi is simply a matter of crossing the river. Either use Phra Pinklao or Memorial/Phra Pokklao **bridge**, take a **cross-river ferry**, or hop on the Chao Phraya **express ferry**, which makes several stops on the Thonburi bank. Useful city **buses** that cross the river into Thonburi include air-con #507 from Thanon Rama IV, Hualamphong Station and Banglamphu; air-con #511 from Thanon Sukhumvit and Banglamphu; and non-air-con #159 from Chatuchak Weekend Market, Hualamphong and Democracy Monument; see the box on p.32 for details.

You might also find yourself taking a train from **Thonburi Station**, 850m west of the Tha Bangkok Noi ferry stop, as this is the departure point for trains to Kanchanaburi – not to be confused with Thonburi's other, even smaller train station, **Wongwian Yai** (for trains to Samut Sakhon), which is further south and served by the Skytrain, to BTS Wongwian Yai (S8). The **Southern Bus Terminal** – for out-of-town southern destinations including Nakhon Pathom, Damnoen Saduak, Samut Songkhram, Phetchaburi and Kanchanaburi is also in Thonburi. Details on all these transport terminals are given on p.131.

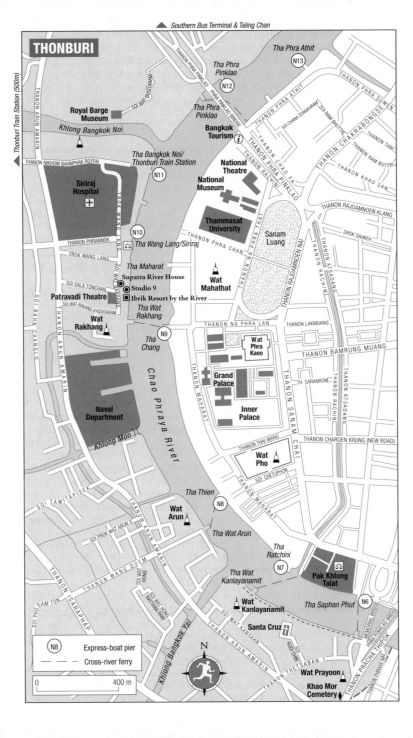

▲ Southern Bus Terminal & Taling Chan

THONBURI

Thonburi Train Station (500m)

Tha Phra Athit

N13

Tha Phra
Pinklao

N12

THANON PHRA PINKLAO

THANON PHRA ATHIT

THANON PHRA SUMEN

THANON CHAKRABONGSE

SOI WAT DUSITARAM

PHRA PINKLAO BRIDGE

Tha Phra Pinklao

SOI CHANA SONGKHRAM

SOI RAM BUTTRI

THANON TANI

Royal Barge
Museum

Khlong Bangkok Noi

THANON CHAO FA

THANON PHRA PINKLAO

Bangkok
Tourism ⓘ

THANON RAM BUTTRI

THANON KHAO SAN

THANON NIKHOM BAHNPHAK ROTFAI

Tha Bangkok Noi/
Thonburi Train Station

N11

National
Theatre

THANON PHRA CHAN

THANON RACHINI

THANON RAJDAMNOEN KLANG

Siriraj
Hospital ✚

National
Museum

TROK WANG LANG

THANON PHRANNOK

N10

Tha Wang Lang/Siriraj

THANON PHRA CHAN

Thammasat
University

Sanam
Luang

DROK SAHKEH

THANON RACHINI

THANON RAJDAMNOEN NAI

THANON NA PHRA THAT

TROK WANG LANG

SOI WAT RAKANG

Tha Maharat

Supatra River House
● Studio 9
■ Ibrik Resort by the River

Wat
Mahathat

SOI SALA TONCHAN

SOI BAHN CHANGLO

SOI WAT RAKANG KHOSITARAM

Patravadi Theatre

Wat
Rakhang

Tha Wat
Rakhang

N9

Tha
Chang

THANON NA PHRA LAN

THANON LAKMUANG

THANON BAMRUNG MUANG

Wat
Phra
Kaeo

TH. SARANROM

THANON MAHARAT

THANON ATSADANG

THANON SANAM CHAI

THANON RACHINI

Chao Phraya River

Grand
Palace

Inner
Palace

THANON CHAROEN KRUNG (NEW ROAD)

Naval
Department

Khlong Mon

THANON ARUN AMARIN

THANON THAI WANG

Wat
Pho

SOI CHETUPHON

THANON MAHARAT

Tha Thien

N8

SOI TAWITAPISEK

SOI PROK WAT ARUN 3

THANON ARUN AMARIN 3

Wat
Arun

Tha Wat Arun

Tha
Ratchini

N7

Pak Khlong
Talat

THANON WANG DOEM

SOI WAT RATTANA RAM

KHLONG MON

Tha Wat
Kanlayanamit

Wat
Kanlayanamit

Tha Saphan Phut

N6

MEMORIAL BRIDGE

PHRA PINKLAO BRIDGE

SOI WAT ARUN 7

SAM TON

SOI PHU

SOI SARAPHAP

Santa Cruz

SOI WAT KANYAHN

KUDI CHIN

THANON PRACHA THIPOK

THANON PHRA NAI

Khlong Bangkok Yai

THANON ARUN AMARIN

THANON THE SABAN

Wat Prayoon

Khao Mor
Cemetery ▼

N8 Express-boat pier

--- Cross-river ferry

0   400 m

N

and far from the marauding Burmese, but the story of his brief reign is a chronicle of battles that left little time and few resources to devote to the building of a city worthy of its predecessor. When General Chao Phraya displaced the by-then demented Taksin to become Rama I, his first decision as founder of the Chakri dynasty was to move the capital to the more defensible site across the river. It wasn't until 1932 that Thonburi was linked to its replacement by Memorial Bridge (Saphan Phut), and Thonburi retained its separate identity for another forty years until, in 1971, it officially became part of Bangkok.

The usual way to explore Thonburi's traditional **canalside neighbourhoods** is on a longtail boat tour (see box opposite), though it's also fun to wander through on foot. The most visited sight is **Wat Arun**, whose distinctive, corncob-shaped profile dominates the area just north of Khlong Bangkok Yai. Broad, busy **Khlong Bangkok Noi** is bordered by some typical stilt-house neighbourhoods and is the site of the popular **Royal Barge Museum**. South of the khlong and gathered along the west bank of the Chao Phraya River, the sprawling Siriraj Hospital dominates a big chunk of waterfront and harbours a collection of curious **medical museums**, after which peaceful **Wat Rakhang** comes as pleasant relief. Some distance downriver, the cemetery at **Wat Prayoon** makes a surprisingly intriguing place to take the kids.

The lack of footbridges over canals means **walking** between sights often involves using the heavily trafficked Thanon Arun Amarin, so for these stretches it's more comfortable to jump onto a motorbike taxi. The slower, more convoluted alternative would be to leapfrog your way up or down the river by **boat**, using the various cross-river ferries that sail from small piers on the Thonburi bank to link up with the Chao Phraya express-boat stops on the other side.

Royal Barge Museum

Since the Ayutthaya era, kings of Thailand have been conveyed along their country's waterways in royal barges. For centuries these slender, exquisitely elegant, black-and-gold wooden vessels were used on all important royal outings, and even up until 1967 the current king used to process down the Chao Phraya River to Wat Arun in a **flotilla of royal barges** at least once a year, on the occasion of Kathin, the annual donation of robes by the laity to the temple at the end of the rainy season. But the hundred-year-old boats are becoming quite frail, so such an event is now rare: the last full-scale royal procession was floated for Kathin in 2007, to mark the king's 80th birthday. A **royal barge procession** along the Chao Phraya River is a magnificent event, all the more spectacular because it happens so infrequently. Fifty or more barges fill the width of the river and stretch for almost 1km, drifting slowly to the measured beat of a drum and the hypnotic strains of ancient boating hymns, chanted by over two thousand oarsmen dressed in luscious brocades.

The eight beautifully crafted vessels at the heart of the ceremony are housed in the **Royal Barge Museum** on the north bank of Khlong Bangkok Noi (daily 9am–5pm; B30; ⓦwww.thailandmuseum.com). Up to 50m long and intricately lacquered and gilded all over, they taper at the prow into imposing mythical figures after a design first used by the kings of Ayutthaya. Rama I had the boats copied and, when those fell into disrepair, Rama VI commissioned the exact reconstructions still in use today. The most important is *Sri Suphanahongse*, which bears the king and queen and is graced by a glittering five-metre-high prow representing the golden swan Hamsa, mount of the Hindu god Brahma.

In front of it floats *Anantanagaraj*, fronted by a magnificent seven-headed naga and bearing a Buddha image. The newest addition to the fleet is *Narai Song Suban*, which was commissioned by the current king for his golden jubilee in 1996; it is a copy of the mid-nineteenth-century original and is crowned with

---

Exploring Thonburi by boat

The most popular way to explore the sights of Thonburi is by **boat**, taking in Wat Arun and the Royal Barge Museum, then continuing along Thonburi's network of small canals. The easiest option is to take a **fixed-price trip** from one of the piers on the Bangkok side of the Chao Phraya River, most conveniently from Tha Phra Arthit in Banglamphu, Tha Chang near Wat Pho or the River City pier off Thanon Charoen Krung; see below for a select list of operators. You can also charter your own longtail from these piers and others such as Tha Sathorn, and from many five-star riverside hotels, but bear the listed prices in mind when negotiating and be specific about your itinerary.

Many of the fixed-price tours include visits to one of Thonburi's two main **floating markets**, both of which are heavily touristed and rather contrived. **Wat Sai** floating market happens daily from Monday to Friday but is very commercialized, and half of it is land-based anyway, while **Taling Chan** floating market is also fairly manufactured but more fun, though it only operates on Saturdays and Sundays (approx 9am–3pm). Taling Chan market is held on Khlong Chak Phra, in front of Taling Chan District Office, a couple of kilometres west of Thonburi train station, and can also be reached by taking bus #79 from Banglamphu. For an authentic floating-market experience, consider heading out of Bangkok to Amphawa, in Samut Songkhram province (see p.145).

Arguably more photogenic, and certainly a lot more genuine, are the individual **floating vendors** who continue to paddle from house-to-house in Thonburi, touting anything from hot food to plastic buckets. You've a good chance of seeing some of them in action on almost any longtail boat tour on any day of the week, particularly in the morning.

Boat trip operators

Mitchaopaya Travel Service Tha Chang ☎02 623 6169. Offers trips of varying durations: in 1hr (B1000/boat), you'll go out along Khlong Bangkok Noi and back via Khlong Mon, passing Wat Arun and the Royal Barge Museum without stopping; in 1hr 30min (B1300), you'd have time to stop at either or you could do a longer route, coming back along Khlong Bangkok Yai; while in 2hr (B1500) you'll have time to go right down the back canals on the Thonburi side and visit an orchid farm. On Sat & Sun, the 90min and 2hr trips take in Taling Chan floating market.

New Road Guest House see p.168. Recommended 4hr longtail trips with a knowledgeable, English-speaking guide that take you deep into Thonburi, passing orchards and taking in an orchid farm, with a drop-off at Wat Pho or the Grand Palace possible on the way back. B700/person.

Real Asia ☎02 665 6364, ⓦwww.realasia.net. Runs guided full-day walking and boat tours of the Thonburi canals for B2000 per person.

River City pier longtails ☎02 237 0077 ext. 180. Private longtail trips for B800 per hour per boat for two people.

Tha Phra Arthit longtails Pier in front of *The Old Phra Arthit Gastronobar*, 200m south of the N13 Tha Phra Arthit express boat pier, Banglamphu. An enjoyable 1 hour 30 minutes loop via Khlong Bangkok Noi, Khlong Chak Phra and Khlong Bangkok Yai that takes in a variety of different khlong-side residences, temples and itinerant floating vendors, but won't include any stops. B850 per hour per boat for two people; B1300 per 1 hour 30 minutes per boat for two to six; B1600/2hr/boat for up to six people.

Wan Fah River City Shopping Centre pier ☎02 639 0704, ⓦwww.wanfahcruise.com. A 2 hourr cruise of the west-bank canals by a combination of longtail and converted rice barge. Daily 2.30pm; B700 per person.

▲ Royal Barge Museum

a black Vishnu (Narai) astride a garuda figurehead. A display of miniaturized royal barges at the back of the museum recreates the exact formation of a traditional procession.

The museum is a feature of most canal tours but is easily visited on your own. Just take the Chao Phraya **express boat** to Tha Phra Pinklao (N12) or, if coming from Banglamphu, take the cheaper, more frequent cross-river ferry (B4) from under Pinklao bridge, beside the tourist information office, to Tha Phra Pinklao across the river, then walk up the road a hundred metres and take the first left down Soi Wat Dusitaram. If coming by **bus** from the Bangkok side (#507, #509 and #511 all cross the river here), get off at the first stop on the Thonburi side, which is right beside the mouth of Soi Wat Dusitaram. Signs from Soi Wat Dusitaram lead you through a jumble of walkways and stilt-houses to the museum, about ten minutes' walk away.

Siriraj Medical Museum

A surprising number of tourists make a point of visiting the **Anatomical Museum**, one of six small collections of medical curiosities at the **Siriraj Medical Museum** (Mon–Sat 9am–4pm; B40; Ⓦ www.si.mahidol.ac.th/eng) in Thonburi's enormous Siriraj teaching hospital. The Anatomical Museum was set up to teach students how to dissect the human body, but its most notorious exhibits are the specimens of conjoined twins kept in jars in a couple of old wooden display cabinets. There is also a picture of the most famous conjoined twins in history, the genuinely Siamese twins Chang and Eng, who were born just outside Bangkok in Samut Songkhran (see box, p.98). The collection was established in 1927 and looks very dated in comparison to modern museums; there is almost no information in English. Exit right from the back door of the Anatomical Building and take the first left to find the potentially more stimulating **Museum of History of Thai Medicine**, whose wax tableaux recreate the traditional medical practices of midwives, masseuses, pharmacists and yogis, though these also have no English-language captions.

Easiest **access** to the hospital is by Chao Phraya express boat to Tha Wang Lang/Siriraj (N10). From the pier walk a few metres up Thanon Phrannok and enter the hospital via its side entrance. Follow the road through the hospital compound for about 350m, turn left just before the (signed) Museum of History of Thai Medicine, and the Anatomical Museum is the first building on your left.

Wat Rakhang

The charming riverside temple of **Wat Rakhang** (Temple of the Bells) gets its name from the five large bells donated by King Rama I and is notable for the hundreds of smaller chimes that tinkle away under the eaves of the main bot and, more accessibly, in the temple courtyard, where devotees come to strike them and hope for a run of good luck. To be extra certain of having wishes granted, visitors also buy loaves of bread from the temple stalls and feed the frenzy of fat fish in the Chao Phraya River below. Behind the bot stands an attractive eighteenth-century wooden *ho trai* (scripture library) that still boasts some original murals on the wooden panels inside, as well as exquisitely renovated gold-leaf paintwork on the window shutters and pillars.

A cross-river **ferry** shuttles between Wat Rakhang's pier and the Tha Chang (Grand Palace) express-boat pier, or you can **walk** to Wat Rakhang in five minutes from the Tha Wang Lang express-boat pier: turn south (left) through the enjoyable **Phrannok pierside market**, which is good for cheap clothes and tempting home-made snacks (especially sweet ones), and continue until you reach the temple, passing the Patravadi Theatre, *Studio 9* theatre-restaurant (see p.197) and tiny *Ibrik Resort by the River* boutique hotel (see p.165) on the way.

Wat Arun

Almost directly across the river from Wat Pho rises the enormous, five-spired prang of **Wat Arun** (daily 8am–5pm; B20; Ⓦ www.watarun.org), the Temple of Dawn, probably Bangkok's most memorable landmark and familiar as the silhouette used in the TAT logo. It looks particularly impressive from the river as you head downstream from the Grand Palace towards the *Oriental Hotel*, and it's well worth stopping off for a closer look. All boat tours include half an hour here, but Wat Arun is also easily visited by yourself, although tour operators will try to persuade you otherwise: just take a cross-river **ferry** from the pier adjacent to the Chao Phraya express-boat pier at Tha Thien. The temple also looks great after dark, when its profile is prettily illuminated – best appreciated from on board one of the dinner cruises that glide nightly up the Chao Phraya; see p.182 for details.

A wat has occupied this site since the Ayutthaya period, but only in 1768 did it become known as the Temple of Dawn, when General Phraya Taksin reputedly reached his new capital at the break of day. The temple served as his royal chapel and housed the recaptured Emerald Buddha for several years until the image was moved to Wat Phra Kaeo in 1785 (see p.62). Despite losing its special status after the relocation, Wat Arun remained important and was reconstructed and enlarged to its present height of 81m by Rama II and Rama III.

The prang that you see today is in classic Ayutthayan style, built as a representation of Mount Meru, the home of the gods in Khmer cosmology. Climbing the two tiers of the square base that supports the **central prang**, you not only enjoy a good view of the river and beyond, but also get a chance to examine the tower's distinctive decorations. Both this main prang and the four minor

Eng and Chang, the Siamese twins

Eng (In) and Chang (Chan), the "original" **Siamese twins**, were born in Samut Songkhram (74km southwest of Bangkok, see p.145) in 1811, when the town was known as Mae Khlong after the estuary on which it sits, and the country was known as Siam. The boys' bodies were joined from breastbone to navel by a short fleshy ligament, but they shared no vital organs and eventually managed to stretch their connecting tissue so that they could stand almost side by side instead of permanently facing each other.

In 1824, the boys were spotted by entrepreneurial Scottish trader Robert Hunter, who returned five years later with an American sea merchant, Captain Abel Coffin, to convince the twins' mother to let them take her sons on a world tour. Hunter and Coffin anticipated a lucrative career as producer-managers of an exotic **freak show**, and were not disappointed. They launched the twins in Boston, advertising them as "the Monster" and charging the public fifty cents to watch the boys demonstrate how they walked and ran. Though shabbily treated and poorly paid, the twins soon developed a more theatrical show, enthralling their audiences with impressive acrobatics and feats of strength, and earning the sobriquet "the eighth wonder of the world". At the age of 21, having split from their exploitative managers, the twins became self-employed, but continued to tour with other companies across the world. Wherever they went, they would always be given a thorough examination by local **medics**, partly to counter accusations of fakery, but also because this was the first time the world and its doctors had been introduced to conjoined twins. Such was the twins' international celebrity that the term "Siamese twins" has been used ever since. Chang and Eng also sought advice from these doctors on surgical separation – an issue they returned to repeatedly right up until their deaths but never acted upon, despite plenty of gruesome suggestions.

By 1840 the twins had become quite wealthy and decided to settle down. They were granted American citizenship, assumed the family name Bunker, and became slave-owning **plantation farmers** in North Carolina. Three years later they married two local sisters, Addie and Sally Yates, and between them went on to father 21 children. The families lived in separate houses and the twins shuttled between the two, keeping to a strict timetable of three days in each household; for an intriguing imagined account of this bizarre state of affairs, read Darin Strauss's novel *Chang and Eng*, reviewed on p.244. Chang and Eng had quite different personalities, and relations between the families soured, leading to the division of their assets, with Chang's family getting most of the land, and Eng's most of the slaves. To support their dependants, the twins were obliged to take their show back on the road several times, on occasion working with the infamous showman P.T. Barnum. Their final tour was born out of financial desperation following the 1861–65 Civil War, which had wiped out most of the twins' riches and led to the liberation of all their slaves.

In 1874, Chang succumbed to bronchitis and died; Eng, who might have survived on his own if an operation had been performed immediately, died a few hours later, possibly of shock. They were 62. The twins are buried in White Plains in North Carolina, but there's a memorial to them near their birthplace in Samut Songkhram.

ones that encircle it are studded all over with bits of broken porcelain, ceramic shards and tiny bowls that have been fashioned into an amazing array of polychromatic flowers. The statues of mythical *yaksha* demons and half-bird, half-human *kinnari* that support the different levels are similarly decorated. The crockery probably came from China, possibly from commercial shipments that were damaged at sea, but whatever its provenance, the overall effect is highly decorative and far more subtle than the dazzling glass mosaics that clad most wat buildings. On the first terrace, the mondops at each cardinal point contain statues of the Buddha at the most important stages of his life: at birth (north), in meditation (east), preaching his first sermon (south) and entering Nirvana (west). The second platform surrounds the base of the prang proper, whose closed entranceways are guarded by four statues of the Hindu god Indra on his three-headed elephant Erawan. In the niches of the smaller prangs stand statues of Phra Pai, the god of the wind, on horseback.

Wat Prayoon

Just west of the Thonburi approach to Memorial Bridge, the unusual **Khao Mor cemetery** makes an unexpectedly enjoyable place to take the kids, with its miniaturized shrines and resident turtles. Its dollshouse-sized chedis and shrines are set on an artificial hillock, which was constructed by Rama III to replicate the pleasing shapes made by dripping candle wax. Wedged in among the grottoes, caverns and ledges of this uneven mass are numerous memorials to the departed, forming a not-at-all sombre gallery of different styles, from traditional Thai chedis, bots and prangs to more foreign designs like the tiny Wild West house complete with cactuses at the front door. Turtles fill the pond surrounding the mound and you can feed them with the bags of banana and papaya sold nearby. The cemetery is part of **Wat Prayoon** (officially Wat Prayurawongsawat) but located in a separate compound to the southeast side of the wat, just off Thanon Pracha Thipok, three minutes' walk from Memorial Bridge. Though it's on the Thonburi bank, it's easiest to reach from the Bangkok side, by walking over Memorial Bridge from the express ferry stop at Tha Saphan Phut (N6).

5

Dusit

Connected to Ratanakosin via the boulevards of Rajdamnoen Klang and Rajdamnoen Nok, the unusually spacious, leafy area known as **Dusit** has been a royal district since the reign of Rama V, King Chulalongkorn (1868–1910). The broad tree-lined avenues, grand, widely spaced government buildings and almost total absence of shops, restaurants and residential developments lend it a dignified ambience. It's also one of the calmer Bangkok neighbourhoods – save for the inevitable thundering traffic – and makes an agreeably uncluttered contrast to the livelier streets of Ratanakosin and Chinatown. However, be prepared to do a fair bit of walking, as the main sights are quite spread out.

Rama V was the first Thai monarch to visit Europe and he returned with radical plans for the modernization of his capital, the fruits of which are most visible in Dusit – notably at **Vimanmek Palace** and **Wat Benjamabophit**, the so-called "Marble Temple". Even now, Rama V still commands a loyal following and his statue, which stands at the Thanon U-Thong–Thanon Sri Ayutthaya crossroads, is presented with offerings every week and is also the focus of celebrations on Chulalongkorn Day (Oct 23).

Today, the Dusit area retains its European feel, and much of the country's decision-making goes on behind the high fences and impressive facades: the building housing the National Parliament is here, as is Government House (which is used mainly for official functions), and the king's official residence, Chitrlada Palace, occupies the eastern edge of the area. On December 2 Dusit is also the venue for the spectacular annual **Trooping the Colour**, when hundreds of magnificently uniformed Royal Guards demonstrate their allegiance to the king by parading around Suan Amporn, across the road from the Rama V statue. Across from Chitrlada Palace, **Dusit Zoo** makes a pleasant enough place to take the kids. The **restaurants** and **guest houses** of Thewet are within walking distance of Dusit; they are marked on the Banglamphu map on p.76 and reviewed under Banglamphu on p.176 and p.162.

Getting to and from Dusit

From Banglamphu, you can get to Dusit by taking the #70 (non-expressway) **bus** from Rajdamnoen Klang and getting off outside the zoo and Elephant Museum on Thanon U-Thong Nai, or the #56 from Thanon Phra Sumen and alighting at the Thanon Ratchasima entrance to Vimanmek Palace (see box, p.78); alternatively, take the **express boat** to Tha Thewet (N15) and then walk. From downtown Bangkok, easiest access is by bus from the Skytrain and subway stops at Victory Monument; there are many services from here, including #28 and #108.

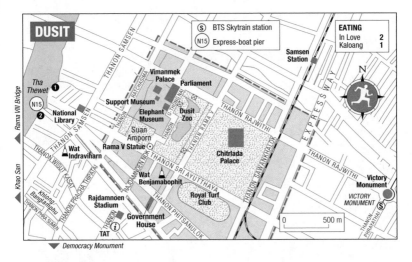

Dusit Park

The ticket price for Vimanmek Palace (daily 9.30am–4pm; compulsory free guided tours every 30min, last tour 3.15pm; B250, or free with a Grand Palace ticket, which remains valid for one week; Ⓦwww.palaces.thai.net) also covers entry to half a dozen other specialist collections in **Dusit Park**'s extensive palace grounds, including the Support Museum and Elephant Museum. Note that the same **dress rules** apply to Vimanmek Palace as to the Grand Palace (see p.59). All visitors to the **Vimanmek compound** are treated to free outdoor performances of traditional Thai dance daily at 10.30am and 2pm. The main entrance to the compound is on Thanon Rajwithi, but there are also ticket gates on Thanon Ratchasima, and opposite Dusit Zoo on Thanon U-Thong Nai.

Vimanmek Palace

Constructed almost entirely of golden teak, without a single nail, breezy, elegant **Vimanmek Palace** is a beautiful coffee-coloured colonial-style mansion, designed in an L-shape to accommodate 81 rooms and encircled by delicate latticework verandas that look out onto carefully tended lawns, flower gardens and lotus ponds. It was originally built in 1868 by Rama V as a summer retreat on the tiny east-coast island of Ko Si Chang, but he had it transported bit by bit to Dusit in 1901, where the "Celestial Residence" soon became his favourite palace. The king and his enormous retinue of officials, concubines and children stayed here for lengthy periods between 1902 and 1906. All of Vimanmek's 81 rooms were out of bounds to male visitors, except for the king's own apartments, in the octagonal tower, which were entered by a separate staircase.

On display inside the palace is Rama V's collection of artefacts from all over the world, including *bencharong* ceramics, European furniture and bejewelled Thai betel-nut sets. Considered progressive in his day, Rama V introduced many newfangled ideas to Thailand: the country's first indoor bathroom is here, as is the earliest typewriter with Thai characters, and some of the first portrait

▲ Vimanmek Palace

paintings – portraiture had until then been seen as a way of stealing part of the sitter's soul.

The Support Museum

Elsewhere in the Vimanmek grounds a dozen handsome, pastel-painted royal residences and small throne halls have been converted into tiny, specialist interest museums, including collections of antique textiles, photographs taken by the king, royal ceremonial objects and antique clocks. The most interesting of these is the **Support Museum Abhisek Dusit Throne Hall**, which is housed in another very pretty building of complementary design, formerly used for meetings and banquets, immediately behind (to the east of) Vimanmek. The Support Museum showcases the exquisite handicrafts produced under Queen Sirikit's charity project, Support, which works to revitalize traditional Thai arts and crafts. Outstanding exhibits include a collection of handbags, baskets and pots woven from the *lipao* fern that grows wild in southern Thailand; jewellery and figurines inlaid with the iridescent wings of beetles; gold and silver nielloware; and lengths of intricately woven silk from the northeast.

Chang Ton Royal Elephant National Museum

Just behind (to the east of) the Support Museum, inside the Thanon U-Thong Nai entrance to the Vimanmek compound, stand two whitewashed buildings that once served as the stables for the king's white elephants. Now that the sacred pachyderms have been relocated, the stables have been turned into the **Royal Elephant National Museum** (Ⓦwww.thailandmuseum.com). Inside you'll find some interesting pieces of elephant paraphernalia, including sacred ropes, mahouts' amulets and magic formulae, as well as photos of the all-important ceremony in which a white elephant is granted royal status (see box opposite).

Dusit Zoo (Khao Din)

Across Thanon U-Thong Nai from the Elephant Museum is the side entrance into **Dusit Zoo**, also known as **Khao Din** (daily 8am–9pm; B100, children B50), which was once part of the Chitrlada Palace gardens, but is now a public park; the main entrance is on Thanon Rajwithi and there's a third gate on Thanon Rama V, within walking distance of Wat Benjamabophit. All the usual suspects are here in the zoo, including big cats, elephants, orang-utans, chimpanzees and a reptile house, but the enclosures are pretty basic. However, it's a reasonable place for kids to let off steam, with plenty of shade, a full complement of English-language signs, a lake with pedalos and lots of foodstalls.

Wat Benjamabophit

Commissioned by Rama V in 1899, **Wat Benjamabophit** (aka Wat Bencha; daily 7am–5pm; B20) is the last major temple to have been built in Bangkok. It's an interesting fusion of classical Thai and nineteenth-century European design, with its Carrara marble walls – hence the touristic tag "**the Marble Temple**" – complemented by the bot's unusual stained-glass windows, Victorian in style but depicting figures from Thai mythology. Inside, a fine replica of the highly revered Phra Buddha Chinnarat image that resides in the

The royal white elephants

In Thailand the most revered of all elephants are the so-called **white elephants** – actually tawny brown albinos – which are considered so sacred that they all, whether wild or captive, belong to the king by law. Their special status originates from Buddhist mythology, which tells how the previously barren Queen Maya became pregnant with the future Buddha after dreaming one night that a white elephant had entered her womb. The thirteenth-century King Ramkhamhaeng of Sukhothai adopted the beast as a symbol of the great and the divine, and ever since, a Thai king's greatness is said to be measured by the number of white elephants he owns. The present monarch, King Bhumibol, has twelve, the largest royal collection to date.

Before an elephant can be granted official "white elephant" status, it has to pass a stringent assessment of its physical and behavioural **characteristics**. Key qualities include a paleness of seven crucial areas – eyes, nails, palate, hair, outer edges of the ears, tail and testicles – and an all-round genteel demeanour, manifested, for instance, in the way in which it cleans its food before eating, or in a tendency to sleep in a kneeling position. Tradition holds that an elaborate ceremony should take place every time a new white elephant is presented to the king: the animal is paraded with great pomp from its place of capture to Dusit, where it's anointed with holy water in front of an audience of priests and dignitaries, before being housed in the royal stables. Recently though, the king has called time on this exorbitantly expensive ritual, and only one of the royal white elephants is now kept inside the palace compound; the others live in less luxurious rural accommodation.

The expression "**white elephant**" to describe an unwanted possession probably derives from the legend that the kings used to present certain enemies with one of these exotic creatures. The animal required expensive attention but, being royal, could not be put to work in order to pay for its upkeep – the recipient thus went bust trying to keep it.

northern Thai city of Phitsanulok presides over the small room containing Rama V's ashes. The courtyard behind the bot houses a gallery of Buddha images from all over Asia, established by Rama V as an overview of different representations of the Buddha.

Wat Benjamabophit is one of the best temples in Bangkok to see religious **festivals** and rituals. Whereas monks elsewhere tend to go out on the streets every morning in search of alms, at the Marble Temple the ritual is reversed, and merit-makers come to them. Between about 6 and 7.30am, the monks line up on Thanon Nakhon Pathom, their bowls ready to receive donations of curry and rice, lotus buds, incense, even toilet paper and Coca-Cola; the demure row of saffron-robed monks is a sight well worth getting up early for. The monks' evening candlelight processions around the bot during the Buddhist festivals of Maha Puja (in Feb) and Visakha Puja (in May) are among the most entrancing in the country.

Wat Benjamabophit is just a two-hundred-metre walk south of the zoo's Thanon Rama V entrance, or about 600m from Vimanmek's U–Thong Nai gate. Coming by bus #70 from Banglamphu, get off at the crossroads in front of the Rama V statue and walk east along Thanon Sri Ayutthaya.

Downtown Bangkok

xtending east from the main rail line and south to Thanon Sathorn, **downtown Bangkok** is central to the colossal expanse of Bangkok as a whole but rather peripheral in a sightseer's perception of the city. This modern high-rise area is where you'll find the main financial district, around Thanon Silom, and the chief shopping centres, around Siam Square and Thanon Ploenchit, in addition to the smart hotels, restaurants and bars, embassies and airline offices. Scattered widely across the downtown area are four attractive museums housed in traditional teak buildings: **Jim Thompson's House** near Siam Square, the **Suan Pakkad Palace Museum** to the north, **M.R. Kukrit's Heritage Home** in southern

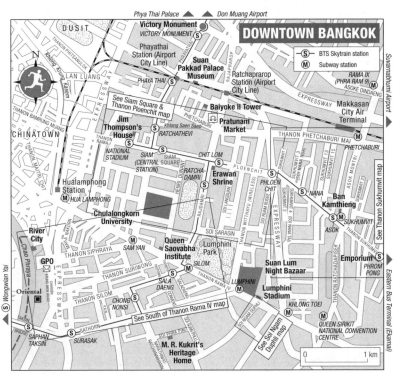

Phya Thai Palace — Don Muang Airport

DOWNTOWN BANGKOK

- (S) BTS Skytrain station
- (M) Subway station

DUSIT

Victory Monument
VICTORY MONUMENT (S)

Phayathai Station (Airport City Line)
PHAYA THAI (S)

Suan Pakkad Palace Museum

Ratchaprarop Station (Airport City Line)

RAMA IX (PHRA RAM 9)
ASOKE DINDAENG

LAN LUANG

Baiyoke II Tower

Makkasan City Air Terminal

See Siam Square & Thanon Ploenchit map

PHETCHABURI

Jim Thompson's House

Klong Saen Saeb

Pratunam Market

THANON PHETCHABURI MAI (M) PHETCHABURI

CHINATOWN

RATCHATHEWI (S)

NATIONAL STADIUM

SIAM (CENTRAL STATION) (S)

SIAM SQUARE

CHIT LOM (S)

PLOENCHIT

NANA (S) SUKHUMVIT

Ban Kamthieng

Hualamphong Station
(M) HUA LAMPHONG

RATCHA-DAMRI

Erawan Shrine

PHLOEN CHIT

Chulalongkorn University

SOI SARASIN

ASOK (S)(M) SUKHUMVIT

River City

SAM YAN (M)

Queen Saovabha Institute

Lumphini Park

Emporium (S) PHROM PONG

GPO

THANON SIPHRAYA

SILOM (M)

Suan Lum Night Bazaar

Oriental

THANON SURIWONG

SALA DAENG (S)

THANON RAMA IV

LUMPHINI (M)

Lumphini Stadium

THANON SILOM

CHONG NONSI (S)

See South of Thanon Rama IV map

KHLONG TOEI (M)

SAPHAN TAKSIN (S) SATHORN

SURASAK

QUEEN SIRIKIT NATIONAL CONVENTION CENTRE (M)

M.R. Kukrit's Heritage Home

0 _____ 1 km

downtown, and the **Ban Kamthieng** off Thanon Sukhumvit. Downtown's other tourist highlights are far more diverse: **Siam Ocean World**, a hi-tech aquarium that both kids and adults can enjoy; the noisy and glittering **Erawan Shrine**; and the Art Nouveau **Phya Thai Palace**, a quirky, half-restored royal dwelling.

If you're heading downtown from Banglamphu, allow at least an hour to get to any of the places mentioned here by **bus**. Depending on the time of day, it may be quicker to take an **express boat** downriver and then change onto the **Skytrain**. It might also be worth considering the regular **boats** on Khlong Saen Saeb. For more detailed information on transport to each of the three main downtown areas, see the boxes on p.107, p.115 and p.121.

Siam Square, Thanon Ploenchit and northern downtown

Though **Siam Square** has just about everything to satisfy the Thai consumer boom – big shopping centres, Western fast-food restaurants, cinemas – don't come looking for an elegant commercial piazza: the "square" is in fact a grid of small streets to the southeast of **Pathumwan intersection** (the corner of Thanon Rama I and Thanon Phrayathai) and the name is applied freely to the surrounding area. Further east, you'll find yet more shopping malls around the Erawan Shrine, where Rama I becomes Thanon Ploenchit, an intersection sometimes known as **Ratchaprasong**. It's possible to stroll in peace here on an elevated **walkway**, beneath the Skytrain lines but above the cracked pavements, noise and fumes of Thanon Rama I, all the way from Siam Centre to the Erawan Shrine (further progress is blocked by Central and Chitlom Skytrain

▲ Siam Square

Getting to and from Siam Square, Thanon Ploenchit and northern downtown

This area is well served by the **Skytrain**, with Siam (Central Station), the junction of the Silom and Sukhumvit lines, hard by Siam Square, while the National Stadium Station (Silom Line) puts you right on the doorstep of Jim Thompson's House and the Soi Kasemsan 1 guest houses. To the east of Central Station, the Sukhumvit Line runs the length of Thanon Ploenchit, while to the north, it will whisk you up to Phaya Thai Station, just five minutes' walk from Suan Pakkad and Victory Monument Station, ten minutes' walk from Phya Thai Palace. Dozens of **buses** of all kinds run through the area, most passing the focal Ratchaprasong intersection by the Erawan Shrine. Probably the most useful for travellers are those which stop near Soi Kasemsan 1, including air-con #508 and ordinary #15, which both run west to Chinatown and Ratanakosin. Soi Kasemsan 1 and Jim Thompson's House are each five minutes' walk from Tha Saphan Hua Chang, the Khlong Saen Saeb longtail boat stop at Thanon Phrayathai, while Tha Pratunam is within walking distance of Pratunam market, Baiyoke II Tower and even the Erawan Shrine.

stations). Life becomes marginally less frenetic around **Ploenchit**, which is flanked by several grand old embassies and sharply delineated by the Expressway flyover, marking the start of Thanon Sukhumvit.

Things also quieten down a little in the **northern part of downtown**, where besides Suan Pakkad and Phya Thai Palace, only the Baiyoke II Tower, Bangkok's tallest building, and the Pratunam covered market in its shadow might draw you into the area. One other landmark you're likely to spot here is the stone obelisk of **Victory Monument** (*Anu Sawari Chaisamoraphum*, or just *Anu Sawari*), which can be seen most spectacularly from Skytrains as they snake their way round it. It was erected after the Indo-Chinese War of 1940–41, when Thailand took back some territory in Laos and Cambodia while the French government was otherwise occupied in World War II, though nowadays it commemorates all of Thailand's past military glories.

Jim Thompson's House

Just off Siam Square at the north end of Soi Kasemsan 2, Thanon Rama I, **Jim Thompson's House** (daily from 9am, viewing on frequent 30–40min guided tours in several languages, last tour 5pm; B100, students & under-25s B50; ☎02 216 7368, ⓦ www.jimthompsonhouse.org) is a kind of Ideal Home in elegant Thai style, and a peaceful refuge from downtown chaos. The house was the residence of the legendary American adventurer, entrepreneur, art collector and all-round character whose mysterious disappearance in the jungles of Malaysia in 1967 has made him even more of a legend among Thailand's farang community (see box, p.110) . National Stadium is the closest **Skytrain** station, but the house is walkable from Central Station (Siam) and a canalside path presents a shortcut from the Khlong Saen Saeb **pier** at Saphan Hua Chang.

Apart from putting together this beautiful home, Thompson's most concrete contribution was to turn traditional silk-weaving from a dying art into the highly successful international industry it is today. The complex now includes a **shop** (closes 6pm), part of the Jim Thompson Thai Silk Company chain (see p.207). Above the shop, the **Jim Thompson Center for the Arts** is a fascinating gallery that hosts both traditional and modern temporary exhibitions on textiles and the arts, such as royal maps of Siam in the nineteenth century or an interactive show that celebrated the hundredth anniversary of Thompson's birth

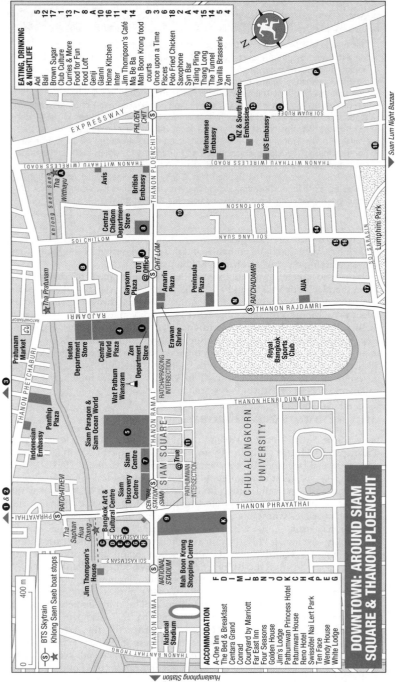

▲ *Thanon Sukhumvit*

EATING, DRINKING & NIGHTLIFE
Aoi	5
Bali	12
Brown Sugar	17
Club Culture	1
Curries & More	13
Food for Fun	7
Food Loft	8
Genji	A
Gianni	10
Home Kitchen	16
Inter	11
Jim Thompson's Café	14
Ma Be Ba	4
Mah Boon Krong food courts	
Once upon a Time	9
Pisces	3
Polo Fried Chicken	6
Saxophone	18
Syn Bar	2
Taling Pling	A
Thang Long	4
The Tunnel	15
Vanilla Brasserie	14
Zen	5
	4

EXPRESSWAY

THANON WITHAYU (WIRELESS ROAD)

THANON PHETCHABURI

THANON PHRAYATHAI

THANON RAMA I

THANON HENRI DUNANT

THANON PHRAYATHAI

Vietnamese Embassy

NZ & South African Embassies

US Embassy

SOI RUAM RUDEE

Suan Lum Night Bazaar ▶

British Embassy

Avis

Central Chidlom Department Store

SOI CHITLOM

Gaysorn Plaza

TOT @ Office

Amarin Plaza

Peninsula Plaza

AUA

SOI TONSON

SOI LANG SUAN

Lumphini Park

SOI SARASIN

THANON RAJDAMRI

RATCHADAMRI

Erawan Shrine

RATCHAPRASONG INTERSECTION

Royal Bangkok Sports Club

Isetan Department Store

Central World Plaza

Zen Department Store

Pratunam Market

Panthip Plaza

Indonesian Embassy

Siam Paragon & Siam Ocean World

Wat Pathum Wanaram

Siam Centre

Siam Discovery Centre

Bangkok Art & Cultural Centre

Jim Thompson's House

Tha Saphan Hua Chang

SOI KASEMSAN 1

SOI KASEMSAN 2

National Stadium

Mah Boon Krong Shopping Centre

SIAM SQUARE

True

PATHUMWAN INTERSECTION

CHULALONGKORN UNIVERSITY

BTS Skytrain

Khlong Saen Saeb boat stops

Khlong Saen Saeb

Tha Pratunam

Tha Withayu

0   400 m

Hualamphong Station ▶

ACCOMMODATION
A-One Inn	F
The Bed & Breakfast	D
Centara Grand	I
Conrad	M
Courtyard by Marriott	L
Far East Inn	B
Four Seasons	N
Golden House	J
Jim's Lodge	O
Pathumwan Princess Hotel	K
Patumwan House	C
Reno Hotel	H
Swissôtel Nai Lert Park	P
Ten Face	E
Wendy House	G
White Lodge	A

DOWNTOWN: AROUND SIAM SQUARE & THANON PLOENCHIT

and the vibrant evolution of Bangkok over the same period. There's also an excellent **bar-restaurant** (last food orders 4.45pm), which serves a similar menu to *Jim Thompson's Saladaeng Café* (see p.181). Ignore any con men at the entrance to the soi looking for mugs to escort on rip-off shopping trips, who'll tell you that the house is closed when it isn't.

The grand, rambling **house** is in fact a combination of six teak houses, some from as far afield as Ayutthaya and most more than 200 years old. Like all traditional houses, they were built in wall sections hung together without nails on a frame of wooden pillars, which made it easy to dismantle them, pile them onto a barge and float them to their new location. Although he had trained as an architect, Thompson had more difficulty in putting them back together again; in the end, he had to go back to Ayutthaya to hunt down a group of carpenters who still practised the old house-building methods. Thompson added a few unconventional touches of his own, incorporating the elaborately carved front wall of a Chinese pawnshop between the drawing room and the bedroom, and reversing the other walls in the drawing room so that their carvings faced into the room.

The impeccably tasteful **interior** has been left as it was during Jim Thompson's life, even down to the place settings on the dining table – Thompson entertained guests most nights and to that end designed the house like a stage set. Complementing the fine artefacts from throughout Southeast Asia is a stunning array of Thai arts and crafts, including one of the best collections of traditional Thai paintings in the world. Thompson picked up plenty of bargains from the Thieves' Quarter (Nakhon Kasem) in Chinatown, before collecting Thai art became fashionable and expensive. Other pieces were liberated from decay and destruction in upcountry temples, while many of the Buddha images were turned over by ploughs, especially around Ayutthaya. Some of the exhibits are very rare, such as a headless but elegant seventh-century Dvaravati Buddha and a seventeenth-century Ayutthayan teak Buddha, but Thompson also bought pieces of little value and fakes simply for their looks – a shopping strategy that's all the more sensible in the jungle of today's Thai antiques trade.

After the guided tour, you're free to look again, at your leisure, at the former rice barn and gardener's and maid's houses in the small, jungly **garden**, which display some gorgeous traditional Thai paintings and drawings, as well as small-scale statues and Chinese ceramics.

Bangkok Art and Cultural Centre

A striking white hunk of modernity, the **Bangkok Art and Cultural Centre** overlooks the junction of Rama I and Phrayathai roads from its northwest corner (Tues–Sun 10am–9pm; ☎02 214 6630–1, ⓦwww.bacc.or.th). Connected by a walkway to National Stadium Skytrain station, this prestigious new centre houses several galleries on its upper floors, connected by spiralling ramps like New York's Guggenheim, as well as an auditorium and studio, and space for planned shops and restaurants. Its aim is to host temporary shows by contemporary artists from Thailand and abroad across all media, from the visual arts to music and design.

Siam Ocean World

Spreading over two spacious basement floors at the east end of the Siam Paragon shopping centre on Thanon Rama I, **Siam Ocean World** is a highly impressive, Australian-built aquarium (daily 9am–10pm, last admission 9pm; B750, children 80–120cm tall B600, under 80cm free; ☎02 687 2000, ⓦwww.siamoceanworld .com). Despite the relatively high admission price, it gets packed at weekends and during holidays, and can be busy with school groups on weekday afternoons –

The legend of Jim Thompson

Thai silk-weavers, art-dealers and conspiracy theorists all owe a debt to **Jim Thompson**, who even now, forty years after his disappearance, remains Thailand's most famous farang. An architect by trade, Thompson left his New York practice in 1940 to join the Office of Strategic Services (later to become the CIA), a tour of duty that was to see him involved in clandestine operations in North Africa, Europe and, in 1945, the Far East, where he was detailed to a unit preparing for the invasion of Thailand. When the mission was pre-empted by the Japanese surrender, he served for a year as OSS station chief in Bangkok, forming links that were later to provide grist for endless speculation.

After an unhappy and short-lived stint as part-owner of the *Oriental Hotel*, Thompson found his calling with the struggling **silk-weavers** of the area near the present Jim Thompson House, whose traditional product was unknown in the West and had been all but abandoned by Thais in favour of less costly imported textiles. Encouragement from society friends and an enthusiastic write-up in *Vogue* convinced him there was a foreign market for Thai silk, and by 1948 he had founded the Thai Silk Company Ltd. Success was assured when, two years later, the company was commissioned to make the costumes for the Broadway run of *The King and I*. Thompson's celebrated eye for colour combinations and his tireless promotion – in the early days, he could often be seen in the lobby of the *Oriental* with bolts of silk slung over his shoulder, waiting to pounce on any remotely curious tourist – quickly made his name synonymous with Thai silk.

Like a character in a Somerset Maugham novel, Thompson played the role of Western exile to the hilt. Though he spoke no Thai, he made it his personal mission to preserve traditional arts and architecture (at a time when most Thais were more keen to emulate the West), assembling his famous Thai house and stuffing it with all manner of Oriental *objets d'art*. At the same time he held firmly to his farang roots and society connections: no foreign gathering in Bangkok was complete without Jim Thompson, and virtually every Western luminary passing through Bangkok – from Truman Capote to Ethel Merman – dined at his table.

If Thompson's life was the stuff of legend, his disappearance and presumed death only added to the mystique. On Easter Sunday, 1967, Thompson, while staying with friends in a cottage in Malaysia's Cameron Highlands, went out for a stroll and never came back. A massive search of the area, employing local guides, tracker dogs and even shamans, turned up no clues, provoking a rash of fascinating but entirely unsubstantiated theories. The grandfather of them all, advanced by a Dutch psychic, held that Thompson had been lured into an ambush by the disgraced former prime minister of Thailand, Pridi Panyonyong, and spirited off to Cambodia for indeterminate purposes; later versions, supposing that Thompson had remained a covert CIA operative all his life, proposed that he was abducted by Vietnamese Communists and brainwashed to be displayed as a high-profile defector to Communism. More recently, an amateur sleuth claims to have found evidence that Thompson met a more mundane fate, having been killed by a careless truck driver and hastily buried.

there are often long queues for the twenty-minute glass-bottomed boat rides (normally B150, though free at the time of writing, on special promotion), which give a behind-the-scenes look at the aquarium's workings.

Among other outstanding features of this US$30-million development are an eight-metre-deep glass-walled tank, which displays the multi-coloured variety of a coral reef drop-off to great effect, touch tanks for handling starfish, and a long, under-ocean tunnel where you can watch sharks and rays swimming over your head. In this global piscatorial display of around four hundred species, locals such as the Mekong giant catfish and the Siamese tigerfish are not forgotten, while regularly spaced touch-screen terminals provide information in English about the creatures on view. Popular daily highlights include shark feeds (currently 1pm & 4pm), and it's even possible to walk with the sharks (wearing a diving helmet; B2000 for 15min) or dive with them for thirty minutes, costing from B5300 for an experienced diver to B6600 for a first-timer (including admission price; ⓦwww.sharkdive.org). You can also watch – through 3D glasses – underwater and other nature films in "4D X-venture", where the chairs move and there are occasional sprays of water (normally B250, though free at the time of writing, on special promotion).

The Erawan Shrine

For a glimpse of the variety and ubiquity of Thai religion, drop in on the **Erawan Shrine** (*Saan Phra Prom* in Thai), at the corner of Thanon Ploenchit and Thanon Rajdamri underneath Chit Lom Skytrain station. Remarkable as much for its setting as anything else, this shrine to Brahma, the ancient Hindu creation god, and Erawan, his elephant, squeezes in on one of the busiest and noisiest intersections in modern Bangkok. And it's not the only one: half a dozen other Hindu shrines are dotted around Ratchaphrasong intersection, most notably **Trimurti**, who combines the three main gods, Brahma, Vishnu and Shiva, on the opposite corner outside Central World Plaza. Modern residents see Trimurti as a sort of Cupid figure, and those looking for love bring red offerings.

Towering over the Erawan Shrine, the *Grand Hyatt Erawan Hotel* is the reason for its existence and its name. When a string of calamities held up the building of the original hotel in the 1950s, spirit doctors were called in, who instructed the owners to build a new home for the offended local spirits: the hotel was then finished without further mishap. Ill fortune struck the shrine itself, however, in early 2006, when a young, mentally disturbed, Muslim man smashed the Brahma statue to pieces with a hammer – and was then brutally beaten to death by an angry mob. An exact replica of the statue was quickly installed, incorporating the remains of the old statue to preserve the spirit of the deity.

Be prepared for sensory overload here: the main structure shines with lurid glass of all colours and the overcrowded precinct around it is almost buried under scented garlands and incense candles. You might also catch a group of traditional dancers performing here to the strains of a small classical orchestra – worshippers hire them to give thanks for a stroke of good fortune. To increase their future chances of such good fortune, visitors buy a bird or two from the flocks incarcerated in cages here; the bird-seller transfers the requested number of captives to a tiny hand-held cage, from which the customer duly liberates the animals, thereby accruing merit. People set on less abstract rewards will invest in a lottery ticket from one of the physically disabled sellers: they're thought to be the luckiest you can buy.

Pratunam Market and Baiyoke II Tower

Ten minutes' walk north of the Erawan Shrine and extending northwest from the corner of Rajaprarop and Phetchaburi roads, **Pratunam Market** is famous for its low-cost, low-quality casual clothes. The vast, dark warren of stalls is becoming touristy near the hotels on its north side, but there are still bargains to be had elsewhere, especially along the market's western side. On the north side of the market rises Bangkok's tallest building, **Baiyoke II Tower**, where high-speed lifts whisk you to the revolving observation deck on the 84th floor (daily 10.30am–10.30pm; B200, including one drink at the bar on the 83rd floor), for breathtaking views of the city.

Suan Pakkad Palace Museum

The **Suan Pakkad Palace Museum** (daily 9am–4pm; B100; Ⓦwww
.suanpakkad.com), five minutes' walk from Phaya Thai Skytrain station at
352–4 Thanon Sri Ayutthaya, stands on what was once a cabbage patch but is
now one of the finest gardens in Bangkok. Most of this private collection of
beautiful Thai objects from all periods is displayed in four groups of traditional wooden houses, which were transported to Bangkok from various parts
of the country. You can either take a guided tour in English (free) or explore
the loosely arranged collection yourself (a leaflet and bamboo fan are handed
out at the ticket office, and some of the exhibits are labelled). The attached
Marsi Gallery, in the modern Chumbhot-Pantip Center of Arts on the east
side of the garden, displays some interesting temporary exhibitions of
contemporary art (Ⓣ02 246 1775–6 ext. 229 for details).

The highlight of Suan Pakkad is the renovated **Lacquer Pavilion**, across the
reedy pond at the back of the grounds. Set on stilts, the pavilion is actually an
amalgam of two eighteenth- or late seventeenth-century temple buildings, a *ho
trai* (library) and a *ho khien* (writing room), one inside the other, which were
found between Ayutthaya and Bang Pa-In. The interior walls are beautifully
decorated with gilt on black lacquer: the upper panels depict the life of the
Buddha while the lower ones show scenes from the *Ramayana*. Look out
especially for the grisly details in the tableau on the back wall, showing the
earth goddess drowning the evil forces of Mara. Underneath are depicted some
European dandies on horseback, probably merchants, whose presence suggests
that the work was executed before the fall of Ayutthaya in 1767. The carefully
observed details of daily life and nature are skilful and lively, especially considering the restraints which the lacquering technique places on the artist, who has
no opportunity for corrections or touching up.

Divided between House no. 8 and the Ban Chiang Gallery in the Chumbhot-
Pantip Center of Arts is a very good collection of elegant, whorled pottery and
bronze jewellery, which the former owner of Suan Pakkad Palace, Princess
Chumbhot, excavated from tombs at Ban Chiang, the major Bronze Age settle-
ment in northeastern Thailand. Scattered around the rest of the museum are
some attractive Thai and Khmer religious sculptures among an eclectic jumble
of artefacts, including fine ceramics and some intriguing kiln-wasters, failed pots
which have melted together in the kiln to form weird, almost rubbery pieces
of sculpture; an extensive collection of colourful papier-mâché *khon* masks;
monks' elegant ceremonial fans; and some rich teak carvings, including a
200-year-old temple door showing episodes from *Sang Thong*, a folk tale about
a childless king and queen who discover a handsome son in a conch shell.

Phya Thai Palace

An intriguing way to spend a Saturday in Bangkok is to explore **Phya Thai
Palace** (Ⓦwww.phyathaipalace.org), a grandiose and eccentric relic of the
early twentieth century on Thanon Rajwithi, about ten minutes' walk west of
Victory Monument and its Skytrain station. Built mostly by **Vajiravudh**,
Rama VI, who lived here from 1919 for the last six years of his reign, it initially
became the most luxurious hotel in Southeast Asia after his death, incorpo-
rating Thailand's first radio station, then after the 1932 coup, a military hospital.
Parts of the airy, rambling complex have been splendidly restored by the Palace
Fan Club, while others show nearly a century's worth of wear and tear, and
one building is still used as offices by Phra Mongkutklao Army Hospital; you're

quite likely to come across a musical performance or rehearsal as you're being guided round the otherwise empty rooms. Engaging **tours** in Thai and English (1hr 30min–2hr; free, donations towards the palace upkeep welcome), led by volunteer guides, usually kick off at 9.30am and 1.30pm on Saturdays, though it's best to phone in advance to check. It's also possible to visit on weekdays, as long as you make an appointment and pay B500. For further information, contact Miss Pisadaporn Rupramarn at the hospital on ☎02 354 7660 (Mon–Fri ext. 93646 or 93694, Sat ext. 93698) or on 089 672 3477. It's well worth buying the excellent guidebook, not only to help the palace restoration fund, but also to read the extraordinary story of **Dusit Thani**: this miniature utopian city was set up by King Vajiravudh on an acre of the palace grounds (now dismantled) as a political experiment complete with two daily newspapers, elections and a constitution – only a decade or so before a real constitution was forcibly imposed on the monarchy after the coup of 1932.

Most of the central building, the **Phiman Chakri Hall**, is in a sumptuous, English, Art Nouveau style, featuring silk wallpaper, ornate murals, Italian marble – and an extravagant but unusable fireplace that reminded Vajiravudh of his schooling in England. The king's first bedroom, decorated in royal red and appointed with a huge, step-down, marble bath, later went for B120 a night as a hotel suite. Outside in the grounds, between a pond used for bathing and the canal which gave access to Khlong Samsen, Vajiravudh first constructed for himself a simple wooden house so that he could keep an eye on the builders, the **Mekhala Ruchi Pavilion**, which later became the king's barber's. In front of the Phiman Chakri Hall, the **Thewarat Sapharom Hall**, a neo-Byzantine teak audience hall, is still used for occasional **classical concerts**. Don't leave without sampling the lovely, Art Nouveau **coffee shop**, a former waiting room covered in ornate teak carving.

Southern downtown

South of Thanon Rama I, commercial development gives way to a dispersed assortment of large institutions, dominated by Thailand's most prestigious centre of higher learning, Chulalongkorn University, and the green expanse of **Lumphini Park**. Thanon Rama IV marks another change of character: downtown proper, centring British English on the high-rise, American-style boulevard of Thanon Silom – the heart of the financial district – extends from here to the river. Alongside the smoked-glass banks and offices, the plush hotels and tourist shops, and opposite Convent Road (site of Bangkok's Carmelite nunnery) lies the dark heart of Bangkok nightlife, **Patpong**.

Further west along Silom, in a still-thriving South Indian enclave, lies the colourful landmark of the Maha Uma Devi Temple (also known as Sri Mahamariamman or Wat Khaek) – a gaudy, Hindu shrine built in 1895 in honour of Shiva's consort, Uma. Carrying on to the river, the strip west of Charoen Krung (New Rd) reveals some of the history of Bangkok's early dealings with foreigners in the fading grandeur of the old trading quarter. Here you'll find the only place in Bangkok where you might be able to eke out an architectural walk, though it's hardly compelling. Incongruous churches and "colonial" buildings – the best being the Authors' Wing of the *Oriental Hotel*, where nostalgic afternoon teas are served – are hemmed in by the spice shops and *halal* canteens of the growing Muslim area around Thanon Charoen Krung.

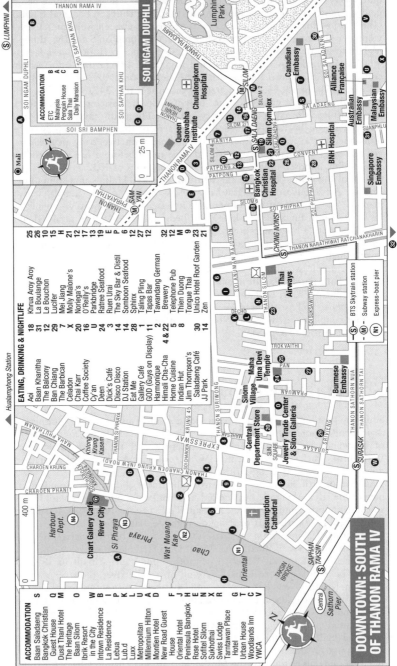

DOWNTOWN: SOUTH OF THANON RAMA IV

SOI NGAM DUPHLI

ACCOMMODATION
ETC	B
Malaysia	A
Penguin House	C
Sala Thai	
Daily Mansion	D

ACCOMMODATION
Baan Saladaeng	S
Bangkok Christian Guest House	Q
Dusit Thani Hotel	M
The Heritage	O
Baan Silom	W
Ibrik Resort in the City	B
Intown Residence	I
La Residence	P
Lebua	L
Lub.d	A
Luxx	U
Metropolitan	K
Millennium Hilton	A
Monten Hotel	D
New Road Guest House	F
Oriental Hotel	J
Peninsula Bangkok	H
Rose Hotel	N
Sofitel Silom	X
Sukhothai	R
Swiss Lodge	G
Tarntawan Place Hotel	T
Urban House	C
Woodlands Inn	V
YWCA	

EATING, DRINKING & NIGHTLIFE
Aoi	18	Khrua Aroy Aroy	25
Baan Khanitha	31	La Boulange	26
The Balcony	12	Le Bouchon	10
Ban Chiang	29	Lucifer	15
The Barbican	7	Mei Jiang	X
Celadon	X	Molly Malone's	21
Chai Karr	20	Noriega's	12
Coffee Society	16	O'Reilly's	17
Cy'an	U	Parkbridge	13
Deen	24	Ratree Seafood	19
Dick's Café	3	Ruen Urai	E
Disco Disco	14	The Sky Bar & Distil	P
DJ Station	14	Somboon Seafood	6
Eat Me	28	Sphinx	12
Gallery Café	1	Taling Pling	27
GOD (Guys on Display)	11	Tapas Bar	12
Harmonique	2	Tawandang German Brewery	32
Himali Cha-Cha	4 & 22	Thien Duong	12
Home Cuisine	5	Telephone Pub	M
Indian Hut	8	Tongue Thai	9
Jim Thompson's Saladaeng Café	30	Unico Hotel Roof Garden	23
JJ Park	14	Zen	21

The Queen Saovabha Memorial Institute (Snake Farm)

The **Queen Saovabha Memorial Institute** (*Sathan Saovabha*), at the corner of Thanon Rama IV and Thanon Henri Dunant (a 10min walk from Sala Daeng Skytrain station or Sam Yan or Si Lom subway stations), is a bit of a circus act but an entertaining, informative and worthy one at that. It's often simply known as the **Snake Farm** but takes its formal name from one of Rama V's wives, who was a notable campaigner. Run by the Thai Red Cross, the institute has a double function: to produce snake-bite serums and to educate the public on the dangers of Thai snakes. The latter mission involves putting on live demonstrations of snake handling and feeding and venom extraction (Mon–Fri 11am & 2.30pm, Sat, Sun & hols 11am; B200, children B50; ☎02 252 0161–4, ⊛www.redcross .or.th). Well presented and safe, these displays gain a perverse fascination from the knowledge that the strongest venoms of the snakes on show can kill in only three minutes. If you're still not herpetologically sated you can look round the grounds, where a wide range of Thai snakes live in cages; some specimens are also preserved and bottled in a small snake museum.

Lumphini Park

If you're sick of cars and concrete, head for **Lumphini Park** (*Suan Lum*; daily 5am–7pm), at the east end of Thanon Silom, where the air is almost fresh and the traffic noise dies down to a low murmur. Named after the town in Nepal where the Buddha was born, it was the country's first public park, donated by Rama VI, whose statue by Silpa Bhirasri (see p.237) stands at the main, southwest entrance. The park is arrayed around two lakes, where you can join the locals in feeding the turtles and fish with bread or take out a pedalo or rowing boat, and is landscaped with a wide variety of local trees and numerous pagodas and pavilions, usually occupied by chess-players. In the early morning and at dusk, exercise freaks hit the outdoor gym on the southwest side of the park, or en masse do aerobics, balletic t'ai chi or jogging along the yellow-marked circuit, stopping for the twice-daily broadcast of the national anthem. On Sunday afternoons in the cool season, free classical concerts draw in scores of urban picnickers. To recharge your batteries, make for the inexpensive garden restaurant in the northwest corner.

Getting to and from the southern downtown area

The Silom Line of the **Skytrain** runs through this area, flying over much of Thanon Silom, before veering down Thanon Narathiwat Ratchanakharin then along Thanon Sathorn to the river. The big advantage of staying at the western edge of this area is that you'll be handily placed for Chao Phraya **express boats**, with piers at Si Phraya, Wat Muang Kae, the Oriental and Sathorn. Indeed, if you're staying anywhere in this area and travelling by public transport to Ratanakosin, you're best off catching a bus to the nearest express-boat stop, or the Skytrain to Saphan Taksin station, and finishing your journey on the water.

At the other side of this area, the **subway** runs from Hualamphong Station under Thanon Rama IV, with stations at Sam Yan (for the Snake Farm), Silom and Lumphini (for the budget accommodation area of Soi Ngam Duphli and Suan Lum Night Bazaar). The most useful **bus** for Soi Ngam Duphli is likely to be air-con #507, which connects you with Hualamphong Station, Chinatown, Ratanakosin, Banglamphu and the Southern Bus Terminal, while countless buses run along Thanon Silom.

Patpong

Concentrated into a small area between the eastern ends of Thanon Silom and Thanon Suriwong, the neon-lit go-go bars of the **Patpong** district loom like rides in a tawdry sexual Disneyland. In front of each bar, girls cajole passers-by with a lifeless sensuality while insistent touts proffer printed menus and photographs detailing the degradations on show. Inside, bikini-clad women gyrate to Western music and play hostess to the (almost exclusively male) spectators; upstairs, live shows feature women who, to use Spalding Gray's phrase in *Swimming to Cambodia*, "do everything with their vaginas except have babies".

Patpong was no more than a sea of mud when the capital was founded on the marshy river bank to the west, but by the 1960s it had grown into a flash district

Thailand's sex industry

Bangkok owes its reputation as the carnal capital of the world to a **sex industry** adept at peddling fantasies of cheap thrills on tap. More than a thousand sex-related businesses operate in the city, but the gaudy neon fleshpots of Patpong and Sukhumvit's Soi Nana and Soi Cowboy give a misleading impression of an activity that is deeply rooted in Thai culture: the overwhelming majority of Thailand's prostitutes of both sexes (estimated at anywhere between 200,000 and 700,000) work with Thai men, not farangs.

Prostitution and **polygamy** have long been intrinsic to the Thai way of life. Until Rama VI broke with the custom in 1910, Thai kings had always kept concubines, only a few of whom would be elevated to royal mothers. The practice was aped by the nobility and, from the early nineteenth century, by newly rich merchants keen to have lots of sons. Though the monarch is now monogamous, many men of all classes still keep **mistresses**, known as *mia noi* (minor wives); the common view is that an official wife (*mia luang*) should be treated like the temple's main Buddha image – respected and elevated upon the altar – whereas the minor wife is like an amulet, to be taken along wherever you go. For less wealthy men, prostitution is a far cheaper option: at least two-fifths of sexually active Thai men are thought to visit brothels twice a month.

The **farang sex industry** is a relatively new development, having started during the Vietnam War, when the American military set up seven bases around Thailand. The GIs' appetite for "entertainment" attracted women from surrounding rural areas to cash in on the boom, and Bangkok joined the fray in 1967. By the mid-1970s, the GIs had left, but tourists replaced them, lured by advertising that diverted most of the traffic to Bangkok and the beach resort of Pattaya. Sex tourism has since grown to become an established part of the Thai economy.

The majority of the women who work in the country's go-go bars and "bar beers" (outdoor hostess bars) come from the poorest rural areas of north and northeast Thailand. **Economic refugees**, they're easily drawn into an industry in which they can make in a single night what it takes a month to earn in the rice fields. In some villages, money sent home by prostitutes in Bangkok far exceeds financial aid given by the government. Many women from rural communities opt for a couple of lucrative years in the sex bars to help pay off family debts and improve the living conditions of parents stuck in the poverty trap.

Many bar girls, and male prostitutes too, are looking for longer-term **relationships** with their farang customers, bringing a temporary respite from bar work and perhaps even a ticket out. A surprising number of one-night transactions do develop into some sort of holiday romance, with the young woman accompanying her farang "boyfriend" (often twice her age) around the country and maintaining contact after he's returned home. It's a common joke that some bar girls field half a dozen mobile of dance halls for rich Thais, owned by a Chinese millionaire godfather, educated at the London School of Economics and by the OSS (forerunner of the CIA), who gave his name to the area. In 1969, an American entrepreneur turned an existing teahouse into a luxurious nightclub to satisfy the tastes of soldiers on R&R trips from Vietnam, and so Patpong's transformation into a Western sex reservation began. At first, the area was rough and violent, but over the years it has wised up to the desires of the affluent farang, and now markets itself as a packaged concept of Oriental decadence. The centre of the skin trade lies along the interconnected sois of **Patpong 1 and 2**, where lines of go-go bars share their patch with respectable restaurants, a 24-hour supermarket and an overabundance of pharmacies. By night, it's a thumping theme park, whose blazing neon promises tend towards self-parody, with names like *Thigh Bar* and

phones so they can juggle all their various "sponsors". An entire sub-genre of novels and confessional memoirs (among them the classic *Hello, My Big Big Honey!: Letters to Bangkok Bar Girls and Their Revealing Interviews*) testifies to the role money plays in all this, and highlights the delusions common to both parties, not to mention the cross-cultural incomprehension.

Despite its ubiquity, prostitution has been **illegal** in Thailand since 1960, though sex-industry bosses easily circumvent the law by registering their establishments as clubs, karaoke bars or massage parlours, and making payoffs to the police. Sex workers, on the other hand, often endure exploitation and violence from pimps and customers rather than face fines and long rehabilitation sentences. Hardly surprising that many prefer to go freelance, working the clubs and bars in non-red-light zones such as Thanon Khao San. Life is made even more difficult because abortion is illegal in Thailand. The **anti-prostitution law** does attempt to treat sex workers as victims rather than criminals, penalizing parents who sell their children and punishing venue managers and customers with a jail sentence or heavy fine, though this is reportedly haphazardly enforced, owing to the number of influential police and politicians allegedly involved in the sex industry. A high-profile voice in the struggle to improve the **rights of sex workers** is the Empower Foundation (@www.empowerfoundation .org), which organizes campaigns and runs education centres for bar workers.

Inevitably, **child prostitution** is a significant issue in Thailand, but NGOs such as ECPAT (@www.ecpat.net) say numbers have declined over the last decade, due to zero-tolerance and awareness campaigns. The government has also strengthened legislation against hiring a prostitute under the age of 18, and anyone caught having sex with an under-15 is now charged with rape. The disadvantaged are still targeted by traffickers however, who "buy" children from desperately poor hill-tribe and other minority families and keep them as bonded slaves until the debt has been repaid. Street kids and other orphans, including those displaced by the 2004 tsunami and by the ongoing conflict in the deep south, are especially vulnerable to pimps and predators.

The spectre of **AIDS** also puts the problems of the sex industry into sharp focus. UN AIDS statistics from 2007 reported that about one in twenty female sex workers in Bangkok was infected with HIV/AIDS and approximately one in 110 of the general adult Thai population. These figures do, however, show an improvement on the infection rate from 2001, thanks to aggressive AIDS awareness campaigns, particularly those of the Population and Community Development Association (PDA; @www.pda.or.th/eng), a Bangkok-based NGO, which also runs the famous *Cabbages and Condom* restaurant on Thanon Sukhumvit (see p.184). It continues to campaign and educate the public, spurred on by fears that young Thais are too complacent about the virus.

Chicken Divine. Budget travellers, purposeful besuited businessmen and noisy lager louts throng the streets, and even the most demure tourists – of both sexes – turn out to do some shopping at the night market down the middle of Patpong 1, where hawkers sell fake watches, bags and designer T-shirts. By day, a relaxed hangover descends on the place. Bar girls hang out at foodstalls and cafés in respectable dress, often recognizable by faces that are pinched and strained from the continuous use of antibiotics and heroin in an attempt to ward off venereal disease and boredom. Farang men slump at the bars on Patpong 2, drinking and watching videos, unable to find anything else to do in the whole of Bangkok.

The small dead-end alley to the east of Patpong 2, **Silom 4** (ie Soi 4, Thanon Silom), hosts some of Bangkok's hippest nightlife, its bars, clubs and pavements heaving at weekends with the capital's bright young things. There are many gay venues on Silom 4, but the focus of the scene has shifted to **Silom 2**, while in between, **Soi Thaniya**'s hostess bars and restaurants cater to Japanese tourists.

M.R. Kukrit's Heritage Home

Ten minutes' walk south of Thanon Sathorn and twenty minutes from Chong Nonsi Skytrain station, at 19 Soi Phra Pinit (Soi 7, Thanon Narathiwat Ratchanakharin), lies **M.R. Kukrit's Heritage Home**, the beautiful traditional house and gardens of one of Thailand's leading figures of the twentieth century (*Baan Mom Kukrit*; Sat, Sun & public hols 9.30am–5pm; B50; ⓣ02 286 8185, ⓦ www.kukritshousefund.com). M.R. (*Mom Rajawongse*, a princely title) **Kukrit Pramoj** (1911–95) was a remarkable all-rounder, descended from Rama II on his father's side and, on his mother's side, from the influential ministerial family, the Bunnags. Kukrit graduated in Philosophy, Politics and Economics from Oxford University and went on to become a university lecturer back in Thailand, but his greatest claim to fame is probably as a writer:

▲ M.R. Kukrit's Heritage Home

he founded, owned and penned a daily column for *Siam Rath*, the most influential Thai-language newspaper, and wrote short stories, novels, plays and poetry. He was also a respected performer in classical dance-drama (*khon*), and he starred as an Asian prime minister, opposite Marlon Brando, in the Hollywood film, *The Ugly American*. In 1974, during an especially turbulent period for Thailand, life imitated art, when Kukrit was called on to become Thailand's prime minister at the head of a coalition of seventeen parties. However, just four hundred days into his premiership, the Thai military leadership dismissed him for being too anti-American.

The **residence**, which has been left just as it was when Kukrit was alive, reflects his complex character. In the large, open-sided *sala* (pavilion) for public functions near the entrance is an attractive display of *khon* masks, including a gold one which Kukrit wore when he played the demon king, Totsagan (Ravana). In and around the adjoining Khmer-styled garden, keep your eyes peeled for the *mai dut*, sculpted miniature trees similar to bonsai, some of which Kukrit worked on for decades. The living quarters beyond are made up of five teak houses on stilts, assembled from various parts of central Thailand and joined by an open veranda. The bedroom, study and various sitting rooms are decked out with beautiful *objets d'art*; look out especially for the carved bed that belonged to Rama II and the very delicate, 200-year-old nielloware (gold inlay) from Nakhon Si Thammarat in the formal reception room. In the small family prayer room, Kukrit Pramoj's ashes are enshrined in the base of a reproduction of the Emerald Buddha.

Thanon Sukhumvit

Thanon Sukhumvit is Bangkok's longest road – it keeps going east all the way to Cambodia – but for such an important artery it's way too narrow for the volume of traffic that needs to use it, and is further hemmed in by the overhead Skytrain line. Packed with high-rise hotels and office blocks, an impressive array of specialist restaurants (from Lebanese to Lao), tailors, bookstores and stall after stall selling cheap souvenirs and T-shirts, it's a lively part of town that also attracts a high proportion of single male tourists to its enclaves of girlie bars on Soi Nana Tai, Soi Cowboy and the Clinton Entertainment Plaza. But for the most part it's not a seedy area, and is home to many expats and middle-class Thais. Shops, restaurants (see p.183) and bars (see p.190) are Sukhumvit's main attractions, though the museum-like northern Thai house **Ban Kamthieng** offers a refreshing alternative to the area's pervasive consumer culture, while the **Thailand Creative and Design Centre** aims to give you an insight into the nation's style and aesthetic.

Ban Kamthieng (Kamthieng House)

Another reconstructed traditional Thai residence, **Ban Kamthieng** (Tues–Sat 9am–5pm; B100; Ⓦwww.siam-society.org) was moved in the 1960s from the northern province of Chiang Mai to 131 Thanon Asok Montri (Soi 21), off Thanon Sukhumvit, and set up as an ethnological museum by the Siam Society. The delightful complex of polished teak buildings makes a pleasing oasis beneath the towering glass skyscrapers that dominate the rest of Sukhumvit, and is easily reached from the Asok Skytrain and Sukhumvit subway stops. It differs from Suan Pakkad, Jim Thompson's House and M.R. Kukrit's Heritage Home in being the home of a rural family, and the objects on display give a fair insight into country life for the well-heeled in northern Thailand.

The house was built on the banks of the Ping River in the mid-nineteenth century, and the **ground-level** display of farming tools and fish traps evokes the upcountry custom of fishing in flooded rice paddies to supplement the supply from the rivers. **Upstairs**, the main display focuses on the ritual life of a typical northern Thai household, explaining the role of the spirits, the practice of

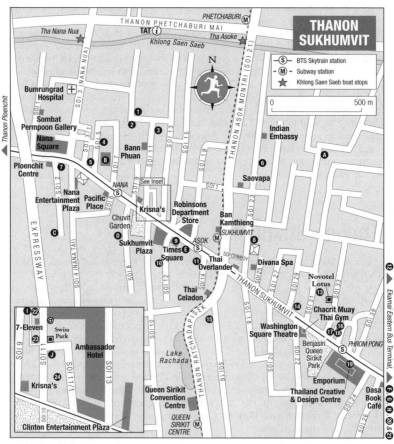

THANON SUKHUMVIT

- Ⓢ – BTS Skytrain station
- Ⓜ – Subway station
- ★ Khlong Saen Saeb boat stops

ACCOMMODATION			EATING, DRINKING & NIGHTLIFE		Face Bangkok (La Na Thai & Hazara)	21
Amari Boulevard Hotel	B		Al Ferdoss	5	Gaeng Pa Lerd Rod	18
The Atlanta	C		Aoi	19	Gulliver's Traveler's Tavern	4
The Eugenia	A		Baan Khanitha	6	Himali Cha-Cha	13
Grand Business Inn	J		The Ball in Hand	9	Le Dalat Indochine	8
Imm Fusion	G		Bangkok Baking Company	7	Londoner Brew Pub	17
PS Guesthouse	D		Basil	E	Long Table	15
Rex Hotel	F		Bed Supperclub	3	MahaNaga	14
Sheraton Grande			The Bull's Head	16	Nest	2
Sukhumvit	E		Cabbages and Condoms	10	Q Bar	1
Suk 11	I		Cheap Charlie's	23	Spring Summer Winter	12
Sukhumvit On-Nut			Dosa King	24	Suda Restaurant	11
Guesthouse	H		Eleven Gallery	22	Vientiane Kitchen (Khrua Vientiane)	20

The **Skytrain** (see p.34) has stops all the way along Thanon Sukhumvit, making journeys to places such as Siam Square and Chatuchak Weekend Market a fast and hassle-free undertaking, and giving you the chance to link up with the Chao Phraya express boats at Saphan Taksin/Tha Sathorn (for a calmish ride to Ratanakosin, for example). Similarly, the Sukhumvit **subway** stop at the mouth of Soi 21 (Thanon Asok Montri) makes it easy to get to Hualamphong Station and Chinatown.

The volume of traffic on Sukhumvit means that travelling by **bus** across town – to Ratanakosin or Banglamphu, for example – can take an age. If possible, try to travel to and from Thanon Sukhumvit outside rush hour (7–9am & 3–7pm); it's almost as bad in a taxi, which will often take at least an hour to reach Ratanakosin. Useful buses for getting to Ratanakosin include #508 and #25, both of which run via Siam Square, so you could also take the Skytrain to Siam Square and then change on to the bus; full details of bus routes are given on p.32.

A much faster way of getting across town is to hop on one of the **longtail boats** that ply Khlong Saen Saeb; the canal service begins at Tha Phan Fah near Democracy Monument in the west of the city, runs parallel with part of Thanon Sukhumvit and has stops at the northern ends of Soi Nana Nua (Soi 3) and Thanon Asok Montri (Soi 21), from where you can either walk down to Thanon Sukhumvit, grab a bus or take a motorbike taxi. This reduces the journey between Thanon Sukhumvit and the Banglamphu/Ratanakosin area to about thirty minutes; for more details on boat routes, see p.33.

making offerings and the belief in talismans, magic shirts and male tattoos. The rectangular lintel above the door is a *hum yon*, carved in floral patterns that represent testicles and designed to ward off evil spirits. Walk along the open veranda to the authentically equipped kitchen to see a video lesson in making spicy frog soup, and to the granary to find an interesting exhibition on the rituals associated with rice-farming. Elsewhere in the Siam Society compound you'll find an esoteric bookshop (see p.211) and an antiques outlet.

Thailand Creative and Design Centre (TCDC)

Appropriately located on the sixth floor of the Emporium, one of Bangkok's most fashion-conscious shopping plazas, the **Thailand Creative and Design Centre** (Tues–Sun 10.30am–9pm; free; Ⓦ www.tcdc.or.th) seeks to celebrate, promote and inspire innovative design through exhibitions, talks, a resource centre and shop (see p.207). The concise but thought-provoking permanent bilingual display focuses on the cultural contexts of design classics from ten countries (including Spain, Japan, Finland and Brazil but sadly excluding Thailand), beginning with the Louis Vuitton trunk of 1854 and culminating with the iPod of 2001. Temporary exhibitions often focus more on Asian trends. The Emporium Shopping Centre is on Thanon Sukhumvit between sois 22 and 24, alongside BTS Phrom Pong station.

7

Chatuchak and the outskirts

The amorphous clutter of Greater Bangkok doesn't harbour many attractions, but there are a handful of places on the outskirts of the city that make pleasant half-day outings. Nearly all the places described in this chapter can be reached fairly painlessly by some sort of city transport, either by ferry up the Chao Phraya River or by Skytrain, subway or city bus.

If you're in Bangkok on a Saturday or Sunday, it's well worth making the effort to visit the enormous **Chatuchak Weekend Market**, where you could browse away an entire day among the thousands of stalls selling everything from handmade paper to bargain-priced sarongs. The open-air **Prasart Museum** boasts many finely crafted replicas of traditional Thai buildings and is recommended for anyone who hasn't got the time to go upcountry and admire Thailand's temples and palaces in situ. Taking a boat ride up the Chao Phraya River makes a nice change to sitting in city-centre traffic, and the upstream town of **Nonthaburi** and the tranquil but less easily accessible island of **Ko Kred** provide the ideal excuse for doing just that.

Chatuchak Weekend Market ("JJ")

With over eight thousand open-air stalls to peruse, and wares as diverse as Lao silk, Siamese kittens and designer lamps, the enormous **Chatuchak Weekend Market**, or "**JJ**" as it's usually abbreviated, from "Jatu Jak" (Sat & Sun 7am–6pm), is Bangkok's most enjoyable – and exhausting – shopping experience. It occupies a huge patch of ground between the Northern Bus Terminal and Mo Chit Skytrain (N8)/Chatuchak Park subway stations, and is best reached by Skytrain or subway if you're coming from downtown areas; Kamphaeng Phet subway station is the most convenient as it exits right into the most interesting, southwestern, corner of the market. Coming from Banglamphu, you can either get a bus to the nearest Skytrain stop (probably National Stadium or Ratchathewi) and then take the train, or take the #59, #503 (non-expressway version) or #509 bus all the way from Rajdamnoen Klang (about 1hr); see p.78 for details.

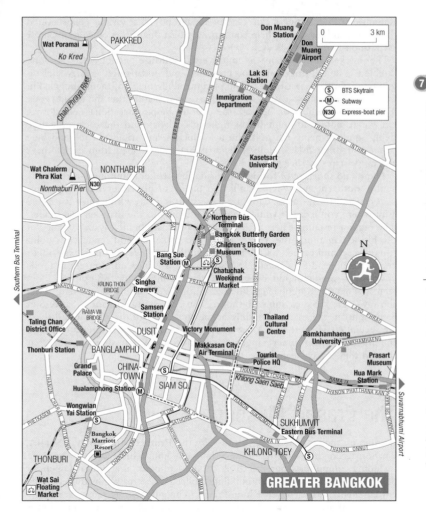

Aside from trendy one-off clothes and accessories, **best buys** include antique lacquerware, unusual sarongs, traditional cotton clothing and crafts from the north, jeans, silver jewellery and ceramics, particularly the five-coloured *bencharong*. The market is divided into 26 numbered **sections**, plus a dozen unnumbered ones, each of them more or less dedicated to a particular genre, for example household items, young fashions, plants, secondhand books or crafts. If you have several hours to spare, it's fun just to browse at whim, but if you're looking for souvenirs, handicrafts or traditional textiles you should start with sections 22, 24, 25 and 26, which are all in a cluster at the southwest (Kamphaeng Phet subway) end of the market; sections A, B and C, behind the market's head office and information centre, are also full of interesting artefacts. *Nancy Chandler's Map of Bangkok* has a fabulously detailed and informatively annotated **map** of all the sections in the market: it's best bought before you arrive but is available at Teak House Art in Section 2, near

Kamphaeng Phet subway's exit 2. Maps are also posted at various points around the market and for specific help you can also ask at the market office near Gate 1 off Thanon Kamphaeng Phet 2.

The market also contains a controversial **wildlife** section that has long doubled as a clearing-house for protected and endangered species such as gibbons, palm cockatoos and Indian pied hornbills, many of them smuggled in from Laos and Cambodia and sold to private animal collectors and foreign zoos. The illegal trade goes on beneath the counter, despite occasional crackdowns, but you're bound to come across fighting cocks around the back, miniature flying squirrels being fed milk through pipettes, and iridescent red and blue Siamese fighting fish, kept in individual jars and shielded from each other's aggressive stares by sheets of cardboard.

There's no shortage of **foodstalls** inside the market compound, particularly at the southern end, where you'll find plenty of places serving inexpensive *phat thai* and Isaan snacks. Close by these stalls is a classy little juice bar called *Viva* where you can rest your feet while listening to the manager's jazz tapes. The biggest restaurant here is *Toh Plue*, whose main branch is on the edge of the block containing the market office and makes a good rendezvous point (there's a second branch beside Kamphaeng Phet subway station's exit 1). For veggie food, head for *Chamlong's* (also known as *Asoke*), an ultra-cheap food-court-style restaurant just outside the market on Thanon Kamphaeng Phet (across Thanon Kamphaeng Phet 2; 5min walk from Kamphaeng Phet subway's exit 1; Sat & Sun 8am–noon). You can **change money** (Sat & Sun 8am–6pm) in the market building at the south end of the market and there are several ATMs here too. A few very small electric **trams** circulate around the market's main inner ringroad, transporting weary shoppers for free, though they always seem to be full.

The Prasart Museum

Located on the far eastern edge of the city, the **Prasart Museum** at 9 Soi 4A, Thanon Krungthep Kreetha (Tues–Sun 10am–3pm; B1000 for 1 or 2 people including compulsory tour; call ☎02 379 3601 to book) is an unusual open-air exhibition of traditional Asian buildings, collected and reassembled by wealthy entrepreneur and art-lover Khun Prasart. The museum is rarely visited by independent tourists – partly because of the intentionally limited opening hours and inflated admission price, and partly because it takes a long time to get there by public transport – but it makes a pleasant day out and is worth the effort.

Set in a gorgeously lush tropical garden, the museum comprises about a dozen beautifully crafted replicas of **traditional buildings**, including a golden teak palace inspired by the royal residence now housed at the National Museum, a Chinese temple and water garden, a Khmer shrine and a Sukhothai-era teak library set over a lotus pond. Some have been pieced together from ruined originals, while others were constructed from scratch. Many are filled with antique **artefacts**, including Burmese woodcarvings, prehistoric pottery from Ban Chiang and Lopburi-era statuettes. There's also an exquisite collection of *bencharong* ceramics. Khun Prasart also owns a ceramics workshop, which produces reproductions of famous designs; they can be bought either at the museum, or at his showroom, the Prasart Collection, on the second floor of the Peninsula Plaza shopping centre on Thanon Rajdamri.

Regular and air-con **bus** #93 runs almost to the door: pick it up near its starting point on Thanon Si Phraya near River City and the GPO, or anywhere along its route on Phetchaburi and Phetchaburi Mai roads (both the Khlong Saen Saeb canal boats and the subway have potentially useful stops at the Thanon Asok Montri/Sukhumvit Soi 21 junction with Thanon Phetchaburi Mai). The #93 terminates on Thanon Krungthep Kreetha but you should get off a couple of stops before the terminus, at the first stop on Thanon Krungthep Kreetha, as soon as you see the sign for the Prasart Museum (about 1hr 15min by bus from Si Phraya). Follow the sign down Soi Krungthep Kreetha, go past the golf course and, after about a fifteen-minute walk, turn off down Soi 4A. To speed things up, you could instead take the Khlong Saen Saeb canal boat all the way to Tha The Mall Bangkapi (about 40min from Phan Fah, four stops after the confusingly similar Tha The Mall 3 stop), which leaves you within a very short taxi ride of the museum.

Nonthaburi

A trip to **NONTHABURI**, the first town beyond the northern boundary of Bangkok, is the easiest excursion you can make from the centre of the city and affords a perfect opportunity to recharge your batteries. Nonthaburi is the last stop upriver for most express boats (N30), under an hour from Central Pier (Sathorn) on an orange-flag boat. The ride itself is most of the fun, weaving

> ## Durians
>
> The naturalist Alfred Russel Wallace, eulogizing the taste of the **durian**, compared it to "rich butter-like custard highly flavoured with almonds, but intermingled with wafts of flavour that call to mind cream cheese, onion sauce, brown sherry and other incongruities". He neglected to discuss the smell of the fruit's skin, which is so bad – somewhere between detergent and dogshit – that durians are barred from Thai hotels and aeroplanes. The different **varieties** bear strange names which do nothing to make them more appetizing: "frog", "golden pillow", "gibbon" and so on. However, the durian has fervent admirers, perhaps because it's such an acquired taste and because it's considered a strong aphrodisiac. Aficionados discuss the varieties with as much subtlety as if they were vintage champagnes and treat the durian as a social fruit, to be shared around, despite a price tag of up to B3000 each. They also pour scorn on the Thai government scientists who have recently genetically developed an odourless variety, the Chanthaburi 1 durian.
>
> Durian season is roughly April to June and the most famous durian orchards are around Nonthaburi, where the fruits are said to have an incomparably rich and nutty flavour due to the fine clay soil. To see these and other plantations such as mango, pomelo and jackfruit, your best bet is to hire a longtail from Nonthaburi pier to take you west along Khlong Om Non. If you don't smell them first, you can recognize durians by their sci-fi appearance: the shape and size of a rugby ball, but slightly deflated, they're covered in a thick, pale-green shell which is heavily armoured with short, sharp spikes (*duri* means "thorn" in Malay). By cutting along one of the faint seams with a good knife, you'll reveal a white pith in which are set a handful of yellow blobs with the texture of a wrinkled soufflé: this is what you eat. The taste is best when the smell is at its highest, about three days after the fruit has dropped. Be careful when out walking near the trees: because of its great weight and sharp spikes, a falling durian can lead to serious injury, or even an ignominious death.

▲ Detail of ceramic at Wat Chalerm Phra Kiat

round huge, crawling sand barges and tiny canoes, and the slow pace of the boat gives you plenty of time to take in the sights on the way. On the north side of Banglamphu, beyond the elegant, new Rama VIII Bridge, which shelters the Mekong whisky distillery on the west bank, you'll pass in turn, on the east bank: the Art Nouveau Bangkhunprom Palace and the adjacent, Neoclassical Devaves Palace, both former princely residences; Thewet flower market; the royal boat house in front of the National Library, where you can glimpse the minor ceremonial boats that escort the grand royal barges; the city's first Catholic church, Holy Conception, founded in the seventeenth century during King Narai of Ayutthaya's reign and rebuilt in the early nineteenth; and, beyond Krungthon Bridge, the Singha brewery. Along the route are dazzling Buddhist temples and drably painted mosques, catering for Bangkok's growing Muslim population, as well as a few remaining communities who still live in houses on stilts or houseboats – around Krungthon Bridge, for example, you'll see people living on the huge teak vessels used to carry rice, sand and charcoal.

Disembarking at suburban Nonthaburi, on the east bank of the river, you won't find a great deal to do, in truth. There's a market that's famous for the quality of its fruit, while the attractive, old Provincial Office across the road is covered in rickety wooden latticework. To break up your trip with a slow, scenic drink or lunch, you'll find a floating seafood restaurant, *Rim Fang*, to the right at the end of the prom.

Set in relaxing grounds about 1km north of Nonthaburi pier on the west bank of the river, elegant **Wat Chalerm Phra Kiat** injects a splash of urban refinement among a grove of breadfruit trees. You can get there from the express-boat pier by taking the ferry straight across the Chao Phraya River and then catching a motorbike taxi. The beautifully proportioned temple, which has been lavishly restored, was built by Rama III in memory of his mother, whose family lived and presided over vast orchards in the area. Inside the walls of the temple compound, you feel as if you've come upon a stately folly in a secret garden, and a strong Chinese influence shows itself in the unusual ribbed roofs and elegantly curved gables, decorated with pastel ceramics. The restorers have done their best work inside: look out especially for the simple, delicate landscapes on the shutters.

Ko Kred

About 7km north of Nonthaburi, the tiny island of **KO KRED** lies in a particularly sharp bend in the Chao Phraya River, cut off from the east bank by a waterway created to make the cargo route from Ayutthaya to the Gulf of Thailand just that little bit faster. Although it's been discovered by day-trippers from Bangkok, this artificial island remains something of a time capsule, a little oasis of village life completely at odds with the metropolitan chaos downriver. Roughly ten square kilometres in all, Ko Kred has no roads, just a concrete path that follows its circumference, with a few arterial walkways branching off towards the interior. Villagers, the majority of whom are Mon, descendants of immigrants from Burma during the reigns of Taksin and Rama II, use a small fleet of motorbike taxis to cross their island, but as a sightseer you're much better off on a rental bicycle or just on foot: a round-island walk takes less than an hour and a half.

There are few sights as such on Ko Kred, though its lushness and comparative emptiness make it a perfect place in which to wander. You'll no doubt come across one of the island's potteries and kilns, which churn out the regionally famous earthenware flower-pots and small water-storage jars and employ a large percentage of the village workforce. The island's clay is very rich in nutrients and therefore excellent for fruit-growing, and banana trees, coconut palms, pomelo, papaya, mango and durian trees all grow in abundance on Ko Kred, fed by an intricate network of irrigation channels that criss-crosses the interior. In among the orchards, the Mons have built their wooden houses, mostly in traditional style and raised high above the marshy ground on stilts. A handful of attractive riverside wats complete the picture, most notably **Wat Paramaiyikawat** (also called **Wat Poramai**), at the main pier at the northeast tip of the island. This engagingly ramshackle eighteenth-century temple was restored by Rama V in honour of his grandmother, with a Buddha relic placed in its white, riverside chedi, which is a replica of the Mutao Pagoda in Hanthawadi, capital of the Mon kingdom in Burma. Among an open-air scattering of Burmese-style alabaster Buddha images, the tall bot shelters some fascinating nineteenth-century murals, depicting scenes from temple life at ground level and the life of the Buddha above, all set in delicate imaginary landscapes.

Practicalities

The easiest but busiest time to go to Ko Kred is on Sunday, when the Chao Phraya Express Boat Company (B300; ☎02 623 6143, ⓦwww.chaophrayaboat .co.th) and Mitchaopaya Travel Service (B300; ☎02 623 6169) run **boat tours** there from central Bangkok. They both take in Wat Chalerm Phra Kiat in Nonthaburi (see opposite), and Wat Poramai and Ban Khanom Thai on Ko Kred, where you can buy traditional sweets and watch them being made. The Chao Phraya express boat departs from Tha Sathorn at 10am, calling at Tha

Maharat in Ratanakosin at 10.30am, returning to the latter at 4.30pm, the former at 4.45pm. Mitchaopaya leaves Tha Chang at 9am, calling at the Royal Barge Museum (see p.94) and cruising up Khlong Bangkok Noi, returning at 4.30pm.

At other times, the main drawback of a day-trip to Ko Kred is the difficulty of **getting there**. Your best option is to take a Chao Phraya express boat to Nonthaburi, then a chartered longtail boat direct to Ko Kred (about B300) or bus #32 (ordinary and air-con, coming from Wat Pho via Banglamphu) to Pakkred, the suburb opposite Ko Kred on the river's east bank. There are also fast, air-con #166 buses from Victory Monument (accessible by Skytrain) to Pakkred, which are probably your best option for getting back as the #32 stops a fair way from Nonthaburi pier on its inbound journey. From Pakkred, the easiest way of getting across to the island is to hire a longtail boat, although shuttle boats cross at the river's narrowest point to Wat Poramai from Wat Sanam Neua, about a kilometre's walk or motorbike-taxi ride south of the Pakkred pier (getting off the bus at Tesco Lotus in Pakkred will cut down the walk to Wat Sanam Neua).

Excursions from Bangkok

Regular bus and train services from Bangkok give access to a number of enjoyable **excursions**, all of which are perfectly feasible as day-trips, though some also merit an overnight stay. The fertile plain to the north of the capital is bisected by the country's main artery, the Chao Phraya River, which carries boat tours to supplement the area's trains and buses. The monumental kitsch of the nineteenth-century palace at **Bang Pa-In** provides a sharp contrast with the atmospheric ruins further upriver at the former capital of **Ayutthaya**, where ancient temples, some crumbling and overgrown, others

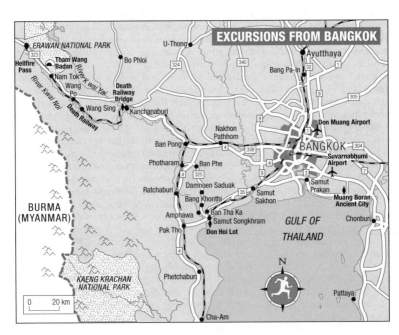

still very much in use, are arrayed in a leafy setting. You could visit the two sites on a long day-trip from Bangkok, but separate outings or an overnight stay in Ayutthaya will let you make the most of the former capital's many attractions.

To the west of the capital, the enormous nineteenth-century stupa at **Nakhon Pathom** is undeniably impressive and well worth the short journey from Bangkok; it's often visited in conjunction with an early-morning outing to the floating markets of **Damnoen Saduak**, though these are so popular with tourists that they seem staged and contrived. Better to venture a few kilometres further south to the more authentic floating markets around **Amphawa**, near **Samut Songkhram**, whose quaint canalside neighbourhoods are complemented by a stylish riverside resort that makes this a perfect overnight break from Bangkok. Getting there – on a rural, single-track train line – is half the fun. Tradition is also central to the untouristed town of **Phetchaburi**, with its many charming temples and hilltop royal palace.

Northwest of the capital, **Kanchanaburi** has long attracted visitors to the notorious **Bridge over the River Kwai**, and the extraordinary, POW-built Death Railway that crosses it. But the town harbours many, much more affecting World War II memorials and occupies a gloriously scenic riverside location, best savoured by spending a night in a raft house moored to the riverbank. Finally, for a taste of Thailand's finest monuments and temples in just one rewarding bite, there's the well-designed open-air museum at **Muang Boran Ancient City**, which contains beautifully crafted replicas of the country's top buildings and is just beyond Bangkok's southeastern suburbs.

Muang Boran Ancient City

A day-trip out to the **Muang Boran Ancient City** open-air museum (daily 8am–5pm; B300, children B200; Ⓦwww.ancientcity.com), 33km southeast of Bangkok, is a great way to enjoy the best of Thailand's architectural heritage in relative peace and without much effort. Occupying a huge park shaped like Thailand itself, the museum comprises more than 116 traditional Thai buildings scattered around pleasantly landscaped grounds and is best toured by rented **bicycle** (B50; B150/tandem; B200/three-seater), though you can also make use of the circulating **tram** (B150 round trip, children B75), and doing it on foot is just about possible. Many of the buildings are copies of the country's most famous monuments and are located in the appropriate "region" of the park, with everything from Bangkok's Grand Palace (central region) to the spectacularly sited hilltop Khmer Khao Phra Viharn sanctuary (northeast) represented here. There are also some original structures, including a rare scripture library rescued from Samut Songkhram (south), as well as some painstaking reconstructions from contemporary documents of long-vanished gems, of which the Ayutthaya-period Sanphet Prasat palace (central) is a particularly fine example. A sizeable team of restorers and skilled craftspeople maintains the buildings and helps keep some of the traditional techniques alive; if you come here during the week you can watch them at work.

To get to Muang Boran from Bangkok, take air-conditioned **bus** #511 to **Samut Prakan** on the edge of built-up Greater Bangkok, then change onto songthaew #36, which passes the entrance to Muang Boran. Although bus #511 runs from Banglamphu via Thanon Rama I and Thanon Sukhumvit (see p.32), the journey is likely to be much faster if you cross downtown Bangkok by Skytrain (and boat and/or subway if necessary) and pick up the #511 at the Ekamai Skytrain stop.

By train

Nearly all trains depart from **Hualamphong Station**. The 24-hour "Information" booth at Hualamphong Station keeps English-language **timetables**, detailing types of trains and classes available on each route, as well as fares and supplementary charges; a third-class ticket in a non-air-con carriage on an Ordinary train (the slowest) from Hualamphong to Ayutthaya, for example, will set you back just B15. Otherwise you can try phoning the Train Information Hotline on ☏1690, while the State Railway of Thailand website (⊛www.railway.co.th) carries a timetable and fare chart for major destinations. For details on city transport to and from Hualamphong and left-luggage facilities at the station, see p.27.

The main exception is the twice-daily service to Kanchanaburi and Nam Tok via Nakhon Pathom, which leaves from **Thonburi Station** (sometimes still referred to by its former name, **Bangkok Noi Station**), across the river from Banglamphu in Thonburi. The station is about an 850m walk west of the Railway Station N11 express boat stop (in use Mon–Fri rush hours only; at other times get off at N10 and walk an extra 500m to N11, through the Siriraj Hospital compound); frequent red *songthaews* (public pick-ups) run passengers between the N10 pier and the train station (5min), or you can walk it in about fifteen minutes by heading up the only road that runs away from the pier, passing a temple, walking alongside (under) the flyover and turning right at the far edge of the market when you see the station sign.

The other non-Hualamphong departure is the service to Samut Sakhon (aka Mahachai), for connections to Samut Songkhram, that leaves from **Wongwian Yai Station**, also in Thonburi. Access is by Skytrain to Wongwian Yai (S8) or by bus #3 from Thanon Phra Arthit in Banglamphu.

By bus

Destinations in this chapter are served by air-conditioned buses (*rot air*) from two major terminals in Bangkok, both on the outskirts of the city. As regards fares, a one-way ticket to Ayutthaya, for example, typically costs B55.

The huge, airport-like **Southern Bus Terminal**, or **Sathaanii Sai Tai Mai** (☏02 434 7192), is at the junction of Thanon Borom Ratchonni and Thanon Phutthamonthon Sai 1 in Taling Chan, an interminable 11km west of the Chao Phraya River and Banglamphu, so access to and from city accommodation can take an age, even in a taxi. It handles departures to destinations west of Bangkok, such as Nakhon Pathom, Damnoen Saduak, Samut Songkhran, Phetchaburi and Kanchanaburi, and to all points south of the capital. To reach the terminal, take city bus #124, #511 or #516 from Banglamphu, #516 from Thewet, or #511 from Thanon Sukhumvit; see box on p.32 for bus route details.

The **Northern Bus Terminal**, or **Sathaanii Mo Chit** (☏02 936 2852–66), is the departure point for buses to Bang Pa-In, Ayutthaya and all northern and northeastern towns. It's on Thanon Kamphaeng Phet 2, near Chatuchak Weekend Market in the far north of the city; Mo Chit Skytrain station and Chatuchak Park subway station are within a short motorbike taxi or tuk-tuk ride, or take a city bus direct to the bus terminal: air-con #3, #159, #509 and #512 run from Banglamphu; see box on p.32 for bus route details.

Bang Pa-In

Little more than a roadside market, the village of **BANG PA-IN**, 60km north of Bangkok, has been put on the tourist map by its extravagant and rather surreal **Royal Palace** (daily 8.30am–5pm, ticket office closes 3.30pm; visitors are asked to dress respectfully, so no vests, shorts or sandals; B100;

Ⓦ www.palaces.thai.net), even though most of the buildings can be seen only from the outside. King Prasat Thong of Ayutthaya first built a palace on this site, 20km down the Chao Phraya River from his capital, in the middle of the seventeenth century. It remained a popular royal country residence until it was abandoned a century later, when the Thai capital was moved from Ayutthaya to Bangkok. In the middle of the nineteenth century, however, the advent of steamboats shortened the journey time upriver and the palace enjoyed a revival: King Mongkut (Rama IV) built a modest residence here, which his son King Chulalongkorn (Rama V), in his passion for Westernization, knocked down to make room for the eccentric melange of European, Thai and Chinese architectural styles visible today.

Set in manicured grounds on an island in the Chao Phraya River, and ranged around an ornamental lake, the palace complex is flat and compact – a free brochure from the ticket office gives a diagram of the layout. On the north side of the lake stand a two-storey, colonial-style residence for the royal relatives and the Italianate **Varobhas Bimarn** (Warophat Phiman, "Excellent and Shining Heavenly Abode"), which housed Chulalongkorn's throne hall and still contains private apartments where the present royal family sometimes stays. A covered bridge links this outer part of the palace to the **Pratu Thewarat Khanlai** ("The King of the Gods Goes Forth Gate"), the main entrance to the inner palace, which was reserved for the king and his immediate family. The high fence that encloses half of the bridge allowed the women of the harem to cross without being seen by male courtiers. You can't miss the glittering **Aisawan Thiphya-art** ("Divine Seat of Personal Freedom") in the middle of the lake: named after King Prasat Thong's original palace, it's the only example of pure Thai architecture at Bang Pa-In. The elegant tiers of the pavilion's roof shelter a bronze statue of Chulalongkorn.

In the inner palace, the **Uthayan Phumisathian** ("Garden of the Secured Land"), recently rebuilt by Queen Sirikit in grand, neo-colonial style, was Chulalongkorn's favourite house. After passing the **Ho Withun Thasana** ("Sage's Lookout Tower"), built so that the king could survey the surrounding countryside, you'll come to the main attraction of Bang Pa-In, the **Phra Thinang Wehart Chamrun** Residential Hall ("Palace of Heavenly Light"). A masterpiece of Chinese design, the mansion and its contents were shipped from China and presented as a gift to Chulalongkorn in 1889 by the Chinese Chamber of Commerce in Bangkok. The sumptuous interior gleams with fantastically intricate lacquered and gilded wooden screens, hand-painted porcelain floor tiles and ebony furniture inlaid with mother-of-pearl.

The simple marble **obelisk** behind the Uthayan Phumisathian was erected by Chulalongkorn to hold the ashes of Queen Sunandakumariratana, his favourite wife. In 1881, Sunanda, who was then 21 and expecting a child, was taking a trip on the river here when her boat capsized. She could have been rescued quite easily, but the laws concerning the sanctity of the royal family left those around her no option: "If a boat founders, the boatmen must swim away; if they remain near the boat [or] if they lay hold of him [the royal person] to rescue him, they are to be executed." Following the tragedy, King Chulalongkorn became a zealous reformer of Thai customs and strove to make the monarchy more accessible.

Practicalities

Bang Pa-In can easily be visited on a day-trip from Bangkok. At a pinch, you could also take in a visit to Ayutthaya (see opposite) on the same day, although

▲ Aisawan Thiphya-art pavilion, Bang Pa-In

this doesn't really leave enough time to get the most out of the extensive remains of the former capital. The best way of getting to Bang Pa-In from Bangkok is by **train** from Hualamphong station. The journey takes just over an hour and all trains continue to Ayutthaya (30 daily; 30min). From Bang Pa-In station (note the separate station hall built by Chulalongkorn for the royal family) it's a two-kilometre hike to the palace, or you can take a motorbike taxi for about B30. Slow **buses** leave Bangkok's Northern Terminal roughly every half-hour and stop at **Bang Pa-In market**, about 300m southwest of the palace entrance. This is also the easiest place to catch a motorized samlor back to the train station. Many **day-tours from Bangkok** to Ayutthaya feature a stop at Bang Pa-In; see p.136.

From Ayutthaya, large songthaews leave Thanon Naresuan roughly every half-hour for the forty-minute journey to Bang Pa-In market; trains are quicker (15min) and more frequent than the English-language timetable implies (most Ayutthaya guest houses keep the full Thai timetable).

There are **foodstalls** just outside the palace gates, at the back of the parking lot and at Bang Pa-In market.

Ayutthaya

In its heyday as the capital of the Thai kingdom (from the fourteenth to the eighteenth centuries), **AYUTTHAYA** was so well endowed with temples that sunlight reflecting off their gilt decoration was said to dazzle from three miles away. Wide, grassy spaces today occupy much of the atmospheric site 80km north of Bangkok, which now resembles a graveyard for temples: grand, brooding red-brick ruins rise out of the fields, evoking the city's bygone grandeur. A few intact buildings help form an image of what the capital must have looked like, while three fine museums flesh out the picture.

The core of the ancient capital was a four-kilometre-wide **island** at the confluence of the Lopburi, Pasak and Chao Phraya rivers, which was once encircled by a twelve-kilometre wall, crumbling parts of which can be seen at the **Phom Phet fortress** in the southeast corner. A grid of broad roads now crosses the island, known as Ko Muang: the hub of the small modern town occupies its northeast corner, around the Thanon U Thong and Thanon Naresuan junction, but the rest is mostly uncongested and ideal for exploring by bicycle.

There is also much pleasure to be had from soaking up life on and along the encircling **rivers**, either by taking a boat tour or by dining at one of the

◀ Suphanburi

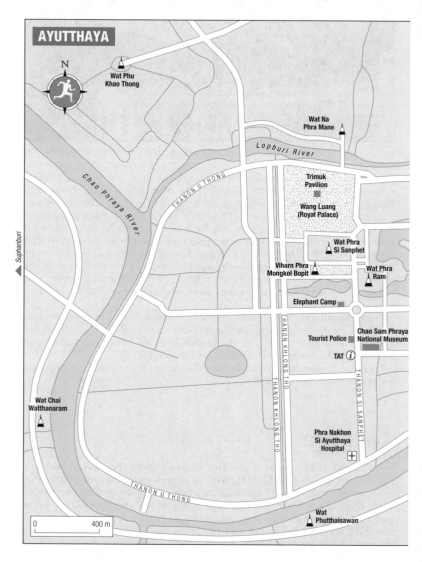

AYUTTHAYA

N

Wat Phu
Khao Thong

Wat Na
Phra Mane

Lopburi River

Chao Phraya River

THANON U THONG

Trimuk
Pavilion

Wang Luang
(Royal Palace)

Wat Phra
Si Sanphet

Viharn Phra
Mongkol Bopit

Wat Phra
Ram

Elephant Camp

Tourist Police

Chao Sam Phraya
National Museum

TAT ⓘ

THANON KHLONG THO

THANON KHLONG THO

THANON SI SANPHET

Wat Chai
Watthanaram

Phra Nakhon
Si Ayutthaya
Hospital

THANON U THONG

Wat
Phutthaisawan

0   400 m

waterside restaurants. It's very much a working waterway, busy with barges carrying cement, rice and other heavy loads to and from Bangkok and the Gulf, and with cross-river ferry services that compensate for the lack of bridges.

Ayutthaya comes alive each year for a week in mid-December, with a **festival** that commemorates the town's listing as a **World Heritage Site** by UNESCO on December 13, 1991. The highlight is the nightly *son et lumière* show, featuring fireworks and elephant-back fights, staged around the ruins.

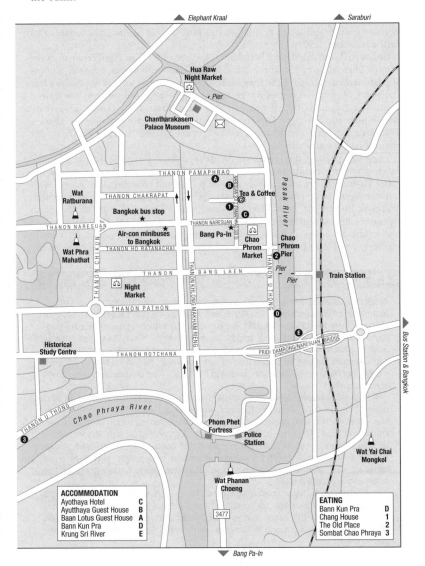

Arrival and information

Ayutthaya can easily be visited on a day-trip from Bangkok, though dedicated ruin-baggers might want to stay overnight (see p.141). The best way of getting there is **by train** from Hualamphong Station (about 30 daily, mostly in the early morning and evening; 90min). To get to the centre of town from the station on the east bank of the Pasak, take the ferry from the jetty 100m west of the station (last ferry around 8pm; B4) across and upriver to Chao Phrom pier; it's then a five-minute walk to the junction of Thanon U Thong and Thanon Naresuan (if you're going to eat or stay at Bann Kun Pra, take the other ferry from the neighbouring jetty, which runs directly across the river and back). A tuk-tuk from the station to the guest houses area will cost about B50.

Buses to Ayutthaya depart Bangkok's Northern Mo Chit Bus Terminal (every 20min; 2hr). Most pull in at the bus stop on Thanon Naresuan, near the accommodation area, though some long-distance services only stop at Ayutthaya's Bus Terminal, 5km to the east of the centre on Highway 1, from where you'll need a tuk-tuk (about B100). Private, air-con **minibuses** from Bangkok's Victory Monument and Southern Bus Terminal finish their routes opposite the Thanon Naresuan bus stop (both about every 20min during daylight hours; 1–2hr depending on traffic; B80).

The most popular **day-trips to Ayutthaya** from Bangkok feature only the briefest whizz around the old city's three main temples, making a stop at the Bang Pa-In summer palace en route (see p.131) and rounding the day off with a three-hour river cruise back down the Chao Phraya from the northern Bangkok suburb of Nonthaburi; Grand Pearl Cruise is one of the main operators (ⓦwww.grandpearlcruise.com; B1700, under 11s B1100). You can also cruise the river in more style, spending one or more nights on plushly converted teak rice barges such as the *Mekhala* (ⓦwww.asian-oasis.com) or the

The golden age of Ayutthaya

Ayutthaya takes its name from the Indian city of Ayodhya ("invincible"), legendary birthplace of Rama, hero of the *Ramayana* epic (see p.63). Founded in 1351 by U Thong, later **King Ramathibodi I**, it rose rapidly by exploiting the expanding trade routes between India and China, and by the mid-fifteenth century its empire covered most of what is now Thailand. Ayutthaya grew into a vast amphibious city built on a 140-kilometre network of canals (few of which survive); by 1685 a million people – roughly double the population of London at the time – lived on its waterways, mostly in houseboats.

By the seventeenth century, Ayutthaya's wealth had attracted **traders** of forty different nationalities, including Chinese, Portuguese, Dutch, English and French. Many lived in their own ghettos, with their own docks for the export of rice, spices, timber and hides. The kings of Ayutthaya deftly maintained their independence from outside powers, while embracing the benefits of contact: they employed foreign architects and navigators, and Japanese samurai as bodyguards; even their prime ministers were often outsiders, who could look after foreign trade without getting embroiled in court intrigues.

This four-hundred-year **golden age** came to an abrupt end in 1767 when the Burmese sacked Ayutthaya, taking tens of thousands of prisoners. The ruined city was abandoned to the jungle, but its memory endured: the architects of the new capital on Ratanakosin island in Bangkok perpetuated Ayutthaya's layout in every possible way.

Manohra 2 (☎02 477 0770, ⓦwww.manohracruises.com). Day-trips by minibus to Ayutthaya start at B600 per person.

Once in Ayutthaya, the helpful **TAT** office (daily 8.30am–4.30pm; ☎035 322730, ⓔtatyutya@tat.or.th) can be found in the former city hall on the west side of Thanon Si Sanphet, opposite the Chao Sam Phraya National Museum. It's well worth heading upstairs here to the smartly presented multimedia **exhibition** on Ayutthaya (daily except Wed 8.30am–4.30pm; free), which provides an engaging introduction to the city's history, an overview of all the sights including a scale-model reconstruction of Wat Phra Si Sanphet, and insights into local traditional ways of life. The **tourist police** (☎035 242352 or 1155) have their office just to the north of TAT on Thanon Si Sanphet.

City transport

Distances are deceptive, so it's best not to walk everywhere: **bicycles** (B30–50 per day) can be rented at guest houses, around the train station and from the tourist police. Some guest houses and a few cheaper outlets in front of the station rent small **motorbikes** (B150–250 a day). Otherwise, **tuk-tuks** charge about B50 for medium-range journeys, **motorbike taxis** around B40.

If you're pushed for time you could hire a tuk-tuk for a whistle-stop **tour** of the old city for B200 an hour (the current going rate set by the tourist police), either from the train station or from Chao Phrom market. **Sunset tuk-tuk tours** organized by guest houses are also popular, taking in some of the illuminated ruins (the main five central ruins are lit nightly 7–9pm) and ending at the night market (about 2hr; B160 per person), or there are the guided **bicycle tours** run by Ayutthaya Boat & Travel (☎081 733 5687, ⓦwww.ayutthaya-boat .com), whose itineraries include the ruins by day or night, a combination cycle and boat tour and a dinner cruise. For a serious **guided tour** of the ruins, local expert Professor Monton at Classic Tour (B1500 per day; ☎081 832 4849) comes highly recommended.

Circumnavigating Ayutthaya by **boat** is a very enjoyable way to take in some of the outlying temples and possibly a few lesser visited ones too; many of the temples were designed to be approached, and admired, from the river, and you also get a leisurely look at twenty-first-century riverine residences. All guest houses and agencies offer boat tours, typically charging B300 per person for a two-hour trip; they can also be chartered from the pier outside the Chanthara-kasem Palace museum.

It's also possible to take a brief **elephant ride** (B400 per person for 20min, B500 for 30min) past a couple of the central ruins from the roadside elephant "camp" on Thanon Pathon. The elephants and their mahouts are photogenically clad in period costume and you can buy them bananas while they wait for custom.

The City

The majority of Ayutthaya's ancient remains are spread out across the western half of the island in a patchwork of parkland: two of the most evocative temples, **Wat Phra Mahathat** and **Wat Ratburana**, stand near the modern centre, while a broad band runs down the middle of the parkland, containing the scant vestiges of the royal palace and temple, the town's most revered Buddha image at **Viharn Phra Mongkol Bopit**, and the two main **museums**. To the north of the island you'll find the best-preserved temple, **Wat Na Phra Mane**, to the west stands the Khmer-style **Wat Chai Watthanaram**, while to the southeast lie the giant chedi of **Wat Yai Chai Mongkol** and **Wat Phanan Choeng**, still a vibrant place of worship.

Wat Phra Mahathat

Heading west out of the new town centre along Thanon Naresuan, after about 1km you'll come to the first set of ruins, a pair of temples on opposite sides of the road. The overgrown **Wat Phra Mahathat**, on the left (daily 8am–6pm; B30), is the epitome of Ayutthaya's nostalgic atmosphere of faded majesty. The name "Mahathat" (Great Relic Chedi) indicates that the temple was built to house remains of the Buddha himself: according to the royal chronicles – never renowned for historical accuracy – King Ramesuan (1388–95) was looking out of his palace one morning when ashes of the Buddha materialized out of thin air here. A gold casket containing the ashes was duly enshrined in a grand 38-metre-high prang. The prang later collapsed, but the reliquary was unearthed in the 1950s, along with a hoard of other treasures including a gorgeous marble fish which opened to reveal gold, amber, crystal and porcelain ornaments – all now on show in the Chao Sam Phraya National Museum (see opposite).

You can climb what remains of the prang to get a good view of the broad, grassy complex, with dozens of brick spires tilting at impossible angles and headless Buddhas scattered around like spare parts in a scrapyard – look out for the serene head of a stone Buddha which has become nestled in the embrace of a bodhi tree's roots.

Wat Ratburana

Across the road from Wat Phra Mahathat, the towering **Wat Ratburana** (daily 8am–6pm; B30) was built in 1424 by King Boromraja II to commemorate his elder brothers Ay and Yi, who managed to kill each other in an elephant-back duel over the succession to the throne, thus leaving it vacant for him. Four elegant Sri Lankan chedis lean outwards as if in deference to the main prang, on which some of the original stucco work can still be seen, including fine statues of garudas swooping down on nagas.

It's possible to go down steep steps inside the prang to the crypt, where on two levels you can make out fragmentary murals of the early Ayutthaya period.

Wat Phra Si Sanphet

Nearly a kilometre west of Wat Ratburana is **Wat Phra Si Sanphet** (daily 8am–6pm; B30), built in 1448 by King Boromatrailokanat as his private chapel. Formerly the grandest of Ayutthaya's temples, and still one of the best preserved, it took its name from one of the largest standing metal images of the Buddha ever known, the **Phra Si Sanphet**, erected here in 1503. Towering 16m high and covered in 173kg of gold, it was smashed to pieces when the Burmese sacked the city, though Rama I rescued the fragments and placed them inside a chedi at Wat Pho in Bangkok. The three remaining grey chedis were built to house the ashes of three kings; their style is characteristic of the old capital, and they have now become the most hackneyed image of Ayutthaya.

The vast **Wang Luang** (Royal Palace) to the north of Wat Phra Si Sanphet was destroyed by the Burmese in 1767 and then plundered for bricks by Rama I to build Bangkok. Now you can only trace the outlines of a few walls in the grass – the only way to form a picture of this huge complex is to consult the model in the Historical Study Centre (see opposite).

Viharn Phra Mongkol Bopit

Viharn Phra Mongkol Bopit (Mon–Fri 8.30am–4.30pm, Sat & Sun 8.30am–5.30pm; free), on the south side of Wat Phra Si Sanphet, attracts tourists and Thai pilgrims in about equal measure. The pristine hall – a replica of a typical Ayutthayan viharn with its characteristic chunky lotus-capped columns around the outside – was built in 1956 (with help from the Burmese to atone for their flattening of the city two centuries earlier) in order to shelter the revered **Phra Mongkol Bopit**, one of the largest bronze Buddhas in Thailand. The powerfully austere image, with its flashing mother-of-pearl eyes, was cast in the fifteenth century, then sat exposed to the elements from the time of the Burmese invasion until its new home was built. During restoration, the hollow image was found to contain hundreds of Buddha statuettes, some of which were later buried around the shrine to protect it.

Chao Sam Phraya National Museum

A ten-minute walk south of the viharn brings you to the largest of the town's three museums, the **Chao Sam Phraya National Museum** (Wed–Sun 9am–4pm; B30; Ⓦ www.thailandmuseum.com), where most of the movable remains of Ayutthaya's glory – those which weren't plundered by treasure hunters or taken to the National Museum in Bangkok – are exhibited. Apart from numerous Buddhas and some fine woodcarving, the museum is bursting with **gold treasures**, including the original relic casket from Wat Mahathat, betel-nut sets and model chedis, and a gem-encrusted fifteenth-century crouching elephant that was found in the crypt at Wat Ratburana.

Historical Study Centre

The **Historical Study Centre** (daily 8.30am–4.30pm; B100), five minutes' walk from the National Museum along Thanon Rotchana, is a more modern showpiece museum. The visitors' exhibition upstairs puts the ruins in context, dramatically presenting a broad social history of Ayutthaya through videos, sound effects and reconstructions of temple murals, along with model ships, a peasant's wooden house and a small-scale model of the Royal Palace.

Chantharakasem Palace

The museum of the **Chantharakasem Palace** (Wed–Sun 8.30am–4.30pm; B30; Ⓦ www.thailandmuseum.com) was traditionally the home of the heir to the Ayutthayan throne. The Black Prince, Naresuan, built the first *wang na* (palace of the front) here in about 1577 so that he could guard the area of the city wall which was most vulnerable to enemy attack. Rama IV had the palace rebuilt in the mid-nineteenth century and it now displays many of his possessions, including a throne platform overhung by a white *chat*, a ceremonial nine-tiered parasol which is a vital part of a king's insignia. The rest of the museum features some beautiful ceramics and Buddha images, and a small arsenal of cannon and musketry from the late Ayutthaya and early Bangkok periods.

Wat Na Phra Mane

Wat Na Phra Mane (daily 8am–6pm; B20), on the north bank of the Lopburi River opposite the Wang Luang, is Ayutthaya's most immediately rewarding temple, as it's the only one from the town's golden age that survived the ravages of the Burmese.

The main **bot**, built in 1503, shows the distinctive features of Ayutthayan architecture: outside columns topped with lotus cups, and slits in the walls instead of windows to let the wind pass through. Inside, underneath a rich red-and-gold coffered ceiling representing the stars around the moon, sits a powerful six-metre-high Buddha in the disdainful, over-decorated royal style characteristic of the later Ayutthaya period.

In sharp contrast is the dark green **Phra Khan Thavaraj** Buddha that dominates the tiny viharn behind to the right. Seated in the "European position", with its robe delicately pleated and its feet up on a large lotus leaf, the gentle figure conveys a reassuring serenity. It's advertised as being from Sri Lanka, the source of Thai Buddhism, but is more likely a Mon image from Wat Phra Mane at Nakhon Pathom, dating from the seventh to ninth centuries.

Wat Phu Khao Thong

Head 2km northwest of Wat Na Phra Mane and you're in open country, where the fifty-metre chedi of **Wat Phu Khao Thong** rises steeply out of the fields. In 1569, after a temporary occupation of Ayutthaya, the Burmese erected a Mon-style chedi here to commemorate their victory. Forbidden by Buddhist law from pulling down a sacred monument, the Thais had to put up with this galling reminder of the enemy's success until it collapsed nearly two hundred years later, when King Borommakot promptly built a truly Ayutthayan chedi on the old Burmese base – just in time for the Burmese to return in 1767 and flatten the town. This "Golden Mount" has been restored and painted tooth-paste-white, with a colossal equestrian statue of King Naresuan, conqueror of the Burmese, to keep it company. You can climb 25m of steps up the side of the chedi to look out over the countryside and the town, with glimpses of Wat Phra Si Sanphet and Viharn Phra Mongkol Bopit in the distance.

Wat Chai Watthanaram

It's worth the ride to reach the elegant brick and stucco latticework of Khmer-style stupas at **Wat Chai Watthanaram** (daily 8am–6pm; B30), across the river to the southwest of the island. These graceful ruins used to be a common stop on boat tours but because of recurrent flooding a wall now protects them from the river and access is only viable by road. Late afternoon is a popular time to visit as the sun sinks photogenically behind the main tower.

King Prasat Thong built Wat Chai Watthanaram in 1630, possibly to commemorate a victory over Cambodia, designing it as a sort of Angkorian homage, around a towering **central Khmer corncob prang** (tower) encircled by a constellation of four minor prangs and eight tiered and tapered chedis. Most of the stucco facing has weathered away to reveal the red brick innards in pretty contrast, though a few tantalizing fragments of stucco relief remain on the outside of the chedis, depicting episodes from the Buddha's life. Around the gallery that connects them sits a solemn phalanx of 120 headless seated Buddhas, each on its own red-brick dais but showing no trace of their original skins, which may have been done in black lacquer and gold-leaf. To the east a couple of larger seated Buddhas look out across the river from the foundations of the old bot. You can share their view by climbing the steep steps of the central prang behind them, which also gives you the chance to admire the tower's robust redented structure at close quarters.

Wat Yai Chai Mongkol

Across the Pasak River southeast of the island, you pass through Ayutthaya's new business zone and some rustic suburbia before reaching the ancient but still functioning **Wat Yai Chai Mongkol**, about 2km from the station (daily 8am–5pm; B20). If you're on a bicycle, avoid the frantic multi-laned Pridi Damrong/Naresuan Bridge and Bangkok road by taking the river ferry across to the train station and then heading south 1.5km before turning east to the temple. Surrounded by formal lawns, flowerbeds and much-photographed saffron-draped Buddhas, the wat was established by Ramathibodi I in 1357 as a meditation site for monks returning from study in Sri Lanka. King Naresuan put up the beautifully curvaceous chedi to mark the decisive victory over the Burmese at Suphanburi in 1593, when he himself had sent the enemy packing by slaying the Burmese crown prince in an elephant-back duel. Built on a colossal scale to outshine the Burmese Golden Mount on the opposite side of Ayutthaya, the chedi has come to symbolize the prowess and devotion of Naresuan and, by implication, his descendants right down to the present king. By the entrance, a reclining Buddha, now gleamingly restored in white, was also constructed by Naresuan. A huge modern glass-walled shrine to the revered king dominates the back of the temple compound.

Wat Phanan Choeng

In Ayutthaya's most prosperous period the docks and main trading area were located near the confluence of the Chao Phraya and Pasak rivers, to the west of Wat Yai Chai Mongkol. This is where you'll find the oldest and liveliest working temple in town, **Wat Phanan Choeng** (daily 8am–5pm; B20). The main viharn is often filled with the sights, sounds and smells of an incredible variety of merit-making activities, as devotees burn huge pink Chinese incense candles, offer food and rattle fortune sticks. It's even possible to buy tiny golden statues of the Buddha to be placed in one of the hundreds of niches which line the walls, a form of votive offering peculiar to this temple. If you can get here during a festival, especially Chinese New Year, you're in for an overpowering experience.

  The nineteen-metre-high Buddha, which almost fills the hall, has survived since 1324, shortly before the founding of the capital, and tears are said to have flowed from its eyes when Ayutthaya was sacked by the Burmese. However, the reason for the temple's popularity with the Chinese is to be found in the early eighteenth-century shrine by the pier, with its image of a beautiful Chinese princess who drowned herself here because of the infidelity of the local ruler to whom she was betrothed: his remorse led him to build the shrine at the place where she had walked into the river.

Accommodation

Although Ayutthaya is usually visited on a day-trip, for those who want to make a little more of it there is a good choice of **accommodation**. Many of the budget guest houses are ghettoized on the lane that runs north from Chao Phrom market to Thanon Pamaphrao; it's sometimes known as Soi Farang but is actually signed as Naresuan Soi 2 at the southern end and Pamaphrao Soi 5 at the northern. For details of the accommodation price codes used in the listings below, see p.159.

Ayothaya Hotel Thanon Naresuan ☏ 035 232855. Central, good-value hotel with unexciting air-con motel rooms in the "standard" wing behind the car park and much more salubrious superior rooms in the hotel building. All guests can use the inviting swimming pool. Nice staff and a handy location. Budget ❹, superior ❺
Ayutthaya Guest House Naresuan Soi 2 ☏ 035 232658. Large, friendly and efficiently managed establishment that's very clued up

about travellers' requirements and offers bike and motorbike rental. Rooms are spread across two buildings and vary in size and facilities from tiny fan singles with shared bathrooms to large air-con en suites for four. Fan ❶–❷, air-con ❸
Baan Lotus Guest House Thanon Pamaphrao ☏ 035 251988. Tranquil traditional-style house with wooden floors and large plain en-suite rooms, fan and air-con, in a quiet spot at the end of a long garden with a lotus pond

at the back. Keeps good local information and offers simple breakfasts. ❸

🏃 **Bann Kun Pra** Thanon U Thong, just north of Pridi Damrong Bridge ☏ 035 241978, ⓦ www.bannkunpra.com. Airy, attractive rooms spread across two buildings: a rambling, hundred-year-old riverside teak house with a large, comfy chill-out terrace, where the nicest rooms have river-view balconies (and shared bathrooms); and a newer, noisier block near the road, where all rooms have en-suite cold-water bathrooms and some have air-con. There's also a dorm (B250) with mattresses on the teak floor and

individual lockable tin trunks. Internet access, bike rental, river tours and a warm welcome. ❸–❹

Krung Sri River 27/2, Thanon Rojana ☏ 035 244333, ⓦ www.krungsririver.com. Ayutthaya's best hotel occupies nine storeys in a prime if noisy position beside the Pridi Damrong Bridge, with some standard and en-suite rooms enjoying river views. Furnishings fall some way short of contemporary chic but there's air-con and TVs throughout, an attractive third-floor pool and a car park. Standard rooms are good value. Standard ❻, suite ❾

Eating

Other than the **restaurants** listed below, after dark there are a couple of **night markets**: beside the river at Hua Raw, about ten minutes' walk north of Naresuan Soi 2, and at the west end of Thanon Bang Laen, 150m south of Wat Phra Mahathat. Competing singers – including local boy Lek ("Little") Clapton – at the clutch of **bar-restaurants** can make Naresuan Soi 2 a bit of a battle of the bands after 9pm but it's fun and lively and free with your beer.

Bann Kun Pra Thanon U Thong. The riverside dining terrace is just as atmospheric as the lovely guest house upstairs and enjoys fine views. It specializes in reasonably priced fish and seafood, notably prawns, and the pork and pumpkin curry is good too. Most mains about B100.

Chang House Naresuan Soi 2. A chilled and inviting streetside travellers' restaurant that lives up to its motto: "Good food, good beer and good cheer" by serving tasty Thai standards and lots of seafood freshly cooked to authentic spiciness if requested (B70–100). Also does veggie dishes, a few Western classics and Indian curries. Imported wine, B90 cocktails and good sounds before the nightly live crooner takes over about 9pm.

🏃 **The Old Place** K-102 Thanon U Thong. Great Thai food and a breezy, always interesting riverside location across and up a bit from the station pier, make this place a hit with locals and tourists alike. Tables are on a wooden deck over the water, shaded by a venerable century-old kapok tree. Seafood is tip-top, especially the fish cakes and the sweet and sour prawns; cheap cocktails too. Mains B80–200.

Sombat Chao Phraya Thanon U Thong on the south side of town. Congenial spot where, on river bank terraces or a moored boat with views of Wat Phutthaisawan's white prang, you can dine on such delicacies as royal tofu with wild mushrooms, crab, cashew nuts and prawns.

Nakhon Pathom

NAKHON PATHOM is probably Thailand's oldest town, and is thought to be the point at which Buddhism first entered the region over two thousand years ago. The modern city's star attraction is the enormous Phra Pathom Chedi, an imposing stupa that dominates the skyline from every direction; nearly everything described below is within ten minutes' walk of this landmark. The town is 56km west of Bangkok and easily reached from the capital by train or bus.

Phra Pathom Chedi

At a phenomenal 120m high, **Phra Pathom Chedi** (daily dawn–dusk; B40) stands as tall as St Paul's Cathedral in London, and is a popular place of pilgrimage for Thais from all parts of the kingdom. Although the Buddha never actually came to Thailand, legend has it that he rested here after wandering the country, and the original 39-metre-high Indian-style chedi may have been erected to commemorate this. Since then, the chedi has been rebuilt twice; its earliest fragments are entombed within the later layers, and its origin has become indistinguishable from folklore.

Approaching the chedi from the main (northern) staircase, you're greeted by the eight-metre-high Buddha image known as **Phra Ruang Rojanarit**, standing in front of the north viharn. Each of the viharns – there's one at each of the cardinal points – has an inner and an outer chamber containing tableaux of the life of the Buddha. Proceeding clockwise around the monument – as is the custom at all Buddhist chedis – you can weave between the outer promenade and the inner cloister via ornate doors that punctuate the dividing wall; the promenade is dotted with trees, many of which have religious significance, such as the **bodhi tree** (*ficus religiosa*) under which the Buddha was meditating when he achieved enlightenment.

The museums

There are two museums within the chedi compound and, confusingly, they have similar names. The newer, more formal setup, the **Phra Pathom Chedi National Museum** (Wed–Sun 9am–noon & 1–4pm; B30; Ⓦwww.thailand museum.com), is just east from the bottom of the chedi's south staircase. It displays a good collection of Dvaravati-era (sixth to eleventh centuries) artefacts excavated nearby, including Wheels of Law – an emblem introduced by Theravada Buddhists before naturalistic images were permitted – and Buddha statuary with the U-shaped robe and thick facial features characteristic of Dvaravati sculpture. More a curiosity shop than a museum, the **Phra Pathom Chedi Museum** (Wed–Sun 9am–noon & 1–4pm; free), halfway up the steps near the east viharn, is an Aladdin's cave of Buddhist amulets, seashells, Chinese ceramics, Thai musical instruments and ancient statues.

Sanam Chandra Palace

A ten-minute walk west of the chedi along Thanon Rajdamnoen brings you into a large park filled with the elegant wooden buildings of **Sanam Chandra Palace** (daily 9.30am–4pm; B50 or free if you have retained your ticket for Bangkok's Grand Palace; Ⓦwww.palaces.thai.net; free classical dance shows every Sat & Sun at 11am & 2pm), which was built as the country retreat of Rama VI in 1907. Sanam Chandra is located across the road from the main campus of Silpakorn University and can also be reached by following signs for the university; it's a B30 ride on a motorbike taxi.

The **palace** was designed to blend Western and Eastern styles, and half a dozen of its main buildings are now open to the public. Its principal structure, the **Chaleemongkolasana Residence**, evokes a miniature Bavarian castle, complete with turrets and red-tiled roof; the **Mareerajaratabulung Residence** is a more oriental-style pavilion, built of teak and painted a deep rose colour inside and out; and the **Thub Kwan Residence** is an unadorned traditional Thai-style house of polished, unpainted golden teak. They each contain royal artefacts and memorabilia.

Practicalities

Trains leave Bangkok's Hualamphong Station twelve times a day (1hr 30min); there are also six trains a day from Bangkok's Thonburi Station (1hr 10min). A 200-metre walk south down Thanon Rotfai from Nakhon Pathom's train station, across the khlong and past the covered market will get you to the chedi compound's north gate. **Buses** leave Bangkok's Southern Bus Terminal every ten minutes and take about an hour; try to avoid being dumped at Nakhon Pathom's bus terminal, which is about 1km east of the town centre – most buses circle the chedi first, so get off there instead. Buses bound for Bangkok pick up from Thanon Phaya Pan on the north bank of the khlong, across from the *Mitpaisal Hotel*.

The obvious places to **eat** are the hot-food stalls just outside the chedi compound's southern wall, near the museum. There are most options here, from noodle soup to grilled chicken and rice dishes. The market in front of the station serves the usual takeaway goodies, including reputedly the tastiest khao laam (bamboo cylinders filled with steamed rice and coconut) in Thailand. For a quality cappuccino or iced mocha, head for the air-con coffee salon *Boncafé Tongmesang* (daily 8am–9pm), beside Soi 3 on Thanon Rajdamnoen, about 300m west of the chedi's west gate; it has internet access too.

Damnoen Saduak floating markets

To get an idea of what shopping in Bangkok used to be like before all the canals were concreted over, many people take an early-morning trip to the **floating markets** (*talat khlong*) of **DAMNOEN SADUAK**, 109km southwest of Bangkok. Vineyards and orchards here back onto a labyrinth of narrow canals, and every morning between 6am and 11am local market gardeners ply these waterways in paddle boats full of fresh fruit and vegetables, and tourist-tempting soft drinks and souvenirs. As most of the vendors dress in the deep-blue jacket and high-topped straw hat traditionally favoured by Thai farmers, it's all richly atmospheric, though the setup feels increasingly manufactured and some visitors have complained of seeing more tourists than vendors, however early they arrive.

The target for most tourists is the main **Talat Khlong Ton Kem**, 2km west of Damnoen Saduak's tiny town centre at the intersection of Khlong Damnoen Saduak and Khlong Thong Lang. Many of the wooden houses here have been converted into warehouse-style souvenir shops and tourist restaurants, diverting trade away from the khlong vendors and into the hands of large commercial enterprises. But, for the moment at least, a semblance of the traditional water trade continues, and the two bridges between Ton Kem and **Talat Khlong Hia Kui** (a little further south down Khlong Thong Lang) make decent vantage points. Touts invariably congregate at the Ton Kem pier to hassle you into taking a **boat trip** around the khlong network (asking an hourly rate of around B300 per person), but there are distinct disadvantages in being propelled between markets at top speed in a noisy motorized boat. For a less hectic and more sensitive look at the markets, explore via the walkways beside the canals.

Practicalities

To reach the market in good time you have to catch one of the earliest **buses** from Bangkok's Southern Bus Terminal (every 40min from 5.50am;

2hr 30min). Or you could join one of the many day-trips (from B500 per person). Damnoen Saduak's bus terminal is just north of Thanarat Bridge and Khlong Damnoen Saduak, on the main Bangkok/Nakhon Pathom–Samut Songkhram road, Highway 325. Frequent yellow **songthaews** (pick-up buses) cover the 2km to Ton Kem, but walk if you've got the time: a walkway follows the canal, which you can get to from Thanarat Bridge, or you can cross the bridge and take the road to the right (west), Thanon Sukhaphiban 1, through the orchards. Drivers on the earliest buses from Bangkok sometimes do not terminate at the bus station but instead cross Thanarat Bridge and then drop tourists at a pier a few hundred metres along Thanon Sukhaphiban 1.

The best way to see the markets is to stay overnight in Damnoen Saduak and get up at dawn, well before the buses and coach tours from Bangkok arrive. There's decent budget **accommodation** at the *Little Bird Hotel*, also known as *Noknoi* (☎032 254382; fan ❶, air-con ❷), whose sign is clearly visible from the main road and Thanarat Bridge. Rooms here are good value with enormous en-suite bathrooms and air-con if you want it. Staff can also arrange floating market boat trips.

Samut Songkhram and Amphawa

Rarely visited by foreign tourists and yet within easy reach of Bangkok, the tiny estuarine province of **Samut Songkhram** is nourished by the Mae Khlong River as it meanders through on the last leg of its route to the Gulf. Fishing is an important industry round here, as is market gardening, but for visitors it is the network of three hundred canals woven around the river, and the traditional way of life the waterways still support, that is most intriguing. As well as some of the most genuine floating markets in Thailand, there are chances to witness traditional cottage industries such as palm-sugar production and *bencharong* ceramic painting, plus more than a hundred historic temples to admire, a number of them dating back to the reign of Rama II, who was born in the province. The other famous sons of the region are Eng and Chang, the "original" Siamese twins (see box, p.98), who grew up in Samut Songkhram and are commemorated at the tiny, makeshift In-Chan Museum (Mon–Fri 8.30am–4.30pm; free), 4km north of the town centre on Thanon Ekachai (Route 3092).

If you're dependent on public transport, your first stop will be the provincial capital of Samut Songkhram, also commonly known as **Mae Khlong**, after the river that cuts through it, but there's little reason to linger here as the sights and most of the accommodation are out of town, mainly in the **Amphawa** district a few kilometres upriver.

Arrival and transport

The traditional way of travelling to Samut Songkhram from Bangkok – by **train** – is still the most scenic, albeit rather convoluted. It's a very unusual line, being single track and for much of its route literally squeezed in between homes, palms and mangroves, and, most memorably, between market stalls, so that at both the Samut Sakhon and Samut Songkhram termini the train really does chug to a standstill amid the trays of seafood. Trains leave from tiny

Wongwian Yai station in Thonburi (see p.131) and arrive in **Samut Sakhon**, also known as **Mahachai**, about an hour later (approximately hourly, but for the fastest onward connections catch the 5.30am, 8.35am, 12.15pm or 3.25pm). At Samut Sakhon you take a ferry across the Tha Chin River (there's no rail bridge) and then wait for the departure of the connecting train from **Ban Laem** on the other bank to Samut Songkhram at the end of the line (4 daily; 1hr). The **bus** ride to Samut Songkhram from Bangkok's Southern Bus Terminal (every 20min; 1hr 30min) is faster, but the views are dominated by urban sprawl. Buses also run direct to **Amphawa** from Bangkok's Southern Bus Terminal (every 20min; 2hr).

Once in Samut Songkhram, you have various options for getting around, though the public transport network is limited and doesn't encompass all the sights. **Taxi-boats** and other chartered river transport operate from the Mae Khlong River pier, which is close to the train station and market in the town centre. **Songthaews** to Amphawa and **local buses** to Amphawa and Damnoen Saduak, via Highway 325, leave from the central market, between the train and bus stations. A big part of this area's appeal is that it's best explored by boat, most rewardingly on a **tour** from *Baan Tai Had Resort*, though it's also possible to charter a boat from the town-centre pier in Samut Songkhram. Independent exploration is possible if you have your own vehicle, and *Baan Tai Had* rents out bicycles, kayaks and Jet Skis. Alternatively, you could join a one-day **cycling tour** from Bangkok with Spice Roads (T02 712 5305, W www.spiceroads.com).

Accommodation and eating

With its contemporary, comfortable **bungalows** set around a Bali-style garden, swimming pool and restaurant, luxurious but good-value *Baan Tai Had Resort* (T034 767220, W www.baantaihad.com; 6) makes a great escape from Bangkok, not least because of its local tour programmes and English-speaking guides. It's located beside the Mae Khlong River in the Amphawa district, about 6km upstream from Samut Songkhram (15min by taxi-boat from Samut Songkhram's pier).

Seafood is the obvious regional speciality and the most famous local dish is *hoi lot pat cha*, a spicy stir-fry that centres on the tubular molluscs – *hoi lot* – that are harvested in their sackloads at low tide from a muddy sandbank known as **Don Hoi Lot** at the mouth of the Mae Khlong estuary. A dozen restaurants occupy the area around the Don Hoi Lot pier, many offering views out over the gulf and its abundant sandbar; the pier is 5km south of Highway 35 and served by songthaews from Samut Songkhram market. In Samut Songkhram itself, the foodstalls alongside the pier make a pleasant spot for a lunch of cheap seafood *phat thai*.

Amphawa

The district town of **Amphawa** retains much traditional charm alongside its modern development. Its old neighbourhoods hug the banks of the Mae Khlong River and the Khlong Amphawa tributary, the wooden homes and shops facing the water and accessed either by boat or on foot along one of the waterfront walkways. Frequent songthaews (pick-up buses) and local buses (both approximately every 30min; 15min) connect Samut Songkhram market with Amphawa market, which sets up beside the khlong, just back from its confluence with the river.

King Rama II Memorial Park and Wat Amphawan

King Rama II was born in Amphawa (his mother's home town) in 1767 and is honoured with a memorial park and temple erected on the site of his probable birthplace, beside the Mae Khlong River on the western edge of Amphawa town, five-minutes' walk west of Amphawa market and khlong. It's accessible both by boat and by road, 6km from Samut Songkhram on the Amphawa–Bang Khonthi road.

Rama II, or Phra Buddhalertla Naphalai as he is known in Thai, was a famously cultured king and a respected poet and playwright, and the **museum** (Wed–Sun 9am–4pm; B10) at the heart of the **King Rama II Memorial Park** (daily 9am–6pm) displays lots of rather esoteric Rama II memorabilia, including a big collection of nineteenth-century musical instruments and a gallery of *khon* masks used in traditional theatre. On the edge of the park, **Wat Amphawan** is graced with a statue of the king and decorated with murals that depict scenes from his life, including a behind-the-altar panorama of nineteenth-century Bangkok, with Ratanakosin Island's Grand Palace, Wat Pho and Sanam Luang still recognizable to modern eyes. The tradition of holding a **floating market** on the canal near Wat Amphawan has recently been revived for tourists: Talat Nam Amphawa Yamyen is held here every Fri, Sat & Sun (4–8pm).

Wat Chulamani and Ban Pinsuwan bencharong workshop

The canalside **Wat Chulamani** was until the late 1980s the domain of the locally famous abbot Luang Pho Nuang, a man believed by many to be able to perform miracles, and followers still come to the temple to pay respects to his body, which is preserved in a glass-sided coffin in the main viharn. The breathtakingly detailed decor inside the viharn is testament to the devotion he inspired: the intricate black-and-gold lacquered artwork that covers every surface has taken years and cost millions of baht to complete. Across the temple compound, the bot's modern, pastel-toned murals tell the story of the Buddha's life, beginning inside the door on the right with a scene showing the young Buddha emerging from a tent (his birth) and being able to walk on lilypads straightaway. The death of the Buddha and his entry into nirvana is depicted on the wall behind the altar. Wat Chulamani is located beside Khlong Amphawa, a twenty-minute walk east of Amphawa market, or a five-minute boat ride. It is also signed off Highway 325, so any bus going to Damnoen Saduak from Samut Songkhram will drop you within reach.

A few hundred metres down the road from Wat Chulamani, and also accessible on foot, by bus and by canal, the Ban Pinsuwan **bencharong workshop** specializes in reproductions of famous antique *bencharong* ceramics, the exquisite five-coloured pottery that used to be the tableware of choice for the Thai aristocracy and is now a prized collector's item.

Tha Ka Floating Market and the palm-sugar centres

Unlike at the over-touristed markets of nearby Damnoen Saduak, the **floating market at Tha Ka** is still the province of local residents, with market gardeners either paddling up here in their small wooden sampans, or motoring along in their noisy longtails, the boats piled high with whatever is in season, be it pomelos or betel nuts, rambutans or okra, or with perennially popular snacks like hot noodle soup and freshly cooked satay. Thai tourist groups do visit, but mainly if market day happens to fall on a weekend. The Tha Ka market operates only six times a month, on a **timetable** that's dependent on the tides (for boat access) and is therefore dictated by the moon; thus market days are restricted to the second, seventh and twelfth mornings of every fifteen–day lunar cycle, from around 7am to 11am (contact any TAT office for exact dates). The market takes place on Khlong Phanla in the village of Ban Tha Ka, a half-hour **boat ride** from Amphawa's *Baan Tai Had Resort*, or about an hour from Damnoen Saduak; it's usually incorporated into a day-trip. The boat ride to the market is half the fun, but you can also get there by **road**, following Highway 325 out of Samut Songkhram for 10km, then taking a five-kilometre access road to Ban Tha Ka.

Most boat trips to Tha Ka also make a stop at one of the nearby **palm–sugar-making centres**. The sap of the coconut palm is a crucial ingredient in many Thai sweets and the fertile soil of Samut Songkhram province supports many small-scale sugar-palm plantations. There are several palm-sugar cottage industries between Amphawa and Ban Tha Ka, off Highway 325, accessible by car, by Damnoen Saduak-bound bus or by longtail boat.

Phetchaburi

Straddling the Phet River about 120km south of Bangkok, **PHETCHABURI** has long had a reputation as a cultural centre and became a favourite country retreat of Rama IV, who had a hilltop palace built here in the 1850s. Modern Phetchaburi has lost relatively little of the ambience that so attracted the king: the central riverside area is hemmed in by historic wats in varying states of repair, along with plenty of traditional wooden shophouses. Many Bangkok tour operators combine the floating markets of Damnoen Saduak (see p.144) with Phetchaburi as a day-trip package, but the town is also served by trains and frequent buses from the capital.

The Town

The pinnacles and rooftops of the town's thirty-odd wats are visible in every direction, but only a few are worth stopping off to investigate; the following description takes in the three most interesting, as well as Rama IV's palace, and can be done on a long, leisurely walk. Alternatively, hop on one of the public **songthaews** (pic-kup taxis) that circulate round the town, hire a **samlor** (cycle rickshaw) or rent a **bicycle** or **motorbike** from *Rabieng Rimnum Guest House*.

Wat Yai Suwannaram

Of all Phetchaburi's temples, the most attractive is the still-functioning seventeenth-century **Wat Yai Suwannaram** on Thanon Phongsuriya, about 700m east of Chomrut Bridge. The temple's fine old teak hall has elaborately carved doors and stands near a traditional scripture library that was built on stilts in the middle of a pond, to prevent ants destroying the precious documents.

Across from the pond and hidden behind high whitewashed walls stands the windowless Ayutthayan-style bot. Enter the walled compound from the south and pass through the statue-filled cloisters into the bot itself, which is supported by intricately patterned red-and-gold pillars and contains a remarkable, if rather faded, set of murals, depicting Indra, Brahma and other lower-ranking divinities ranged in five rows of ascending importance. If you climb the steps in front of the Buddha image seated against the far back wall you'll get a close-up of the left foot, which for some reason was cast with six toes.

Wat Kamphaeng Laeng

Fifteen minutes' walk east and then south of Wat Yai, the five tumbledown prangs of **Wat Kamphaeng Laeng** on Thanon Phra Song mark out Phetchaburi as the probable southernmost outpost of the Khmer empire. Built to enshrine Hindu deities and set out in a cruciform arrangement facing east, the laterite corncob-style prangs were later adapted for Buddhist use, as you can see from the two which now house Buddha images. There has been some attempt to restore a few of the carvings and false balustraded windows, but these days worshippers congregate in the modern whitewashed wat behind these shrines, leaving the atmospheric and appealingly quaint collection of decaying prangs and casuarina topiary to chickens, stray dogs and the occasional tourist.

Wat Mahathat

Continuing west along Thanon Phra Song from Wat Kamphaeng Laeng, across the river, you can see the prangs of Phetchaburi's most fully restored and important temple, **Wat Mahathat**, long before you reach them. The five landmark prangs at its heart are adorned with stucco figures of mythical creatures, though these are nothing compared with those on the roofs of the main viharn and the bot. Instead of tapering off into the usual serpentine *chofa*, the gables are studded with miniature figures of angels and gods, which

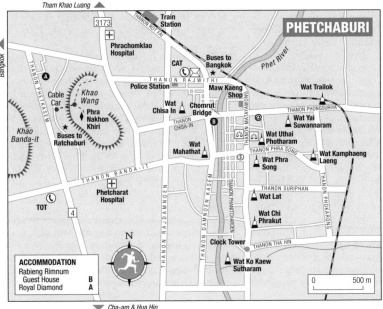

add an almost mischievous vitality to the place. In a similar vein, a couple of gold-embossed crocodiles snarl above the entrance to the bot, and a caricature carving of a bespectacled man rubs shoulders with mythical giants in a relief around the base of the gold Buddha, housed in a separate mondop nearby.

Khao Wang

Scattered over the crest of the hill known as **Khao Wang**, about thirty minutes' walk from Wat Mahathat on the western outskirts of town, the assorted structures that make up Rama IV's palace are a strange medley of mid-nineteenth-century Thai and European styles. Whenever the king came on an excursion here, he stayed in the airy summerhouse on the summit, **Phra Nakhon Khiri** (daily 9am–4pm; B40; Ⓦwww.thailandmuseum.com), with its Mediterranean-style shutters and verandas. Now a museum, it houses a moderately interesting collection of ceramics, furniture and other artefacts given to the royal family by foreign friends.

A **cable car** (daily 8.30am–4.30pm; B70 return, including admission to Phra Nakhon Khiri) runs to the summit from a spot at the base of the western flank of the hill that's just off Highway 4; there's also a path up the eastern flank, starting near Thanon Rajwithi.

Practicalities

Phetchaburi air-con **buses** from Bangkok's Southern Bus Terminal (every 40min; 2hr 15min) arrive at the air-con bus terminal just off Thanon Rajwithi, from where it's about ten minutes' walk south to the town centre and Chomrut Bridge. If you happen to catch a through-bus that's heading further south on Highway 4, you'll be set down at the corner of Thanon Banda-It on the western edge of town. Eleven **trains** a day run from Bangkok's Hualamphong Station (2hr 45min–3hr 45min) to Phetchaburi train station, which is on the northern outskirts of town, not far from Khao Wang, but about 1500m from the town centre.

There is no TAT office in town, but *Rabieng Rimnum Guest House* is a good source of local **information**. Phetchaburi's plushest **accommodation** is the *Royal Diamond* (Ⓣ032 411061, Ⓦwww.royaldiamondhotel.com; ❺), which has comfortable air-con rooms with hot water and is located west of Khao Wang on the outskirts of town, on Soi Sam Chao Phet, which is just off the Phetkasem Highway. Most travellers, however, stay at the *Rabieng Rimnum (Rim Nam) Guest House*, centrally located at 1 Thanon Chisa-in, on the southwest corner of Chomrut Bridge (Ⓣ032 425707 or 089 919 7446, Ⓦwww.rabiengrimnum .com; ❶). Occupying a century-old wooden house next to the Phet River and, less appealingly, a noisy main road, it has nine simple rooms with shared bathrooms and the best restaurant in town, offering an interesting menu of inexpensive Thai dishes, from banana blossom salad to tasty sugar-palm fruit curry with prawns, at its riverside tables.

Almost half the shops in the town centre stock Phetchaburi's famous **sweet snacks** (*khanom*), as do many of the souvenir stalls crowding the base of Khao Wang and vendors at the day market on Thanon Matayawong. The most well-known local speciality is *maw kaeng* (best sampled from a shop on the west side of Thanon Matayawong just north of Phongsuriya), a baked sweet egg custard made with mung beans and coconut and sometimes flavoured with lotus seeds, durian or taro.

Kanchanaburi and the River Kwai

Set in a landscape of limestone hills 121km northwest of Bangkok, **KANCHANABURI** is most famous as the location of the Bridge over the River Kwai. However, it has a lot more to offer, including fine riverine scenery and some moving relics from World War II, when the town served as a POW camp and base for construction work on the notorious Thailand–Burma Death Railway. It's possible to see the Bridge and ride the railway on a day-trip from Bangkok, but if you have the time, the town makes a pleasant spot for an overnight stay; there are many guest houses and hotels prettily set alongside the river, including some with accommodation in raft houses moored beside the river bank. The Bridge forms the dramatic centrepiece of the annual *sonet lumière* **River Kwai Bridge Festival**, which is held over ten nights from the end of November to commemorate the first Allied bombing of the Bridge on November 28, 1944.

Arrival, transport and information

The most enjoyable way to get to Kanchanaburi is by **train** from Thonburi station in Bangkok (2 daily; 2hr 40min) or Nakhon Pathom (2 daily; 1hr 30min). The main Kanchanaburi train station is on Thanon Saeng Chuto, about 2km north of the town centre, but if you're doing a day-trip and want to see the Bridge, get off at River Kwai Bridge train station, five minutes further on. Faster than the train are the **buses** from Bangkok's Southern Bus Terminal (every 15min; 2hr) and Northern Bus Terminal (hourly; 2hr 30min), arriving at the bus station off Thanon Saeng Chuto. The speediest transport option from Bangkok is to take a **minibus**: tourist minibuses leave from Thanon Khao San tour agencies (2hr; B120) or there's a private air-con minibus service from outside the *Royal Hotel* at the west end of Ratchadamnoen Klang in Banglamphu (approximately hourly; 2hr; B120).

Kanchanaburi is best explored by **bicycle** (B30–50 per day from guest houses and tour agents). Alternatively, orange public **songthaews** (pick-ups) run along Thanon Saeng Chuto, originating from outside the Focus Optic optician's, one block north of the bus station, and travelling north via the Kanchanaburi War Cemetery (Don Rak), Death Railway Museum, train station and access road to the Bridge (#2; every 15min until 6pm; 15min to the Bridge turn-off; B10). There are also plenty of **samlor** (cycle rickshaws) available for hire, or you could charter a **longtail boat** from the Bridge (around B700 for two hours).

The **TAT** office (daily 8.30am–4.30pm; ☎034 511200, ✉tatkan@tat.or.th) is on Thanon Saeng Chuto, a few hundred metres south of the bus station. Several banks on Thanon Saeng Chuto have ATMs and offer money-changing facilities.

The Town

Strung out along the east bank of the River Kwai and its continuation, as the Mae Khlong River, south of the Kwai Noi confluence, Kanchanaburi is a long, narrow ribbon of a town. The **war sights** are sandwiched between the river and the busy main drag, Thanon Saeng Chuto, with the Bridge over the River Kwai marking the northern limit, and the JEATH War Museum towards the town's southern edge.

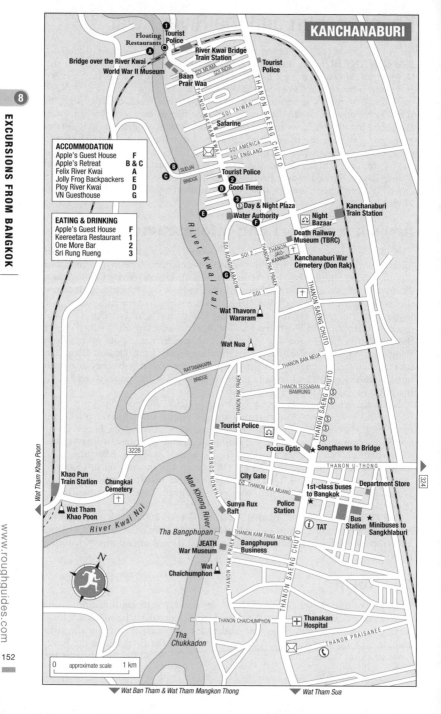

KANCHANABURI

ACCOMMODATION
Apple's Guest House	F
Apple's Retreat	B & C
Felix River Kwai	A
Jolly Frog Backpackers	E
Ploy River Kwai	D
VN Guesthouse	G

EATING & DRINKING
Apple's Guest House	F
Keereetara Restaurant	1
One More Bar	2
Sri Rung Rueng	3

Floating Restaurants
Tourist Police
River Kwai Bridge Train Station
Tourist Police
Bridge over the River Kwai
World War II Museum
Baan Prair Waa
SOI MEIMA
SOI INDIA
THANON MAENAM KWAI
SOI TAIWAN
Safarine
SOI AMERICA
SOI ENGLAND
SUDJAI BRIDGE
THANON SAENG CHUTO
Tourist Police
Good Times
Day & Night Plaza
Water Authority
Night Bazaar
Kanchanaburi Train Station
River Kwai Yai
Death Railway Museum (TBRC)
SOI RONGHEBAOW
THANON JAO-KANNUN
THANON PAK PRAEK
Kanchanaburi War Cemetery (Don Rak)
SOI 2
SOI 1
Wat Thavorn Wararam
Wat Nua
THANON BAN NEUA
RATTANAKARIN BRIDGE
THANON PAK PRAEK
THANON TESSABAN BAMRUNG
THANON SAENG CHUTO
Tourist Police
Focus Optic
Songthaews to Bridge
THANON SONG KWAI
3228
THANON U-THONG
Khao Pun Train Station
Chungkai Cemetery
Wat Tham Khao Poon
City Gate
THANON LAK MUANG
Mae Khlong River
1st-class buses to Bangkok
Department Store
Police Station
River Kwai Noi
Sunya Rux Raft
TAT
Bus Station
Minibuses to Sangkhlaburi
324
Tha Bangphupan
THANON KAM PANG MOENG
JEATH War Museum
Bangphupun Business
THANON PAK PRAEK
Wat Chaichumphon
THANON CHAICHUMPHON
Thanakan Hospital
THANON PRAISANEE
Tha Chukkadon
0   approximate scale   1 km

Wat Tham Khao Poon

Wat Ban Tham & Wat Tham Mangkon Thong

Wat Tham Sua

Death Railway Museum (Thailand–Burma Railway Centre)

The **Death Railway Museum** (formerly known as the Thailand–Burma Railway Centre; daily 9am–5pm; B100, children B50; ⓦ www.tbrconline.com) is the best place to start any tour of Kanchanaburi's World War II memorials. Located on Thanon Jaokannun, across the road from the train station and next to the Don Rak Kanchanaburi War Cemetery, it aims to provide an informed context for the thousands of people who visit the POW graves every week, presenting a sophisticated history of the Death Railway line itself, with the help of original artefacts, illustrations and scale models. The human stories are well documented too, notably via some unique original photographs and video footage shot by Japanese engineers, as well as through interviews with surviving Asian labourers on the railway.

Kanchanaburi War Cemetery (Don Rak)

Many of the Allied POWs who died during the construction of the Thailand–Burma Railway are buried in the **Kanchanaburi War Cemetery**, also called **Don Rak** (daily 8am–4pm; free), opposite the train station on Thanon Saeng Chuto. The 6982 POW graves are laid out in straight lines amid immaculate lawns and flowering shrubs. Many of the identical stone memorial slabs state simply "A man who died for his country" – at the upcountry camps, bodies were thrown onto mass funeral pyres, making identification impossible. Others, inscribed with names, dates and regiments, indicate that the overwhelming majority of the dead were under 25 years old.

The Bridge over the River Kwai

For many people the plain steel arches of the **Bridge over the River Kwai** come as a disappointment: it lacks drama and looks nothing like as hard to construct as it does in David Lean's famous 1957 film *The Bridge on the River Kwai* (which was in fact shot in Sri Lanka). But it is the film, of course, that draws tour buses here by the dozen, and makes the Bridge approach seethe with trinket-sellers and touts. **To get here**, either take any songthaew (pick-up) heading north up Thanon Saeng Chuto and then walk the 850m from the junction, hire a samlor (cycle rickshaw), or cycle – it's 5km from the bus station.

The Death Railway

Shortly after entering World War II in December 1941, Japan began looking for a supply route to connect its newly acquired territories that now stretched from Singapore to the Burma-India border. In spite of the almost impenetrable terrain, the River Kwai basin was chosen as the route for a new 415-kilometre-long **Thailand–Burma Railway**.

About 60,000 Allied POWs were shipped up from captured Southeast Asian territories to work on the link, their numbers later augmented by as many as 200,000 conscripted Asian labourers. Work began at both ends in June 1942. Three million cubic metres of rock were shifted and 14km of bridges built with little else but picks and shovels, dynamite and pulleys. By the time the line was completed fifteen months later it had more than earned its nickname, the **Death Railway**: an estimated 16,000 POWs and 100,000 Asian labourers died while working on it.

Food rations were completely inadequate for men forced into backbreaking eighteen-hour shifts, often followed by night-long marches to the next camp. Many suffered from beri-beri, many more died of dysentery-induced starvation, but the biggest killers were cholera and malaria, particularly during the monsoon. It is said that one man died for every sleeper laid on the track.

The fording of the Kwai Yai at this point was one of the first major obstacles in the construction of the Thailand–Burma Railway. Sections of a steel bridge were brought up from Java and reassembled by POWs using only pulleys and derricks. A temporary **wooden bridge** was built alongside it, taking its first train in February 1943; three months later the steel bridge was finished. Both bridges were severely damaged by Allied bombers (rather than commando-saboteurs as in the film) in 1944 and 1945, but the steel bridge was repaired after the war and is still in use today. In fact the best way to see the Bridge is by taking the **train** over it: the Kanchanaburi–Nam Tok train crosses it three times a day in each direction, stopping briefly at the River Kwai Bridge station on the east bank of the river (see below for details). You can also walk over the Bridge to the souvenir stalls on the west bank.

World War II Museum and Art Gallery

You're strongly advised to avoid the poorly designed and in some places tasteless **World War II Museum** (daily 8am–6.30pm; B40), just steps from the Bridge. The so-called World War II Museum is actually a bizarre hotchpotch of a private collection featuring all sorts of oddities, from coins and stamps to Allied motorbikes and distasteful tableaux of dying POWs, with barely any sensible captions.

JEATH War Museum

Founded by the chief abbot of Wat Chaichumpon and housed within the temple grounds in a reconstructed Allied POW hut of thatched palm, the ramshackle and unashamedly low-tech **JEATH War Museum** (daily 8.30am–6pm; B30) was the town's first public repository for the photographs, letters and memorabilia of the POWs who worked on the Death Railway. These items are now rather faded and seem poorly presented when compared to the slicker, more informative exhibitions at the Death Railway Museum, but the JEATH Museum is still an inevitable stop on any organized tour of the town. JEATH is an acronym of six of the countries involved in the railway: Japan, England, Australia, America, Thailand and Holland. The museum is located beside the Mae Khlong on Thanon Pak Praek, at the southern end of town. It's about 700m from the TAT office, or 5km from the Bridge.

Riding the Death Railway

The two-hour rail journey along the notorious Thailand–Burma **Death Railway** from Kanchanaburi to Nam Tok is one of Thailand's most scenic. Leaving Kanchanaburi via the Bridge over the River Kwai, the train chugs through the Kwai Noi valley, stopping frequently at pretty flower-decked country stations.

The most hair-raising section of track begins shortly after Tha Kilen at **Wang Sing**, also known as Arrow Hill, when the train squeezes through thirty-metre solid rock cuttings, dug at the cost of numerous POW lives. Six kilometres further, it slows to a crawl at the approach to the **Wang Po viaduct**, where a 300-metre-long trestle bridge clings to the cliff face as it curves with the Kwai Noi – almost every man who worked on this part of the railway died. Half an hour later, the train reaches its terminus at the small town of **Nam Tok**.

Three **trains** operate daily along the Death Railway in both directions, but they often run very late. At the time of writing, they're scheduled to leave Kanchanaburi at 5.57am, 10.24am and 4.19pm and to return from Nam Tok

▲ Bridge over the River Kwai, Kanchanaburi

at 5.20am, 12.50pm and 3.15pm; Kanchanaburi TAT keeps up-to-date **timetables**. If you're up at the Bridge, you can join the train five minutes later. Tourists are charged an inflated flat fare of B100. Many Kanchanaburi tour operators offer a day-trip that includes other war sights and waterfalls as well as a ride on the railway. Though it's possible to do the **Bangkok–Kanchanaburi–Nam Tok round trip** in one day, bear in mind that this leaves no time for exploring, and that only third class, hard seats are available. The 7.45am train from Bangkok's Thonburi station arrives in Nam Tok at 12.20pm and turns around at 12.50pm, returning to the capital at 5.35pm.

Accommodation

Many people choose to make the most of the inspiring scenery by staying on or near the river, in either a **raft house** (often just a rattan hut balanced on a raft of logs) or a **guest house**. The most popular area is around **Thanon Maenam Kwai**, which is crammed with bars, restaurants and tour agents; most guest houses are at the riverside end of the small sois running off this thoroughfare.

Apple's Guest House East off Thanon Maenam Kwai and **Apple's Retreat** Across Sudjai Bridge ☎034 512017, ⓦ www.applenoi-kanchanaburi .com. Run by a welcoming duo in two different locations: *Apple's Guest House* is set round a swimming pool and garden and has smart, modern fan and air-con rooms behind the airy two-storey restaurant. Across the river, *Apple's Retreat* sits in a green and tranquil spot, with a lovely Kwai-side restaurant and terrace. Rooms

are across the road in a two-storey building, with views across farmland to the hills beyond, plus a swimming pool and garden. There's wi-fi throughout both places and free transport between the two. Fan ❸, air-con ❹

Felix River Kwai On the west bank of the Kwai Yai ☎034 551000, ⓦ www.felixriverkwaihotel .com. Occupying a lovely riverside spot within walking distance of the Bridge (or a 2km drive from Thanon Maenam Kwai – a little inconvenient if you don't have transport), this is one of the top hotels in the area, though it's starting to look dated and a little faded. It has over 200 large air-con rooms, plus two swimming pools. Rates depend on whether you want a river view and are sometimes discounted during the week; reservations are essential for weekends. ❼–❾

Jolly Frog Backpackers **28 Soi China, Thanon Maenam Kwai** ☎ **034 514579.** Many backpackers' first choice, this large, efficiently run complex occupies a lovely stretch of the riverfront, fronted by a grassy lawn and flowering shrubs, and has a popular restaurant (good for fresh coffee and home-made bread from 7am). Aside from some cheap single rooms and a few doubles with shared bathrooms, it mostly comprises bright and comfortable en-suite rooms in two-storey bamboo-walled blocks around the shady garden. You can swim

off the jetty, though be careful of the strong current. Fan ❶, air-con ❸

Ploy River Kwai **Thanon Maenam Kwai** ☎ **034 515804,** ⓦ **www.ploygh.com.** Strikingly different in style from other guest houses on this road, this is a smart little enclave set back off the road but with distant river views only from the restaurant. The chic, sleek, contemporary-look rooms each have a platform bed and air-con, with extra charged for those with garden-style bathrooms or TVs. Good discounts if you book a week ahead. ❹–❺

VN Guesthouse **44 Soi Rongheabaow** ☎ **034 514082,** ⓦ **www.vnguesthouse.net.** In a pretty location on a quiet stretch of the river just south of the Maenam Kwai hub, this place offers very good rafthouse rooms: they're large and en suite and come with either fan or air-con; the best have lovely outlooks and they all have terraces and wi-fi. Rooms on dry land are unexceptional. Fan ❷, air-con ❸

Eating and drinking

Apple's Guest House **East off Thanon Maenam Kwai.** Exceptionally delicious food, prepared to traditional Thai recipes by Kanchanaburi's most famous cooking school. The extensive menu (B65–180) includes coconut- and cashew-laced matsaman curries – both meat and vegetarian varieties – as well as outstanding yellow curries and multi-course set dinners.

Keereetara Restaurant **Just north of the Bridge.** Classy Thai food, especially seafood, contemporary styling and great views of the Bridge from the terrace make this the top place to eat near the Bridge, and a favourite haunt of celebs and movie stars filming at the nearby Promitr Studios. Most mains B100–300.

One More Bar **Thanon Maenam Kwai.** The current backpackers' favourite is a lively, sociable place to spend an evening, not least because it has a refreshing no-bar-girls policy, hosts regular free-barbecues and occasional parties and has Nintendo Wii and DVDs in its backroom lounge.

Sri Rung Rueng **Thanon Maenam Kwai.** Popular, well-priced, bamboo-roofed restaurant with a huge menu of *tom kha, tom yam* and curries (yellow, red, green, *phanaeng* and matsaman), all available in veggie and non-veggie versions (from B60), plus steaks, seafood and cocktails.

Listings

Listings

Accommodation

B angkok has appalling traffic jams, so think carefully about what you want to see and do before deciding which part of town to stay in: easy access to relevant train networks and river transport can be crucial. Advance **reservations** are recommended where possible during high season (Nov–Feb), though some guest houses will only take cash deposits.

For ultra-cheap double rooms under B400, your widest choice lies with the no-frills guest houses on and around **Banglamphu**'s Thanon Khao San. The most inexpensive rooms here are no-frills crash-pads – small and often window-less, with thin walls and shared bathrooms – but Banglamphu also offers plenty of well-appointed mid-priced options with air-con, wi-fi and swimming pools. Other, far smaller and less interesting travellers' ghettoes that might be worth considering are the generally dingy **Soi Ngam Duphli**, off the south side of Thanon Rama IV, which nevertheless harbours a couple of decent shoestring options, as well as mid-range and expensive rooms; and **Soi Kasemsan I**, which is very handily placed next to Siam Square and occupies the moderate range, averaging B700 for a double, though with a few rooms for B500. The majority of the city's moderate and expensive rooms are scattered widely across the **downtown areas**, around Siam Square and Thanon Ploenchit, to the south of Thanon Rama IV and along **Thanon Sukhumvit**, and to a lesser extent in **Chinatown**. As well as easy access to transport links and shops, the downtown views from accommodation in these areas are a real plus. For accommodation **near Suvarnabhumi Airport** see p.27.

Bangkok boasts an increasing number of exceptionally stylish **super-deluxe** hotels, many of them designed as intimate, small-scale **boutique** hotels, with chic minimalist decor and excellent facilities that often include a **spa** (see p.200). The cream of this accommodation, with rates starting from B4500, is

Accommodation prices

Throughout this guide, accommodation has been categorized according to the **price codes** given below. These categories represent the **minimum** you can expect to pay in the **high season** (roughly July, Aug and Nov–Feb) for a **double room**, booked via the hotel website where available; there may however be an extra "peak" supplement for the Christmas–New Year period. If travelling on your own, expect to pay between sixty and one hundred percent of the rates quoted for a double room. Top-end hotels will add **seven percent tax** and **ten percent service charge** to your bill; the price codes below include taxes.

❶ B250 and under	❹ B601–900	❼ B2001–3000
❷ B251–400	❺ B901–1400	❽ B3001–4500
❸ B401–600	❻ B1401–2000	❾ B4501 and over

Online booking agents

Asia Hotels ⓦ www.asia-hotels.com
Hotel Thailand ⓦ www.hotelthailand.com
Passion Asia ⓦ www.passionasia.com

Sawadee ⓦ www.sawadee.com
Thai Focus ⓦ www.thaifocus.com

scenically sited along the banks of the Chao Phraya River, though there are a few top-notch hotels in the downtown area, which is also where you'll find the best business hotels. Many luxury hotels quote rates in US dollars, though you can always pay in baht.

Many of the expensive hotels listed offer special deals for **families**, usually allowing one or two under-12s to share their parents' room for free, so long as no extra bedding is required. It's also often possible to cram two adults and two children into the double rooms in inexpensive and mid-priced hotels (as opposed to guest houses), as beds in these places are usually big enough for two. A number of guest houses offer three-person rooms.

For **long-stay accommodation**, the most economical option is usually a room with a bathroom in an apartment building, which is likely to cost at least B6000 a month. Many foreigners end up living in apartments off Thanon Sukhumvit, around Victory Monument and Pratunam, or on Soi Boonprarop, off Thanon Rajaprarop just north of Pratunam. Visit the Teaching in Thailand website, ⓦ www.ajarn.com, for links to a room-finder website and tips on living in Bangkok, or try ⓦ www.sabaai.com for serviced apartments.

Banglamphu

Nearly all backpackers head straight for **Banglamphu** (ⓦ www.khaosanroad .com), Bangkok's long-established travellers' ghetto and arguably the most enjoyable area to base yourself in the city. It has the cheapest accommodation and some of the best nightlife in Bangkok, though some people find its insularity tiresome after just a few hours. It's also within easy reach of the Grand Palace and other major sights in **Ratanakosin**.

The increasingly sophisticated nightlife scene has enticed more moneyed travellers into Banglamphu and a growing number of Khao San **guest houses** are reinventing themselves as good-value mini-hotels boasting chic decor, wi-fi, swimming pools, and even views from the windows. Yet the cheapish sleeps are still there, particularly immediately west of Khao San, around the neighbourhood temple **Wat Chana Songkhram**, and along riverside **Thanon Phra Arthit**, where you'll also find some upscale places offering prime views. About ten minutes' walk north from Thanon Khao San, the handful of guest houses scattered amongst the shophouses of the **Thanon Samsen sois** enjoy a more authentically Thai environment, while the **Thewet** area, a further fifteen minutes' walk in the same direction or a seven-minute walk from the Thewet express-boat stop, is more local still. Heading south from Khao San into the area immediately **south of Democracy** also puts you in the middle of an interesting old neighbourhood – one that's not only easy walking distance to the big Ratanakosin sights, but is also famous for its specialist traditional shophouse restaurants.

Only the cream of what's on offer in each enclave of Banglamphu is listed: if your first choice is full there'll almost certainly be a vacancy somewhere just along the soi, if not right next door. **Theft** is a problem in Banglamphu, particularly at the cheaper guest houses, so don't leave anything valuable in your room and heed the guest houses' notices about padlocks and safety lockers.

Banglamphu is well served by **public transport** (see box, p.78). Banglamphu accommodation is marked on the **map** on p.76.

Thanon Khao San and around

Buddy Lodge 265 Thanon Khao San ☎02 629 4477, ⓦwww.buddylodge.com. N13 Tha Phra Arthit express boats. The most stylish and expensive hotel on Khao San and right in the thick of the action. The charming, colonial-style rooms are done out in cream, with louvred shutters, balconies, air-con and polished dark-wood floors, though they aren't as pristine as you might expect for the price. There's a beautiful rooftop pool, a spa, in-room wi-fi and several bars and restaurants downstairs in the Buddy Village complex. Specify an upper-floor location away from Khao San to ensure a quieter night's sleep.

D & D Inn 68–70 Thanon Khao San ☎02 629 0526, ⓦwww.khaosanby.com. N13 Tha Phra Arthit express boats. The attractive seventh-floor rooftop pool, with expansive views (and wi-fi), is the clincher at this good-value, mid-sized hotel located in the midst of the throng. Rooms all have air-con and TVs and are comfortably furnished and perfectly acceptable, if not immaculate. The cheapest single rooms don't have windows. ❹

Khao San Palace Hotel 139 Thanon Khao San ☎02 282 0578. N13 Tha Phra Arthit express boats. Clean and well-appointed hotel with a rooftop pool. All rooms have bathrooms and windows and some also have air-con and TV. The best rooms are in the new wing; they're nicely tiled and some have panoramic views, making them good value. Fan ❸, air-con ❸–❹

Lek House 125 Thanon Khao San ☎02 281 8441. N13 Tha Phra Arthit express boats. Classic old-style Khao San guest house, with twenty small, basic rooms, all with shared bathrooms and thin partition walls but thick mattresses. Less shabby than many others in the same price bracket and friendlier than most. Can get noisy at night as it's right next to the popular *Silk Bar*. ❶

Live Good East off Thanon Tanao ☎02 282 5092. N13 Tha Phra Arthit express boats. Cheap and simple rooms in this friendly, back-alley guest house, just off the veggie restaurants soi, a minute from Khao San.

Budget options have fans, wall views and shared bathrooms. En-suite fan rooms are larger and have outlooks of sorts. Shared bathroom ❶, en suite ❷

Shambara 138 Thanon Khao San ☎02 282 7968, ⓦwww.shambarabangkok.com. N13 Tha Phra Arthit express boats. This calm little hideaway is set down a tiny soi at the eastern end of Khao San and has just nine simple but individually designed fan and air-con rooms, all with shared bathrooms. Very popular, especially with solo women travellers, so book well ahead. Fan ❸, air-con ❹

Siam Oriental 190 Thanon Khao San ☎02 629 0312, ⓦwww.siamorientalgroup.com. N13 Tha Phra Arthit express boats. Small hotel right in the middle of Thanon Khao San, offering slightly scruffy rooms in a cheery shade of mauve, all with attached bathrooms and most with a window. Some rooms have air-con and a few also have balconies. ❷

Wally House 189/1–2 Thanon Khao San ☎02 282 7067. N13 Tha Phra Arthit express boats. Small guest house behind the family restaurant, with very cheap, very small, bottom-budget fan rooms, some of them en suite. Set back from the road so quieter than many. ❶–❷

West: around Wat Chana Songkhram, Phra Arthit and the river

Bella Bella House Soi Ram Bhuttri ☎02 629 3090. N13 Tha Phra Arthit express boats. The pastel-coloured rooms in this guest house are no frills but well priced and a few boast lovely views over Wat Chana Songkhram. The cheapest share bathrooms, and the most expensive have air-con. In-room wi-fi available throughout. Fan ❷–❸, air-con ❸

KC Guest House 64 Trok Kai Chae, off Thanon Phra Sumen ☎02 282 0618, ⓦwww.kcguest house.com. N13 Tha Phra Arthit express boats. Friendly, family-run little guest house with exceptionally clean, tiled-floor rooms, with and without private bathrooms and air-con, and a terrace eating area on the soi. Fan ❷, air-con ❸

Lamphu House 75 Soi Ram Bhuttri ☎02 629 5861, ⓦwww.lamphuhouse.com. N13 Tha Phra

Arthit express boats. With smart bamboo beds, coconut-wood clothes rails, and elegant rattan lamps in even its cheapest rooms, this travellers' hotel set round a quiet courtyard has a calm, modern feel. Cheapest rooms share facilities and have no outside view. Wi-fi is available throughout. Fan ❷, en suite ❸, air-con ❹

Merry V Soi Ram Bhuttri ℡02 282 9267. N13 Tha Phra Arthit express boats. Large, efficiently run guest house offering some of the cheapest accommodation in Banglamphu. Bottom-end rooms are basic and small, many share bathrooms and it's pot luck whether you get a window. Better en suites and air-con versions are also available and there's a useful noticeboard in the downstairs restaurant. Fan ❶, en suite ❸, air-con ❸

Navalai River Resort 45/1 Thanon Phra Arthit ℡02 280 9955, ⓦwww.navalai.com. N13 Tha Phra Arthit express boats. Style-conscious riverfront hotel, with an elegant rooftop pool, modishly–furnished rooms, and river views from the most desirable. There's air-con, private balconies and wi-fi throughout and the excellent riverside *Aquatini* restaurant is at ground level (see p.176). ❼–❽

New Siam Riverside 21 Thanon Phra Arthit ℡02 629 3535, ⓦwww.newsiam.net. N13 Tha Phra Arthit express boats. Occupying a prime riverside spot, this latest in the New Siam empire offers well-designed, good value rooms, all with air-con, full amenities and wi-fi; the best of them have fabulous river views from windows or private balconies. Also has a large riverside swimming pool and terrace restaurant. ❻–❼

New Siam 2 50 Trok Rong Mai ℡02 282 2795, ⓦwww.newsiam.net. N13 Tha Phra Arthit express boats. Very pleasant and well run small hotel whose en-suite fan and air-con rooms stand out for their thoughtfully designed extras such as in-room safes, cable TV and drying rails on the balconies. Occupies a quiet but convenient location and has a small streetside pool. Popular with families and triple rooms are also available. ❹

Peachy Guest House 10 Thanon Phra Arthit ℡02 281 6471. N13 Tha Phra Arthit express boats. Popular, good value, very cheap Bangkok institution set round a small, late-night courtyard bar. Offers lots of clean, simple, wooden-floored rooms, most with shared bathrooms but some with air-con. Fan and

shared bathroom ❶, air-con and shared bathroom ❶, air-con and bathroom ❸

North: Samsen sois and Thewet

Lamphu Treehouse 155 Saphan Wanchat, Thanon Phracha Thipatai ℡02 282 0991, ⓦwww.lamphutreehotel.com. Named after the *lamphu* trees (as in Banglamphu, "place with *lamphu* trees") that line the adjacent canal, this attractively turned-out mid-range guest house offers smart, modish air-con rooms, all with balconies and plenty of polished teakwood fittings. There's a pool, and wi-fi in the lobby. It's in a quiet neighbourhood but just a few minutes' walk from Democracy, Khao San and the river. ❺

🏃 **Old Bangkok Inn** 609 Thanon Phra Sumen ℡02 629 1787, ⓦwww.oldbangkokinn .com. This chic little boutique guest house has just ten air-con rooms, each individually styled in dark wood, with antique north-Thai partitions, Burmese doors, beds and ironwork lamps, plus elegant contemporary-accented bathrooms. All rooms have a PC with free broadband access, wi-fi and DVD player. Some also have a tiny private garden. A 10min walk from Khao San. ❽–❾

🏃 **Phra Nakorn Norn Len** 46 Thewet Soi 1, Thewet ℡02 628 8188, ⓦwww .phranakorn-nornlen.com. N15 Tha Thewet express boats. What was once a seedy short-time motel has been transformed into a bohemian haven with genuine eco-conscious and socially engaged sensibilities and a tangible fair-trade philosophy. Every one of the thirty comfortable, though not luxurious, rooms has been hand-painted to a different retro Thai design, and each has a platform bed, cute modern bathroom, balcony, CD player, wi-fi and air-con. The downstairs areas are filled with the owner's twentieth-century collectibles; the rooftop enjoys unrivalled views of Wat Indraviharn's huge standing Buddha and is partly given over to growing organic veg for the restaurant. ❼

Sawatdee Guest House 71 Soi 16, Thanon Sri Ayutthaya, Thewet ℡02 281 0757. N15 Tha Thewet express boats. Cheap and basic, but friendlier than many in the Thewet area, this long-running old-style guest house offers no-frills fan rooms with partition walls, either with or without private bathroom. ❷–❸

Sri Ayutthaya 23/11 Soi 14, Thanon Sri Ayutthaya, Thewet ℡02 282 5942. N15 Tha

Thewet express boats. The most attractive guest house in Thewet, where the good-sized rooms (choose between fan rooms with or without private bathroom and en suites with air-con) are elegantly done out with wood-panelled walls and beautiful polished wood floors. ❸–❹

Thamna Hometaurant 175 Thanon Samsen, between sois 3 and 5, ☎ 02 282 4979, Ⓔ thamnahome@yahoo.com. **N14 Tha Saphan Rama VIII express boats.** Upscale homestay comprising just two guest rooms on the floor above the young owners' organic veggie restaurant and below their own home. The look is simple but arty, with wooden floors, polished concrete walls and understated fabrics. Bathrooms are private but not en suite and the cheaper room has no window. Air-con and wi-fi throughout. Rates include a full veggie breakfast. ❹

Vimol Guest House 358 Samsen Soi 4 ☎ 02 281 4615. Old-style, family-run guest house in a quiet but interesting neighbourhood that has just a smattering of other tourist places. The simple, cramped, hardboard-walled rooms are ultra basic and have shared

bathrooms but are possibly the cheapest in Banglamphu. ❶

South: south of Democracy

Baan Dinso 113 Trok Sin, Thanon Dinso ☎ 02 622 0560, Ⓦ www.baandinso.com. This tasteful, upmarket little guest house of just nine rooms occupies an elegant 1920s Thai house all done out in cool buttermilk paintwork and polished teak floors. Prices are a little steep considering all but the deluxe rooms have to use shared ground-floor bathrooms, but they all have air-con, TVs and DVD players and there's free wi-fi. Youth Hostel members get a ten percent discount. ❻

Boonsiri Place 55 Thanon Buranasart ☎ 02 622 2189, Ⓦ www.boonsiriplace.com. Two charming sisters run this mid-range hotel, notable for its warm welcome, environmentally conscious policies and location in an old-Bangkok neighbourhood less than 10min walk from the Grand Palace. Each of its 48 air-con rooms is hung with a different painting commissioned from Thai traditional temple artist Chanok Chunchob, whose work is also on sale in the adjacent gallery. ❻

Ratanakosin

Several small, upmarket hotels have recently opened on Ratanakosin's west side. It's a peerless location, in a quiet, traditional, heavily Chinese neighbourhood of low-rise shophouses, overlooking the river and on the doorsteps of Wat Pho and the Grand Palace. The restaurants and nightlife of Banglamphu are within walking distance, while the sights of Thonburi and Chinatown, as well as Saphan Taksin Skytrain station, are a public boat ride away. All accommodation listed below is marked on the map on p.58. For **public transport** details, see the box on p.57.

Arun Residence 36 Soi Pratu Nokyung, Thanon Maharat ☎ 02 221 9158, Ⓦ www.arunresidence .com. **N8 Tha Thien express boats.** Stunning views of Wat Arun and charming, wooden-floored rooms that mix traditional and contemporary Thai styles. Occupying an eccentrically converted shophouse (plumbing can sometimes be a problem), the hotel also has a library with internet access, a rooftop bar and a good European and Thai restaurant, *The Deck*, where breakfast (included in the price) is served. ❽

Aurum: The River Place 394/27–29 Soi Pansook, Thanon Maharat ☎ 02 622 2248, Ⓦ www .aurum-bangkok.com. **N8 Tha Thien express boats.** Modelled on a French townhouse,

with wooden shutters and wrought-iron balconies, this spruce, four-storey hotel is set back slightly from the river but offers views of the water from most bedrooms. Splashed with colourful Thai fabrics and sporting heavily varnished wooden floors, the well-equipped rooms are a little on the small side, apart from those on the top floor. There's a daytime riverside café, *The Coffee Place*, where complimentary breakfast is served. ❽

Chakrabongse Villas 396 Thanon Maharat ☎ 02 224 6686, Ⓦ www.thaivillas.com. **N8 Tha Thien express boats.** In the luxuriant, riverside gardens of 100-year-old Chakrabongse House overlooking Wat Arun are four tranquil villas beautifully furnished in dark wood and silk, with polished teak floors. All have air-con and cable TV, and there's a small, attractive swimming pool and an open-sided riverfront pavilion for relaxing or dining (if ordered in advance). ⑨

Chinatown and Hualamphong Station area

Close to the Ratanakosin sights, and within fifteen minutes' walk of Siam Square, **Chinatown** (**Sampeng**) is among the most frantic and fume-choked parts of Bangkok – and there's quite some competition. Still, it's got plenty of interest, sees barely any Western overnighters and is very handy for **Hualamphong Station**.

Hualamphong is on the **subway** system, and a number of useful **bus** routes (see box, p.85) serve Chinatown. All accommodation listed below is marked on the map on p.86.

Baan Hualamphong 336/20 Soi Chalong Krung ☏02 639 8054, ⊛www.baanhualampong.com. Hualamphong subway (5min walk). This once strikingly stylish, now slightly faded wooden guest house is still the most welcoming in the soi, not least for its traveller-friendly vibe. There are big, bright, double rooms plus five-person dorms at B220 per bed, but all bar one room share bathrooms. Has kitchen facilities, inviting lounging areas and a small roof terrace, provides a left-luggage service and is open 24hr. Fan ❸, air-con ❹

Bangkok Centre 328 Thanon Rama IV ☏02 238 4848, ⊛www.bangkokcentrehotel.com. Hualamphong subway (exit 4). The most interesting thing about this otherwise rather mediocre, old-fashioned hotel is its location, a couple of steps from the subway exit and just across the road from the train station. Rooms are air-con and adequate for the price and there's a pool, restaurant and wi-fi throughout. ❻

FF Guest House 338/10 Trok La-O, off Thanon Rama IV ☏02 233 4168. Hualamphong subway (5min walk). Tiny, family-run guest house offering ten cheap, cell-like but perfectly acceptable wooden-floored fan rooms with shared bathrooms. No other facilities, nor much English spoken. ❶

Grand China Princess 215 Thanon Yaowarat ☏02 224 9977, ⊛www.grandchina.com. N5 Tha Rachawongse express boats. The poshest hotel in Chinatown boasts fairly luxurious accommodation in its 27-storey tower close to the heart of the bustle, with stunning views over all the city landmarks (the best take in the river), a small rooftop swimming pool, revolving panoramic restaurant and broadband in every room. ❽

🏃 **Shanghai Mansion** 479 Thanon Yaowarat, next to Scala Shark's Fin restaurant

☏02 221 2121, ⊛www.shanghai-inn.com. N5 Tha Rachawongse express boats or Hualamphong subway (15min walk from either). The most design-conscious accommodation in Chinatown has embraced the modern Chinoiserie look with gusto. Rooms are prettily done out in silks, lacquer-look furniture and lanterns, featuring a lot of sumptuous reds and purples. There's barely any daylight in the hotel (only the noisy street-front suites have windows and views) but standard rooms are cosily isolated from the Chinatown frenzy and all have air-con, TV and free wi-fi. ❼–❽

The Train Inn 428 Thanon Rong Muang ☏02 215 3055, ⊛www.thetraininn.com. Hualamphong subway. Just a couple of minutes' walk from Hualamphong Railway Station's side exit off platform 3, and open 24hr, is a decent, traveller-oriented choice for weary rail passengers. Rooms – "first", "second" and "third class" – mostly share bathrooms and can be a bit scruffy, but are all air-con and the majority are a reasonable size. ❸–❹

TT2 Guest House 516 Soi Kaeo Fa (formerly Soi Sawang and known to taxi drivers as such), off Thanon Maha Nakorn ☏02 236 2946, ⓔttguesthouse@hotmail.com. Hualamphong subway or N3 Tha Si Phraya express boats (15min walk from either). A long-running, traveller-friendly budget place, this guest house is clean and well run, has simple singles, doubles and triples, and stores left luggage at B15–20 per day. All rooms share bathrooms. From Hualamphong, cross Thanon Rama IV, then walk left for 250m, cross Thanon Maha Nakorn and walk down it for 275m as far as Soi Kaeo Fa, where you turn left and then first right. The guest house is opposite Wat Kaeo Jam Fa. No check-in between midnight and 5.30am. ❷

Thonburi

Few tourists stay on the **Thonburi** side of the river, though many visit its canals and temples. It enjoys a refreshingly authentic neighbourhood vibe and is surprisingly convenient, with express boats and cross-river shuttles serving Banglamphu and Ratanakosin across on the other bank. See map on p.93.

Ibrik Resort by the River 256 Soi Wat Rakang ☎02 848 9220, ⊛www .ibrikresort.com. N10 Tha Wang Lang express boats. With just three rooms, this is the most bijou of boutique resorts. Each room is beautifully appointed in boho-chic style, with traditional wood floors, modernist white walls and sparkling silk accessories – and two of them have balconies right over the Chao Phraya River. It's just like staying at a trendy friend's home in a neighbourhood that sees hardly any other tourists. Located next door to *Supatra River House* restaurant. ❽

Siam Square, Thanon Ploenchit and northern downtown

Siam Square and nearby **Thanon Ploenchit** are as central as Bangkok gets: all the accommodation listed here is within walking distance of a Skytrain station. On hand are the city's best shopping possibilities – notably the phalanx of malls along Thanon Rama I – and a wide choice of Thai and international restaurants and food courts. There's no ultra-cheap accommodation around here, but a few scaled-up guest houses complement the expensive hotels. Concentrated in their own small "ghetto" on **Soi Kasemsan 1**, which runs north off Thanon Rama I, between the Bangkok Metropolitan Art Museum and Jim Thompson's House, these offer typical travellers' facilities and basic hotel comforts – air-conditioning and en-suite hot-water bathrooms – at moderate prices; the Khlong Saen Saeb canal-boat pier, Tha Saphan Hua Chang (easily accessed via Thanon Phrayathai), is handy for heading west to the Golden Mount and beyond, to Ratanakosin.

All accommodation listed below is marked on the map on p.108, unless otherwise stated. For **public transport** details see the box on p.107.

Inexpensive and moderate

A-One Inn 25/13 Soi Kasemsan 1, Thanon Rama I ☎02 215 3029 or 02 216 4770, ⊛www .aoneinn.com. BTS National Stadium. The original upscale guest house, and still justifiably popular, with a 24hr internet café, wi-fi and a reliable left-luggage room. Bedrooms all have satellite TV and come in a variety of sizes, including family rooms; discounts for longer stays. ❹

The Bed & Breakfast 36/42 Soi Kasemsan 1, Thanon Rama I ☎02 215 3004, ⊕02 215 2493. BTS National Stadium. Bright, clean and family-run, though some of the rooms are a bit cramped. As the name suggests, a simple breakfast – coffee, toast and fruit – is included. ❹

Far East Inn 20/8–11 Soi Bangkok Bazaar, Soi Chitlom ☎02 255 4041–5, ⊛www.fareastinn .webs.com or www.tyha.org. BTS Chit Lom. The large rooms here are unexceptional but well-equipped – air-con, cable TV, mini-bars and baths with hot water – and the place is friendly, very central and reasonably quiet. Breakfast included in the price. Discounts for YHA members. ❺

Golden House (VIP Guest House) 1025/5–9 Thanon Ploenchit ☎02 252 9535–7, ⊛www .goldenhouses.net. BTS Chit Lom. Very clean and welcoming, small hotel in a peerless location. The plain but attractive, parquet-floored bedrooms are equipped with air-con, hot water, cable TV, free wi-fi and mini-bar – ask for one of the three larger front rooms with bay windows, which leave just enough space for a couple of armchairs. Breakfast included. Weekly and monthly discounts available. ❻

Jim's Lodge 125/7 Soi Ruam Rudee, Thanon Ploenchit ☎02 255 3100, ⊛www.jimslodge .com. BTS Ploen Chit. In a relatively peaceful residential area, with friendly and helpful staff; offers international standards –

including satellite TV and mini-bars – on a smaller scale and at bargain prices; no swimming pool, but there is a roof garden with outdoor jacuzzi. ⑥

Patumwan House 22 Soi Kasemsan 1, Thanon Rama I ☎02 612 3580–99, ⊛www.patumwan house.com. BTS National Stadium. Around the corner to the left at the far end of the soi, with very large, though rather bare rooms with satellite TV, fridges, wardrobes and wi-fi; facilities include a café and internet terminals. Discounted weekly and monthly rates. ⑤

Reno Hotel 40 Soi Kasemsan 1, Thanon Rama I ☎02 215 0026–7, ⊛www.renohotel.co.th. BTS National Stadium. Friendly hotel, boasting large, comfortable, en-suite rooms (some with fridges) with air-con, hot water, baths, TV, and a small swimming pool. Far more stylish than the bedrooms is the bar-restaurant, refurbished in contemporary Thai style, where breakfast is served (included in the price). Internet access. ⑤

Wendy House 36/2 Soi Kasemsan 1, Thanon Rama I ☎02 214 1149–50, ⊛www .wendyguesthouse.com. BTS National Stadium. Friendly and well-run guest house, with smart, clean and comfortable rooms, all with fridge, cable TV and wi-fi. Internet terminals in the ground-floor café, where breakfast (included in the price) is served. Discounted weekly rates. Internet bookings accepted. ⑤

White Lodge 36/8 Soi Kasemsan 1, Thanon Rama I ☎02 216 8867 or 02 215 3041, ℻02 216 8228. BTS National Stadium. Cheapest guest house on the soi, with shining white cubicles and a lively, welcoming atmosphere – the best rooms, bright and quiet, are on the upper floors. ③

Expensive

Centara Grand at Central World 999/99 Thanon Rama 1 ☎02 100 1234, ⊛www.centarahotels resorts.com/cgcw. BTS Chit Lom. Occupying Floors 23 to 55 atop the huge, glossy Central World Plaza mall and its fifty restaurants and fifteen cinema screens, this is a luxurious cocoon high above the hot, noisy city. The views from rooms and restaurants – particularly the appealingly laid-back, indoor-outdoor *Globe* lounge bar – are panoramic, and shared by the invitingly large swimming pool. Broadband access throughout. ⑧

Conrad All Seasons Place, 87 Thanon Witthayu ☎02 690 9999, ⊛www.conradhotels.com. BTS Ploen Chit. The *Conrad* places a high premium on design, aiming to add a cutting edge to traditional Thai style, and on service, including tailor-made itineraries by the concierge. Bathroom fittings include free-standing baths, glass walls and huge shower heads, and there's an enticing pool, spa, gym and two floodlit tennis courts. Restaurants include the modern Chinese *Liu* and authentic Japanese *Drinking Tea Eating Rice*, while the *Diplomat Bar* hosts live jazz Mon–Sat eve. ⑨

Courtyard by Marriott 155/1 Soi Mahadlekluang 1, Thanon Rajdamri ☎02 690 1888, ⊛www .courtyardbangkok.com. BTS Ratchadamri. On a quiet, but very handy soi, this hotel offers most of the facilities of a five-star, but at more manageable prices. The modern design is seductive, gleaming white outside, candy colours and plenty of natural light inside, and there's a long, narrow, infinity pool, a fitness centre and reasonably priced massage rooms. ⑧

Four Seasons 155 Thanon Rajdamri ☎02 250 1000, ⊛www.fourseasons.com. BTS Ratchadamri. The stately home of Bangkok's top hotels formerly the *Regent*. Afternoon tea is still served in the monumental lobby, which is adorned with magnificent, vibrant eighteenth-century-style murals depicting the Thai cosmology, and flanked by acclaimed Thai, Italian and Japanese restaurants and a steakhouse. Large and luxurious rooms are decorated in warm Thai colours and dark wood, and there's an excellent concierge service. ⑨

Pathumwan Princess Hotel 444 Thanon Phrayathai ☎02 216 3700, ⊛www.pprincess.com. BTS Central. At the southern end of MBK Shopping Centre, affordable luxury (at the lower end of this price range) that's recently been refurbished in a crisp, modern style and is popular with families and businessmen. With Korean and Italian restaurants, a large, saltwater swimming pool with hot and cold jacuzzis, a health spa and a huge fitness club. ⑨

Reflections 224/2–9 Thanon Pradiphat (between sois 18 and 20; see the colour Skytrain and Subway map at the back of the book) ☎02 270 3344, ⊛www.reflections-thai.com. BTS Saphan Kwai. Urban guerrilla meets kitsch at this idiosyncratic pop-art hotel, where every room was designed by a different artist.

Browse the website to make your choice. The 36 rooms come in two sizes and all have air-con, a balcony or terrace, and in-room wi-fi, though few are luxurious. The location in an unfashionable neighbourhood is not great: it's a 10min walk south then west from the BTS, but Chatuchak Weekend Market is only 20min away. There's a spa and art shop on site. **❼**

Siam City Hotel 477 Thanon Sri Ayutthaya (see main colour map at the back of the book) ☏ 02 247 0123, ⓦ www.siamhotels.com. BTS Phaya Thai. Elegant, welcoming luxury hotel north of downtown (opposite Suan Pakkad). Choose between an "Ayutthaya" room, done out in sharp, modern Thai style, and a larger "Siam" room with a soothing, more traditional flavour. There's a spa, health club, swimming pool and a comprehensive array of restaurants including Chinese, Japanese and Italian. At the lower end of this price code. **❾**

Swissôtel Nai Lert Park 2 Thanon Witthayu ☏ 02 253 0123, ⓦ www .swissotel.com. BTS Ploen Chit. This welcoming, low-rise hotel is distinguished by its lushly beautiful gardens, overlooked by many of the chic and spacious, balconied bedrooms; set into the grounds are a landscaped swimming pool, tennis courts, squash court and popular spa and health club. Good deli-café, cool bar (see p.189) and Japanese (see p.179), French and Chinese restaurants. **❾**

Ten Face 81 Soi 2, Soi Ruam Rudee ☏ 02 695 4242, ⓦ www.tenfacebangkok.com. BTS Ploen Chit. The name comes from Totsagan, the ten-faced demon of the Ramakien (see p.63), and without being gimmicky, this place ingeniously combines sleek, contemporary design with striking artworks inspired by the national myth. All the rooms are spacious suites with espresso machines, free wi-fi, SIM cards and iPods, some with small kitchens; ask for a room at the back if you're worried about noise from the nearby expressway. There's a fusion restaurant, fitness centre, long, narrow "dipping" pool and shuttle service to the Skytrain, plus a special concierge, who DJs in the ultra-hip *Sita Bar* and dispenses the lowdown on Bangkok parties and happenings. **❾**

Downtown: south of Thanon Rama IV

South of Thanon Rama IV, the area sometimes known as **Bangrak** contains a full cross-section of places to stay. Tucked away at its eastern edge, there are a few decent, cheap guest houses in the small travellers' ghetto of **Soi ̀ Ngam Duphli** and adjacent Soi Sri Bamphen and Soi Saphan Khu. The neighbourhood is often traffic-clogged and occasionally seedy, but is close to Lumphini Park and subway station and handy for Suvarnabhumi Airport.

Some medium-range places are scattered between Thanon Rama IV and the river, ranging from the notorious (the *Malaysia*) to the sedate (the *Bangkok Christian Guest House*). Bangrak also lays claim to the capital's biggest selection of top hotels, which are among the most opulent in the world. Traversed by the Skytrain, this area is especially good for eating and for gay and straight nightlife, mostly near the east end of **Thanon Silom** (around which several gay-friendly hotels are scattered), and has its fair share of interesting shops. Staying by the river itself in the atmospheric area around **Thanon Charoen Krung**, also known as **New Road**, has the added advantage of easy access to express boats.

Accommodation in this area is marked on the **map** on p.114, unless otherwise noted. For **public transport** details, see the box on p.115.

Inexpensive

ETC Guest House 5/3 Soi Ngam Duphli ☏ 02 287 1477–8, ⓦ www.etc.co.th. Lumphini subway. Above a branch of the recommended travel agent of the same name, and very handy for Thanon Rama IV, though consequently a little noisy. Helpful and very clean, catering mainly to Japanese travellers. Rooms come with fans and are further cooled by air-conditioning in the corridors; hot-water bathrooms are either shared or en suite. Breakfast is included and free internet and wi-fi are available. **❷**

New Road Guest House 1216/1 Thanon Charoen Krung, between sois 34 and 36 ☏02 630 6994–8, ⓦwww.jysktravel.com. N2 Wat Muang Kae express boats. Thai headquarters of Danish backpacker travel agent and tour operator Jysk, offering a wide choice of accommodation around a courtyard off New Rd, as well as interesting canal tours (see p.95). There are ten-bunk dorms (with air-con planned) and basic bunk-bedded twins sharing bathrooms, as well as free hammocks on the roof. En-suite rooms, some with air-con and cable TV, sport attractive wooden floors, mini-bars, Thai decorative touches and well-equipped, hot-water bathrooms. Guests hang out in the restaurant, the sociable bar with pool table and the DVD room; internet access and free baggage storage are available, as well as showers for guests with an evening departure. Dorms from B90, fan ❷–❸, air-con ❺

Sala Thai Daily Mansion 15 Soi Saphan Khu ☏02 287 1436. Lumphini subway. The pick of the area, at the end of a quiet, shaded alley off Soi Saphan Khu, near Soi Sri Bamphen. A clean and efficiently run place, with bright, modern rooms with wall fans, sharing hot- and cold-water bathrooms, and a large, leafy roof garden. Good rates for single rooms. Fan ❸, air-con ❹

Moderate

Baan Saladaeng 69/2 Soi 3, Thanon Saladaeng ☏02 636 3038, ⓦwww .baansaladaeng.com. BTS Sala Daeng. On a tiny, central alley, this chic designer guest house offers nine individually styled rooms, such as the Pop Art Mania Room and the Moroccan Suite, some with outdoor shower/bath and terrace. Air-con, rain showers, mini-bars, cable TV, comfy beds and free wi-fi throughout. No children. Continental breakfast included. ❺–❼

Bangkok Christian Guest House 123 Soi 2, Thanon Saladaeng ☏02 233 6303, ⓦwww .bcgh.org. BTS Sala Daeng. Well-run, orderly missionary house in a shiny, modern building overlooking a neat garden, where plain but immaculately kept rooms come with air-con and hot-water bathrooms. Decent rates for singles, and plenty of family rooms. Breakfast included. ❻

Intown Residence 1086/6 Thanon Charoen Krung ☏02 639 0960–2, ⓦwww.tarad.com /intownbkk. N3 Si Phraya express boats. Clean, welcoming, rather old-fashioned and very good-value Thai-Chinese hotel with a coffee shop, where most bedrooms are set back from the noisy main road. There's a wide variety of comfortable, old and new rooms, in plain or slightly chintzy styles, all with air-con, hot-water bathrooms, mini-bars and satellite TVs. Good weekly and monthly discounts available. ❹

Lub.d 4 Thanon Decho ☏02 634 7999, ⓦwww .lubd.com. BTS Chong Nonsi. Buzzing, upmarket hostel with air-con and hot water throughout and an industrial feel to the stylishly lit decor. This crisp modernity extends to the bedrooms, among which the dorms (some women-only) and the cheaper, bunk-bedded private rooms share large bathroom areas, while the top-of-the-range en-suite doubles boast TVs. There's wi-fi throughout, a popular bar and café, a travel agency, washing machines, storage facilities and free internet terminals, but no kitchen. Discounts in the private rooms for single travellers. Dorms B520–750 (towels extra), rooms ❺–❻

Malaysia Hotel 54 Soi Ngam Duphli ☏02 679 7127–36, ⓦwww.malaysiahotelbkk.com. Lumphini subway. Once a travellers' legend famous for its compendious noticeboard, now better known for its seedy 24hr coffeeshop and massage parlour. The accommodation itself is reasonable value though: the rooms are large and have air-con, mini-bars and hot-water bathrooms; some have cable TV. There's a swimming pool (B50 per day for non-guests) and internet access. Gay-friendly. ❹

Penguin House 27/23 Soi Sri Bamphen ☏02 679 9991. Lumphini subway. Modern block with a ground-floor café, wi-fi and large, reasonably attractive rooms above, featuring air-con, hot water, cable TV and fridges; ask for one away from the busy road. Discounted monthly rates available. ❹

Urban House 35/13 Soi Yommarat, Thanon Saladaeng ☏02 636 3244 or 081 492 7778, ⓦwww.urbanh.com. BTS Sala Daeng. On a quiet but very central sub-soi, this modern, cubist building is more impressive from outside than in, but the six rooms are smart, bright and well equipped, done out in browns and creams. Air-con, hot water, fridges and cable TV in all rooms, small kitchens in half of them. Free internet and wi-fi. No children under 10. Light breakfast included. ❺

Woodlands Inn 1158/5–7 Soi 32, Thanon Charoen Krung ☏02 235 3894, ⓦwww .woodlandsinn.org. N3 Si Phraya express boats. Simple but recently refurbished and well-run hotel next to the GPO. Under Indian management, which will appeal to world travellers who are homesick for the subcontinent. All rooms have air-con, cable TV and hot-water bathrooms, and there's a good-value South Indian restaurant on the ground floor, where complimentary American breakfast is served. ❹

YWCA 13 Thanon Sathorn Tai ☏02 287 3136, ⓦwww.ywcabangkok.com. Lumphini subway. Reliable, low-rise accommodation for women in neat standard or bright, spacious deluxe rooms, all with air-con and hot water. Decent reductions for singles and deeply discounted long-term rates. ❺

Expensive

🏃 **Bangkok Marriott Resort** 257 Thanon Charoennakorn ☏02 476 0022, ⓦwww .marriott.com. A luxury retreat from the frenetic city centre, well to the south on the Thonburi bank (see map, p.123), but connected to Taksin Bridge (for the Skytrain and Chao Phraya express boats), 10min away, by hotel ferries every 15min. Arrayed around a highly appealing, landscaped swimming pool, the tranquil, riverside gardens are filled with birdsong, while the stylish and spacious bedrooms come with varnished hardwood floors and balconies. There's a fitness centre, a branch of the classy Mandara Spas, and among a wide choice of food outlets, a good Japanese teppanyaki house and a bakery-café. ❾

Dusit Thani Hotel 946 Thanon Rama IV, on the corner of Thanon Silom ☏02 200 9000, ⓦwww .dusit.com. BTS Sala Daeng & Silom subway. Elegant, centrally placed top-class hotel, geared for both business and leisure, with very high standards of service. It's famous for its eight restaurants, including *Thien Duong* (see p.183) and the French *D'Sens*, which has some spectacular top-floor views. ❾

The Heritage Baan Silom 659 Soi 19, Thanon Silom ☏02 236 8388, ⓦwww.theheritage hotels.com. Just off Silom in a shopping arcade, the colonial-style facade of this new hotel doesn't prepare you for the interior's striking contemporary design, mostly in black and cream. All bedrooms enjoy rain

showers, mini-bars and turn-down service; despite the name, "Studio" rooms are fairly spacious, while "Deluxe" have balconies and "Superior" bathtubs. There's a restaurant and free internet access, but no pool. ❽

Ibrik Resort in the City 235/16 Thanon Sathorn Tai ☏02 211 3470, ⓦwww.ibrikresort.com. BTS Surasak. Downtown copy of the Thonburi boutique hotel (see p.165), also with just three rooms. Slightly off the beaten track, but near the Expressway and handy for the BTS. ❽

La Residence 173/8–9 Thanon Suriwong ☏02 266 5400–1, ⓦwww.laresidencebangkok.com. BTS Chong Nonsi. A small, intimate boutique hotel where the tasteful, individually decorated bedrooms – including proper single rooms at proper single rates – stretch to mini-bars, safes and cable TV. Continental breakfast included. ❼

Lebua 1055 Thanon Silom ☏02 624 9999, ⓦwww.lebua.com. Occupying part of the landmark State Tower on the corner of Thanon Charoen Krung, Lebua offers extravagant suites with kitchen areas, decorated in a restrained contemporary style; it's worth paying US$40 extra for "Riverview", for the lofty vista from the balcony, over 200m above the Chao Phraya. Staff are very solicitous and there's a gym and outdoor pool on Floor 13. Outlets include *Breeze*, for contemporary Asian seafood, and, beneath the golden, Neoclassical dome on the top floor, Italian food at *Mezzaluna* and Mediterranean *Sirocco*, the world's highest al fresco restaurant; also up here are *Sky Bar* and *Distil* (see p.189). ❾

Luxx 6/11 Thanon Decho ☏02 635 8800, ⓦwww.staywithluxx.com. BTS Chong Nonsi. Welcoming boutique hotel offering a good dose of contemporary style at reasonable prices (with a new, larger branch with a pool, XL, about to open on Soi Lang Suan). Decorated in white, grey and natural teak, the rooms feature DVD players, free wi-fi and cute wooden baths surmounted by rain showers. Breakfast included. ❼

Metropolitan 27 Thanon Sathorn Tai ☏02 625 3333, ⓦwww.metropolitan.como.bz. Lumphini subway. The height of chic, minimalist urban living, where the rooms are stylishly decorated in dark wood, creamy Portuguese limestone and lotus-themed contemporary artworks. There's a very seductive pool, a fine spa, a well-equipped fitness centre, an excellent restaurant, *Cy'an* (see p.181) and a fiercely hip bar. ❾

Millennium Hilton 123 Thanon Charoennakorn ☏02 442 2000, ⓦwww.hilton.com. Impressive new hotel with a twelve-storey lobby atrium, decorated throughout in modern Asian style. Its fourth-floor saltwater pool, fringed with white sand, is known as The Beach. There's also a secluded spa and a top-floor bar, *Three Sixty*, 130m above the river with huge picture windows, while every restaurant also boasts views of the Chao Phraya: Cantonese *Yuan*, with good-value lunchtime dim sum, a steakhouse and an international buffet with its own refrigerated cheese room. On the Thonburi bank, with shuttle boats across to River City shopping centre and Taksin Bridge. ❾

Montien Hotel 54 Thanon Surawongse, on the corner of Rama IV ☏02 233 7060–9, ⓦwww.montien.com. Grand, airy and solicitous luxury hotel, with a strongly Thai character. It's had a recent face-lift but retains a quaintly old-fashioned demeanour – astrologers on the mezzanine, Latin and ballroom dancing in the nightclub and live muzak in the lobby. ❾

Oriental Hotel 48 Oriental Avenue, off Thanon Charoen Krung ☏02 659 9000, ⓦwww.mandarinoriental.com. N1 Tha Oriental express boats. One of the world's best, this effortlessly stylish riverside hotel boasts immaculate standards of service. ❾

🏃 **Peninsula Bangkok** 333 Thanon Charoennakorn ☏02 861 2888, ⓦwww.peninsula.com. Superb top-class hotel to rival the *Oriental* across the river. Service is flawless, the ultra-luxurious decor stylishly blends traditional Western and Asian design, and every room has a panoramic view of the Chao Phraya River. The lovely riverside gardens shelter a three-tiered pool, a beautiful spa run by ESPA, a fitness centre and tennis courts. On the Thonburi bank, with shuttle boats across to a reception area by the *Shangri-La Hotel* off Thanon Charoen Krung and down to Taksin Bridge. ❾

Rose Hotel 118 Thanon Suriwong ☏02 266 8268–72, ⓦwww.rosehotelbkk.com. BTS Sala Daeng. Set back from the main road but very handy for the city's nightlife, this 30-year-old hotel has been cleverly refurbished: the compact rooms (all with bathtubs) now boast a simple but stylish,

retro look, in keeping with the age of the place. Suites and the ground-floor public rooms, where continental breakfast (included in the price) is served, are more elegant again, and there's a beautiful, new swimming pool at the back. Frequent discounts. ❼

Sofitel Silom 188 Thanon Silom ☏02 238 1991, ⓦwww.sofitel.com. BTS Chong Nonsi. Towards the quieter end of Thanon Silom, a clever renovation combines contemporary Asian artworks and furnishings with understated French elegance. A wine bar and Mediterranean and rooftop Chinese restaurants, as well as a fitness club and small pool, complete the picture. ❾

🏃 **Sukhothai** 13/3 Thanon Sathorn Tai ☏02 344 8888, ⓦwww.sukhothai.com. Lumphini subway. The most elegant of Bangkok's top hotels, its decor inspired by the walled city of Sukhothai: low-rise accommodation, as well as a beautiful garden spa, all coolly furnished in silks, teak and granite. Service is of the highest standard and the architecture makes the most of the views of the surrounding six acres of gardens, lotus ponds and pools dotted with statuary. Health club, 25m infinity pool, squash and tennis courts, and excellent restaurants including *Celadon* (see p.180). ❾

Swiss Lodge 3 Thanon Convent ☏02 233 5345, ⓦwww.swisslodge.com. BTS Sala Daeng. Swish, friendly, good-value, boutique hotel, with high standards of service, just off Thanon Silom and ideally placed for business and nightlife. The tiny terrace swimming pool confirms the national stereotypes of neatness and clever design, while the *Three on Convent* restaurant branches out into North Californian wine-country cuisine. ❽

Tarntawan Place Hotel 119/5–10 Thanon Suriwong ☏02 238 2620, ⓦwww.tarntawan.com. Set back from the main road, a pretty, flower-strewn lobby announces this gracious, well-run, gay-friendly hotel. The decent-sized, well-equipped rooms are pleasant and homely, with free wi-fi. Guests also receive free breakfast and internet access, as well as reduced-price entry to a gym and swimming pool on Soi Thaniya. Discounted fortnightly and monthly rates; in the off-season, excellent-value three-night packages. ❼

Thanon Sukhumvit

Staying on **Thanon Sukhumvit** puts you within walking distance of a huge choice of restaurants, bars, clubs and shops, but you're a long way from the main Ratanakosin sights, and the volume of traffic on Sukhumvit itself means travelling by bus or taxi across town can take ages; access to downtown areas, however, is made easy by Sukhumvit's Skytrain and subway stops.

This isn't the place to come if you're on a tight budget, but Sukhumvit has a couple of exceptional mid-priced guest houses; the area's four- and five-star hotels tend to be oriented towards business travellers, though facilities are good and the downtown views from high-rise rooms a plus. The most central accommodation is between and along sois (side roads) 1 to 21; hotels further east are handy for Ekamai Eastern Bus Station and, traffic permitting, can be quite convenient for **Suvarnabhumi Airport**, but are far from the main shopping and eating hubs. Even in central Sukhumvit, many of the sois are refreshingly quiet, even leafy; transport down the longer sois is provided by motorbike–taxi drivers who wait at the soi's mouth, clad in numbered waistcoats.

For details of **public transport** in the Sukhumvit area see the box on p.121. Sukhumvit accommodation is marked on the **map** on p.120.

Central Sukhumvit

Amari Boulevard Hotel Soi 5 ☎ 02 255 2930, ⓦ www.amari.com. BTS Nana. Rooms in the deluxe category and above at this modernised four-star tourist hotel enjoy fine views of the Bangkok skyline and have either wi-fi or broadband. The attractive sixth-floor rooftop swimming pool and garden terrace becomes the Thai-food restaurant *Season* in the evenings. ❽–❾

The Atlanta At the far southern end of Soi 2 ☎ 02 252 1650, ⓦ www.theatlantahotel.bizland.com. BTS Nana. A Bangkok institution, this classic, five-storey budget hotel was built in 1952 around a famously photogenic Art Deco-style lobby and continues to emphasize an old-fashioned hospitality. It offers some of the cheapest accommodation on Sukhumvit: rooms are simple and some are pretty scruffy, though they are all en suite and some have air-con while others have small balconies. There's a swimming pool, wi-fi and internet access and a left-luggage facility. The hotel restaurant serves an extensive Thai menu, including lots of vegetarian dishes, and shows classic movies set in Asia. ❹

The Eugenia 267, off Soi 31 ☎ 02 259 9017, ⓦ www.theeugenia.com. BTS Phrom Pong (15min walk or free hotel transfer). This cosy little Relais & Chateaux hideaway of just twelve rooms recreates an ambience of old-fashioned Indochinese charm with four-poster beds, freestanding copper bathtubs,

mellow colour schemes and a bijou courtyard pool. ❾

Grand Business Inn 2/4-2/11 Soi 11 ☎ 02 254 7981, ⓦ www.grandbusinessinn.net. BTS Nana. Popular, good-value and very central mid-range hotel offering 127 large, comfortable, standard-issue air-con rooms, all with bathtubs, cable TV and broadband access. Advance reservations essential. ❻

PS Guesthouse 26/1 Soi 8 ☎ 02 255 2309, ⓔ psguesthouse@hotmail.com. BTS Nana. This small, calm, friendly guesthouse offers huge, airy, well-equipped rooms, each with air-con, TV, safe, fridge, free tea and coffee and refreshingly green, plant-screened balconies. Pay a little extra for in-room kitchen facilities. Complimentary wi-fi in the lobby and some rooms. ❺

Sheraton Grande Sukhumvit Between sois 12 and 14 ☎ 02 649 8888, ⓦ www.sheratongrandesukhumvit.com. BTS Asok. Deluxe accommodation in large, stylishly understated rooms, all of which offer fine views of the cityscape. Facilities include a gorgeous free-form swimming pool and tropical garden on the ninth floor, a spa, the trendy *Basil* Thai restaurant, and the *Living Room* bar, which is famous for its jazz singers. ❾

Suk 11 Behind the 7–Eleven store at 1/3 Soi 11 ☎ 02 253 5927, ⓦ www.suk11.com. BTS Nana. One of the most unusual little hotels in Bangkok, this is also the most backpacker-orientated guest house in the area. The interior of the apparently

▲ Suk 11 guest house, Thanon Sukhumvit

ordinary apartment-style building has been transformed to resemble a village of traditional wooden houses, accessed by a dimly lit plankway that winds past a variety of guest rooms, terraces and lounging areas. The rooms are simple but comfortable, all air-con and some en suite. It's well run and thoughtfully appointed, keeps informative noticeboards, provides free breakfast, has wi-fi and washing machines, stores left luggage (B20 per day), and accepts advance reservations via the website. **④**–**⑤**

Eastern Sukhumvit

Imm Fusion 1594/50 Thanon Sukhumvit, between sois 48 and 50 ☎02 331 5555, ⓦwww.immhotel.com. BTS On Nut (30m west from exit 2). Step through the entrance of this attractive and welcoming mid-range hotel and you're in another world, a Moroccan themed one done out in rich earthy colours, wrought ironwork, pretty tiles and plenty of Moorish arches. Rooms are comfortable and equally tasteful, and come with air-con, TV, safe and wi-fi. There's a gorgeous indoor pool, spa and restaurant and the staff are charming. **⑥**

Rex Hotel Between sois 32 and 34 (opposite Soi 49) ☎02 259 0106. BTS Thong Lo (300m west from exit 2). The best value accommodation close to the Eastern Bus Terminal (one stop on the BTS), this old-fashioned hotel is comfortable and run with an old-world graciousness. A rooftop pool and a restaurant complement the spacious air-con rooms and rates include breakfast. **⑤**

Sukhumvit On-Nut Guesthouse 125/2 Sukhumvit Soi 89 ☎02 742 4525 ext 2, ⓦwww.bangkok -guesthouse.com. BTS On Nut (12min walk east from exit 3, or a B20 motorcycle taxi ride from the mouth of adjacent Soi 81). This backpacker-oriented guest house shares premises with a small language school on a quiet residential soi in a low-rise, unpretentious neighbourhood and makes for a calm introduction to the city. Many rooms have air-con but all share bathrooms; options range from four- and eight-bed fan and air-con dorms (from B169 per bed) to doubles with private balconies and a mattress on the floor; facilities include a café and internet access. **④**

⑩

Eating

angkok boasts an astonishing fifty thousand places to eat – that's almost one for every hundred citizens – ranging from makeshift streetside noodle shops to the most elegant of restaurants. Despite this glut, an awful lot of visitors venture no further than the front doorstep of their guest house, preferring the dining room's ersatz Thai or Western dishes to the more adventurous food to be found in even the most touristy accommodation areas.

Thai restaurants of all types are found all over the city. The best **gourmet Thai** restaurants operate from the downtown districts around Thanon Sukhumvit and Thanon Silom, proffering wonderful royal, traditional and regional cuisines that definitely merit an occasional splurge – though even here, you'd have to push the boat out to spend more than B500 per person. Over in Banglamphu, Thanon Phra Arthit is known for its idiosyncratic little restaurant-bars angled at young Thai diners. At the other end of the scale, as well as the **food courts** of shopping centres and department stores listed below, which usually run on a coupon system, there are the **night markets** and **street stalls**, where you can generally get a lip-smacking feast for around B100 or less. These are so numerous in Bangkok that we can only flag a few promising areas – but wherever you're staying, you'll hardly have to walk a block in any direction before encountering something appealing.

For the non-Thai cuisines, Chinatown naturally rates as the most authentic district for pure **Chinese** food; likewise neighbouring Pahurat, the capital's Indian enclave, is best for unadulterated **Indian** dishes, while there's a sprinkling of Indian and (mostly southern Thai) **Muslim** restaurants around Silom's Maha Uma Devi Temple and nearby Thanon Charoen Krung. Sukhumvit's Soi 3 is a hub for **Middle Eastern** cafés, complete with hookah pipes at the outdoor tables; and good, comparatively cheap **Japanese** restaurants are concentrated on Soi Thaniya, at the east end of Thanon Silom. The place to head for inexpensive, Western, **travellers' food** – from herbal teas and hamburgers to muesli – as well as a hearty range of veggie options, is Thanon Khao San; standards vary, but there are some definite gems among the blander establishments. Meanwhile, downtown Bangkok has a good quota of **coffee shops**, including several branches of local company *Black Canyon*.

Few Thais are **vegetarian**, but in the capital it's fairly easy to find specially concocted Thai and Western veggie dishes, usually at tourist-oriented restaurants. Even at the plainest street stall, it's usually possible to persuade the cook

The glorious range and flavours of **Thai cuisine** are discussed in our colour insert. For a detailed **food and drink glossary**, turn to p.252. Information about Thai **cookery courses** is given on p.48.

How to eat Thai food

Thai food is eaten with a **fork** (left hand) and a **spoon** (right hand); there is no need for a knife as food is served in bite-sized chunks, which are forked onto the spoon and fed into the mouth. Cutlery is often delivered to the table wrapped in a perplexingly tiny pink napkin: Thais use this, not for their lap, but to give their fork, spoon and plate an extra wipe-down before they eat. Steamed **rice** (*khao*) is served with most meals, and indeed the most commonly heard phrase for "to eat" is *kin khao* (literally, "eat rice"). **Chopsticks** are provided only for noodle dishes.

Instead of being divided into courses, a Thai meal – even the soup – is served all at once, and shared communally, so that complementary taste combinations can be enjoyed. The more people, the more taste and texture sensations; if there are only two of you, it's best to order at least three dishes, plus your own individual plates of steamed rice, while three diners would order at least four dishes and so on. Only put a serving of one dish on your rice plate at each time, and then only one or two spoonfuls.

Bland food is anathema to Thais, and restaurant tables come decked out with a **condiment** set featuring the four basic flavours, salty, sour, sweet and spicy: usually fish sauce with chopped chillies; vinegar with chopped chillies; sugar; and dried and ground red chillies – and often extra ground peanuts and a bottle of chilli ketchup as well. If you do bite into a chilli, the way to combat the searing heat is to take a mouthful of plain rice and/or milk – swigging water just exacerbates the sensation.

to rustle up a vegetable-only fried rice or noodle dish. If you're **vegan** you'll need to make clear you don't want egg when you order, as eggs get used a lot; cheese and other dairy produce don't feature at all in Thai cuisine.

Hygiene is a consideration when eating anywhere in Bangkok, but being too cautious means you'll end up spending a lot of money and missing out on some real treats – you can be pretty sure any noodle stall or curry shop that's permanently packed with customers is a safe bet. Foods that are generally considered high risk include salads, shellfish, raw or undercooked meat, fish or eggs, ice and ice cream. If you're really concerned about health standards you could stick to restaurants and foodstalls displaying a "Clean Food Good Taste" sign, part of a food sanitation project set up by the Ministry of Public Health, TAT and the Ministry of Interior. Thais don't drink **water** straight from the tap and nor should you: plastic bottles of drinking water (*nam plao*) are sold everywhere for around B10, as well as the usual multinational panoply of soft drinks.

In the more expensive restaurants listed below you may have to pay a ten percent **service charge** and seven percent government tax. Most restaurants in Bangkok are open every day for lunch and dinner; we've noted exceptions in the listings below.

Banglamphu and the Democracy Monument area

Copycat entrepreneurship means Khao San is stacked full of **backpacker restaurants** serving near-identical Western and (mostly) watered-down Thai food; there's even a lane, one block east, parallel to Thanon Tanao (behind *Burger King*), dominated by **vegetarian** cafés, following a trend started by *May Kaidee*. Hot-food stalls selling very cheap **night-market** snacks operate until the early hours. Things are more varied down on Thanon Phra Arthit, with its arty little **café-restaurants** favoured by Thammasat University students, while the riverside places, on Phra Arthit and further north off Thanon Samsen and in

Thewet, tend to be best for **seafood** with a view. For the real old-fashioned Thai taste, browse southern Thanon Tanao and its network of sois south of Democracy and west of Sao Ching Cha (the Giant Swing), where traditional shophouses have been selling **specialist sweets and savouries** for generations; none have signs or numbers in English. For restaurant locations see the map on p.76 and for public transport details see the box on p.78.

Around Khao San

Chabad House 96 Thanon Ram Bhuttri ⓦ www .jewishthailand.com. N13 Tha Phra Arthit express boats. A little piece of Israel, run by the Bangkok branch of the Jewish outreach Chabad-Lubavitch movement. Serves a well-priced kosher menu (B75–150) of falafel, baba ghanoush, schnitzels, hummus, salads and Jewish breads in air-conditioned calm, on the ground floor of a long-established community centre and guest house. Sun–Thurs 10am–10pm, Fri 10am–3pm.

Lotash Seed Thanon Ram Bhuttri. N13 Tha Phra Arthit express boats. A tiny pocket of Buddhist calm in an increasingly frantic street, this cosy restaurant has understated lotus imagery and a menu full of delicious Thai classics and one-offs, plus cocktails and wines. The roll-your-own *miang* stuffed tea-leaf starters are a

▲ Food stalls at Chatuchak Weekend Market

delicious opener and there are great curries, plus *yam taleh* (seafood salad) and a long vegetarian menu. Mains B80–150.

🏃 **May Kaidee East off Thanon Tanao** ⓦwww.maykaidee.com. **N13 Tha Phra Arthit express boats.** Simple, neighbourhood Thai vegetarian restaurant, with two outlets on opposite sides of the soi, that still serves some of the best veggie food in Banglamphu despite having spawned a row of competitors on the same alley. Try the tasty green curry with coconut, the Vietnamese-style veggie spring rolls or the sticky black-rice pudding. May Kaidee herself also runs vegetarian cookery classes (see p.49). Most dishes B60–70.

Popaing Soi Ram Bhuttri. N13 Tha Phra Arthit express boats. Popular place for cheap seafood: mussels and cockles cost just B50 per plate, squid B70, or you can get a large helping of seafood noodles for B100. Eat in the low-rent restaurant area or on the street beneath the temple wall.

Prakorb House Thanon Khao San. N13 Tha Phra Arthit express boats. Archetypal travellers' haven, with only a few tables and an emphasis on wholesome ingredients. Herbal teas, mango shakes, delicious pumpkin curry, and more (B50–90).

Sunset Bar Sunset St, 197–201 Thanon Khao San. N13 Tha Phra Arthit express boats. Follow the passageway behind *Sabai Bar* as it opens out into a tranquil, shrub-filled courtyard occupied by this coffee shop and restaurant – the perfect place to escape the Khao San hustle with a mid-priced juice or snack. The courtyard's handsome, mango-coloured, 1907 villa is another enticement: a discreet branch of Starbucks, with sofas, occupies its ground floor.

Tom Yam Kung Thanon Khao San ⓦwww .tomyumkungkhaosan.com. **N13 Tha Phra Arthit express boats.** Occasionally mouth-blastingly authentic Thai food served in the courtyard of a beautiful early twentieth-century villa hidden behind Khao San's modern clutter. The menu (B115–300) includes spicy fried catfish, coconut-palm curry with tofu and shrimps in sugar cane. Well-priced cocktails, draught beer and a small wine list.

Phra Arthit area

🏃 **Aquatini Navalai River Resort, 45/1 Thanon Phra Arthit** ⓦwww.navalai.com. **N13 Tha Phra Arthit express boats.** Occupying a nice wooden deck in a perfect breezy riverfront spot beside the express-boat pier (even better after sunset when the boats stop running), this hotel restaurant does exceptionally good mid-priced Thai food. Seafood's a speciality: the deep-fried ruby fish served with cashew nuts and bell peppers is very good, and their tangy coconut milk *tom kha kai* soup is especially delicious. Most seafood mains B200–300.

🏃 **Hemlock 56 Thanon Phra Arthit** ☎02 282 7507. **N13 Tha Phra Arthit express boats.** Small, stylish, air-con restaurant that's very popular with students and young Thai couples. Offers a long and interesting menu of unusual Thai dishes (mostly about B80), including banana-flower salad, coconut and mushroom curry, grand lotus rice and various *laap* and fish dishes. The traditional *miang* starters (shiny green wild tea leaves filled with chopped vegetables, fish and meat) are also very tasty, and there's a good vegetarian selection. Mon–Sat 5pm– midnight; worth reserving a table on Friday and Saturday nights.

Roti Mataba 136 Thanon Phra Arthit. N13 Tha Phra Arthit express boats. Famous outlet for the ever-popular fried Indian breads, or rotis, served here in lots of sweet and savoury varieties, including with vegetable and meat curries, and with bananas and condensed milk (from B10). Mon–Sat 8.30am–10pm.

Thanon Samsen and Thewet

In Love 2/1 Thanon Krung Kasem. N15 Tha Thewet express boats. Popular place for good Thai seafood – and riverine breezes – right next to the express-boat pier, with decent Chao Phraya views, an airy upstairs terrace, and a huge menu including baked cotton-fish in mango sauce, steamed sea bass with lime and chilli, and *tom yam kung*. Most dishes B160–300.

Kaloang Beside the river at the far western end of Thanon Sri Ayutthaya. N15 Tha Thewet express boats. Flamboyant service and excellent seafood attracts an almost exclusively Thai clientele to this open-air riverside restaurant. Dishes worth sampling include the fried rolled shrimps served with a sweet dip, the roast squid cooked in a piquant sauce and the steamed butter fish (mains B150–300).

Kinlom Chom Saphan Riverside end of Thanon Samsen Soi 3 ⓦwww.khinlomchomsaphan.com. **N14 Tha Saphan Rama VIII express boats.** This sprawling, waterside seafood restaurant

Thai food is now hugely popular in the West, but nothing, of course, beats coming to Thailand to experience the full range of subtle and fiery flavours, constructed from the freshest ingredients. Four fundamental tastes are identified in Thai cuisine – spiciness, sourness, saltiness and sweetness. Lemon grass, basil, coriander, galangal, chilli, garlic, lime juice, coconut milk and fermented fish sauce (used instead of salt) are just some of the distinctive components that bring these tastes to life.

Street food, Bangkok ▲

A bowl of *tom yam kung* ▼

Curries

Thai curries (**kaeng**) have as their foundation a variety of curry pastes, elaborate blends of herbs, spices, garlic, shallots and chilli peppers traditionally ground together with a pestle and mortar. The use of some of these spices, as well as of coconut cream, was imported from India long ago; curries without coconut cream are naturally less sweet and thinner, with the consistency of soups.

While some curries, such as *kaeng karii* (mild and yellow) and *kaeng matsaman* (literally "Muslim curry", with potatoes, peanuts and usually beef), still show their roots, others have been adapted into quintessentially Thai dishes, notably *kaeng khiaw wan* (sweet and green), *kaeng phet* (red and hot) and *kaeng phanaeng* (thick and savoury, with peanuts). *Kaeng som* generally contains vegetables and fish and takes its distinctive sourness from the addition of tamarind or, in the northeast, okra leaves. Traditionally eaten during the cool season, *kaeng liang* uses up gourds or other bland vegetables, but is made aromatic by the heat of peppercorns and shallots and the fragrance of basil leaves.

Soups

Thai soups (**tom**), an essential component of most shared meals, are eaten simultaneously with other dishes, not as a starter. They are often flavoured with the distinctive tang of lemon grass, kaffir lime leaves and galangal, and garnished with fresh coriander – and can be extremely hot, if the cook adds liberal handfuls of chillies to the pot. Two favourites are *tom kha kai,* a creamy coconut chicken soup; and *tom yam kung,* a hot and sour prawn soup without coconut milk. *Khao tom,* a starchy rice soup often eaten for breakfast, meets the approval of few Westerners, except as a traditional hangover cure.

Salads

One of the lesser-known delights of Thai cuisine is the **yam** or salad, which can often impart all four of the fundamental flavours in an unusual and refreshing harmony. *Yam* can be made in many permutations – with noodles, meat, seafood or vegetables – but at the heart of every variety is fresh lime juice and a fiery sprinkling of chopped chillies. As well as *som tam*, *laap* and *nam tok* (described overleaf in the box), salads to look out for include *yam som oh* (pomelo), *yam hua plee* (banana flowers) and *yam plaa duk foo* (deep-fried catfish).

Noodle and rice dishes

Thais eat **noodles** when Westerners would dig into a sandwich – for lunch or as a late-night snack. Sold on street stalls everywhere, they come in assorted varieties – including *kway tiaw* (made with rice flour) and *ba mii* (egg noodles), *sen yai* (wide) and *sen lek* (thin) – and get boiled up as soups (*nam*), doused in gravy (*rat na*) or stir-fried (*haeng*, "dry", or *phat*, "fried"). Most famous of noodle dishes is *kway tiaw phat thai* – usually abbreviated to **phat thai**, meaning "Thai fry-up" – a delicious mix of fried noodles, bean sprouts, egg, tofu and spring onions, sprinkled with ground peanuts and lime juice, and often spiked with tiny dried shrimps.

Fried **rice** (*khao phat*) is the other faithful standby that features on menus right across the country. Also popular are cheap, one-dish meals served on a bed of steamed rice, notably *khao kaeng* (with curry), *khao na pet* (with roast duck) and *khao muu daeng* (with red-roasted pork).

▲ Seafood salad and sticky rice in a rattan basket

▼ Bottles of fish sauce

Desserts

Desserts (**khanom**) don't really figure on most restaurant menus, though a few places offer bowls of *luk taan cheum*, a jellied concoction of lotus or palm seeds floating in a syrup scented with jasmine or other aromatic flowers. Coconut milk is a feature of most other desserts, notably delicious coconut ice cream; *khao niaw mamuang/thurian* (sticky rice with mango or durian); *khao niaw daeng*, sticky red rice mixed with coconut cream; *takoh*, which consists of squares of transparent jelly (jello) topped with coconut cream); and a royal Thai cuisine special of coconut custard (*sangkhayaa*) cooked inside a small pumpkin, whose flesh you can also eat.

Thai desserts ▲

Foodstall at Chatuchak Weekend Market ▼

Northeastern food

In Bangkok, northeastern food is the most prevalent of Thailand's several regional cuisines, partly due to the large numbers of migrants from the northeast (or Isaan) who work in the capital. Their staple food is **sticky rice** (*khao niaw*), which is more suited to the infertile lands of Isaan than the standard grain. Served in its own special rattan basket, it's usually eaten with the fingers – rolled up into small balls and dipped into chilli sauces. A classic combination is sticky rice with **som tam**, a spicy green-papaya salad with garlic, raw chillies, green beans, tomatoes, peanuts and dried shrimps (or fresh crab), and **kai yaang**, basted and barbecued chicken on a stick. Raw minced pork, beef or chicken is the basis of another popular Isaan dish, laap, a salad that's subtly flavoured with mint and lime. A similar northeastern salad is **nam tok**, featuring grilled beef or pork and roasted rice powder, which takes its name, "waterfall", from its refreshing blend of complex tastes.

boasts close-up views of the lyre-like Rama VIII Bridge and is always busy with a youngish Thai crowd. The predominantly seafood menu (B130–300) features everything from crab to grouper cooked in multiple ways, including with curry, garlic or sweet basil sauces, but never with MSG. As well as the usual complement of *tom yam* and *tom kha* soups, there are yam salads and meat options including stir-fried ostrich with herbs.

May Kaidee 2 33 Thanon Samsen, between the khlong and Soi 1 ⓦwww.maykaidee.com. N13 Tha Phra Arthit express boats. Air-con branch of Banglamphu's best loved Thai veggie restaurant and cooking school; see p.49.

see p.49.

South: Thanon Tanao and around

Gor Panit 431–433 Thanon Tanao, on the east side, directly opposite Soi Phraeng Phuton. Outstanding take-away coconut-laced sticky rice with mango (or banana) has been sold here since 1932. No English sign but look for the mango vendors outside, where you can choose your variety if you want. Open during the mango season only; June–Dec Mon–Sat 6.30am–8pm.

Kai Yang Boran 474–476 Thanon Tanao, immediately to the south of the Chao Poh Seua Chinese shrine (no English sign). Locally famous grilled chicken and *som tam* restaurant (with air-con). Daily 9am–8pm.

Nattaporn 94 Soi Phraeng Phuton, west off southern Thanon Tanao. This family has been specializing in its famous home-made fresh coconut ice cream for over sixty years, topping it with classic Thai condiments like sweetcorn, red beans and taro balls. They also do chocolate, coffee and ice-tea flavours. To find it, take the first left off Soi Phraeng Phuton and follow it round until you reach *Nattaporn*, on the corner of the next sub-soi. Mon–Sat 9am–4pm.

Padthai Thipsamai 313 Thanon Mahachai (no English sign), near Wat Rajnadda ⓦwww .thipsamai.com. The most famous *phat thai* in Bangkok, flash-fried by the same husband–and–wife team since 1966. The "extra" option is huge, comes with especially juicy prawns, and is wrapped in a translucent, paper-thin omelette. Best washed down with fresh coconut juice. Daily except alternate Wed, from 5.30pm.

Ratanakosin

The places reviewed below are especially handy for sightseers, but there are also plenty of street stalls around Tha Chang and a load of simple, studenty restaurants off the north end of Thanon Maharat near Thammasat University, as well as a decent restaurant at *Arun Residence* and a daytime café at *Aurum* (see p.163). See the map on p.58 for locations of the places listed below; for public transport details, see the box on p.57.

(see p.163). See the map on p.58 for locations of the places listed below; for public transport details, see the box on p.57.

Na Pralan Café Thanon Na Phra Lan. N9 Tha Chang express boats. This small, cheap café is ideally placed for refreshment after your tour of the Grand Palace. Popular with students, it occupies a quaint old air-con shophouse with battered, artsy decor. The menu, well thought out with some unusual twists, offers mostly Thai salads and one-dish meals with rice, and a range of ice creams, coffees, teas and beers. Mon–Sat 10.30am–10pm, Sun 10.30am–6pm.

Rub Ar Roon Opposite Wat Pho at 310–2 Thanon Maharat. N8 Tha Thien express boats. Among many open-fronted, century-old shophouses on this stretch, this cosy, congenial café used to be a dispensary and still has its original teak cabinets. The Thai food is varied and very reasonably priced, and there are sandwiches, espressos, Thai herbal teas and fruit shakes. Daily 8am–6pm.

Chinatown and Pahurat

Much of the fun of Chinatown dining is in the browsing of the night-time hot-food stalls that open up all along Thanon Yaowarat, around the mouth of Soi Issaranuphap (Yaowarat Soi 11) and along Soi Phadungdao; wherever there's a

Yellow-flag heaven for veggies

Every autumn, for nine days during the ninth lunar month (between late Sept and Nov), Thailand's Chinese community goes on a meat-free diet in order to mark the onset of the **Vegetarian Festival** (Ngan Kin Jeh), a sort of Taoist version of Lent. Though the Chinese citizens of Bangkok don't go in for acts of extreme self-mortification like their compatriots in south Thailand, they do celebrate the Vegetarian Festival with gusto. Some people choose to wear only white for the duration, all the temples throng with activity, and nearly every restaurant and foodstall in Chinatown turns vegetarian for the period, flying small yellow flags to show they are upholding the tradition and participating in what's essentially a nightly veggie food jamboree.

For vegetarian tourists this is a great time to be in town – just look for the yellow flag and you can be sure all dishes will be one hundred percent vegan. Soya substitutes are a popular feature on the vegetarian Chinese menu, so don't be surprised to find pink prawn-shaped objects floating in your noodle soup or unappetizingly realistic slices of fake duck. Many hotel restaurants also get in on the act during the festival, running special veggie promotions for a week or two.

crowd you'll be sure of a good feed. Pan Siam's *Good Eats: Chinatown* map, available from major bookshops, is also a great resource for the weirder local specialities.

The places listed below are marked on the map on p.86; for public transport details, see the box on p.85.

Chong Kee 84 Soi Sukon 1, near Wat Traimit. Hualamphong subway. Delicious and moreishly cheap pork satay and sweet toast. Tues–Sun 9.30am–7pm, Mon 9.30am–2pm.

Hua Seng Hong 371 Thanon Yaowarat. N5 Tha Rachawongse express boats. Braised goose feet is one of the specialities here, but more familiar alternatives include wonton noodle soup and stir-fried crab noodles. Dishes from B160.

Royal India Just off Thanon Chakraphet at 392/1. N6 Tha Saphan Phut express boats. Great dhal, perfect parathas and famously good north Indian curries (from B90) served in a dark little café in the heart of Bangkok's most Punjabi of neighbourhoods to an almost exclusively South Asian clientele.

S&P Next to Sala Chalermkrung Theatre and Old Siam Plaza, Thanon Triphet/Charoen Krung intersection. N6 Tha Saphan Phut express boats. Moccachino frosts, blueberry smoothies (B70), iced fruit teas and various cakes all help make this chain restaurant a good place to cool down during a Chinatown circuit. It's hardly haute cuisine, but there's air-con and it's comfy.

Shangri-La 306 Thanon Yaowarat (cnr of Thanon Rajawong). N5 Tha Rachawongse express boats. Cavernous banquet-hall serving Cantonese classics (B100–1000), including lots of seafood, and lunchtime dim sum. Very popular, especially for family gatherings.

T&K (Toi & Kid's Seafood) 49 Soi Phadungdao, just off Thanon Yaowarat. N5 Tha Rachawongse express boats or Hualamphong subway (15min walk from either). Known for their barbecued seafood, with everything from prawns (B150 a serving) to oysters (B30 each) on offer. Eat at streetside tables or inside with air-con. Daily 4.30pm–2am.

White Orchid Hotel 409–421 Thanon Yaowarat. N5 Tha Rachawongse express boats or Hualamphong subway (15min walk from either). Recommended for its dim sum, with bamboo baskets of prawn dumplings, spicy spare ribs, stuffed bean curd and the like, served in three different portion sizes at fairly high prices. Dim sum 11am–2pm & 5–10pm. All-you-can-eat lunchtime buffets also worth stopping by for.

Downtown: Around Siam Square and Thanon Ploenchit

In this area, there are also branches of *Taling Pling* (see p.183), on Floor 3, Central World Plaza (☎02 613 1360–1); *Jim Thompson's Café* (see p.181), on the ground floor of Central World Plaza (℡02 255 9813–4) and at Jim Thompson's House; and *Aoi* (see p.180), in the Siam Paragon shopping centre on Thanon Rama I (℡02 129 4348–50). See the map on p.108 for locations of the places listed below; for details of public transport to this area, see the box on p.107.

Bali 15/3 Soi Ruam Rudee ℡02 250 0711. BTS Ploen Chit. Top-notch, reasonably priced Indonesian food in a cosy nook, including plenty of options for veggies and authentic desserts. Blow out on the seven-course rijstaffel for B400 or restrain yourself with the excellent four-course version for B260. Closed Sun.

Curries & More 63/3 Soi Ruam Rudee ℡02 253 5408–9. BTS Ploen Chit. And a whole lot more…this offshoot of Baan Khanitha (see p.183) offers something for everyone, including European-style fish, steaks and pasta, as well as curries from around the country (from B240). Try the delicious *chu chi khung nang*, deep-fried freshwater prawns with mild, Indian-style curry, or the prawn and pomelo salad. The modern, white-painted interior is hung with contemporary paintings, but the garden, surrounded by waterfalls and with water flowing over the transparent roof, is the place to be.

Food for Fun Floor 4, Siam Centre, Thanon Rama I. BTS Central. Highly enjoyable, inexpensive, new food court, decorated in startling primary colours. Lots of traditional Thai drinks and all manner of tasty one-dish meals – *khao man kai*, and *laap* and *som tam* from the Isaan counter – as well as pizza, pastas, Chinese and Indian food. Daily 10am–9pm.

Food Loft Floor 7, Central Chidlom, Thanon Ploenchit. BTS Chit Lom. Bangkok's top department store lays on a suitably upscale food court of all hues – Thai, Vietnamese, Malay, Chinese, Japanese, Indian, Italian (by Gianni – see below). Choose your own ingredients and watch them cooked in front of you, eat in the stylish, minimalist seating areas and then ponder whether you have room for a Thai or Western dessert. There's another, recently opened branch of *Food Loft* on Floor 7 of Zen department store in Central World Plaza.

Genji Swissôtel Nai Lert Park, 2 Thanon Witthayu ℡02 253 0123. BTS Ploen Chit. Excellent, genteel Japanese restaurant, serving authentic food in a contemporary setting overlooking the hotel's beautiful gardens, with a sushi bar, teppanyaki grill tables and private dining rooms.

Gianni 34/1 Soi Tonson, Thanon Ploenchit ℡02 252 1619, ⓦwww.giannibkk.com. BTS Chit Lom. One of Bangkok's best independent Italian restaurants, offering a sophisticated blend of traditional and modern in both its decor and food. Offerings include a belt- (and wallet-) busting tasting menu for B1290 and innovative pastas. Gianni also runs a couple of classy *Bar Italia* café-restaurants, on the ground floor of Gaysorn Plaza and on Floor 6 of Central World Plaza.

Home Kitchen (Khrua Nai Baan) 94 Soi Lang Suan ℡02 253 1888. Like an upcountry restaurant in the heart of the city, this congenial, unpretentious spot offers a choice between air-con and outdoor tables behind a huge open kitchen. On the inexpensive picture menu you're bound to find something delicious, among dozens of soups – how about the *kaeng liang*, with shrimp, pumpkin and mixed vegetables, for B150? – six kinds of *laap* and a huge array of seafood. There's a smarter new branch with the same menu two doors away. Daily 8am–midnight.

Inter 432/1–2 Soi 9, Siam Square. BTS Central. Honest, efficient Thai restaurant that's popular with students and shoppers, serving good one-dish meals from B50, as well as curries, soups, salads and seafood, in a no-frills, fluorescent-lit canteen atmosphere.

Ma Be Ba 93 Soi Lang Suan ℡02 254 9595. Lively, spacious, late-opening Italian restaurant, extravagantly decorated with mosaics in an authentic "grotto" style, which dishes up a good variety of antipasti, excellent pastas (B375 and upwards) and pizzas (in two sizes), and traditional main courses strong on seafood. Live music, mostly pop covers, country and Latin, Mon–Sat eve. Daily noon–3pm & 6pm–midnight.

Mah Boon Krong Shopping Centre corner of Rama I and Phrayathai roads. BTS Central. Two good food courts, operating on a coupon system, at the north end of MBK: the long-running area on Floor 6 is a great introduction to Thai food, with English names and pictures of a huge variety of tasty, cheap one-dish meals from all over the country displayed at the various stalls, as well as fresh juices and a wide range of desserts; the slightly upmarket version on Floor 5 is an international affair, spanning India, Italy, Vietnam, China and Japan, plus good homegrown cuisine at *Nara Thai*. Both daily 10am–10pm.

Once upon a Time 32 Soi 17, Thanon Phetchaburi ☎02 252 8629. The antique, rustic feel of this restaurant verges on the kitsch, but it's a genteel, quiet place, spread across several old wooden houses in a lush compound. And the Thai food, which includes traditional appetisers and desserts and lots of salads, is very good – try the omelette with sweet basil leaves and the pomelo salad. It's halfway down the soi directly opposite Panthip Plaza, on the right.

Pisces 36/6 Soi Kasemsan 1, Thanon Rama I. BTS National Stadium. Drawing plenty of custom from the local guest houses, a friendly, family-run restaurant, neat and colourful, serving a wide variety of breakfasts and cheap, tasty Thai food, with lots of vegetarian options. Daily 8am–1pm & 5–10pm.

Polo Fried Chicken (Kai Thawt Jay Kee Soi Polo) Soi Polo, Thanon Witthayu ☎02 655 8489. On the access road to the snobby polo club, Bangkok's most famous purveyor of the ultimate Thai peasant dish, fried chicken. All manner of northeastern dishes, including fish, sausages and loads of salads, fill out the menu, but it would be a bit perverse to come to this basic, air-con restaurant and not have the classic combo of finger-licking chicken (B80 for a half), *som tam* and sticky rice. Daily 7am–10pm.

Thang Long 82/5 Soi Lang Suan ☎02 251 3504. Excellent Vietnamese food, such as lemon grass fish (B215) in this stylish, minimalist and popular restaurant, all stone floors, ornamental plants and whitewashed walls.

Vanilla Brasserie Ground floor, Siam Paragon shopping centre ☎02 610 9383. BTS Central. Sophisticated restaurant, patisserie, crêperie, glacier and chocolatier that's a shrine to Western gourmet delights: delicious parma ham and mascarpone crêpes, salads and other main courses, spot-on desserts, and excellent teas and coffees. Their small *Vanilla Industry* café on Siam Square Soi 11 should have reopened by the time you read this. Daily 10am–11pm.

Zen Floor 6 (north end), Central World Plaza ☎02 255 6462; Floor 3, MBK shopping centre ☎02 620 9007–8; and Floor 4, Siam Centre ☎02 658 1183–4. Good-value Japanese restaurant with wacky and colourful modern wooden design and a sushi bar. Among a huge range of dishes, the complete meal sets (with pictures to help you choose) are filling and particularly good. The recently opened, slightly upmarket *Cucina Zen*, towards the south end of Floor 3, Central World Plaza (☎02 613 1580–1), promises contemporary Japanese cuisine.

Downtown: south of Thanon Rama IV

Two popular groupings of street stalls off Thanon Silom are worth noting: the top end of Thanon Convent and, away to the west opposite the Maha Uma Devi Temple, Soi 20. In this area, there are also branches of *Baan Khanitha* (see p.183) at 69 Thanon Sathorn Tai, at the corner of Soi Suan Phlu (☎02 675 4200–1), and *Zen* (see above), at 1/1 Thanon Convent (☎02 266 7150–1). The places listed below are marked on the map on p.114 unless otherwise stated; for public transport details, see the box on p.115.

Aoi 132/10–11 Soi 6, Thanon Silom ☎02 235 2321–2. BTS Sala Daeng. The best place in town for a Japanese blowout, justifiably popular with the expat community. Excellent authentic food and elegant decor. Good-value lunch sets (from B250) available and a superb sushi bar. Aoi also operates two *Ramentei* noodle restaurants in this area, at 11/1 Thanon Suriwong (☎02 235 4326) and 23/8–9 Soi Thaniya (☎02 234 8082).

Ban Chiang 14 Soi Srivieng, off Thanon Surasak, between Thanon Silom and Thanon Sathorn ☎02 236 7045. BTS Surasak. Fine, reasonably priced central and northeastern Thai cuisine in an elegant, surprisingly quiet wooden house with garden tables.

Celadon Sukhothai Hotel, 13/3 Thanon Sathorn Tai ☎02 344 8888. Consistently rated as one of the best hotel restaurants in Bangkok and a favourite with locals, serving outstanding traditional and contemporary

Thai food – try the banana-flower salad and the red curry with chicken rolls and salted egg – in an elegant setting surrounded by lotus ponds.

Chai Karr 312/3 Thanon Silom, opposite Holiday Inn ☎02 233 2549. Folksy, traditional-style wooden decor is the welcoming setting for a wide variety of well-prepared, modestly priced Thai and Chinese dishes, followed by home-made coconut ice cream. Closed Sun.

Cy'an Metropolitan Hotel, 27 Thanon Sathorn Tai ☎02 625 3388. Expensive but highly inventive cooking, fusing Asian and Mediterranean (especially North African) elements to produce strong, clean flavours, with great attention to detail. Charming service to go with it, in a stylish room with the best tables on a terrace overlooking the pool.

Deen 761 Thanon Silom, almost opposite Silom Village ☎02 635 0441. Small, basic, air-con Muslim café (espresso coffee, but no alcohol), which offers mostly southern Thai and Malay dishes, including spicy Indian-style curries, crispy grouper fish with pepper and garlic and roti kaeng (pancakes with curry).

Eat Me 1/6 Soi Phiphat 2, Thanon Convent ☎02 238 0931. BTS Sala Daeng. Highly fashionable art gallery and restaurant in a striking, white, modernist building, with changing exhibitions on the walls and a temptingly relaxing balcony. The pricey, far-reaching menu is more international – with dishes such as tenderloin steak fillet with Dijon sauce – than fusion, though the lemon grass crème brûlée is not to be missed. Daily 3pm–1am.

Gallery Café 86–100 Soi 30, Thanon Charoen Krung ☎02 639 5580. N3 Si Phraya express boats. At this civilized all-rounder, as well as having a massage and shopping for jewellery and handbags, you can sit down at antique Chinese tables and chairs to enjoy some tasty Thai grub: a wide choice of starters and salads, such as prawn and pomelo (B180), plenty of fish and even nam phrik, highly traditional but hard-to-find pastes served with raw green vegetables.

Harmonique 22 Soi 34, Thanon Charoen Krung, on the lane between Wat Muang Kae express-boat pier and the GPO ☎02 237 8175. A relaxing, welcoming, moderately priced restaurant that's well worth a trip: tables are scattered throughout several converted shophouses, decorated with antiques and bric-a-brac, and a quiet, leafy courtyard, and the Thai food is varied and excellent – among

the seafood specialities, try the crab (B160) or red shrimp (B85) curries. Closed Sun.

Himali Cha-Cha 1229/11 Soi 47/1, Thanon Charoen Krung, south of GPO ☎02 235 1569. Fine, moderately priced North Indian restaurant, founded by a character who was chef to numerous Indian ambassadors, and now run by his son. Homely atmosphere, attentive service and a good vegetarian selection. There's also a branch from a short alley off the north end of Thanon Convent, opposite *Molly Malone's* (BTS Sala Daeng).

Home Cuisine Islamic Restaurant 186 Soi 36, Thanon Charoen Krung ☎02 234 7911. The short, cheap menu of Indian and southern Thai dishes here has proved popular enough to warrant a spruce refurbishment in green and white, with comfy booths, pot plants and a few outdoor tables overlooking the colonial-style French embassy. The *khao mok kai* (B60), a typical hybrid version of a chicken biryani, served with aubergine curry, is delicious. Closed Sun lunch.

Indian Hut 311/2–5 Thanon Suriwong ☎02 237 8812. Bright, white-tablecloth, North Indian restaurant – look out for the Pizza Hut-style sign – that's fairly reasonably priced (mains from B180) and justly popular with local Indians. For carnivores, tandoori's the thing, with especially good kebabs. There's a wide selection of mostly vegetarian appetizers, as well as plenty of veggie main courses and breads, and a hard-to-resist house dhal.

Jim Thompson's Saladaeng Café 120/1 Soi 1, Thanon Saladaeng ☎02 266 9167. A civilized, reasonably priced haven with tables in the elegantly informal air-con interior or out in the leafy garden. Thai food stretches to some unusual dishes such as southern *khao yam*, a refreshing salad of dried cooked rice, dried shrimps and grated coconut with a sweet sauce. There's pasta, salads and other Western dishes, plus a few stabs at fusion including linguini *tom yam kung*. The array of desserts is mouthwatering, rounded off by good coffee and a wide choice of teas. Daily 11am–11pm.

Khrua Aroy Aroy 3/1 Thanon Pan. Aptly named "Delicious, Delicious Kitchen", this simple shophouse restaurant stands out for its choice of inexpensive, tasty, well-prepared dishes from all around the kingdom, notably *khao soi* (curried noodle soup from the north) and *kaeng matsaman*. Lunch only.

La Boulange 2–2/1 Thanon Convent ☎02 631 0354. BTS Sala Daeng. A fine choice for breakfast with great croissants and all sorts of tempting patisserie made on the premises. For savoury lunches and dinners, choose from a variety of quiches, plates of charcuterie, sandwiches, salads and simple brasserie dishes such as lamb Provençal.

Le Bouchon 37/17 Patpong 2, near Thanon Suriwong ☎02 234 9109. BTS Sala Daeng. Cosy bar-bistro that's much frequented by the city's French expats, offering French home-cooking, such as lamb shank in a white bean sauce (B580); booking is strongly recommended. Closed Sun lunchtime.

Le Café Siam 4 Soi Sri Akson, Thanon Chua Ploeng ☎02 671 0030, ⓦwww.lecafesiam .com (see the main colour map at the back of the book). An early twentieth-century Sino-Thai mansion in a tranquil garden that's difficult to find off the eastern end of Soi Sri Bamphen, but well worth the effort (the restaurant suggests a taxi company, ☎02 611 6499; or you can download a map from their website). The French and Thai food, with main courses starting at B250, is superb, served in a relaxing ambience that subtly blends Chinese and French styles, with an especially seductive bar area upstairs. Eve only.

Le Lys 104 Soi Phra Pinit (Soi 7, Thanon Narathiwat Ratchanakharin) ☎02 287 1898–9 (see the main colour map at the back of the book). In a large, characterful compound – with an air-con room, outdoor tables under a pergola, a bar and a petanque court – opposite M.R. Kukrit's Heritage Home, the French-Thai owners rustle up excellent, authentic Thai food, supplemented by daily bistro specials such as *assiette de rillettes*.

Mali Soi Jusmag, just off Soi Ngam Duphli ☎02 679 8693. Lumphini subway. Cosy, informal, low-lit restaurant, mostly air-con with a few cramped tables out front. The Thai menu specializes in salads and northeastern food, with plenty of veggie options, while pricier Western options run as far as burgers (B180), potato salad, all-day breakfasts, delicious banana pancakes and a few Mexican dishes.

Mei Jiang Peninsula Hotel (see p.170) ☎02 861 2888. Probably Bangkok's best Chinese restaurant, with beautiful views of the hotel's riverside gardens night and day, and very attentive and graceful staff. Cantonese specialities include delicious teas, lobster rolls, smoked duck with tea and excellent lunchtime dim sum such as crystal prawn dumplings – a bargain, starting at B80 a dish.

Dinner and cocktail cruises

The **Chao Phraya River** looks fabulous at night, when most of the noisy longtails have stopped terrorizing the ferries, and the riverside temples and other grand monuments – including the Grand Palace and Wat Arun – are elegantly illuminated. Joining one of the nightly **dinner cruises** along the river is a great way to appreciate it all. Call ahead to reserve a table and check departure details – some places offer free transport from hotels, and some cruises may not run during the rainy season (May to Oct). If you have other plans for dinner, it's now also possible to take a **cocktail cruise** on the *Manohra* (see below), between 6 and 7pm (B900).

Grand Pearl of Siam ☎02 861 0255, ext 201–4, ⓦwww.grandpearlcruise.com. A large modern boat which departs River City at 7.30pm, returning at 9.30pm. Thai and international buffet. B1400.

Loy Nava ☎02 235 3108. This long-running converted rice barge departs Si Phraya pier twice nightly, at 6pm and 8pm. Thai or seafood meal. B1300.

Maeyanang Run by the *Oriental Hotel* ☎02 659 9000; mid-Oct to April Tues–Sun. After cocktails in the *Oriental* gardens (7pm), this former rice barge departs at 7.30pm, returning at 10pm. Thai set meal. B1950.

Manohra Beautiful converted rice barge operated by the *Bangkok Marriott Resort*, south of Taksin Bridge in Thonburi ☎02 476 0022 ext 1416, ⓦwww.manohracruises .com. Departs hotel at 7.30pm, returning at 10pm, with pick-ups at Tha Sathorn possible. Thai set dinner, accompanied by live traditional music. B1990.

Wan Fah ☎02 222 8679, ⓦwww.wanfahcruise.com. Departs River City at 7pm, returning at 9pm. Thai or seafood set menu. B1200.

Ratree Seafood Soi 1, Thanon Silom, opposite Soi Thaniya. BTS Sala Daeng. Famous and popular streetside stall in the heart of the urban maelstrom, with half-a-dozen tables on the Silom pavement and down the soi behind. The *rot khen* (pushcart kitchen), laden with glistening seafood and even a small water tank for giant shrimp, rolls up about 6pm and barbecues away until around midnight.

Ruen Urai Rose Hotel, 118 Thanon Suriwong ☎02 266 8268–72. **BTS Sala Daeng.** Set back behind the hotel, this peaceful, hundred-year-old, traditional house, with fine balcony tables overlooking the beautiful hotel pool, comes as a welcome surprise in this full-on downtown area. The varied Thai food is of a high quality (though you can forget the house wine): try the *tom khlong talay* (B200) and don't be misled by the name – "seafood canal soup" – it's a delicious, refined, spicy and sour soup from the northeast, with tamarind juice and herbs.

Sarah Jane's 55/21 Thanon Narathiwat Ratchanakharin, between sois 4 & 6 ☎02 676 3338–9 **(see the main colour map at the back of the book).** Long-standing restaurant, popular with Bangkok's Issan population, serving excellent, simple northeastern dishes, including a huge array of *nam tok* (B85), *laap* and *som tam*, as well as Italian food.

Somboon Seafood Thanon Suriwong, corner of Thanon Narathiwat Ratchanakharin ☎02 234 4499. **BTS Chong Nonsi.** Highly favoured, bustling seafood restaurant, known for its crab curry (B250) and soy-steamed sea bass, with simple, functional, modern decor

and an array of marine life lined up in tanks outside awaiting its gastronomic fate. Daily 4–11.30pm.

Taling Pling 60 Thanon Pan ☎02 234 4872. One of the best Thai restaurants in the city outside of the big hotels, specializing in classic dishes from the four corners of the kingdom. The house deep-fried fish salad (B120) is delicious and refreshing, while the toothsome, deeply flavoured green beef curry with roti (B155) is recommended by the leading Thai restaurant guides. The atmosphere's convivial and relaxing, too.

Thien Duong Dusit Thani Hotel, corner Silom and Rama IV roads ☎02 236 9999. **BTS Sala Daeng & Silom subway.** Probably Bangkok's finest Vietnamese, a classy and expensive restaurant serving beautifully prepared dishes such as succulent *salat cua*, deep-fried soft-shell crab salad with cashew nuts and herb dressing, and zesty *goi ngo sen*, lotus-stem salad with shrimp and pork.

Tongue Thai 18–20 Soi 38, Thanon Charoen Krung, in front of the Oriental Place shopping mall ☎02 630 9918–9. **N1 Oriental express boats.** Very high standards of food and cleanliness, with charming, unpretentious service, in a hundred-year-old shophouse elegantly decorated with Thai and Chinese antiques and contemporary art. Veggies are very well catered for with delicious dishes such as tofu in black bean sauce and deep-fried banana-flower and corn cakes, while carnivores should try the fantastic beef curry (*panaeng neua*; B170).

Thanon Sukhumvit

In this area, there are also branches of the sushi restaurant *Aoi* (see p.180), Floor 4, Emporium shopping centre (☎02 664 8590), and the north–Indian *Himali Cha-Cha* (see p.181), on Soi 31 (☎02 259 6677). For dessert heaven take a stroll around the fifth-floor food stalls in the Emporium, which overflows with luscious gateaux, gelati, mango surprises and other blissful sweets.

See the map on p.120 for locations of the places listed below. For those restaurants east of Sois 39 and 26 that are not shown on the map, we've given directions from the nearest Skytrain station. For public transport details, see the box on p.121.

Al Ferdoss Soi 3/1. BTS Nana. Long-running Lebanese and Turkish restaurant in the heart of Sukhumvit's Middle Eastern soi, where you can smoke hookah pipes on the streetside terrace and choose from a menu

(B80–200) that encompasses shish, hummus, tabouleh and the rest.

Baan Khanitha 36/1 Soi 23 ☎02 258 4128, ⓦwww.baan-khanitha.com. **BTS Asok.** The big attraction at this long-running favourite haunt of Sukhumvit expats is the setting in a traditional Thai house. The food is upmarket Thai and fairly pricey, and includes lots of fiery salads (*yam*), and a good range of *tom yam* soups, green curries and seafood curries. Most mains cost B190–490.

Bangkok Baking Company Ground Floor, JW Marriott Hotel, between sois 2 and 4. BTS Nana. Exceptionally delicious cakes, pastries and breads: everything from rosemary focaccia to tiramisu cheesecake (B65–120). Daily 6am–11pm.

Basil Sheraton Grande Sukhumvit Hotel, between sois 12 and 14 ☎02 649 8888, ⊛www.sheratongrandesukhumvit.com. BTS Asok. Mouthwateringly fine traditional Thai food with a modern twist is the order of the day at this trendy, relatively informal though high-priced restaurant in the deluxe five-star *Sheraton*. Recommendations include the grilled river prawns with chilli, the *matsaman* curry (both served with red and green rice) and the surprisingly delicious durian cheesecake. Vegetarian menu on request. Daily 6.30–10.30pm.

Cabbages and Condoms 6–8 Soi 12 ⊛www .pda.or.th/restaurant. BTS Asok. The Population and Community Development Association of Thailand (PDA; see p.117) runs this restaurant – "our food is guaranteed not to cause pregnancy" – so diners are treated to authentic Thai food in the Condom Room, and relaxed scoffing of barbecued seafood in the rainforest beer-garden. Try the spicy catfish salad (B130) or the prawns steamed in a whole coconut (B250). All proceeds go to the PDA, and there's an adjacent shop selling double-entendre T-shirts, cards, key rings and of course, condoms.

Dosa King Soi 11/1 ⊛www.dosaking.net. BTS Nana. Usually busy with expat Indian diners, this vegetarian Indian restaurant serves good food from both north and south, including twenty different dosa (southern pancake) dishes, tandooris and the like. It's an alcohol-free zone so you'll have to make do with sweet lassi instead. Most dishes B100–180.

Eleven Gallery Soi 11 ☎02 651 2672, ⊛www.11-gallery.com. BTS Nana. Sharing the traffic-free sub-soi with the idiosyncratic *Suk 11* guest house, this restaurant also re-creates an atmosphere of old-fashioned village Thailand, with its wooden building, plentiful foliage, lamplight and staff dressed in late nineteenth-century

fashions. The food is good, authentic, mid-priced Thai (mostly B100–200), with plenty of spicy *yam* salads, delicious chicken *laap*, tasty *phanaeng* curry plus Thai desserts, cocktails and imported wines by the glass. It all adds up to a special occasion ambience, but without the pretension or high prices of its better known competitors. Daily 10am–1am.

Face Bangkok: La Na Thai and Hazara 29 Soi 38 ☎02 713 6048, ⊛www.facebars.com. BTS Thong Lo (150m from exit 4). Two restaurants, a bar, a bakery and a spa occupy this attractive compound of traditional, steeply gabled wooden Thai houses. Each restaurant is tastefully styled with appropriate artefacts and fabrics, and the adjacent *Face Bar* makes a chic 'n' funky place for a pre- or post-dinner drink. The very upmarket *Lan Na Thai* restaurant (daily 11.30am–2.30pm & 6.30–11.30pm) serves quality Thai food such as Chiang Mai-style pork curry and deep-fried grouper with tamarind sauce (mains from B400), while the Hazara (daily 6.30–11.30pm) specializes in Afghani and north-Indian tandoor cuisine, including murgh Peshawar chicken and the signature cardamom–marinated lamb (B400 and up).

Gaeng Pa Lerd Rod Soi 33/1 (no English sign), just before the Bull's Head. BTS Phrom Pong. Hugely popular outdoor restaurant whose tables are clustered under trees in a streetside yard and get packed with office workers at lunchtime. Thai curries (from B50) are the speciality here, with dishes ranging from conventional versions, like catfish and beef curries, to more adventurous offerings like fried cobra with chilli, and curried frog.

Le Dalat Indochine 14 Soi 23 ☎02 661 7967. BTS Asok. There's Indochinese romance aplenty at this delightful early twentieth-century villa decked out in homely and eclectic curiosities. The extensive, Vietnamese menu (B250–1200) features favourites such as a *goi ca* salad of aromatic herbs and shredded pork, *chao tom* shrimp sticks and *ga sa gung*, chicken curry with caramelized ginger.

MahaNaga 2 Soi 29 ⊛www.mahanaga.com. BTS Phrom Pong. The dining experience at this tranquil enclave is best appreciated after dark, when the fountain-courtyard tables are romantically lit and the air-con interior seduces with its burgundy velvet drapes. Cuisine is fusion fine-dining, though some east-west combos work better than others and the vegetarian selection is underwhelming. Grilled salmon in red curry is a winner, or you might brave the rack of lamb served with spicy vegetables, egg noodles and mango sauce. Set lunch B250; à la carte mains B400–600.

Spring Summer Winter 199 Soi Promsri 1 ☎02 392 2747, ⓦ www.springnsummer.com. BTS Phrom Pong (15min walk: 700m north up Soi 39 then 350m east along Soi Promsri 1). A fashionable three-in one experience occupying a pair of chic twentieth-century modern buildings set round a grassy lawn in a residential soi. *Spring* (daily 11.30am–2.30am & 6–11pm) serves delicious Thai and Japanese fusion cuisine – scrumptiously tangy pomelo and wingbean salad, fried rice with seared salmon and avocado (B290), snow fish with sweet tandoori sauce; *Summer* (midday–midnight) indulges chocoholics with all manner of treats from frozen forest gateaux to cheesecakes and chocolate hotpots; and *Winter* (7pm–midnight, weather permitting) sets up a bar on the lawn in between, with food from Spring and Summer, and lounging cushions.

Suda Restaurant Soi 14. BTS Asok. Unpretentious shophouse restaurant whose formica tables and plastic chairs spill out onto the soi and are mainly patronized by budget-conscious expats and their Thai friends. The friendly proprietor serves a good, long menu of Thai favourites (mostly B50–80), including deep-fried chicken in banana leaves, battered shrimps, fried tuna with cashews and chilli, and sticky rice with mango. Mon–Sat 11am–midnight, Sun 4pm–midnight.

🏃 **Vientiane Kitchen (Khrua Vientiane)** 8 Soi 36, about 50m south off Thanon Sukhumvit. BTS Thong Lo (3min walk west then south from exit 2). Just a short swerve off Sukhumvit and you're transported into a little piece of Isaan (northeast Thailand), where the menu's stocked full of north-eastern delicacies, a live band sets the mood with heart-felt folk songs, and there are even occasional performances by a troupe of upcountry dancers. The Lao- and Isaan-accented menu (B120–300) includes vegetable curry with ants' eggs, spicy-fried frog, jackfruit curry, and farm chicken with cashews, plus there's a decent range of veggie options such as meat-free *laap* and sweet and sour dishes. With its airy, barn-like interior and mixed clientele of Thais and expats, it's a very enjoyable dining experience.

⑪

Nightlife

For many of Bangkok's male visitors, nightfall is the signal to hit the city's sex bars, most notoriously in the area off the east end of Thanon Silom known as Patpong (see p.116). Fortunately, Bangkok's **nightlife** has thoroughly grown up and left these neon sumps behind in the past ten years, offering everything from microbreweries and vertiginous, roof-top cocktail bars to fiercely chic clubs and dance bars, hosting top-class DJs: within spitting distance of the beer bellies flopped onto Patpong's bars, for example, lies Soi 4, Thanon Silom, one of the city's most happening after-dark haunts. Though Silom 4 started out as a purely **gay** area (for details of Bangkok's gay nightlife, see p.193), it now offers a range of styles in gay, mixed and straight pubs, DJ bars and clubs. Along with Silom 4, the high-concept clubs and bars of Sukhumvit and the lively, teeming venues of Banglamphu pull in the style-conscious cream of Thai youth and are tempting an increasing number of travellers to stuff their party gear into their rucksacks.

Most bars and clubs **open** nightly until 1am, while clubs on Silom 4 can stay open until 2am. In the past few years, there have been regular "social order" clampdowns by the police, strictly enforcing these closing times, conducting occasional urine tests for drugs on bar customers, and setting up widespread ID checks to curb under-age drinking (you have to be 20 or over to drink in bars and clubs). However, at the time of writing, probably partly due to the political turmoil, things were much more chilled, with clubs staying open into the wee hours on busy nights and little sign of ID checks. It's hard to predict how the

Drink

The two most famous local **beers** (*bia*) are Singha, which has five percent alcohol content (ask for "*bia sing*"), and Chang, which delivers 6.4 percent alcohol at slightly cheaper prices: in shops around B30 for a 330ml bottle, B50 for a 660ml bottle. All manner of foreign beers are now brewed in Thailand, including Heineken and Asahi, and in Bangkok you'll find imported bottles from all over the world.

Wine is now found on plenty of upmarket and tourist-oriented restaurant menus, but expect to be disappointed both by the quality and by the price, which is jacked up by heavy taxation. At about B80 for a hip-flask-sized 375ml bottle, the local **whisky** is a lot better value, and Thais think nothing of consuming a bottle a night, heavily diluted with ice and soda or Coke. The most palatable and widely available of these is Mekong, which is very pleasant once you've stopped expecting it to taste like Scotch; distilled from rice, Mekong is deep gold in colour and tastes slightly sweet. If that's not to your taste, a pricier Thai **rum** is also available, Sang Som, made from sugar cane, and even stronger than the whisky. Check the menu carefully when ordering a bottle of Mekong from a bar in a tourist area, as they often ask up to five times more than you'd pay in a guest house or shop.

situation might develop, but you'll soon get an idea of how the wind is blowing when you arrive in Bangkok – and there's little harm in taking your passport out with you, just in case.

The travellers' enclave of **Banglamphu** takes on a new personality after dark, when its hub, Thanon Khao San, becomes a "walking street", closed to all traffic but open to almost any kind of makeshift stall, selling everything from fried bananas and buckets of "very strong" cocktails to share, to bargain fashions and one-off art works. Young Thais crowd the area to browse and snack before piling in to Banglamphu's more stylish bars and indie live-music clubs, most of which are free to enter (though some ask you to show ID first).

Downtown, there's a small knot of bars that are popular with both foreigners and Thais on Soi Sarasin (along the north side of Lumphini Park), as well as a larger concentration around the east end of Thanon Silom. Sarasin's western end (between *Brown Sugar* and Thanon Rajdamri) supports a gaggle of good-time DJ bars, gay and straight, such as the *Seventies Bar*, that heave at weekends. On Silom 4, while most of the gay venues have been around for some years now, other bars and clubs have opened and closed with bewildering speed. All the same, on a short, slow bar-crawl around this wide, traffic-free alley lined with pavement tables, it would be hard not to find somewhere to enjoy yourself.

If, among all the choice of nightlife around Silom, you do end up in one of Patpong's sex shows, watch out for hyper-inflated bar bills and other cons – plenty of customers get ripped off in some way, and stories of menacing bouncers are legion. A night out on **Thanon Sukhumvit** could also be subsumed by the girlie bars and hostess-run bar-beers (open-sided drinking halls with huge circular bars) on Sois Nana and Cowboy, but there's plenty of style on Sukhumvit too, especially in the rooftop bars and enjoyably trendy clubs.

During the cool season (Nov–Feb), an evening out at one of the seasonal **beer gardens** is a pleasant way of soaking up the urban atmosphere (and the traffic fumes). You'll find them in hotel forecourts or sprawled in front of dozens of shopping centres all over the city, most notably Central World Plaza.

Getting back to your lodgings should be no problem in the small hours: many bus routes run a (reduced) service throughout the night, and tuk-tuks and taxis are always at hand – though it's probably best for unaccompanied women to avoid using tuk-tuks late at night.

Banglamphu and Ratanakosin

Except where indicated, all bars listed below are marked on the map on p.76. For advice on getting public transport to this area see the box on p.78.

Ad Here the 13th 13 Thanon Samsen. N13 Tha Phra Arthit express boats. Relaxed, sociable little neighbourhood live-music joint where half-a-dozen tables of Thai and expat musos congregate to listen to nightly sets from the in-house blues 'n' jazz quartet (10pm onwards). Well-priced beer and plenty of cocktails. Daily 6pm–midnight.

Bangkok Bar Next to Sawasdee Inn at 149 Soi Ram Bhuttri ⓦ www.bkkbar.com. N13 Tha Phra Arthit express boats. Small, dark, tastefully furnished air-con bar-restaurant whose DJs and live indie-rock bands – including

occasional big-name appearances – are popular with young Thais and can be a fun introduction to the neighbourhood live-music scene. Daily 6pm–1am.

Bar Bali 58 Thanon Phra Athit. N13 Tha Phra Arthit express boats. Typical Phra Arthit bar-restaurant, with just a handful of tables, a small menu of drinking foods and a decent selection of well-priced cocktails. Live music from student singer-songwriters (usually one rather soulful man and his guitar) most nights. Daily 6pm–1am.

Brick Bar Buddy Village complex, 265 Thanon Khao San @www.brickbarkhaosan.com. N13 Tha Phra Arthit express boats. Massive red-brick vault of a live-music bar whose regular roster of reggae, ska and blues bands, and occasional one-off appearances, are hugely popular with Thai twenty-somethings and teens. Big, sociable tables are set right under the stage and there's food too. The liveliest nights are Fridays and Saturdays when there's a B150 entry charge, which includes one free drink. Daily 7pm–1am.

Café Democ 78 Thanon Rajdamnoen Klang @www.cafe-democ.com. Fashionable, dark and dinky bar that overlooks Democracy Monument and is spread over one-and-a-half cosy floors, with extra seating on the semi-circular mezzanine. Lots of cocktails, nightly sessions from up-and-coming Thai DJs, and regular trance, techno, house and progressive nights. Tues–Sun 4pm–2am.

The Club 123 Thanon Khao San @www .theclubkhaosan.com. N13 Tha Phra Arthit express boats. High ceilings, a central DJ station spinning mostly house music and an intimate dance floor encircled by tables draw a sophisticated young Thai and international crowd. Free entry except for special events, when one free drink is included in the B300–500 ticket. Daily 8pm–1am.

Gulliver's Traveler's Tavern Thanon Khao San @www.gulliverbangkok.com. N13 Tha Phra Arthit express boats. Infamous, long-established, tourist-oriented air-con pub with pool tables, sports TV, reasonably priced beer (happy hours often till 10pm) and a reputation for being something of a pick-up joint. Has a branch on Thanon Sukhumvit. Daily 11am–1am.

Hippie de Bar 46 Thanon Khao San. N13 Tha Phra Arthit express boats. Invitingly mellow courtyard bar set away from the main fray near *Tom Yam Kung* restaurant. Attracts an indie, mostly Thai crowd, to drink cocktails (B120) and 3.5-litre towers of draft Heineken (B500) at its wrought-iron tables and artily mismatched furniture. Cool sounds too. Daily 6pm–2am.

Po 230 Tha Thien, Thanon Maharat (see map, p.58). When the Chao Phraya express boats start to wind down around 6pm, this bar takes over the rustic wooden pier and the balcony above with their great sunset views across the river to Wat Arun. It's popular with local students and office workers, hence the loud Thai pop music; avoid the food in favour of beer and Thai whisky.

Susie Pub On the soi between Thanon Khao San and Thanon Ram Bhuttri @www.susiepub.com. N13 Tha Phra Arthit express boats. Big, dark, phenomenally popular pub that's often standing-room-only on weekend nights. Has a pool table, cheapish beer and DJs playing mainstream pop and generally gets a mixed crowd of farang and Thais. Daily 11am–1am; ID sometimes required.

Siam Square, Thanon Ploenchit and northern downtown

See the map on p.108 for locations of the venues listed below. For advice on getting public transport to this area see the box on p.107.

Brown Sugar 231/19–20 Soi Sarasin ☏02 250 1826. Tightly packed, pricey and atmospheric bar, with a certain crumpled chic, acknowledged as the capital's top jazz venue, with a popular Sunday night jam session.

Club Culture 346/29 Thanon Sri Ayutthaya, opposite Siam City Hotel @www.club-culture -bkk.com. BTS Phaya Thai. Huge, attractive former ballroom that's handy for Phaya Thai Skytrain station and trendy among Thais and expats. A roster of international and local DJs play house, electronica, trance or drum'n'bass, depending on the night. Tues–Sun 9pm–2am. B400 including two drinks.

▲ Saxophonist playing at Brown Sugar

Saxophone 3/8 Victory Monument (southeast corner), Thanon Phrayathai ☎02 246 5472, Ⓦwww.saxophonepub.com. BTS Victory Monument. Lively, easy-going, spacious venue with decent Thai and Western food and a diverse roster of bands – mostly jazz (Mon–Thurs) and blues (Fri–Sun), plus acoustic guitar, funk, rock and reggae – that attracts a good mix of Thais and foreigners.

Syn Bar Swissôtel Nai Lert Park, 2 Thanon Witthayu. BTS Ploen Chit. Hip hotel bar, popular at weekends, decorated retro style with bubble chairs and a sparkling fibre-optic carpet. Excellent cocktails, including a mean Wasabi Mary, and DJs playing house and Latin.

The Tunnel Soi Lang Suan, behind Ma Be Ba restaurant. The after-hours club of the moment, though it suffers from sporadic police clampdowns, hence the dimly lit entrance. Like the restaurant, decor is grotto-like with a riot of mosaics; music policy is strictly electro and house. Open 10pm till 3–5am or later, depending on the constabulary; busy after 1am. Sun–Thurs free, Fri & Sat B500 including two drinks.

Southern downtown: south of Thanon Rama IV

See the map on p.114 for locations of the venues listed below. For advice on getting public transport to this area see the box on p.115.

The Barbican 9/4–5 Soi Thaniya, east end of Thanon Silom ☎02 233 4141–2. BTS Sala Daeng. Stylishly modern fortress-like decor to match the name: dark woods, metal and undressed stone. With Guinness on tap and a long menu of imported beers, it could almost be a smart City of London pub – until you look out of the windows onto the soi's incongruous Japanese hostess bars. Good food, DJ sessions Tues & Fri and happy hours Mon–Fri 4–7pm.

Lucifer 76/1–3 Patpong 1. BTS Sala Daeng. Popular dance club playing trance, techno and house in the dark heart of Patpong, largely untouched by the sleaze around it. Done out with mosaics and stalactites like a satanic grotto, with balconies to look down on the dance-floor action. Free entry on quiet nights, B150 including one drink when busy. *Radio City*, the interconnected bar downstairs, is only slightly less raucous, with jumping live bands, including famous Elvis and Tom Jones impersonators, and tables out on the sweaty pavement.

Molly Malone's 1/5 Thanon Convent, off the east end of Thanon Silom ☎02 266 7160. BTS Sala Daeng. Blarney Bangkok-style: a popular Irish pub, tastefully done out in dark wood and leather and packed with expats, especially on Friday night. Guinness, Kilkenny Bitter, Hoegaarden and Leffe on tap (happy hours 4–7pm), expensive food such as Irish stew and beef and Guinness pie, TV sports and live cover bands Mon–Sat.

Noriega's Soi 4, Thanon Silom. BTS Sala Daeng. Unpretentious, good-time bar at the end of the alley, with nightly live bands (blues, rock or acoustic, including open mike on Thurs) or DJs. Regular salsa nights; happy hour all night Mon & Tues, till 9pm Wed–Sun.

O'Reilly's Corner of Silom and Thaniya rds. BTS Sala Daeng. Welcoming Irish bar that's especially good for watching TV sport. Guinness and Kilkenny bitter on draught, multifarious drinks offers including 4–7pm happy hours, popular food and varied live music Tues–Sat eve.

Parkbridge Patpong 2 Ⓦwww.theparkbridge .com. BTS Sala Daeng. An extraordinary setting in a glass-walled bridge two floors above the sleazy soi, with decor that melds imperial kitsch and urban art styles – think graffiti and silver antlers – mark out this French-run bar-disco. Throw in a 6–9pm happy hour and an imaginative menu of DJs (after 9pm) stretching from Japanese (Wed) to bring-your-own (Sun), and you might find yourself still there at closing time (currently 3am-ish weekdays, 5am weekends).

🏃 The Sky Bar & Distil Floor 63, State Tower, 1055 Thanon Silom, corner of Thanon Charoen Krung ☎02 624 9555. Thrill-seekers and view addicts shouldn't miss forking out for an al fresco drink here, 275m above the city's pavements – come around 6pm to enjoy the stunning panoramas in both the light and the dark. It's standing only at *The Sky Bar*, a circular restaurant-bar on the edge of the building with almost 360° views, but for the sunset itself, you're better off on the outside terrace of *Distil* on the other side of the building (where bookings are accepted), which has a wider choice of drinks, charming service and huge couches to recline on.

Tapas Bar Soi 4, Thanon Silom. BTS Sala Daeng. Vaguely Spanish-oriented, pricey bar (but no tapas) with Moorish-style decor, whose outside tables are probably the best spot for checking out the comings and goings on the soi; inside, music ranges from house and hip-hop to Latin jazz and funk. Fri & Sat admission B100, Sun free, Mon–Thurs B200 including 1 drink.

Tawandang German Brewery 462/61 Thanon Rama III ☏ 02 678 1114–6. A taxi-ride south of Thanon Sathorn down Thanon Narathiwat Ratchanakharin, this vast all-rounder is well worth the effort (it's best to book a table in advance). Under a huge dome, up to 1600 revellers enjoy good food and great micro-brewed beer every night. Sundays sees cover bands, but the main attraction from Monday to Saturday is the mercurial live music and cabaret, featuring Fong Naam, led by Bruce Gaston, who blend Thai classical and popular music with Western styles.

Unico Hotel Roof Garden Thanon Silom, opposite Thanon Decho. BTS Chong Nonsi. Budget version of Bangkok's famous roof-top bar-restaurants, at lower altitude (only the 19th floor) but with much lower prices – and with few skyscrapers in the immediate vicinity, the city panorama is still pretty special. Fairy lights, patches of lawn and occasional live music complete the picture.

Thanon Sukhumvit

Many clubs in Sukhumvit require you to show ID when you enter, to prove that you are 20 or over. The places listed below are marked on the map on p.120. For advice on getting public transport to this area, see the box on p.121.

Bed Supperclub 26 Soi 11 ☏ 02 651 3537, ⊛ www.bedsupperclub.com. BTS Nana. Worth visiting for the futuristic visuals alone, this seductively curvaceous spacepod bar is still the top nightspot in this happening soi. Inside, the all-white interior is dimly lit and surprisingly cosy, with deep couches inviting drinkers to recline around the edges of the upstairs gallery, getting a good view of the downstairs bar and DJ. The vibe is always welcoming and a lot less pretentious than you might expect; some nights are themed, including a weekly gay night. The cover charge (B700 after 9pm on Wed, Fri & Sat, B600 other nights) is redeemable against two drinks. The restaurant section is starker, lit with glacial ultra-violet, and serving a mostly Asian fusion menu 7.30–9pm (reservations essential). Bar daily 8pm–2am; ID required.

The Bull's Head Soi 33/1. BTS Phrom Pong. A Sukhumvit institution that takes pride in being Bangkok's most authentic British pub, right down to the horse brasses, jukebox and typical pub food. Famous for its Sunday evening "toss the boss" happy hours (5–7pm), when a flip of a coin determines whether or not you have to pay for your round. Daily 11am–1.30am.

Cheap Charlie's Soi 11. BTS Nana. Idiosyncratic open-air pavement bar that's famous for its cheap beer, customers' hall-of-fame gallery and lack of tables and chairs. A few lucky punters get to occupy the bar-stools but otherwise it's simple standing room only. Mon–Sat 5.30pm–12.30am.

Gulliver's Traveler's Tavern 6 Soi 5 ⊛ www .gulliverbangkok.com. BTS Nana. An offshoot of the original Khao San sports bar, this cavernous branch has tables inside and out where you can down draught Guinness (happy hour lasts from kickoff until 7pm) and nosh your way through the international menu. Shows live sporting fixtures and has table football, pool tables and internet access. Daily 10.30am–1am.

Londoner Brew Pub Mouth of Soi 33 ⊛ www .the-londoner.com. BTS Phrom Pong. Aside from the pool table, darts board, big-screen sports TV and live music (nightly from about 9pm), it's the specially brewed pints of Londoner's Pride Cream Bitter and London Pilsner 33 that draw in the punters. Happy hour 4–7pm. Free wi-fi. Daily 11am–1am.

Long Table 25th Floor, Column Tower, 48 Soi 16 ⊛ www.longtablebangkok.com. BTS Asok. This achingly fashionable 25th-floor restaurant, serving contemporary Thai cuisine, is named for its thirty-metre-long communal centrepiece table, which seats seventy. But the real attraction is the sleek, Shanghai-style open-sided balcony bar whose "long-tail" cocktails give you ample time to lounge glamorously on the leather sofas and soak up the wraparound panoramas across downtown skyscrapers. Daily midday–1am.

Nest 9th Floor, Le Fenix hotel, Soi 11 ⓦ www .lefenix-sukhumvit.com. **BTS Nana.** Whether you unfurl on a daybed, curl up in a basket-chair or recline under a hooded chaise longue at this aptly named rooftop eyrie, you'll get an airy view of the condo-spiked skyline (there are covers for wet days) and a decent choice of cocktails (mostly B300) plus a few light meals. Not

as slick or spectacular as the more famous downtown sky bars but very pleasant. Daily 5pm–1am.

Q Bar 34 Soi 11 ⓦ www.qbarbangkok.com. **BTS Nana.** Very dark, very trendy, New York-style bar occupying two floors and a terrace. Famous for its wide choice of chilled vodkas, and for its music, Q Bar appeals to a mixed crowd of fashionable people, particularly on Friday and Saturday nights when the DJs have the dance floor zinging. Arrive before 11pm if you want a seat, and don't turn up in shorts, singlets or sandals if you're male. Sun–Thurs B500 including two free drinks, Fri & Sat B700. Daily 8pm–1am; ID required.

12

Gay and lesbian Bangkok

B uddhist tolerance and a national abhorrence of confrontation and victimization combine to make Thai society relatively tolerant of **homosexuality**, if not exactly positive about same-sex relationships. Most Thais are extremely private and discreet about being gay, generally pursuing a "don't ask, don't tell" understanding with their family. Hardly any public figures are out, yet the predilections of several respected social, political and entertainment figures are widely known and accepted. There is no mention of homosexuality at all in Thai law, which means that the age of consent for gay sex is fifteen, the same as for heterosexuals. This also means that gay rights are not protected under Thai law. However, most Thais are horrified by the idea of gay-bashing and generally regard it as unthinkable to spurn a child or relative for being gay. Although excessively physical displays of affection are frowned upon for both heterosexuals and homosexuals, Western **gay couples** should get no hassle about being seen together in public – it's more common, in fact, for friends of the same sex (gay or not) to walk hand-in-hand, than for heterosexual couples to do so.

Transvestites and **transsexuals** (known as *katoey* or "ladyboys") are a lot more visible in Thailand than in the West. You'll find cross-dressers doing

---

Information and contacts for gay travellers

Anjaree PO Box 322, Rajdamnoen PO, Bangkok 10200 ℮ anjaree@loxinfo.com. General information on the lesbian community in Thailand.

Bangkok Lesbian ⓦ www.bangkoklesbian.com. Organized by foreign lesbians living in Thailand, Bangkok Lesbian hosts regular parties and posts general info and listings of the capital's lesbian-friendly hangouts on its website.

Gay People in Thailand ⓦ www.thaivisa.com/forum/Gay-People-Thailand-f27.html. Popular forum for gay expats.

Long Yang Club ⓦ www.longyangclub.org/thailand. This international organization was founded to promote friendship between men of Western and Eastern origin and runs regular socials.

Utopia ⓦ www.utopia-asia.com and www.utopia-asia.com/womthai.htm. Asia's best gay and lesbian website lists clubs, events, accommodation, tour operators and organizations for gays and lesbians and has useful links to other sites in Asia and the rest of the world.

ordinary jobs and there are a number of transvestites and transsexuals in the public eye too – including national volleyball stars and champion *muay thai* boxers. The government tourist office vigorously promotes the transvestite cabarets in Bangkok (see p.198), all of which are advertised as family entertainment. *Katoey* also regularly appear as characters in soap operas, TV comedies and films, where they are depicted as harmless figures of fun. Richard Totman's *The Third Sex* offers an interesting insight into Thai *katoey*, their experiences in society and public attitudes towards them; see "Books" on p.241 for a review.

The gay scene

Bangkok's **gay scene** is mainly focused on mainstream venues like karaoke bars, restaurants, massage parlours, gyms, saunas and escort agencies. Most of the action happens on Silom 4 (near Patpong) and on the more exclusive Silom 2 (towards Thanon Rama IV).

The farang-oriented gay **sex industry** is a tiny but highly visible part of Bangkok's gay scene and, with its tawdry floor shows and host services, it bears a dispiriting resemblance to the straight sex trade. Like their female counterparts in the heterosexual fleshpots, many of the boys working in the gay sex bars that dominate these districts are underage (anyone caught having sex with a prostitute below the age of 18 faces imprisonment). A significant number of gay prostitutes are gay by economic necessity rather than by inclination. As with the straight sex scene, we do not list the commercial gay sex bars.

The gay scene is heavily male, and there are hardly any **lesbian**-only venues, though quite a few gay bars are mixed. Thai lesbians generally eschew the word lesbian, which in Thailand is associated with male fantasies, instead referring to themselves as either *tom* (for tomboy) or *dee* (for lady).

Every year in mid-November, the capital's GLBT community puts on a big show for **Bangkok Pride** (Ⓦ www.bangkokpride.org), strutting its stuff around Thanon Silom in a carnival of parades, cabarets, fancy-dress competitions and sports contests that usually culminates with a jamboree in Lumphini Park.

Gay bars and clubs

The bars, clubs and café–restaurants listed here – all of them walkable from Sala Daeng **Skytrain** station or Silom **subway** station – are the most notable of Bangkok's gay nightlife venues; *Bed Supperclub* (see p.190) also hosts a regular gay night.

The Balcony Soi 4, Thanon Silom. Unpretentious, fun place with plenty of outdoor seats for people-watching, welcoming staff, reasonably priced drinks, karaoke and decent Thai and Western food.

Coffee Society 12/3 Thanon Silom, between sois 2 and 2/1. Gay-friendly, 24hr coffee shop and restaurant with cosy booths and free wi-fi.

Dick's Café Duangthawee Plaza, 894/7–8 Soi Pratuchai, Thanon Suriwong Ⓦ www.dickscafe .com. Stylish day-and-night café-bar-restaurant (daily 10.30am–2am), hung with

exhibitions by gay artists, on a traffic-free soi of go-go bars opposite the prominent Wall St Tower. Ideal for drinking, eating decent Thai and Western food, or just chilling out.

Disco Disco Soi 2, Thanon Silom. Small, pared-down bar-disco with a minimalist, retro feel, playing dance music to a fun young crowd.

DJ Station Soi 2, Thanon Silom. Highly fashionable but unpretentious three-storey club, packed at weekends, attracting a mix of Thais and farangs; cabaret show nightly at 11.30pm. B100 including one drink (B200 including two drinks Fri & Sat).

▲ Bangkok Pride

GOD (Guys on Display) 60/18–21 Soi 2/1, Thanon Silom, in a small soi between Soi Thaniya and Soi 2. Large, busy club, somewhat more Thai-oriented and with later hours (till 3–6am) than *DJ Station*; occasional cabaret shows. B140 including one drink before 1am, B280 including two drinks afterwards. *Richard's* next door is a smart bar-restaurant that's open till 2am.
JJ Park 8/3 Soi 2, Thanon Silom. Classy, Thai-oriented bar, for relaxed socializing rather than raving, with nightly singers and cabaret acts, and a chill-out annexe, *Club Café*, next door.
Sphinx 98–104 Soi 4, Thanon Silom. Plush decor with a vaguely Egyptian theme, terrace seating and very good Thai and Western food attract a sophisticated crowd to this ground-floor bar and restaurant; karaoke upstairs at *Pharoah's*.
Telephone Pub 114/11–13 Soi 4, Thanon Silom. Bangkok's first Western-style gay bar when it opened in 1987, this cruisey, dimly lit eating and drinking venue has a terrace on the alley, telephones on the tables inside for making new friends and karaoke upstairs.

Entertainment

T he most accessible of the capital's performing arts are **Thai dancing**, particularly when served up in bite-size portions in tourist shows, and the graceful and humorous performances at the **Traditional Thai Puppet Theatre**. **Thai boxing** is also well worth watching: the raucous live experience at either of Bangkok's two main national stadia far outshines the TV coverage.

For something unclassifiably different, try **bowling** at SF Strike Bowl, at the Rama I end of Floor 7 in the MBK Shopping Centre (Sun–Thurs 10am–1am, Fri & Sat 10am–2pm; ☎02 611 4555). Designed by the same team as *Bed Supperclub* (see p.190), the alleys glow in shades of luminous purple, blue and green, and thump to the sounds of a DJ. There are pool tables, a bar and karaoke, and you can even book a VIP lounge with two lanes from B600 per hour.

Drama, dance and music

Drama pretty much equals dance in classical Thai theatre, and many of the **traditional dance-dramas** are based on the Hindu epic the *Ramayana* (in Thai, *Ramakien*), a classic adventure tale of good versus evil which is taught in all the schools (see p.63 for an outline of the story). Not understanding the plots can be a major disadvantage, so try reading an abridged version beforehand (see "Books", p.242) and check out the wonderfully imaginative murals at Wat Phra Kaeo (see p.64), after which you'll certainly be able to sort the goodies from the baddies, if little else.

The best way to experience the traditional performing arts is usually at a show designed for tourists, where background knowledge and stoic concentration are not essential; the spectacular Siam Niramit cultural extravaganza (see p.196) is a good introduction. Several tourist restaurants offer low-tech versions of the Siam Niramit experience, in the form of nightly **culture shows** that usually feature a medley of Thai dancing and classical music, perhaps with a martial-arts demonstration thrown in. In some cases there's a set fee for dinner and show, in others the performance is free but the à la carte prices are slightly inflated; it's always worth calling ahead to reserve, especially if you want a vegetarian version of the set menu.

Thai dancing is performed for its original ritual purpose, usually several times a day, at the Lak Muang Shrine behind the Grand Palace (see map, p.58) and the Erawan Shrine on the corner of Thanon Ploenchit (see map, p.108). Both shrines have resident troupes of dancers who are hired by worshippers to perform *lakhon chatri*, a sort of *khon* dance-drama, to thank benevolent spirits for answered prayers. The dancers are always dressed up in full gear and accompanied by

▲ *Lakhon chatri* dancers, Erawan shrine

musicians, but the length and complexity of the dance and the number of dancers depend on the amount of money paid by the supplicant: a price list is posted near the dance area. The musicians at the Erawan Shrine are particularly highly rated, though the almost comic apathy of the dancers there doesn't do them justice.

Non-Thai-speaking audiences are likely to struggle with much of the **contemporary Thai theatre** performed in the city, though all the venues listed below occasionally stage shows that will appeal to visitors, be that experimental drama, **classical concerts** or performances by visiting international dance and theatre companies.

Culture shows

Siam Niramit Ratchada Theatre, 19 Thanon Tiam Ruammit (see colour map) ☎02 649 9222, Ⓦwww.siamniramit.com. Thailand Culture Centre subway (5min walk). Unashamedly tourist-oriented but the easiest place to get a glimpse of the variety and spectacle intrinsic to traditional Thai theatre. The eighty-minute show presents a history of regional Thailand's culture and beliefs in a hi-tech spectacular of fantastic costumes and huge chorus numbers, enlivened by acrobatics and flashy special effects. Daily 8pm; B1500; tickets can be bought on the spot or through most travel agents. The complex also includes crafts outlets and a buffet restaurant (dinner B500).

Silom Village Thanon Silom ☎02 234 4581, Ⓦwww.silomvillage.co.th. This complex of tourist shops stages a nightly 50min show at its Ruen Thep theatre (8.30pm; B600) to accompany a set menu of Thai food (available from 7pm), as well as rather desultory free 15min shows at 7.45pm and 8.45pm at its outdoor restaurant.

Other venues

National Theatre Sanam Luang, Ratanakosin ☎02 224 1342 or 02 222 1012. Closed for a lengthy renovation at the time of writing, but has in the past staged roughly weekly shows of music, *lakhon* (classical dance-drama) and *likay* (folk drama), monthly medley shows, plus outdoor shows of classical music and dancing at the National Museum on dry-season weekends – try the nearby Bangkok Tourism Division for the latest information (see p.36).

Patravadi Theatre 69/1 Soi Wat Rakhang, Thonburi (see map, p.93) ☎02 412 7287, ⓦwww.patravaditheatre.com. Free shuttle boat from Tha Maharat. Highly regarded, experimental theatre company rooted in the traditional arts; stages a dinner-theatre experience at its riverside restaurant *Studio 9* (Fri & Sat 7.30pm; à la carte menu). It also runs classes in classical dance and other disciplines, some of which are accessible to non-Thai speakers.

Sala Chalermkrung Theatre 66 Thanon Charoen Krung, junction with Thanon Triphet in Pahurat, next to Old Siam Plaza (see map, p.86) ☎02 224 4499, ⓦwww.salachalermkrung.com. See p.85 for transport info. This renovated historical theatre shows mainstream traditional and contemporary theatre most of the week, but also stages regular tourist-friendly *khon* performances with English subtitles (Fri & Sat 7.30pm; from B1000).

Thailand Cultural Centre Thanon Ratchadapisek ☎02 247 0028 ext 4280. Thailand Cultural Centre subway. The country's most prominent performing arts space puts on traditional and contemporary theatre, mainstream classical concerts, and visiting international dance and theatre shows.

Traditional Thai Puppet Theatre Suan Lum Night Bazaar, Thanon Rama IV ☎02 252 9683–4, ⓦwww.thaipuppet.com. Lumphini subway. Entertaining, tourist-oriented performances that are well worth it for both adults and children, using *hun lakhon lek* (jointed stick-puppets), an art form that was developed in the early twentieth century and had all but died out before the late owner of the theatre, Sakorn Yangkeowsod

Traditional dance-drama

The most spectacular form of traditional Thai theatre is **khon**, a stylized drama performed in masks and elaborate costumes by a troupe of highly trained classical dancers. There's little room for individual interpretation in these dances, as all the movements follow a strict choreography that's been passed down through generations: each graceful, angular gesture depicts a precise event, action or emotion which will be familiar to educated *khon* audiences. The dancers don't speak, and the story is chanted and sung by a chorus who stand at the side of the stage, accompanied by a classical *phipat* orchestra.

A typical *khon* performance features several of the best-known **Ramayana** episodes, in which the main characters are recognized by their masks, headdresses and heavily brocaded costumes. Gods and humans don't wear masks, but it's generally easy enough to distinguish the hero Rama and heroine Sita from the action; they always wear tall gilded headdresses and often appear in a threesome with Rama's brother Lakshaman. Monkey **masks** are always open-mouthed, almost laughing, and come in several colours: monkey army chief Hanuman always wears white, and his two right-hand men – Nilanol, the god of fire, and Nilapat, the god of death – wear red and black respectively. In contrast, the demons have grim mouths, clamped shut or snarling out of usually green faces; Totsagan, king of the demons, wears a green face in battle and a gold one during peace, but always sports a two-tier headdress carved with two rows of faces.

Even if you don't see a show, you're bound to come across copies of the masks worn by the main *khon* characters, which are sold as souvenirs and constitute an art form in their own right.

(aka Joe Louis), came to its rescue in the 1980s. Each sixty-centimetre-tall puppet is manipulated by three puppeteers, who are accomplished Thai classical dancers in their own right, complementing their charges' elegant and precise gestures with graceful movements in a harmonious ensemble.

Hour-long shows (B900, kids B300) are put on daily at the theatre at 8pm, preceded by a video documentary in English at 7.30pm. The puppets perform *khon*, *lakhon* and *likay* stories, accompanied by synopses in English and live traditional music of a high standard.

Cabaret

Glitzy and occasionally ribald entertainment is the order of the day at the capital's two **ladyboy cabaret shows**, where luscious transvestites don glamorous outfits and perform over-the-top song and dance routines. Mambo Cabaret plays at the theatre in Washington Square, between Sukhumvit sois 22 and 24 (☎02 259 5715; nightly 8pm; Nov–Feb also at 10pm; B800), and New Calypso Cabaret performs inside the *Asia Hotel*, on the west side of Ratchathevi Skytrain station at 296 Thanon Phrayathai (☎02 216 8937, ⓦwww.calypsocabaret.com; nightly 8.15 & 9.45pm; B1000 or half-price if booked online 5 days ahead).

Thai boxing

The violence of the average **Thai boxing** (*muay thai*) match may be offputting to some, but spending a couple of hours at one of Bangkok's two main stadia can be immensely entertaining, not least for the enthusiasm of the spectators and the ritualistic aspects of the fights. Bouts, advertised in the English-language newspapers, are held in the capital every night of the week at the **Rajdamnoen Stadium**, next to the TAT office on Rajdamnoen Nok (☎02 281 4205; Mon, Wed & Sun 6pm, Thurs 5pm), and at **Lumphini Stadium** on Thanon Rama IV (☎02 252 8765, ⓦwww.muaythailumpini.com; Tues & Fri 6.30pm, Sat 4.30pm & 8.30pm; Lumphini subway); see the colour map at the back of the book for

Rituals of the ring

Thai boxing (*muay thai*) enjoys a following in Thailand similar to football in Europe. Every province has a stadium and whenever a fight is shown on TV large noisy crowds gather round the sets in streetside restaurants and noodle shops.

There's a strong spiritual and **ritualistic** dimension to *muay thai*, adding grace to an otherwise brutal sport. Each boxer enters the ring to the wailing music of a three-piece *phipat* orchestra, often flamboyantly attired in a lurid silk robe over the statutory red or blue boxer shorts. The fighter then bows, first in the direction of his birthplace and then to the north, south, east and west, honouring both his teachers and the spirit of the ring. Next he performs a slow dance, claiming the audience's attention and demonstrating his prowess as a performer.

Any part of the body except the head may be used as an **offensive weapon** in *muay thai*, and all parts except the groin are fair targets; most knockouts are caused by kicks to the head. As the action hots up, so the orchestra speeds up its tempo and the betting in the audience becomes more frenetic. It can be a gruesome business, but it was far bloodier before modern boxing gloves were made compulsory in the 1930s – combatants used to wrap their fists with hemp impregnated with a face-lacerating dosage of ground glass.

venue locations. **Tickets** cost B1000–2000, though at Rajdamnoen the view from the B1000 seats is partially obscured. Sessions usually feature ten bouts, each consisting of five three-minute rounds (with two-minute rests in between each round), so if you're not a big fan it may be worth turning up an hour late, as the better fights tend to happen later in the billing. It's more fun if you buy one of the less expensive standing tickets, enabling you to witness the wild gesticulations of the betting aficionados at close range.

To engage in a little *muay thai* yourself, visit Sor Vorapin's Gym at 13 Trok Kasap off Thanon Chakrabongse in Banglamphu, which holds **muay thai classes** twice daily (B500 per session; ☎02 282 3551, Ⓦwww.thaiboxings.com) or Chacrit Muay Thai School, next to Washington Square Theatre on Sukhumvit, between Sois 22 and 24 (Mon–Sat 9am–8pm; drop-in sessions B500; ☎02 260 5826, Ⓦwww.chacritmuaythaischool.com). For more serious training there are a couple of well-regarded places for foreigners to train on the outskirts of the city: Jitti's Gym (Ⓦwww.jittigym.com) and the Muay Thai Institute (Ⓦwww.muaythai-institute.net).

Cinemas

Central Bangkok has more than forty **cinemas**, many of which show recent American and European releases with their original dialogue and Thai subtitles. Most cinemas screen shows around four times a day: some programme details are advertised every day in the *Bangkok Post* but your best bet is to go to Ⓦwww.movieseer.com, which allows you to search by movie or by area in Bangkok, up to a week ahead; cinema locations are printed on *Nancy Chandler's Map of Bangkok*. Whatever cinema you're in, you're expected to stand for the king's anthem, which is played before every performance. See p.41 for information about Bangkok's annual film festival.

There are half-a-dozen cinemas in Siam Square, among which the Lido on Soi 1 (☎02 252 6498, Ⓦwww.apexsiam-square.com) is your best bet for independent foreign films. Otherwise, head out to House, an arthouse cinema northeast of the centre in Royal City Avenue Plaza (☎02 641 5177–8, Ⓦwww.houserama.com; nearest subway Phetchaburi). Nearly every major downtown shopping plaza has several screens on its top floor, including Siam Paragon: on Floor 5 here, you can go for a regular auditorium (from B140), super-size to the IMAX, which shows recent Hollywood releases on a giant screen with enhanced sound (B250), or plump for the Enigma, a VIP cinema where for B3000 you get a sofa, food and drink (with waiter service) for four people.

Movies at the French and German cultural centres, the Alliance Française, at 29 Thanon Sathorn Tai (☎02 670 4200, Ⓦwww.alliance-francaise.or.th), and the Goethe Institut, at 18/1 Soi Goethe, between Thanon Sathorn Tai and Soi Ngam Duphli (☎02 287 0942, Ⓦwww.goethe.de), are often subtitled in English, while Thammasat University's Pridi Banomyong Library in Ratanakosin hosts free weekly shows of foreign films (☎02 613 3529–30 or see the *Bangkok Post*).

14

Mind and body

T he last few years have seen an explosion in the number of spas opening in Bangkok – mainly inside the poshest hotels, but also as small, afford-able walk-in centres around the city. With their focus on indulgent self-pampering, spas are usually associated with high-spending tourists, but the treatments on offer at Bangkok's five-star hotels are often little different from those used by traditional medical practitioners, who have long held that massage and herbs are the best way to restore physical and mental well-being. Even in the heart of the city, it's also possible to undergo a bit of highly tradi-tional mental self-help by practising meditation.

Traditional massage and spas

Thai massage (*nuad paen boran*) is based on the principle that many physical and emotional problems are caused by the blocking of vital energy channels within the body. The masseur uses his or her feet, heels, knees and elbows, as well as hands, to exert a gentle pressure on these channels, supplementing this acupressure-style technique by pulling and pushing the limbs into yogic stretches. This distinguishes Thai massage from most other massage styles, which are more concerned with tissue manipulation. One is supposed to emerge from a Thai massage feeling both relaxed and energized, and it is said that regular massages produce long-term benefits in muscles as well as stimulating the circu-lation and aiding natural detoxification.

Thais visit a masseur for many conditions, including fevers, colds and muscle strain, but bodies that are not sick are also considered to benefit from the restorative powers of a massage, and nearly every hotel and guest house will be able to put you in touch with a masseur. Thai masseurs do not use oils or lotions and the client is treated on a mat or mattress; you'll often be given a pair of loose-fitting trousers and perhaps a loose top to change into. A session should ideally last two hours and will cost from around B300–1500, or a lot more in the most exclusive spas.

The **science** behind Thai massage has its roots in Indian Ayurvedic medicine, which classifies each component of the body according to one of the four elements (earth, water, fire and air), and holds that balancing these elements within the body is crucial to good health. Many of the stretches and manipula-tions fundamental to Thai massage are thought to have derived from yogic practices introduced to Thailand from India by Buddhist missionaries in about the second century BC; Chinese acupuncture and reflexology have also had a strong influence. In the nineteenth century, King Rama III ordered a series of murals illustrating the principles of Thai massage to be painted around the courtyard of Bangkok's Wat Pho (see p.66), and they are still in place today, along with statues of ascetics depicted in typical massage poses. **Wat Pho** has been the leading school of Thai massage for hundreds of years, and it's possible to take courses there as well as to receive a massage. Masseurs who trained at Wat Pho are considered to be the best in the country and masseurs all across the city advertise this as a credential, whether it's true or not. Many Thais consider blind masseurs to be especially sensitive practitioners.

The same Indian missionaries who introduced yogic practices to Thailand are also credited with spreading the word about the therapeutic effects of herbal saunas and heated herbal compresses, though the **herbs** themselves are resolutely Thai and feature in Thai cuisine as well as herbal treatments. Among these the most popular are tamarind, whose acidic content makes it a useful skin exfoliant, and turmeric, which is known for its disinfectant and healing properties; both are a common component of the scrubs and body wraps offered at many spas. The same places will also use lemon grass, probably Thailand's most distinctive herb, and the ubiquitous jasmine as soothing agents in aromatherapy treatments.

Spas and massage centres

All **spas** in Bangkok feature traditional Thai massage and herbal therapies in their programmes, but most also offer dozens of other international treatments, including facials, aromatherapy, Swedish massage and various body wraps. Spa centres in upmarket hotels are usually open to non-guests but generally need to be booked in advance; day spas that are not attached to hotels may not require reservations. We've listed a selection of Bangkok's most famous spas and massage centres, but cheaper traditional massage sessions and courses are also held at dozens of guest houses in Banglamphu.

Bann Phuan Sukhumvit Soi 11. BTS Nana. Good, inexpensive Thai massage at this no-frill streetside massage centre (B300 per hour). Daily noon–2am.

Banyan Tree Spa Banyan Tree Hotel, 21/100 Thanon Sathorn Tai ☏02 679 1054, ⊛www .banyantreespa.com. Internationally famous spa hotel with panoramic views of the city (including some hotel suites with their own private spa rooms). Extensive and very expensive programme of massages, body wraps and beauty treatments. Reservations essential. Daily 9am–10pm.

Divana Massage and Spa 7, Sukhumvit Soi 25 ☏02 661 6784, ⊛www.divanaspa.com. BTS **Asok.** Tranquil little garden-haven day spa, with a range of own-product treatments, including spas from B2950 and Thai massage from B1500 for 1hr 40min. Daily 11am–11pm.

Kinnaree Spa Buddy Lodge Hotel, 265 Thanon Khao San, Banglamphu ☏02 629 4477, ⊛www .buddylodge.com. **N13 Tha Phra Arthit express boats.** Luxurious but refreshingly mid-priced hotel spa with a full range of treatments and massages, including body scrubs and steam rooms, in chic minimalist surroundings. Daily 10am–10pm.

Mandara Spa Bangkok Marriott Resort, 257/1–3 Thanon Charoen Nakorn, beside the Krungthep Bridge in southern Thonburi ☏02 476 0021, ⊛www.mandaraspa.com. The famous chain of classy Asian spas has several outlets in Bangkok, including this one set within the extensive tropical gardens of the riverside *Bangkok Marriott Resort*, which offers all the trademark Mandara Spa treatments and massages, at fairly high prices. Phone the spa for complimentary ferry transport from the Saphan Taksin Skytrain station. Reservations essential. Daily 10am–10pm.

Nicolie Sun Square, a small shopping arcade on the south side of Thanon Silom between Soi 21 and 23 ☏02 233 6957, ⊛www.nicolie-th.com. Superb Thai (B1600 for 1hr 30min) and other massages, as well as facials and scrubs, in a soothing environment decorated with Asian objets d'art. Daily 10.30am–9.30pm.

The Oriental Spa Oriental Hotel, 48 Oriental Avenue, off Thanon Charoen Krung ☏02 659 9000, ⊛www.mandarinoriental.com. **N1 Tha Oriental express boats.** This was Bangkok's first hotel spa and, as you'd expect from the city's most famous lodging, it's a superior establishment, housed in a restored hundred-year-old teakwood home across the river from the *Oriental* and accessed by the hotel ferry. Huge range of very expensive treatments including Keralan Ayurvedic sessions and hydrotherapy. Reservations essential. Daily 9am–10pm.

Pian's Massage Center Soi Susie Pub, off Thanon Khao San, Banglamphu ☎02 629 0924. N13 Tha Phra Arthit express boats. Despite looking uninvitingly clinical, this walk-in city massage centre is very popular. It offers inexpensive traditional Thai massage (B180 per hr), foot massages, Swedish and herbal massages. Also runs courses in Thai, Swedish, herbal and foot massage (about B5000 for a 30-hour course, or B250 for a one-hour introduction). Daily 7.30am–12.30am.

Pimmalai Between sois 81 and 83, Thanon Sukhumvit ☎02 742 6452, @www.pimmalai .com. BTS On Nut (50m east from exit 1). Highly regarded, very well priced massage centre in a tranquil, attractively decorated old wooden house. Signature treatments include Lanna aromatic hot stone massage and herbal compress massage. Traditional Thai massage from B250 per hr; hot stone B1400 for 1hr 30min. Daily 10.30am–10pm.

Ruen Nuad 42 Thanon Convent, off Thanon Silom ☎02 632 2662–3. BTS Sala Daeng. Excellent Thai massages (B350 for 1hr, B600 for 2hr), as well as aromatherapy and herbal massages, in an air-con, characterful wooden house, down an alley opposite the BNH Hospital and behind *Naj* restaurant. Daily 10am–10pm.

Wat Pho Ratanakosin @www.watpomassage .com. See p.66.

Meditation

Most of Thailand's retreats are, naturally enough, out in the provinces, but a few temples and centres in Bangkok cater specifically for foreigners by holding **meditation sessions** in English; novices and practised meditators alike are generally welcome. The meditation taught is mostly Vipassana, or "insight", which emphasizes the minute observation of internal sensations; to join a one-off class, call to check times and then just turn up.

Though a little out of date, *A Guide to Buddhist Monasteries and Meditation Centres in Thailand*, published by the World Fellowship of Buddhists, contains plenty of useful general information. An even more useful resource is @www .dhammathai.org, which provides lots of general background, practical advice and details of meditation temples and centres.

House of Dhamma Insight Meditation Centre 26/9 Soi Lardprao 15, Chatuchak, Bangkok ☎02 511 0439, @www.houseofdhamma.com. Lat Phrao subway. Regular introductory two-day courses in Vipassana, and day, weekend and week-long retreats. Courses in *reiki* and other subjects available.

Wat Mahathat Thanon Maharat, Ratanakosin. See p.70.

World Fellowship of Buddhists (WFB) 616 Benjasiri Park, Soi Medhinivet off Soi 24, Thanon Sukhumvit, Bangkok ☎02 661 1284–7, @www .wfb-hq.org. Headquarters of an influential worldwide organization of (mostly Theravada) Buddhists, founded in Sri Lanka in 1950, this is the main information centre for advice on English-speaking retreats in Thailand. Holds a Buddhist discussion group and meditation session in English on the first Sunday of every month, with dharma lectures and discussions on the second Sunday.

15

Shopping

B
angkok is a fabulous place to shop, offering varied, temptingly priced and enjoyable browsing at countless market stalls, craft outlets, chic boutiques and glitzy shopping plazas. Silk, gems, contemporary interior design and fashions are famously good buys, while the city's English-language bookshops carry an exceptional range of Southeast Asian titles, and antiques and handicrafts are very popular purchases. Watch out, however, for **fakes**: cut glass masquerading as precious stones; old or damaged goods being passed off as antiques; counterfeit designer clothes and accessories; or pirated CDs and DVDs. Department stores and tourist-oriented shops in the city keep late hours, opening daily at 10am or 11am and closing at about 9pm; many small, upmarket boutiques, for example along Thanon Charoen Krung and Thanon Silom, close on Sundays. Monday is meant to be no-street-vendor day throughout Bangkok, a chance for the pavements to get cleaned and for pedestrians to finally see where they're going, but plenty of stalls manage to flout the rule.

Downtown Bangkok is full of smart, multi-storeyed **shopping plazas** like Siam Paragon, Siam Centre and Emporium, which is where you'll find the majority of the city's fashion stores, as well as designer lifestyle goods and bookshops. The plazas tend to be pleasantly air-conditioned and thronging with trendy young Thais, but don't hold much interest for tourists unless you happen to be looking for a new outfit. You're more likely to find useful items in one of the city's numerous **department stores**: seven-storey Central Chidlom on Thanon Ploenchit, which boasts handy services like watch-, garment- and shoe-repair booths as well as a huge product selection (including large sizes), is probably the city's best, though the Siam Paragon department store (which also offers garment and shoe repairs), in the shopping centre of the same name on Thanon Rama I, is also good. The British chain of **pharmacies**, Boots the Chemist, has lots of branches across the city, including on Thanon Khao San, in Siam Paragon, on Patpong, in the Times Square complex between Sukhumvit Sois 12 and 14, and in Emporium; Boots is the easiest place in the city to buy tampons.

The best places to buy anything to do with **mobile phones** (see p.54) are the scores of small booths on Floor 4 of Mah Boon Krong (MBK) Shopping Centre at the Rama I/Phrayathai intersection. For **computer** hardware and genuine and pirated software, as well as **digital cameras**, Panthip Plaza, at 604/3 Thanon Phetchaburi (BTS Ratchathewi or canal stop Tha Pratunam) is the best place: staff are often very knowledgeable and there are dozens of repair and secondhand booths, especially towards the back of the shopping centre and on the upper floors.

▲ Siam Paragon, Siam Square

Markets

For travellers, spectating, not shopping, is apt to be the main draw of Bangkok's neighbourhood **markets** – notably the bazaars of Chinatown (see p.88) and the blooms and scents of Pak Khlong Talat, the flower and vegetable market just west of Memorial Bridge (see p.90). The massive Chatuchak Weekend Market is an exception, being both a tourist attraction and a marvellous shopping experience (see p.122 for details). If you're planning on some serious market exploration, get hold of *Nancy Chandler's Map of Bangkok*, an enthusiastically annotated creation with special sections on the main areas of interest. With the chief exception of Chatuchak, most markets operate daily from dawn till early afternoon; early morning is often the best time to go to beat the heat and crowds.

Night-time shoppers will want to make a beeline for **Suan Lum Night Bazaar**, opposite Lumphini Park at the corner of Thanon Rama IV and Thanon Witthayu (Lumphini subway), a huge development of hundreds of booths, which is at its best between 6pm and 10pm. Down the narrow alleys of tiny shops, you'll find colourful street fashions, jewellery and lots of soaps, candles and beauty products, as well as some interesting contemporary decor: lighting, paintings, ceramics and woodcarving. At the centre stands the Traditional Thai Puppet Theatre (see p.197), with a popular Thai terrace-restaurant in front, and the attractive women's clothes and furnishings, notably rugs, of the Doi Tung by Mae Fah Luang shop (see p.206), with a hip *Doi Tung* coffee house attached. Other options for eating and drinking are uninspiring – your best bet is probably the open-air food court and beer garden, with a stage for nightly live music, by Thanon Witthayu. The lease on the night bazaar ran out in 2007, but amid very protracted legal wrangling and plenty of colourful rumour, it looks set to remain open for a good few years yet – though it might be worth checking with your hotel before setting out.

Handicrafts, textiles and contemporary interior design

Samples of nearly all regionally produced **handicrafts** end up in Bangkok, so the selection is phenomenal. Many of the shopping plazas have at least one classy handicraft outlet, and competition keeps prices in the city at upcountry levels, with the main exception of household objects – particularly wickerware and tin bowls and basins – which get palmed off relatively expensively in Bangkok. Handicraft sellers in Banglamphu tend to tout a limited range compared to the shops downtown, but several places on and around Thanon Khao San sell reasonably priced triangular "axe" pillows (*mawn khwaan*; see box, p.206) in traditional fabrics, which make fantastic souvenirs but are heavy to post home; some places sell unstuffed versions which are simple to mail home, but a pain to fill when you return. The cheapest outlet for traditional northern and northeastern textiles – including sarongs, axe pillows and farmers' shirts – is **Chatuchak Weekend Market** (see p.122), where you'll also able to nose out some interesting handicrafts.

Bangkok is also rapidly establishing a reputation for its **contemporary interior design**, fusing minimalist Western ideals with traditional Thai and other Asian craft elements. The best places to sample this, as detailed in the reviews below, are on Floor 4 of the Siam Discovery Centre and Floor 4 of the Siam Paragon shopping centre, both on Thanon Rama I, and Floor 3 of the Gaysorn Plaza on Thanon Ploenchit.

Banglamphu and Ratanakosin

For a map of this area see p.76; for transport information see p.78.

Lofty Bamboo Buddy Hotel complex, 265 Thanon Khao San Ⓦ www.loftybamboo.com. **N13 Tha Phra Arthit express boats.** Fair-trade outlet for Thai crafts, accessories and jewellery, including silver made by Karen people from north and west Thailand, Lahu hill-tribe bags, recycled textile products from tsunami-affected communities in Phang Nga and weaving from Mae Hong Son.

Queen's Support Foundation Grand Palace (on the right just inside the Gate of Glorious Victory; see map, p.60). N9 Tha Chang express boats. Not-for-profit shop that's especially good for beautiful, top-quality *yan lipao* – traditional basketware made from delicately woven fern stems.

Taekee Taekon 118 Thanon Phra Athit. N13 Tha Phra Arthit express boats. Tasteful assortment of traditional textiles and scarves, plus a good selection of Thai art cards, black-and-white photocards and Nancy Chandler greetings cards.

Axe pillows

Traditional triangular pillows (*mawn*) – so named because their shape supposedly resembles an axe head (*khwaan*) – are a lot more comfortable than they look and come in a range of sizes, fabrics and colours, both traditional and contemporary. **Axe pillows** have been used in Thai homes for centuries, where it's normal to sit on the floor and lean against a densely stuffed *mawn khwaan*; in wealthier homes one reclines on a polished teak chaise longue and props one's head against a *mawn khwaan*.

Pillows are made up of seven or more triangular pods, each of which is packed with kapok, although the cheaper (but longer-lasting) versions are bulked out with cardboard. The **design** has been slightly adapted over the years, so it's now also possible to get *mawn khwaan* with up to four flat cushions attached, making lying out more comfortable. The trademark *khit* fabric used in traditional-style pillows is characterized by stripes of (usually yellow) supplementary weft and is mostly woven in north and northeast Thailand. Pillows made from the multi-coloured red, blue and green nylon *khit* are the most durable, but those covered in muted shades of cotton *khit* are softer and more fashionable. The price of a *mawn khwaan* depends on the number of triangular pods in the pillow: a stand-alone ten-triangle pillow costs around B300, or B1200 with three attached cushions, and a fifteen-triangle pillow costs about B600.

Downtown: around Siam Square and Thanon Ploenchit

For a map of this area see p.108; for transport information see p.107.

Ayodhya Floor 4, Siam Paragon (BTS Central), and Floor 3, Gaysorn Plaza (BTS Chit Lom). With the same owners and designers as Panta (see opposite) but specializing in smaller items, such as gorgeous cushion covers, pouffes covered in dried water-hyacinth stalks, bowls, trays and mats.

Come Thai Floor 3, Amarin Plaza, Thanon Ploenchit. BTS Chit Lom. Wide range of unusual handwoven silk and cotton fabrics from all over Southeast Asia.

D & O Shop Floor 3, Gaysorn Plaza Ⓦwww .dandoshop.com. BTS Chit Lom. Ten enterprising local designers have formed the Design and Objects Association to showcase their diverse contemporary wares here: vases, lamps, tableware, jewellery, bags, stationery, even sandals.

Doi Tung by Mae Fah Luang Floor 4, Siam Discovery Centre (BTS Central), and Suan Lum Night Bazaar, Thanon Rama IV (Lumphini subway) Ⓦwww.doitung.org. Part of the late Princess Mother's development project based at Doi Tung in northern Thailand, selling very striking and attractive cotton and linen in warm colours, made up into clothes, cushion covers, rugs and so on, as well as rustic ceramics.

EGG Floor 4, Siam Discovery Centre Ⓦwww .eggthai.com. BTS Central. The main draws here are cushion covers, table settings and boxes which tread a fine line between traditional and modern, featuring floral- and coral-inspired motifs in sumptuous colours.

Exotique Thai Floor 4, Siam Paragon. BTS Central. A collection of small outlets from around the city and the country – including silk-makers and clothes designers down from Chiang Mai – that makes a good, upmarket one-stop shop, much more interesting than Narai Phand (see opposite). There's everything from jewellery to celadon to beauty products, with a focus on home decor and contemporary adaptations of traditional crafts.

Gilles Caffier Floor 4, Siam Discovery Centre Ⓦwww.gillescaffier.com. BTS Central. From a French designer based in Nakhon Pathom, who has spent time in Japan but takes his influences from around the world. Leather cushions, signature brown "spaghetti" bowls, and some lovely, subtly coloured modern vases.

Lamont Contemporary Floor 3, Gaysorn Plaza Ⓦwww.lamont-design.com. BTS Chit Lom. Beautiful lacquerware bowls, vases and boxes, as well as bronze, glass, crystal and ceramic objects, all in imaginative contemporary styles. Lamont also has a pan-Asian antique shop opposite, and sells both contemporary and antique lines at branches in the *Sukhothai* and *Oriental* hotels (see p.170).

Lofty Bamboo Floor 2, MBK, Siam Square. BTS Central. Branch of Banglamphu's fair-trade Thai crafts outlet (see p.205).

Narai Phand Ground floor, President Tower Arcade, just east of Gaysorn Plaza, Thanon Ploenchit ⓦwww.naraiphand.com. BTS Chit Lom. This souvenir centre was set up to ensure the preservation of traditional crafts and to maintain standards of quality, as a joint venture with the Ministry of Industry in the 1930s, and has a duly institutional feel, though it makes a reasonable one-stop shop for last-minute presents. It offers a huge assortment of reasonably priced goods from all over the country, including silk and cotton, *khon* masks, *bencharong*, nielloware and celadon, woodcarving, silver, basketware and beauty products.

Niwat (Aranyik) Floor 3, Gaysorn Plaza. BTS Chit Lom. A good place to buy that chunky, elegant Thai-style cutlery you may have been eating your dinner with in Bangkok's posher restaurants, with both traditional and contemporary handmade designs; plus lovely, handmade stainless-steel bowls.

Panta Floor 4, Siam Discovery Centre, and Floor 4, Siam Paragon ⓦwww.pantathailand.net. BTS Central. Modern design store which stands out for its experimental furniture, including way-out-there items made of woven rattan and wood, and cushions covered in dried water-hyacinth stalks, string and rag clippings.

Thann Native Floor 3, Gaysorn Plaza ⓦwww .thann.info. BTS Chit Lom. Striking contempo-rary rugs, cushion covers and furniture, plus famous spa and beauty products (with a high-concept modern spa next door).

Triphum Floor 3, Gaysorn Plaza (BTS Chit Lom), and Floor 4, Siam Paragon (BTS Central). Affordable, hand-painted reproductions of temple mural paintings, Buddhist manuscripts from Burma, repro Buddha statues in many styles, lacquerware, framed amulets and even Buddha's footprints.

Downtown: south of Thanon Rama IV

For a map of this area see p.114; for transport information see p.115.

Jim Thompson's Thai Silk Company Main shop at 9 Thanon Suriwong, corner of Thanon Rama IV (including a branch of their very good café; see p.181), plus branches at the Jim Thompson House Museum and at many department stores,

malls and hotels around the city; ⓦwww .jimthompson.com. A good place to start looking for traditional Thai fabric, or at least to get an idea of what's out there. Stocks silk and cotton by the yard and ready-made items from dresses to cushion covers, which are well designed and of good quality, though pricey. Also has a home furnishings section and a good tailoring service. A couple of hundred metres along Thanon Suriwong from the main branch, at no. 149/4–6, a Jim Thompson Factory Sales Outlet sells remnant home-furnishing fabrics and home accessories at knock-down prices (if you're really keen on a bargain, they have a much larger factory outlet way out east of the centre on Soi 93, Thanon Sukhumvit).

The Legend Floor 3, Thaniya Plaza, corner of Soi Thaniya and Thanon Silom. BTS Sala Daeng. Stocks a small selection of well-made Thai handicrafts, from wood and wickerware to pretty fabrics and celadon and other ceramics, at reasonable prices. Tamnan Mingmuang, its subsidiary opposite, concentrates on basketry from all over the country: among the unusual items on offer are trays and boxes for tobacco and betel nut made from *yan lipao* (intricately woven fern vines), and bambooware sticky rice containers, baskets and lampshades.

Silom Village 286/1 Thanon Silom. A complex of low-rise shops that attempts to create a relaxing, upcountry atmosphere as a backdrop for its diverse but pricey handicrafts.

Thanon Sukhumvit

For a map of this area see p.120; for transport information see p.121. Also in this area is a branch of Ayodhya (see opposite), on Floor 4 of Emporium.

Krisna's Just west of Soi 11. BTS Nana. Five-floor emporium of mostly mass-produced but good quality artefacts from Thailand and beyond, especially figurines and Buddha statues in wood, lacquer and silver plus some jewellery and trinkets. Mon–Sat 10am–9pm, Sun 4–7pm.

The Shop @ TCDC Thailand Creative and Design Centre, Floor 6, Emporium, Thanon Sukhumvit, between sois 22 and 24. BTS Phrom Pong. The retail outlet at Bangkok's design centre sells innovative products dreamt up by local creatives, mostly fairly funky stocking-fillers, bags and household items, with just a whiff of kitsch. Closed Mon.

Thai Celadon Soi 16 (Thanon Ratchadapisek).
BTS Asok. Classic celadon stoneware made without commercial dyes or clays and glazed with the archetypal blues and greens that were invented by the Chinese to emulate the colour of precious jade. Mainly dinner sets, vases and lamps, plus some figurines.

Tailored clothes

Inexpensive **tailoring shops** crowd Silom, Sukhumvit and Khao San roads, but the best single area to head for is the short stretch of Thanon Charoen Krung between the GPO and Thanon Silom (near the Chao Phraya express boat stops at Tha Oriental and Tha Wat Muang Kae, or ten minutes' walk from Saphan Taksin Skytrain station), where most of the recommended tailors below are. It's generally advisable to avoid tailors in tourist areas such as Thanon Khao San, shopping malls and Thanon Sukhumvit's Soi Nana and Soi 11, although if you're lucky it's still possible to come up trumps here: one that stands apart is

Having clothes tailor-made

Bangkok can be an excellent place to get **tailor-made suits, dresses, shirts and trousers** at a fraction of the price you'd pay in the West. Tailors here can copy a sample brought from home and will also work from any photographs you can provide; most also carry a good selection of catalogues. The bad news is that many tourist-oriented tailors aren't terribly good, often attempting to get away with poor work and shoddy materials (and sometimes trying to delay delivery until just before you leave the city, so that you don't have time to complain). However, with a little effort and thought, both men and women can get some fantastic clothes made to measure.

Choosing a tailor can be tricky, and unless you're particularly knowledgeable about material, shopping around won't necessarily tell you much. However, don't make a decision wholly on prices quoted – picking a tailor simply because they're the cheapest usually leads to poor work, and cheap suits don't last. Special deals offering two suits, two shirts, two ties and a kimono for US$99 should be left well alone. Above all, ignore recommendations by anyone with a vested interest in bringing your custom to a particular shop.

Prices vary widely depending on material and the tailor's skill. As a very rough guide, for labour alone expect to pay B5000–6000 for a two-piece suit, though some tailors will charge rather more (check whether or not the price you're quoted includes the lining). For middling material, expect to pay about the same again, or anything up to four times as much for top-class cloth. With the exception of **silk**, local materials are frequently of poor quality and for suits in particular you're far better off using **English or Italian cloth**. Most tailors stock both imported and local fabrics, but bringing your own from home can work out significantly cheaper.

Give yourself as much time as possible. For suits, insist on two fittings. Most good tailors require around three days for a suit (some require ten days or more), although a few have enough staff to produce good work in a day or two. The more detail you can give the tailor the better. As well as deciding on the obvious features such as single- or double-breasted and number of buttons, think about the width of lapels, style of trousers, whether you want the jacket with vents or not, and so forth. Specifying factors like this will make all the difference to whether you're happy with your suit, so it's worth discussing them with the tailor; a good tailor should be able to give good advice. Finally, don't be afraid to be an awkward customer until you're completely happy with the finished product – after all, the whole point of getting clothes tailor-made is to get exactly what you want.

Banglamphu's well-regarded Chang Torn, located at 95 Thanon Tanao (☎02 282 9390). For cheap and reasonable shirt and dress material other than silk, go for a browse around Pahurat market (see p.90), though the suit materials are mostly poor and best avoided.

A Song Tailor 8 Trok Chartered Bank, off Thanon Charoen Krung, near the Oriental Hotel ☎02 630 9708. Friendly, helpful and a good first port of call if you're on a budget.

Ah Song Tailor 1203 Thanon Charoen Krung, opposite Soi 36 ☎02 233 7574. Younger brother of the above, a meticulous tailor who takes pride in his work. Men's and women's suits.

Golden Wool 1340–1342 Thanon Charoen Krung ☎02 233 0149; **also World Group 1302–1304 Thanon Charoen Krung** ☎02 234 1527, **and 38 Oriental Avenue** ☎02 238 3344–8. All part of the same company, they can turn around decent work in three or four days, though prices are slightly on the high side.

Marco Tailor Soi 7, Siam Square ☎02 252 0689 or 02 251 7633 **(BTS Central), and Floor 2, Amarin Plaza, Thanon Ploenchit (BTS Chit Lom).** Long-established tailor with a good reputation, though not cheap by Bangkok standards; they require two or three weeks for a suit. Men's only.

Marzotto Tailor 3 Soi 42/1 (Soi Shangri-la Hotel), Thanon Charoen Krung ☎02 233 2880. Friendly business which makes everything from trousers to wedding outfits, and can make a suit in two days, with just one fitting, if necessary.

Fashions

Thanon Khao San is lined with stalls selling low-priced **fashions**: the tie-dyed vests, baggy cotton fisherman's trousers and embroidered blouses are all aimed at backpackers, but they're supplemented by cheap contemporary fashions that appeal to urban Thai trendies as well. The stalls of Banglamphu Market, around the edges of the abandoned New World department store, have the biggest range of inexpensive Thai fashions in this area. Downtown, the most famous area for low-cost, low-quality casual clothes is the warren-like Pratunam Market (see p.111) and the surrounding malls, but for the best and latest trends from Thai designers, you should check out the shops in Siam Square and across the road in the more upmarket Siam Centre.

Prices vary considerably: street gear in Siam Square is undoubtedly inexpensive (and look out for outlet stores such as Jaspal's in Amarin Plaza, Thanon Ploenchit), while genuine Western brand names are generally competitive but not breathtakingly cheaper than at home; larger sizes can be hard to find. **Shoes** and **leather goods** are good buys in Bangkok, being generally handmade from high-quality leather and quite a bargain: check out branches of the stylish, Italian-influenced Viera by Ragazze (Ⓦwww.ragazze.co.th) in the Silom Complex (Floor 2), Thanon Silom, in Central World Plaza or in the attached Isetan department store.

Central World Plaza Ratchaprasong Intersection, corner of Rama I and Rajdamri. BTS Chit Lom. This recently refurbished shopping centre is so huge that it defies easy classification, but you'll find plenty of Thai and international fashions on its lower floors and in the attached Zen department store at its southern end.

Emporium Thanon Sukhumvit, between sois 22 and 24. BTS Phrom Pong. Enormous and rather glamorous shopping plaza, with a

good range of fashion outlets, from exclusive designer wear to trendy high-street gear. Brand-name outlets include Versace, Prada, Gucci, Chanel and Louis Vuitton.

Gaysorn Plaza Thanon Ploenchit. BTS Chit Lom. The most chic of the city's shopping plazas: among Burberry, Emporio Armani and Louis Vuitton, a few Thai names have made it onto the second floor, notably Fly Now, which mounts dramatic displays of women's party and formal gear, alongside more casual wear, and Myth, a gathering of six cutting-edge local designers for men and women in one store.

Mah Boon Krong (MBK) At the Rama I/ Phrayathai intersection. BTS Central.
Labyrinthine shopping centre which houses hundreds of small, mostly fairly inexpensive outlets, including plenty of high-street fashion shops.

Siam Centre Thanon Rama I. BTS Central.
Particularly good for hip local labels, many of whom have made the step up from the booths of Siam Square across the road – look out for Baking Soda, Fly Now, Greyhound, Headquarter, Jaspal, Kloset, Senada and Theatre – as well as international names like Nike and Quiksilver.

Siam Square BTS Central. Worth poking around the alleys here, especially near what's styled as the area's "Centerpoint" between sois 3 and 4. All manner of inexpensive boutiques, some little more than booths, sell colourful street gear to the capital's fashionable students and teenagers.

Books

English–language **bookstores** in Bangkok are always well stocked with everything to do with Thailand and the rest of Southeast Asia, and most carry fiction classics and popular paperbacks as well. Imported books are quite pricey, however. The capital's **secondhand** bookstores are not cheap, but you can usually part–exchange your unwanted titles.

Aporia 131 Thanon Tanao, Banglamphu. N13 Tha Phra Arthit express boat. This is one of Banglamphu's main outlets for new books and keeps a good stock of titles on Thai and Southeast Asian culture, a decent selection of travelogues, plus some English-language fiction. Also sells secondhand books.

Asia Books Branches on Thanon Sukhumvit between sois 15 and 19 (BTS Asok); in Landmark Plaza between sois 4 and 6 (BTS Nana); in Times Square between sois 12 and 14 (BTS Asok); and in Emporium between sois 22 and 24 (BTS Phrom Pong); downtown on Thanon Rajdamri in the Peninsula Plaza (BTS Ratchadamri) and Central World Plaza (BTS Chit Lom); in Siam Discovery Centre and Siam Paragon, both on Thanon Rama I (both BTS Central); and in Thaniya Plaza on Soi Thaniya off Thanon Silom (BTS Sala Daeng). English-language bookstore (and publishing house) that's especially recommended for its books on Asia – everything from guidebooks to cookery books, novels to art (the Sukhumvit 15–19 branch has the very best Asian selection). Also stocks bestselling novels and coffee-table books.

B2S Floors 1–3, Central World Plaza, and Floor 7, Central Chidlom, Thanon Ploenchit. BTS Chit Lom. Decent selection of English-language books, but most notable for its huge selection of magazines, newspapers and stationery.

Bookazine Silom Complex, Thanon Silom (BTS Sala Daeng); Soi 4, Siam Square (BTS Central); Gaysorn Plaza, Thanon Ploenchit (BTS Chit Lom); and at the mouth of Sukhumvit Soi 5 (BTS Nana). Alongside a decent selection of novels and English-language books about Asia, these shops stock a wide range of foreign newspapers and magazines.

Books Kinokuniya Third Floor, Emporium Shopping Centre, between sois 22 and 24 on Thanon Sukhumvit (BTS Phrom Pong); plus branches at Floor 6, Isetan, in the Central World Plaza, Thanon Rajdamri (BTS Chit Lom); and Floor 3, Siam Paragon, Thanon Rama I (BTS Central). Huge, efficient English-language bookstore with a wide selection of books ranging from bestsellers to travel literature and from classics to sci-fi; not so hot on books about Asia though.

Dasa Book Cafe Between sois 26 and 28, Thanon Sukhumvit ⓦ www.dasabookcafe.com. BTS Phrom Pong. Appealingly calm secondhand bookshop that's intelligently categorized, with sections on everything from Asia to chick lit, health to gay and lesbian interest. Browse its stock online, or enjoy coffee and cakes in situ.

Orchid Books Silom Complex, Thanon Silom. BTS Sala Daeng. Publishers' shop devoted to scholarly books, fiction and poetry, both new works and reprints, related to Asia.

Rim Khob Fa Bookshop Democracy Monument roundabout, Rajdamnoen Klang, Banglamphu. Useful outlet for the more obscure and esoteric English-language books on Thailand and Southeast Asia, as well as mainstream titles on Thai culture.

Shaman Books Thanon Khao San (3 branches), Banglamphu. N13 Tha Phra Arthit express boats. Well-stocked secondhand bookshop where all books are logged on the computer. Lots of books on Asia (travel, fiction, politics and history) as well as a decent range of novels and general interest books.

Silkworm Books @ The Siam Society 131 Sukhumvit Soi 21, inside the Ban Kamthieng compound. BTS Asok. Extensive collection of esoteric and academic books about Thailand, including many ethnology studies published by White Lotus and by the Siam Society itself. Tues–Sat 9am–5pm.

Ton's Bookseller 327/5 Thanon Ram Bhuttri, Banglamphu. N13 Tha Phra Arthit express boats. Exceptionally well stocked with titles about Thailand and Southeast Asia, particularly political commentary and Buddhist studies.

Jewellery and gems

Bangkok boasts the country's best **gem and jewellery** shops, and some of the finest lapidaries in the world, making this *the* place to buy cut and uncut stones such as rubies, blue sapphires and diamonds. However, countless gem-buying tourists get badly **ripped off**, so be extremely wary. Never buy anything through a tout or from any shop recommended by a "government official", "student", "businessperson" or tuk-tuk driver who just happens to engage you in conversation on the street, and note that there are no government jewellery shops, despite any information you may be given to the contrary. Always check that the shop is a member of the **Thai Gem and Jewelry Traders Association** by calling the association or visiting their website (℡02 630 1390–7, ⓦwww.thaigemjewelry.or.th).

To be doubly sure, you may want to seek out shops that also belong to the TGJTA's **Jewel Fest Club** (ⓦwww.jewelfest.com), which guarantees quality and will offer refunds; see their website for a directory of members. For independent professional advice or precious stones certification, contact the Asian Institute of Gemological Sciences, located on the sixth floor of the Jewelry Trade Center Building, 919/1 Thanon Silom (℡02 267 4325, ⓦwww.aigsthailand.com), which also runs reputable **courses**, such as a five-day (15hr) introduction to gemstones (US$250).

A common **scam** is to charge a lot more than what the gem is worth based on its carat weight. Get it tested on the spot, ask for a written guarantee and receipt. Don't even consider **buying gems in bulk** to sell at a supposedly vast profit elsewhere: many a gullible traveller has invested thousands of dollars on a handful of worthless multi-coloured stones, believing the vendor's reassurance that the goods will fetch at least a hundred percent more when resold at home. Gem scams are so common in Bangkok that TAT has published a brochure about it and there are several websites on the subject, including the very informative ⓦwww.2bangkok.com/2bangkok/Scams/Sapphire.shtml, which describes the typical scam in detail and advises on what to do if you get caught out; it's also updated with details of the latest scammers. Most victims get no recompense at all, but you have more chance of doing so if you contact the website's recommended authorities while still in Thailand.

The most exclusive of the reputable **gem outlets** are on Thanon Silom, notably in the Jewelry Trade Center (Silom Galleria); you can get an idea of prices at the online catalogue ⓦwww.thaigem.com. Other recommended outlets include the nearby, American-owned Lambert, at Silom Shanghai Building, Soi 17, Thanon Silom (℡02 236 4343, ⓦwww.lambertgems.com);

the very upscale Kim's in Oriental Place in front of the *Oriental*; and Johnny's Gems at 199 Thanon Fuang Nakhon, near Wat Rajabophit (☎02 224 4065). Thongtavee, at Floor 2, River City, and in the Jewelry Trade Center, both outlets of a famous Burmese **jade** factory in Mae Sai in northern Thailand, sell beautiful jade jewellery, as well as carved Buddha statues, chopsticks and the like. The hub of Bangkok's **gold** trade is Chinatown, specifically Thanon Yaowarat, which boasts over a hundred outlets. For cheap **silver** earrings, bracelets and necklaces, you can't beat the traveller-orientated jewellery shops along Trok Mayom in Banglamphu.

Antiques and paintings

Bangkok is the entrepôt for the finest Thai, Burmese and Cambodian **antiques**, but the market has long been sewn up, so don't expect to happen upon any undiscovered treasure. Even experts admit that they sometimes find it hard to tell real antiques from fakes, so the best policy is just to buy on the grounds of attractiveness. The **River City** shopping complex off Thanon Charoen Krung, which is near Si Phraya and Harbour Department express-boat piers, and operates a shuttle boat from Saphan Taksin BTS (Ⓦ www.rivercity.co.th), devotes its third, fourth and some of its second floors to a bewildering array of pricey treasures, as well as holding an auction on the first Saturday of every month (viewing during the preceding week; ☎02 237 0077 ext 459 or 461). Worth singling out here are Old Maps and Prints on Floor 4 (Ⓦ www.classic maps.com), which has some lovely old prints of Thailand and Asia (starting at around B3000), as well as rare maps; Ingon Gallery on Floor 3, which specializes in small Chinese pieces made of jade and other precious stones, such as snuff boxes, jewellery, statuettes and amulets; and on the same floor, Beyond the Masks, which is true to its name: Asian tribal masks plus a miscellany of ornamental coconut scrapers, silver jewellery and fabrics.

The other main area for antiques is the section of Charoen Krung that runs between the GPO and the bottom of Thanon Silom, and the stretch of Silom running east from here up to and including the multi-storey Silom Galleria. Here you'll find a good selection of largely reputable individual businesses specializing in woodcarvings, ceramics, bronze statues and stone sculptures culled from all parts of Thailand and neighbouring countries as well. The owners of Old Maps and Prints have a second outlet, the Old Siam Trading Company in the Nailert Building at the mouth of Thanon Sukhumvit Soi 5 (Ⓦ www.oldsiamtrading.com). There are also half-a-dozen shops specializing in Thai and Chinese antiques on Thanon Mahachai, across the road from Wat Rajnadda in Banglamphu. Remember that most antiques require an export permit (see p.49).

Street-corner stalls all over the city sell poor-quality mass-produced traditional Thai **paintings**, but for a huge selection of Thai art, especially oil paintings, visit Sombat Permpoon Gallery at 12, Sukhumvit Soi 1 (Ⓦ www .sombatpermpoongallery.com), which carries thousands of canvases, framed and unframed, spanning the range from classical Ayutthayan-era-style village scenes to twenty-first-century abstracts. The gallery also has works by famous Thai artists like Thawan Duchanee.

Kids' Bangkok

Thais are very tolerant of children, so you can take them almost anywhere without restriction. The only drawback might be the constant attention lavished on your kids by complete strangers, which can get tiring for adults and children alike.

Should you be in Thailand in January, your kids will be able to join in the free entertainments and activities staged all over the city on **National Children's Day** (Wan Dek), which is held on the second Saturday of January. They also get free entry to zoos that day and free rides on public buses.

Practicalities

Kids get **discounts** at most of the theme parks and amusement centres listed on p.214, though not at the majority of the city's museums, and there are no reductions on Bangkok buses and boats.

Many of Bangkok's expensive **hotels** offer special deals for families (see p.160) and an increasing number of guesthouses offer three-person rooms. Decent cots are available free in the bigger hotels as well as at some smaller ones (though cots in these places can be a bit grotty) and top-and mid-range rooms often come with a fridge. Many hotels can also provide a **babysitting service**.

Although most Thai babies don't wear them, **disposable nappies** (diapers) are sold at pharmacies, supermarkets, department stores and convenience stores across the city, as is international-brand formula and baby food (though some parents find restaurant-cooked rice and bananas go down just as well). Thai women do not **breastfeed** in public. A **changing mat** may be worth bringing with you as, although there are public toilets in every shopping plaza and department store, few have baby facilities (toilets at posh hotels being a useful exception).

Opinions are divided on whether or not it's worth bringing a **buggy** or three-wheeled **stroller**. Bangkok's pavements are bumpy at best and there's an almost total absence of ramps. Buggies and strollers do, however, come in handy for feeding and even bedding small children, as highchairs and cots are only provided in the most upmarket hotels. Taxis and car-rental companies almost never provide **children's car seats**; even if you bring your own you'll often find there are no seatbelts to strap them in with.

Should you need to buy a crucial piece of **children's gear** while you're in Bangkok, you should find it in one of the department stores (see p.203), which all have children's sections selling bottles, slings and clothes. There are even several branches of Mothercare in the main shopping plazas, including in the Emporium (between Sukhumvit sois 22 and 24; BTS Phrom Pong; see map, p.120); in Central Chidlom on Thanon Ploenchit (BTS Chit Lom; see map, p.108); and in

Siam Paragon at Siam Square (BTS Central; see map, p.108). Children's clothes are very cheap in Thailand.

Even more than their parents, children need protecting from the sun, unsafe drinking water, heat and unfamiliar **food**. As with adults, you should be careful about unwashed fruit and salads and about dishes that have been left uncovered for a long time (see p.174). As diarrhoea can be dangerous for a child, rehydration solutions (see under "Health", p.38) are vital if your child goes down with it. You should also make sure, if possible, that your child is aware of the dangers of rabies; keep children away from animals, especially dogs and monkeys, and ask your medical adviser about rabies jabs.

Information and other resources

Nancy Chandler's Family Travel ⓦ www .nancychandler.net/travelwkids.asp. Plenty of unusual ideas on Thai-style entertainment for kids, plus tips, links and Thailand-themed kids' books.

Thailand 4 Kids ⓦ www.thailand4kids.com. Sells an e-book guide covering the practicalities of family holidays in Thailand.

Activities for kids

The main drawback with Bangkok's kid-centred **activities** is that most of the theme parks listed below are a long way from the city centre. However, a number of more accessible adult-oriented attractions also go down well with kids, including the Museum of Siam (see p.68), Siam Ocean World aquarium (see p.109), Dusit Zoo (see p.103), the Snake Farm (see p.115), cycling around Muang Boran Ancient City (see p.130), feeding the turtles at Wat Prayoon (see p.99), taking a canal boat through Thonburi (p.95), pedal-boating in Lumphini Park (see p.115) and the Traditional Thai Puppet Theatre (see p.197).

Bangkok Butterfly Garden and Insectarium In Suan Rotfai (Railway Park), just north of Chatuchak Weekend Market ☎02 272 4359. **BTS Mo Chit or Chatuchak Park subway.** Tues–Sun 8.30am–4.30pm; free. Over 500 butterflies inhabit an enormous landscaped dome. Family-oriented cycle routes and bikes for rent in the adjacent park, which also has a kids' playground.

Children's Discovery Museum Opposite Chatuchak Weekend Market on Thanon Kamphaeng Phet 4 ☎02 615 7333. **BTS Mo Chit or Chatuchak Park subway or, from Banglamphu, any bus bound for Chatuchak or the Northern Bus Terminal (see p.78).** Tues–Fri 9am–5pm, Sat & Sun 10am–6pm; B150, kids B120. Interactive displays covering science, the environment, human and animal life.

Dream World 10min drive north of Don Muang Airport at kilometre-stone 7 on Thanon Rangsit-Ongharak ☎02 533 1152, ⓦ www.dreamworld-th .com. **BTS Mo Chit or Chatuchak Park subway, then air-con bus #523; or non-air-con buses #39 or #59 from Banglamphu to Rangsit, then songthaew or tuk-tuk to Dream World.** Mon–Fri 10am–5pm, Sat & Sun 10am–7pm; B120,

children B95. Theme park with different areas such as Snow Land, Dream Garden and Adventure Land. Water rides, a flying carpet and other amusements.

Safari World On the northeastern outskirts at 99 Thanon Ramindra, Minburi ☎02 518 1000, ⓦ www.safariworld.com. **Air-con bus #60 from Banglamphu or air-con #26 from Victory Monument, then a songthaew to Safari World.** Daily 9am–4.30pm; joint ticket to both parks B700, children B450. Drive-through safari park, with monkeys, lions, giraffes and zebras, and separate marine park with dolphins and sea lions. Both stage animal shows (phone for times).

Siam Park On the far eastern edge of town at 101 Thanon Sukhapiban 2 ☎02 919 7200, ⓦ www.siamparkcity.com. **Air-con bus #60 from Banglamphu or air-con #501 from Hualam-phong Station.** Daily 10am–6pm; B400, children B300. Popular water park that boasts some of the longest waterslides in the country, along with all manner of whirl-pools and swimming pools. There's also a mini-zoo, a botanical garden and rollercoasters.

Contexts

Contexts

History

B
angkok is a comparatively new capital, founded in 1782 after Ayutthaya, a short way upriver, had been razed by the Burmese, but it has established an overwhelming dominance in Thailand. Its history over the last two centuries directly mirrors that of the country as a whole, and the city has gathered to itself, in the National Museum and elsewhere, the major relics of Thailand's previous civilizations, principally from the eras of Ayutthaya and its precursor, Sukhothai.

Early history

The region's first distinctive civilization, **Dvaravati**, was established around two thousand years ago by an Austroasiatic-speaking people known as the Mon. One of its mainstays was Theravada Buddhism, which had been introduced to Thailand during the second or third century BC by Indian missionaries. From the discovery of monastery boundary stones (sema), clay votive tablets and Indian-influenced Buddhist sculpture, it's clear that the Dvaravati city-states (including **Nakhon Pathom**) had their greatest flourishing between the sixth and ninth centuries AD. Meanwhile, in the eighth century, peninsular Thailand to the south of Dvaravati came under the control of the **Srivijaya** empire, a Mahayana Buddhist state centred on Sumatra which had strong ties with India.

From the ninth century onwards, however, both Dvaravati and Srivijaya Thailand succumbed to invading **Khmers** from Cambodia, who consolidated their position during the watershed reign of **Jayavarman II** (802–50). To establish his authority, Jayavarman II had himself initiated as a chakravartin or universal ruler, the living embodiment of the **devaraja**, the divine essence of kingship – a concept which was adopted by later Thai rulers. From their capital at **Angkor**, Jayavarman's successors took control over northeastern, central and peninsular Thailand, thus mastering the most important trade routes between India and China. By the thirteenth century, however, the Khmers had overreached themselves and were in no position to resist the onslaught of a vibrant new force in Southeast Asia, the Thais.

The earliest Thais

The earliest traceable history of the **Thai people** picks them up in southern China around the fifth century AD, when they were squeezed by Chinese and Vietnamese expansionism into sparsely inhabited northeastern Laos. Their first significant entry into what is now Thailand seems to have happened in the north, where some time after the seventh century the Thais formed a state known as Yonok. Theravada Buddhism spread to **Yonok** via Dvaravati around the end of the tenth century, which served not only to unify the Thais themselves but also to link them to the wider community of Buddhists.

By the end of the twelfth century they formed the majority of the population in Thailand, then under the control of the Khmer empire. The Khmers' main outpost, at Lopburi, was by this time regarded as the administrative capital of a land called **Syam** (possibly from the Sanskrit *syam*, meaning swarthy) – a mid-twelfth-century bas-relief at Angkor portraying the troops of Lopburi, preceded by a large group of self-confident Syam Kuk mercenaries, shows that the Thais were becoming a force to be reckoned with.

Sukhothai

At some time around 1238, Thais in the upper Chao Phraya valley captured the main Khmer outpost in the region at **Sukhothai** and established a kingdom there. For the first forty years it was merely a local power, but an attack by the ruler of the neighbouring principality of Mae Sot brought a dynamic new leader to the fore: the king's 19-year-old son, Rama, defeated the opposing commander, earning himself the name **Ramkhamhaeng**, "Rama the Bold". When Ramkhamhaeng himself came to the throne around 1278, he seized control of much of the Chao Phraya valley, and over the next twenty years, more by diplomacy than military action, gained the submission of most of Thailand under a complex tribute system.

Although the empire of Sukhothai extended Thai control over a vast area, its greatest contribution to the Thais' development was at home, in cultural and political matters. A famous **inscription** by Ramkhamhaeng, now housed in the Bangkok National Museum, describes a prosperous era of benevolent rule: "In the time of King Ramkhamhaeng this land of Sukhothai is thriving. There is fish in the water and rice in the fields… [The King] has hung a bell in the opening of the gate over there: if any commoner has a grievance which sickens his belly and gripes his heart… he goes and strikes the bell… [and King Ramkhamhaeng] questions the man, examines the case, and decides it justly for him."

Although this plainly smacks of self-promotion, it seems to contain at least a kernel of truth: in deliberate contrast to the Khmer god-kings (*devaraja*), Ramkhamhaeng styled himself as a **dhammaraja**, a king who ruled justly according to Theravada Buddhist doctrine and made himself accessible to his people. A further sign of the Thais' growing self-confidence was the invention of a new script to make their tonal language understood by the non-Thai inhabitants of the land.

The growth of Ayutthaya

After the death of Ramkhamhaeng around 1299, however, his empire quickly fell apart. By 1320 Sukhothai had regressed to being a kingdom of only local significance, though its mantle as the capital of a Thai empire was taken up shortly after at **Ayutthaya** to the south. Soon after founding the city in 1351, the ambitious king Ramathibodi united the principalities of the lower Chao Phraya valley, which had formed the western provinces of the Khmer empire. When he recruited his bureaucracy from the urban elite of Lopburi, **Ramathibodi** set the style of government at Ayutthaya, elements of which persisted into the Bangkok empire and up to the present day. The elaborate etiquette, language and rituals of Angkor were adopted, and, most importantly, the conception of the ruler as *devaraja*: when the king processed through the town, ordinary people were forbidden to look at him and had to be silent while he passed.

The site chosen by Ramathibodi was the best in the region for an international port, and so began Ayutthaya's rise to prosperity, based on exploiting the upswing in trade in the middle of the fourteenth century along the routes between India and China. By 1540, the Kingdom of Ayutthaya had grown to cover most of the area of modern-day Thailand. Despite a 1568 invasion by the Burmese, which led to twenty years of foreign rule, Ayutthaya made a spectacular comeback, and in the seventeenth century its **foreign trade** boomed. In 1511 the Portuguese had become the first Western power to trade with Ayutthaya, and a treaty with Spain was concluded in 1598; relations with Holland and England were initiated in 1608 and 1612 respectively. European merchants flocked to Thailand, not only to buy Thai products, but also to gain access to Chinese and Japanese goods on sale there.

The Burmese invasion

In the mid-eighteenth century, however, the rumbling in the Burmese jungle to the north began to make itself heard again. After an unsuccessful siege in 1760, in February 1766 the Burmese descended upon the city for the last time. The Thais held out for over a year, during which they were afflicted by famine, epidemics and a terrible fire which destroyed ten thousand houses. Finally, in April 1767, the walls were breached and the city taken. The Burmese savagely razed everything to the ground and led off tens of thousands of prisoners to Burma, including most of the royal family. The city was abandoned to the jungle, and Thailand descended into banditry.

Taksin and Thonburi

Out of this lawless mess, however, emerged **Phraya Taksin**, a charismatic and brave general, who had been unfairly blamed for a failed counterattack against the Burmese at Ayutthaya and had quietly slipped away from the besieged city. Taksin was crowned king in December 1768 at his new capital of **Thonburi**, on the opposite bank of the river from modern-day Bangkok. Within two years he had restored all of Ayutthaya's territories; more remarkably, by the end of the next decade Taksin had outdone his Ayutthayan predecessors by bringing Cambodia and much of Laos into a huge new empire.

However, by 1779 all was not well with the king. Taksin was becoming increasingly paranoid about plots against him, a delusion that drove him to imprison and torture even his wife and sons. At the same time he sank into religious excesses, demanding that the monkhood worship him as a god. By March 1782, public outrage at his sadism and dangerously irrational behaviour had reached such fervour that he was ousted in a coup.

Chao Phraya Chakri, Taksin's military commander, was invited to take power and had Taksin executed. In accordance with ancient etiquette, this had to be done without royal blood touching the earth: the mad king was duly wrapped in a black velvet sack and struck on the back of the neck with a sandalwood club. (Popular tradition has it that even this form of execution was too much: an unfortunate substitute got the velvet sack treatment, while Taksin was whisked away to a palace in the hills near Nakhon Si Thammarat, where he is said to have lived until 1825.)

The early Bangkok empire: Rama I

With the support of the Ayutthayan aristocracy, Chakri – reigning as **Rama I** (1782–1809) – set about consolidating the Thai kingdom. His first act was to move the capital across the river to what we know as **Bangkok**, on the more defensible east bank where the French had built a grand but short-lived fort in the 1660s. Borrowing from the layout of Ayutthaya, he built a new royal palace and impressive monasteries in the area of **Ratanakosin** – which remains the city's spiritual heart – within a defensive ring of two (later expanded to three) canals. In the palace temple, Wat Phra Kaeo, he enshrined the talismanic Emerald Buddha, which he had snatched during his campaigns in Laos. Initially, as at Ayutthaya, the city was largely amphibious: only the temples and royal palaces were built on dry land, while ordinary residences floated on thick bamboo rafts on the river and canals, and even shops and warehouses were moored to the river bank.

During Rama I's reign, trade with China revived, and the style of government was put on a more modern footing: while retaining many of the features of a *devaraja*, he shared more responsibility with his courtiers, as a first among equals.

Rama II and Rama III

The peaceful accession of his son as **Rama II** (1809–24) signalled the establishment of the **Chakri dynasty**, which is still in place today. This Second Reign was a quiet interlude, best remembered as a fertile period for Thai literature. The king, himself one of the great Thai poets, gathered round him a group of writers including the famous Sunthorn Phu, who produced scores of masterly love poems, travel accounts and narrative songs.

In contrast, **Rama III** (1824–51) actively discouraged literary development and was a vigorous defender of conservative values. To this end, he embarked on an extraordinary redevelopment of **Wat Pho**, the oldest temple in Bangkok. Hundreds of educational inscriptions and mural paintings, on all manner of secular and religious subjects, were put on show, apparently to preserve traditional culture against the rapid change which the king saw corroding the country.

The danger posed by Western influence became more apparent in the Third Reign. As early as 1825, the Thais were sufficiently alarmed by British colonialism to strengthen Bangkok's defences by stretching a great iron chain across the mouth of the Chao Phraya River, to which every blacksmith in the area had to donate a certain number of links. In 1826 Rama III was obliged to sign the **Burney Treaty**, a limited trade agreement with the British by which the Thais won some political security in return for reducing their taxes on goods passing through Bangkok.

Mongkut

Rama IV, commonly known to foreigners as **Mongkut** (in Thai, *Phra Chom Klao*; 1851–68), had been a Buddhist monk for 27 years when he succeeded his brother. But far from leading a cloistered life, Mongkut had travelled widely throughout Thailand, had maintained scholarly contacts with French and American missionaries, and had taken an interest in Western learning, studying English, Latin and the sciences.

When his kingship faced its first major test, in the form of a threatening British mission in 1855 led by **Sir John Bowring**, Mongkut dealt with it confidently. Realizing that Thailand would be unable to resist the military might of the British, the king reduced import and export taxes, allowed British subjects to live and own land in Thailand and granted them freedom of trade. Furthermore, Mongkut quickly made it known that he would welcome diplomatic contacts from other Western countries: within a decade, agreements similar to the Bowring Treaty had been signed with France, the United States and a score of other nations.

Thus by skilful diplomacy the king avoided a close relationship with just one power, which could easily have led to Thailand's annexation. And as a result of the open-door policy, foreign trade boomed, financing the redevelopment of Bangkok's waterfront and, for the first time, the building of paved roads. However, Mongkut ran out of time for instituting the far-reaching domestic reforms which he saw were needed to drag Thailand into the modern world.

Chulalongkorn

Mongkut's son, **Chulalongkorn**, took the throne as Rama V (1868–1910) at the age of only 15, but he was well prepared by an excellent education which mixed traditional Thai and modern Western elements – provided by Mrs Anna Leonowens, subject of *The King and I*. When Chulalongkorn reached his majority after a five-year regency, he set to work on the reforms envisioned by his father.

One of his first acts was to scrap the custom by which subjects were required to prostrate themselves in the presence of the king. He constructed a new residential palace for the royal family in **Dusit**, north of Ratanakosin, and laid out that area's grand European-style boulevards. In the 1880s Chulalongkorn began to **restructure the government** to meet the country's needs, setting up a host of departments, for education, public health, the army and the like, and bringing in scores of foreign advisers to help with everything from foreign affairs to rail lines.

Throughout this period, however, the Western powers maintained their pressure on the region. The most serious threat to Thai sovereignty was the **Franco-Siamese Crisis** of 1893, which culminated in the French sending gunboats up the Chao Phraya River to Bangkok. Flouting numerous international laws, France claimed control over Laos and made other outrageous demands, which Chulalongkorn had no option but to concede. During the course of his reign the country was obliged to cede almost half of its territory, and forewent huge sums of tax revenue, in order to preserve its independence; but by Chulalongkorn's death in 1910, the frontiers were fixed as they are today.

The end of absolute monarchy

Chulalongkorn was succeeded by a flamboyant, British-educated prince, **Vajiravudh** (Rama VI, 1910–25). However, in 1912 a group of young army lieutenants, disillusioned by the absolute monarchy, plotted a coup. The conspirators were easily broken up, but this was something new in Thai history: the country was used to infighting among the royal family, but not to military intrigue by men from comparatively ordinary backgrounds. By the time the young and inexperienced **Prajadhipok** – seventy-sixth child of Chulalongkorn – was catapulted to the throne as Rama VII (1925–35), Vajiravudh's extravagance had created severe financial problems. The vigorous community of Western-educated intellectuals who had emerged in the lower echelons of the bureaucracy were becoming increasingly dissatisfied with monarchical government. The Great Depression, which ravaged the economy in the 1930s, came as the final shock to an already moribund system.

On June 24, 1932, a small group of middle-ranking officials, led by a lawyer, **Pridi Phanomyong**, and an army major, Luang Phibunsongkhram (**Phibun**), staged a **coup** with only a handful of troops. Prajadhipok weakly submitted to the conspirators, and 150 years of absolute monarchy in Bangkok came to a sudden end. The king was sidelined to a position of symbolic significance, and in 1935 he abdicated in favour of his ten-year-old nephew, **Ananda**, then a schoolboy living in Switzerland.

Up to World War II

The success of the 1932 coup was in large measure attributable to the army officers who gave the conspirators credibility, and it was they who were to dominate the constitutional governments that followed. Phibun emerged as prime minister after the decisive elections of 1938, and encouraged a wave of nationalistic feeling with such measures as the official institution of the name Thailand in 1939 – Siam, it was argued, was a name bestowed by external forces, and the new title made it clear that the country belonged to the Thais rather than the economically dominant Chinese.

The Thais were dragged into **World War II** on December 8, 1941, when, almost at the same time as the assault on Pearl Harbor, the Japanese invaded the east coast of peninsular Thailand, with their sights set on Singapore to the south. The Thais at first resisted fiercely, but realizing that the position was hopeless, Phibun quickly ordered a ceasefire.

The Thai government concluded a military alliance with Japan and declared war against the United States and Great Britain in January 1942, probably in the belief that the Japanese would win. However, the Thai minister in Washington, Seni Pramoj, refused to deliver the declaration of war against the US and, in cooperation with the Americans, began organizing a resistance movement called **Seri Thai**. Pridi Phanomyong, now acting as regent to the young king, furtively coordinated the movement under the noses of the occupying Japanese, smuggling in American agents and housing them in a European prison camp in Bangkok.

By 1944 Japan's defeat looked likely, and in July Phibun, who had been most closely associated with them, was forced to resign by the National Assembly. Once the war was over, American support prevented the British from imposing heavy punishments on the country for its alliance with Japan.

Postwar upheavals

With the fading of the military, the election of January 1946 was for the first time contested by organized political parties, resulting in Pridi becoming prime minister. A new constitution was drafted and the outlook for democratic, civilian government seemed bright. Hopes were shattered, however, on June 9, 1946, when King Ananda was found dead in his bed, with a bullet wound in his forehead. Three palace servants were hurriedly tried and executed, but the murder has never been satisfactorily explained. Pridi resigned as prime minister, and in April 1948 Phibun, playing on the threat of communism, took over the premiership.

As **communism** developed its hold in the region with the takeover of China in 1949 and the French defeat in Indochina in 1954, the US increasingly viewed Thailand as a bulwark against the red menace. Between 1951 and 1957, when its annual state budget was only about $200 million a year, Thailand received a total $149 million in American economic aid and $222 million in military aid. This strengthened Phibun's dictatorship, while enabling leading military figures to divert American money and other funds into their own pockets.

Phibun narrowly won a general election in 1957, but only by blatant vote rigging and coercion. Although there's a strong tradition of foul play in Thai elections, this is remembered as the dirtiest ever: after vehement public outcry, **General Sarit**, the commander-in-chief of the army, overthrew the new government in September 1957. Believing that Thailand would prosper best under a unifying authority, Sarit set about re-establishing the monarchy as the head of the social hierarchy and the source of legitimacy for the government. Ananda's successor, **Bhumibol** (**Rama IX**), was pushed into an active role, while Sarit ruthlessly silenced critics and pressed ahead with a plan for economic development, achieving a large measure of stability and prosperity.

The Vietnam War

Sarit died in 1963, whereupon the military succession passed to **General Thanom**, closely aided by his deputy prime minister, General Praphas. Their most pressing problem was the **Vietnam War**. The Thais, with the backing of the US, quietly began to conduct military operations in Laos, to which North Vietnam and China responded by supporting anti-government insurgency in Thailand. The more the Thais felt threatened by the spread of communism, the more they looked to the Americans for help – by 1968 around 45,000 US military personnel were on Thai soil, which became the base for US bombing raids against North Vietnam and Laos.

The effects of the **American presence** were profound. The economy swelled with dollars, and hundreds of thousands of Thais became reliant on the Americans for a living, with a consequent proliferation of prostitution – centred on Bangkok's infamous Patpong district – and corruption. The sudden exposure to Western culture also led many to question traditional Thai values and the political status quo.

The democracy movement and civil unrest

Poor farmers in particular were becoming increasingly disillusioned with their lot, and many turned against the Bangkok government. At the end of 1964, the Communist Party of Thailand and other groups formed a broad left coalition which soon had the support of several thousand insurgents in remote areas of the northeast and the north. By 1967, a separate threat had arisen in southern Thailand, involving Muslim dissidents and the Chinese-dominated Communist Party of Malaya, as well as local Thais.

Thanom was now facing a major security crisis, especially as the war in Vietnam was going badly. In November 1971 he reimposed repressive military rule, under a triumvirate of himself, his son Colonel Narong and Praphas, who became known as the "Three Tyrants". However, the 1969 experiment with democracy had heightened expectations of power-sharing among the middle classes, especially in the universities. **Student demonstrations** began in June 1973, and in October as many as 500,000 people turned out at Thammasat University in Bangkok to demand a new constitution. King Bhumibol intervened with apparent success, and indeed the demonstrators were starting to disperse on the morning of October 14, when the police tried to control the flow of people away. Tensions quickly mounted and soon a full-scale riot was under way, during which over 350 people were reported killed. The army, however, refused to provide enough troops to suppress this massive uprising, and later the same day, Thanom, Narong and Praphas were forced to resign and leave the country.

In a new climate of openness, **Kukrit Pramoj** formed a coalition of seventeen elected parties and secured a promise of US withdrawal from Thailand, but his government was riven with feuding. In October 1976, the students demonstrated again, protesting against the return of Thanom to Bangkok to become a monk at Wat Bowonniwet. This time there was no restraint: supported by elements of the military and the government, the police and reactionary students launched a massive assault on **Thammasat University**. On October 6, hundreds of students were brutally beaten, scores were lynched and some even burned alive; the military took control and suspended the constitution.

"Premocracy"

Soon after, the military-appointed prime minister, **Thanin Kraivichien**, forced dissidents to undergo anti-communist indoctrination, but his measures seem to have been too repressive even for the military, who forced him to resign in October 1977. **General Kriangsak Chomanand** took over, and began to break up the insurgency with shrewd offers of amnesty. He in turn was displaced in February 1980 by **General Prem Tinsulanonda**, backed by a broad parliamentary coalition.

Untainted by corruption, Prem achieved widespread support, including that of the monarchy. Overseeing a period of rapid economic growth, Prem maintained the premiership until 1988, with a unique mixture of dictatorship and democracy sometimes called **Premocracy**: although never standing for parliament himself, Prem was asked by the legislature after every election to become prime minister. He eventually stepped down because, he said, it was time for the country's leader to be chosen from among its elected representatives.

The 1992 demonstrations and the 1997 constitution

The new prime minister was indeed an elected MP, **Chatichai Choonhavan**, a retired general with a long civilian career in public office. He pursued a vigorous policy of economic development, but this fostered widespread corruption, in which members of the government were often implicated. Following an economic downturn and Chatichai's attempts to downgrade the political role of the military, the armed forces staged a bloodless coup on February 23, 1991, led by Supreme Commander Sunthorn and General Suchinda, the army commander-in-chief, who became premier.

When Suchinda reneged on promises to make democratic amendments to the constitution, hundreds of thousands of ordinary Thais poured onto the streets around Bangkok's Democracy Monument in **mass demonstrations** between May 17 and 20, 1992. Hopelessly misjudging the mood of the country, Suchinda brutally crushed the protests, leaving hundreds dead or injured. Having justified the massacre on the grounds that he was protecting the king from communist agitators, Suchinda was forced to resign when King Bhumibol expressed his disapproval in a ticking-off that was broadcast on world television.

Elections were held in September, with the **Democrat Party**, led by Chuan Leekpai, a noted upholder of democracy and the rule of law, emerging victorious. Chuan was succeeded in turn by Banharn Silpa-archa – nicknamed by the local press "the walking ATM", a reference to his reputation for buying votes – and General Chavalit Yongchaiyudh. The most significant positive event of the latter's tenure was the approval of a **new constitution** in 1997. Drawn up by an independent drafting assembly, its main points included: direct elections to the senate, rather than appointment of senators by the prime minister; acceptance of the right of assembly as the basis of a democratic society and guarantees of individual rights and freedoms; greater public accountability; and increased popular participation in local administration. The eventual aim of the new charter was to end the traditional system of patronage, vested interests and vote-buying.

Tom yam kung: the 1997 economic crisis

In February 1997 foreign-exchange dealers began to mount speculative attacks on the **baht**, alarmed at the size of Thailand's private foreign debt – 250 billion baht in the unproductive property sector alone, much of it accrued through the proliferation of prestigious skyscrapers in Bangkok. Chavalit's government defended the pegged exchange rate, spending $23 billion of the country's formerly healthy foreign-exchange reserves, but at the beginning of July was forced to give up the ghost – the baht was floated and soon went into free-fall. Thailand was forced to seek help from the **IMF**, who in August put together a $17-billion **rescue package**, coupled with severe austerity measures.

In November, the inept Chavalit was replaced by Chuan Leekpai, who immediately took a hard line in following the IMF's advice, which involved maintaining cripplingly high interest rates to protect the baht and slashing government budgets. Although this played well abroad, at home the government encountered increasing hostility from its newly impoverished citizens – the downturn struck with such speed and severity that it was dubbed the **tom yam kung crisis**, after the searingly hot Thai soup. Chuan's tough stance paid off, however, with the baht stabilizing and inflation falling back, and in October 1999 he announced that he was forgoing almost $4 billion of the IMF's package.

Thaksin

The 2001 general election was won by a new party, **Thai Rak Thai** (Thai Loves Thai), led by one of Thailand's wealthiest men, **Thaksin Shinawatra**, an ex-policeman who had made a personal fortune from government telecommunications concessions. Instead of a move towards greater democracy, as envisioned by the new constitution, Thaksin's government seemed to represent a full-blown merger between politics and big business, concentrating economic power in even fewer hands. Furthermore, the prime minister began to apply commercial and legal pressure, including several lawsuits, to try to silence critics in the media and parliament, and to manipulate the Senate and supposedly independent institutions such as the Election Commission to consolidate his own power.

As his standing became more firmly entrenched, he rejected constitutional reforms designed to rein in his power – famously declaring that "democracy is only a tool" for achieving other goals. Thaksin did, however, live up to his billing as a populist reformer. In his first year of government, he issued a three-year loan moratorium for perennially indebted farmers and set up a one-million-baht development fund for each of the country's seventy thousand villages. To improve public health access, a standard charge of B30 per hospital visit was introduced nationwide.

In early 2004, politically and criminally motivated violence in the **Islamic southern provinces** escalated sharply, and since then, there have been over 1200 deaths on both sides in the troubles. The insurgents have targeted any representative of central authority, including monks and teachers, as well as setting off bombs in marketplaces and near tourist hotels. The authorities have inflamed opinion in the south by reacting violently, notably in crushing protests at Tak Bai and the much-revered Krue Se Mosque in Pattani in 2004, in which a total of over two hundred alleged insurgents died. In 2005, the government imposed **martial law** in Pattani, Yala and Narathiwat provinces and in parts of Songkhla province – this, however, has exacerbated economic and unemployment problems in what is Thailand's poorest region. Facing a variety of shadowy groups, whose precise aims are unclear, the authorities' natural instinct has been to get tough – which so far has brought the problem no nearer to a solution.

Despite these problems, but bolstered by his high-profile response to the tsunami on December 26, 2004, in which over eight thousand people died on Thailand's Andaman Coast, Thaksin breezed through the **February 2005 election**, becoming the first prime minister in Thai history to win an outright majority at the polls. The prospect of such a one-party state, however, alarmed a wide spectrum of opposition. When Thaksin's relatives sold their shares in the family's Shin Corporation in January 2006 for £1.1 billion, without paying tax, tens of thousands of mostly middle-class Thais flocked to Bangkok to take part in protracted but peaceful demonstrations, under the umbrella of the **People's Alliance for Democracy (PAD)**. After further allegations of corruption and cronyism, in September Thaksin, while on official business in the United States, was ousted by a military government in a benign **coup**.

Thaksin set up home in London, but in May 2007 his party, TRT, was found guilty of electoral fraud and dissolved. Undeterred, his supporters formed the People's Power Party (PPP), which despite its ill-concealed opposition to the royalist-military elite, won the December 2007 general election; its leader, Samak Sundaravej, an irascible, right-wing TV chef, openly confessed to being a proxy for Thaksin. In response, the PAD – its trademark yellow shirts (the colour of the king) now firmly established – restarted and stepped up its mass protests, eventually occupying the government's offices for several months. Meanwhile, the merry-go-round of tribunals and court cases continued, including the disqualification of Samak from political office – only to be replaced as prime minister by Thaksin's brother-in-law. Much more significantly, Thaksin was finally convicted *in absentia* of corruption and, as a fugitive from justice, was refused a visa extension by the UK.

Matters came to a head in November and December, 2008: the PAD seized and closed down Bangkok's Suvarnabhumi and Don Muang airports; the ruling People's Power Party was declared illegal, which persuaded the yellow shirts to lift their sit-in; and Peua Thai, the PPP's swift reincarnation, found itself unable to form a new coalition government. Instead, led by the young, charismatic **Abhisit Vejjajiva**, who was born in Newcastle-upon-Tyne and educated at Eton and Oxford, the Democratic Party jumped into bed with the Friends of Newin (aka the Bhumjaithai Party), formerly staunch supporters of Thaksin, to take the helm. At the time of writing, however, the divisions between the pro- and anti-Thaksin camps have not been resolved. Thaksin's supporters, now red-shirted and organized into the UDD (United Front for Democracy against Dictatorship), have taken their turn to hold mass protest meetings; in April 2009 they forced the ASEAN (Association of Southeast Asian Nations) summit meeting in Pattaya to be embarrassingly abandoned and closed down central Bangkok for several days before being dispersed by the army. Meanwhile the PAD, who have blotted their copybook internationally by advocating a part-elected, part-appointed system of government for Thailand to try to minimize corruption, have decided to form a political party, the New Politics Party, and have changed their colours to yellow and green (to display their environmentalist credentials).

Religion: Thai Buddhism

O ver 85 percent of Thais consider themselves **Theravada Buddhists**, followers of the teachings of a holy man usually referred to as the Buddha (Enlightened One), though more precisely known as Gautama Buddha to distinguish him from lesser-known Buddhas who preceded him. Theravada Buddhism is one of the two main schools of Buddhism practised in Asia, and in Thailand it has absorbed an eclectic assortment of animist and Hindu elements.

Islam is the biggest of the minority religions in Thailand, practised by between five and ten percent of the population. Most Muslims live in the south, along the Malaysian border. The rest of the Thai population comprises Mahayana Buddhists, Hindus, Sikhs, Christians and animists.

The Buddha: his life and beliefs

Gautama Buddha was born in Nepal as **Prince Gautama Siddhartha** in either the sixth or seventh century BC. At his birth, astrologers predicted that he would become either a famous king or a celebrated holy man, depending on which path he chose. Much preferring the former, the prince's father forbade the boy from leaving the palace grounds, and set about educating Gautama in all aspects of the high life. Most statues of the Buddha depict him with elongated earlobes, which is a reference to this early pampered existence, when he would have worn heavy precious stones in his ears.

The prince married and became a father, but at the age of 29 he flouted his father's authority and sneaked out into the world beyond the palace. On this fateful trip he encountered successively an old man, a sick man, a corpse and a hermit, and thus for the first time was made aware that pain and suffering were intrinsic to human life. Contemplation seemed the only means of discovering why this was so – and therefore Gautama decided to leave the palace and become a **Hindu ascetic**.

For several years he wandered the countryside leading a life of self-denial and self-mortification, but failed to come any closer to the answer. Eventually concluding that the best course of action must be to follow a "Middle Way" – neither indulgent nor overly ascetic – Gautama sat down beneath the famous riverside bodhi tree at **Bodh Gaya** in India, facing the rising sun, to **meditate** until he achieved enlightenment. For 49 days he sat cross-legged in the "lotus position", contemplating the causes of suffering and wrestling with temptations that materialized to distract him. Most of these were sent by **Mara**, the Evil One, who was finally subdued when Gautama summoned the earth goddess **Mae Toranee** by pointing the fingers of his right hand at the ground – the gesture known as **Calling the Earth to Witness**, or *Bhumisparsa Mudra*, which has been immortalized by thousands of Thai sculptors. Mae Toranee wrung torrents of water from her hair and engulfed Mara's demonic emissaries in a flood, an episode that's also commonly reproduced, most famously in the statue in Bangkok's Sanam Luang.

Temptations dealt with, Gautama soon came to attain **enlightenment** and so become a Buddha. As the place of his enlightenment, the **bodhi tree** (or bo tree) has assumed special significance for Buddhists: not only does it appear in many Buddhist paintings, but there's often a real bodhi tree (*Ficus religiosa*) planted in temple compounds as well. In addition, the bot is nearly always built facing either a body of water or facing east (preferably both).

The Buddha preached his **first sermon** in a deer park in India, where he characterized his doctrine, or **Dharma**, as a wheel. From this episode comes the early Buddhist symbol the **Dharmachakra**, known as the Wheel of Law, which is often accompanied by a statue of a deer. Thais celebrate this first sermon with a public holiday in July known as **Asanha Puja**. On another occasion 1250 people spontaneously gathered to hear the Buddha speak, an event remembered in Thailand as **Maha Puja** and marked by a public holiday in February (see p.40).

For the next forty-odd years the Buddha travelled the region converting non-believers and performing miracles. One rainy season he even ascended into the **Tavatimsa heaven** (Heaven of the 33 Gods) to visit his mother and to preach the doctrine to her. His descent from this heaven is quite a common theme of paintings and sculptures, and the **Standing Buddha** pose of numerous Buddha statues comes from this story.

The Buddha "died" at the age of 80 on the banks of a river at Kusinari in India – an event often dated to 543 BC, which is why the **Thai calendar** is 543 years out of synch with the Western one, so that the year 2010 AD becomes 2553 BE (Buddhist Era). Lying on his side, propping up his head on his hand, the Buddha passed into **Nirvana** (giving rise to another classic pose, the **Reclining Buddha**), the unimaginable state of nothingness which knows no suffering and from which there is no reincarnation. Buddhists believe that the day the Buddha entered Nirvana was the same date on which he was born and on which he achieved enlightenment, a triply significant day that Thais honour with the **Visakha Puja** festival in May (see p.41).

Buddhists believe that Gautama Buddha was the five-hundredth incarnation of a single being: the stories of these five hundred lives, collectively known as the **Jataka**, provide the inspiration for a lot of Thai art. Hindus also accept Gautama Buddha into their pantheon, perceiving him as the ninth manifestation of their god Vishnu.

The spread of Buddhism

After the Buddha entered Nirvana, his **doctrine** spread relatively quickly across India, and probably was first promulgated in Thailand in about the third century BC. His teachings, the *Tripitaka*, were written down in the Pali language – a derivative of Sanskrit – in a form that became known as **Theravada**, or "The Doctrine of the Elders".

By the beginning of the first millennium, a new movement called **Mahayana** (Great Vehicle) had emerged within the Theravada school, attempting to make Buddhism more accessible by introducing a pantheon of **bodhisattva**, or Buddhist saints, who, although they had achieved enlightenment, postponed entering Nirvana in order to inspire the populace. Mahayana Buddhism spread north into China, Korea, Vietnam and Japan, also entering southern Thailand via the Srivijayan empire around the eighth century and parts of Khmer Cambodia in about the eleventh century. Meanwhile Theravada Buddhism (which the Mahayanists disparagingly renamed "Hinayana" or "Lesser Vehicle") established itself most significantly in Sri Lanka, northern and central Thailand and Burma.

Buddhist doctrine and practice

Central to Theravada Buddhism is a belief in **karma** – every action has a consequence – and **reincarnation**, along with an understanding that craving is at the root of human suffering. The ultimate aim for a Buddhist is to get off the cycle of perpetual reincarnation and suffering and to instead enter the blissful state of non-being that is **Nirvana**. This enlightened state can take many lifetimes to achieve so the more realistic goal for most is to be reborn slightly higher up the karmic ladder each time. As Thai Buddhists see it, animals are at the bottom of the karmic scale and monks at the top, with women on a lower rung than men.

Living a good life, specifically a life of "pure intention", creates good karma and Buddhist doctrine focuses a great deal on how to achieve this. Psychology and an understanding of human weaknesses play a big part. Key is the concept of **dukka**, which holds that craving is the root cause of all suffering or, to put it simplistically, human unhappiness is caused by the unquenchable dissatisfaction experienced when one's sensual, spiritual or material desires are not met. Accepting the truth of this is known as the **Four Noble Truths** of Buddhism. The route to enlightenment depends on a person being sufficiently detached from earthly desires so that *dukka* can't take hold. One acknowledges that the physical world is impermanent and ever-changing, and that all things – including the self – are therefore not worth craving. A Buddhist works towards this realization by following the **Eightfold Path**, or **Middle Way**, that is by developing a set of highly moral personal qualities such as "right speech", "right action" and "right mindfulness". Meditation is particularly helpful in this.

A devout Thai Buddhist commits to the **five basic precepts**, namely not to kill or steal, to refrain from sexual misconduct and incorrect speech (lies, gossip and abuse) and to eschew intoxicating liquor and drugs. There are **three extra precepts** for special *wan phra* holy days and for those laypeople including foreign students who study meditation at Thai temples: no eating after noon, no entertainment (including TV and music) and no sleeping on a soft bed; in addition, the no sexual misconduct precept turns into no sex at all.

Making merit

Merit-making in popular Thai Buddhism has become slightly skewed, so that some people act on the assumption that they'll climb the karmic ladder faster if they make bigger and better offerings to the temple and its monks. However, it is of course the purity of the intention behind one's merit-making (*tham bun*) that's fundamental.

Merit can be made in many ways, from giving a monk his breakfast to attending a Buddhist service or donating money and gifts to the neighbourhood temple, and most **festivals** are essentially communal merit-making opportunities. Between the big festivals, the most common days for making merit and visiting the temple are **wan phra** (holy days), which are determined by the phase of the moon and occur four times a month. The simplest **offering** inside a temple consists of lotus buds, candles and three incense sticks (representing the three gems of Buddhism – the Buddha himself, the Dharma or doctrine, and the monkhood). One of the more bizarre but common merit-making activities involves **releasing caged birds**: worshippers buy tiny finches from vendors at wat compounds and, by liberating them from their cage, prove their Buddhist compassion towards all living things. The fact that the birds were free until netted earlier that morning doesn't seem to detract from the ritual. In riverside and seaside wats, fish or even baby turtles are released instead.

For an insightful introduction to the philosophy and practice of Thai Buddhism, see Ⓦwww.thaibuddhism.net. Details of Thai temples that welcome foreign students of Buddhism and meditation are on p.202.

The monkhood

It's the duty of Thailand's 200,000-strong **Sangha** (monkhood) to set an example to the Theravada Buddhist community by living a life as close to the Middle Way as possible and by preaching the Dharma to the people. The life of a monk (*bhikkhu*) is governed by 227 precepts that include celibacy and the rejection of all personal possessions except gifts.

Each day begins with an alms round in the neighbourhood so that the laity can donate food and thereby gain themselves merit, and then is chiefly spent in meditation, chanting, teaching and study. As the most respected members of any community, monks act as teachers, counsellors and arbiters in local disputes. They also perform rituals at cremations, weddings and other events, such as the launching of a new business or even the purchase of a new car. Many young boys from poor families find themselves almost obliged to become either a *dek wat* (temple boy) or a **novice monk** because that's the only way they can get accommodation, food and, crucially, an education. This is provided free in exchange for duties around the wat, and novices are required to adhere to ten rather than 227 Buddhist precepts.

Monkhood doesn't have to be for life: a man may leave the Sangha three times without stigma and in fact every Thai male (including royalty) is expected to **enter the monkhood** for a short period, ideally between leaving school and marrying, as a rite of passage into adulthood. Thai government departments and some private companies grant their employees paid leave for their time as a monk, but the custom is in decline as young men increasingly have to consider the effect their absence may have on their career prospects. Instead, many men now enter the monkhood for a brief period after the death of a parent, to make merit both for the deceased and for the rest of the family. The most popular time for temporary ordination is the three-month Buddhist retreat period – **Pansa**, sometimes referred to as "Buddhist Lent" – which begins in July and lasts for the duration of the rainy season. The monks' confinement is said to originate from the earliest years of Buddhist history, when farmers complained that perambulating monks were squashing their sprouting rice crops.

Monks in contemporary society

In recent years, some monks have become influential activists in social and environmental issues, and some upcountry temples have established themselves as successful drug rehabilitation centres. Other monks have acquired such a reputation for giving wise counsel and bringing good fortune and prosperity to their followers that they have become national gurus; their temples now generate great wealth through the production of specially blessed amulets (see p.83) and photographs.

Though the increasing involvement of many monks in the secular world has not met with unanimous approval, far more disappointing to the laity are those monks who **flout the precepts** of the Sangha by succumbing to the temptations of a consumer society, flaunting Raybans, Rolexes and Mercedes (in some cases actually bought with temple funds), chain-smoking and flirting, even making pocket money from predicting lottery results and practising faith-healing. With so much national pride and integrity riding on the sanctity of the Sangha, any whiff of a deeper scandal is bound to strike deep into the national psyche. Cases of monks involved in drug-dealing, gun-running, even rape and murder have prompted a stream of editorials on the state of the Sangha and the collapse of spiritual values at the heart of Thai society. The inclusivity of the monkhood – which is open to just about any male who wants to join – has been highlighted as a particularly vulnerable aspect, not least because donning saffron robes has always been an accepted way for criminals, reformed or otherwise, to repent of their past deeds.

Interestingly, back in the late 1980s, the influential monk Phra Bodhirak (Photirak) was defrocked after criticizing what he saw as a tide of decadence infecting Thai Buddhism. He now preaches his ascetic code of anti-materialism through his breakaway **Santi Asoke** sect, famous across the country for its cheap vegetarian restaurants, its philosophy of self-sufficiency and for the simple blue farmers' shirts worn by many of its followers.

Women and the monkhood

Although the Theravada Buddhist hierarchy in some countries permits the ordination of **female monks**, or *bhikkhuni*, the Thai Sangha does not. Instead, Thai women are officially only allowed to become **nuns**, or *mae chii*, shaving their heads, donning white robes and keeping eight rather than 227 precepts. Their status is lower than that of the monks and they are chiefly occupied with temple upkeep rather than conducting religious ceremonies.

However, the progressives are becoming more vocal, and in 2002 a Thai woman became the first of several to break with the Buddhist authorities and get **ordained** as a novice *bhikkhuni* on Thai soil. Thailand's Sangha Council, however, still recognizes neither her ordination nor the temple, Watra Songdhammakalyani in Nakhon Pathom, where the ordination took place. The Watra (rather than Wat) is run by another Thai *bhikkuni*, Dhammananda Bhikkhuni, the author of several books in English about **women and Buddhism** and of an informative website, Ⓦ www.thaibhikkhunis.org.

Hindu deities and animist spirits

The complicated history of the area now known as Thailand has made Thai Buddhism a confusingly syncretic faith, as you'll realize when you enter a Buddhist temple compound to be confronted by a statue of a Hindu deity. While regular Buddhist merit-making insures a Thai for the next life, there are certain **Hindu gods and animist spirits** that many Thais – sophisticated city dwellers and illiterate farmers alike – also cultivate for help with more immediate problems; and as often as not it's a Buddhist monk who is called in to exorcise a malevolent spirit. Even the Buddhist King Bhumibol employs Brahmin priests and astrologers to determine auspicious days and officiate at certain royal ceremonies and, like his royal predecessors of the Chakri dynasty, he also associates himself with the Hindu god Vishnu by assuming the title Rama IX – Rama, hero of the Hindu epic the *Ramayana*, having been Vishnu's seventh manifestation on earth.

If a Thai wants help in achieving a short-term goal, like passing an exam, becoming pregnant or winning the lottery, he or she will quite likely turn to the **Hindu pantheon**, visiting an enshrined statue of Brahma, Vishnu, Shiva or Ganesh, and making offerings of flowers, incense and maybe food. If the outcome is favourable, the devotee will probably come back to show thanks, bringing more offerings and maybe even hiring a dance troupe to perform a celebratory *lakhon chatri*. Built in honour of Brahma, Bangkok's Erawan Shrine is the most famous place of Hindu-inspired worship in the country.

Spirits and spirit houses

Whereas Hindu deities tend to be benevolent, **spirits** (or *phi*) are not nearly as reliable and need to be mollified more frequently. They come in hundreds of varieties, some more malign than others, and inhabit everything from trees, rivers and caves to public buildings and private homes – even taking over people if they feel like it.

So that these *phi* don't pester human inhabitants, each building has a special **spirit house** (*saan phra phum*) in its vicinity, as a dwelling for spirits ousted by the building's construction. Usually raised on a short column to set it at or above eye-level, the spirit house must occupy an auspicious location – not, for example, in the shadow of the main building. It's generally about the size of a dolls' house and designed to look like a wat or a traditional Thai house, but its ornamentation is supposed to reflect the status of the humans' building, so if that building is enlarged or refurbished, the spirit house should be improved accordingly. And as architects become increasingly bold in their designs, so modernist spirit houses are also beginning to appear in Bangkok, where an eyecatching new skyscraper might be graced by a spirit house of glass or polished concrete. **Figurines** representing the relevant guardian spirit and his aides are sometimes put inside, and daily offerings of incense, lighted candles and garlands of jasmine are placed alongside them to keep the *phi* happy – a disgruntled spirit is a dangerous spirit, liable to cause sickness, accidents and even death.

Art and architecture

side from pockets of Hindu-inspired statuary and architecture, the vast majority of Thailand's cultural monuments take their inspiration from Theravada Buddhism, and so it is **temples** and **religious images** that constitute Bangkok's main sights. Few of these can be attributed to any individual artist, but with a little background information it becomes fairly easy to recognize the major artistic styles. Though Bangkok's temples nearly all date from the eighteenth century or later, many of them display features that originate from a much earlier time. The National Museum (see p.70) is a good place to see some of Thailand's more ancient Hindu and Buddhist statues, and a visit to the fourteenth-century ruins at Ayutthaya (see p.133), less than two hours from Bangkok, is also recommended.

ONTEXTS | Art and architecture

The wat

The **wat** or Buddhist temple complex has a great range of uses: as home to a monastic community, a place of public worship, a shrine for holy images and a shaded meeting place for townspeople and villagers. Wat architecture has evolved in ways as various as its functions, but there remain several essential components which have stayed constant for some fifteen centuries.

The most important wat building is the **bot** (sometimes known as the *ubosot*), a term most accurately translated as the "ordination hall". It usually stands at the heart of the compound and is the preserve of the monks: lay persons are rarely allowed inside and it's generally kept locked when not in use. There's only one bot in any wat complex, and often the only way to distinguish it from other temple buildings is by the eight **sema** or boundary stones which always surround it.

Often almost identical to the bot, the **viharn** or assembly hall is for the lay congregation, and as a tourist this is the building you're most likely to enter, since it usually contains the wat's principal **Buddha image**, and sometimes two or three minor images as well. Large wats may have several viharns, while strict meditation wats, which don't deal with the laity, may not have one at all.

Thirdly, there's the **chedi** or stupa, a tower which was originally conceived as a monument to enshrine relics of the Buddha, but has since become a place to contain the ashes of royalty – and anyone else who can afford it.

Buddhist iconography

In the early days of Buddhism, image-making was considered inadequate to convey the faith's abstract philosophies, so the only approved iconography comprised doctrinal **symbols** such as the Dharmachakra (Wheel of Law, also known as Wheel of Doctrine or Wheel of Life). Gradually these symbols were displaced by **images of the Buddha**, construed chiefly as physical embodiments of the Buddha's teachings rather than as portraits of the man.

Of the four postures in which the Buddha is always depicted – sitting, standing, walking and reclining – the seated Buddha, which represents him in meditation, is the most common in Thailand. A popular variation shows the Buddha **seated** on a coiled serpent, protected by the serpent's hood – a reference to the story about the Buddha meditating during the rainy season, when a serpent offered to raise him off the wet ground and shelter him from the storms. The **reclining** pose symbolizes the Buddha entering Nirvana at his death, while the **standing** and **walking** images both represent his descent from Tavatimsa heaven.

ww.roughguides.com

33

Hindu iconography

Hindu images tend to be a lot livelier than Buddhist ones, partly because there is a panoply of gods to choose from, and partly because these gods have mischievous personalities and reappear in all sorts of bizarre incarnations.

Vishnu has always been a favourite: in his role of "Preserver" he embodies the status quo, representing both stability and the notion of altruistic love. He is most often depicted as the deity, but has ten manifestations in all, of which **Rama** (number seven) is by far the most popular in Thailand. The epitome of ideal manhood, Rama is the superhero of the epic story the *Ramayana* (in Thai, the *Ramakien*; see box, p.63) and appears in storytelling reliefs and murals in every Hindu temple in Thailand; in painted portraits you can usually recognize him by his green face. Manifestation number eight is **Krishna**, more widely known than Rama in the West, but slightly less common in Thailand. Krishna is usually characterized as a flirtatious, flute-playing, blue-skinned cowherd, but he is also a crucial moral figure in the lengthy moral epic poem, the *Mahabharata*. Confusingly, Vishnu's ninth avatar is the **Buddha** – a manifestation adopted many centuries ago to minimize defection to the Buddhist faith. When represented as **the deity**, Vishnu is generally shown sporting a crown and four arms, his hands holding a conch shell (whose music wards off demons), a discus (used as a weapon), a club (symbolizing the power of nature and time), and a lotus (symbol of joyful flowering and renewal). He is often depicted astride a **garuda**, a half-man, half-bird. Even without Vishnu on its back, the garuda is a very important beast: a symbol of strength, it's often shown "supporting" temple buildings.

Statues and representations of **Brahma** (the Creator) are rare. He too has four arms, but holds no objects; he has four faces (sometimes painted red), is generally borne by a goose-like creature called a *hamsa*, and is associated with the direction north.

Shiva (the Destroyer) is the most volatile member of the pantheon. He stands for extreme behaviour, for beginnings and endings, as enacted in his frenzied Dance of Destruction, and for fertility, and is a symbol of great energy and power. His godlike form typically has four, eight or ten arms, sometimes holding a trident (representing creation, protection and destruction) and a drum (to beat the rhythm of creation). In his most famous role, as **Nataraja**, or Lord of the Dance, he is usually shown in a stylized standing position with legs bent into a balletic position and the full complement of arms outstretched above his head. Three stripes on a figure's forehead also indicate Shiva, or one of his followers. In abstract form, he is represented by a **lingam** (once found at the heart of every Khmer temple in the northeast). Primarily a symbol of energy and godly power, the lingam also embodies fertility, particularly when set upright in a vulva-shaped vessel known as a **yoni**. The yoni doubles as a receptacle for the holy water that worshippers pour over the lingam.

Close associates of Shiva include **Parvati**, his wife, and **Ganesh**, his elephant-headed son. As the god of knowledge and overcomer of obstacles (in the path of learning), Ganesh is used as the symbol of the Fine Arts Department, so his image features on all entrance tickets to national museums and historical parks.

Lesser mythological figures include the **yaksha** giants who ward off evil spirits (like the enormous freestanding ones guarding Bangkok's Wat Phra Kaeo); the graceful half-woman, half-bird **kinnari**; and the ubiquitous **naga**, or serpent king of the underworld, often depicted with seven heads.

The schools

In the 1920s art historians and academics began compiling a classification system for Thai art and architecture that was modelled along the lines of the country's historical periods. The following brief overview starts in the sixth century, when Buddhism began to take a hold on the country.

Dvaravati (sixth to eleventh centuries)

Centred on the towns of Nakhon Pathom, U Thong, Lopburi and Haripunjaya (modern-day Lamphun), the Dvaravati state was populated by Theravada Buddhists who were strongly influenced by Indian culture.

In an effort to combat the defects inherent in the poor-quality limestone at their disposal, Dvaravati-era **sculptors** made their Buddhas quite stocky, cleverly dressing the figures in a sheet-like drape that dropped down to ankle level from each raised wrist, forming a U-shaped hemline – a style which they used when casting in bronze as well. Nonetheless many **statues** have cracked, leaving them headless or limbless. Where the faces have survived, Dvaravati statues display some of the most naturalistic features ever produced in Thailand, distinguished by their thick lips, flattened noses and wide cheekbones.

Srivijaya (eighth to thirteenth centuries)

While Dvaravati's Theravada Buddhists were influencing the central plains, southern Thailand was paying allegiance to the Mahayana Buddhists of the **Srivijayan** empire. Mahayanists believe that those who have achieved enlightenment should postpone their entry into Nirvana in order to help others along the way. These stay-behinds, revered like saints both during and after life, are called **bodhisattva**, and statues of them were the mainstay of Srivijayan art.

The finest Srivijayan *bodhisattva* statues were cast in bronze and show such grace and sinuosity that they rank among the finest sculpture ever produced in the country. Many are lavishly adorned and some were even bedecked in real jewels when first made. By far the most popular *bodhisattva* subject was *Avalokitesvara*, worshipped as compassion incarnate and generally shown with four or more arms and clad in an animal skin. Bangkok's National Museum holds a beautiful example.

Khmer and Lopburi (tenth to fourteenth centuries)

By the end of the ninth century the **Khmers** of Cambodia were starting to expand from their capital at Angkor into the Dvaravati states, bringing with them the Hindu faith and the cult of the god-king (*devaraja*). As lasting testaments to the sacred power of their kings, the Khmers built hundreds of imposing stone sanctuaries across their newly acquired territory.

Each magnificent castle-temple – known in Khmer as a **prasat** – was constructed primarily as a shrine for a shiva lingam, the phallic representation of the god Shiva. Almost every surface of the sanctuary was adorned with intricate **carvings**, usually gouged from sandstone, depicting Hindu deities (notably Vishnu Reclining on the Milky Sea of Eternity in the National Museum – see p.71) and stories, especially episodes from the *Ramayana* (see p.63).

During the Khmer period the former Theravada Buddhist principality of Lopburi produced a distinctive style of Buddha statue. Broad-faced and muscular, the classic **Lopburi** Buddha wears a diadem or ornamental headband – a nod to the Khmers' ideological fusion of earthly and heavenly power – and the *ushnisha* (the sign of enlightenment) becomes distinctly conical rather than a mere bump on the head.

Sukhothai (thirteenth to fifteenth centuries)

Two Thai generals established the first real Thai kingdom in **Sukhothai** (some 400km north of modern-day Bangkok, in the northern plains) in 1238, and over the next two hundred years the artists of this realm produced some of Thailand's most refined art. Sukhothai's artistic reputation rests above all on its **sculpture**. More sinuous even than the Srivijayan images, Sukhothai Buddhas tend towards elegant androgyny, with slim oval faces and slender curvaceous bodies usually clad in a plain, skintight robe that fastens with a tassle close to the navel. Fine examples include the Phra Buddha Chinnarat image at Bangkok's Wat Benjamabophit, and the enormous Phra Sri Sakyamuni in Bangkok's Wat Suthat. Sukhothai sculptors were the first to represent the walking Buddha, a supremely graceful figure with his right leg poised to move forwards.

Sukhothai-era architects also devised a new type of chedi, as elegant in its way as the images their sculptor colleagues were producing. This was the **lotus-bud chedi**, a slender tower topped with a tapered finial that was to become a hallmark of the Sukhothai era.

Ancient Sukhothai is also renowned for the skill of its potters, who produced a **ceramic ware** known as Sawankhalok, after the name of one of the nearby kiln towns. It is distinguished by its grey-green celadon glazes and by the fish and chrysanthemum motifs used to decorate bowls and plates.

Ayutthaya (fourteenth to eighteenth centuries)

From 1351 Thailand's central plains came under the thrall of a new power centred on **Ayutthaya**, and over the next four centuries, the Ayutthayan rulers commissioned some four hundred grand wats as symbols of their wealth and power. Though essentially Theravada Buddhists, the kings also adopted some Hindu and Brahmin beliefs from the Khmers – most significantly the concept of *devaraja* or god-kingship, whereby the monarch became a mediator between the people and the Hindu gods.

Retaining the concentric layout of the typical Khmer **temple complex**, Ayutthayan builders refined and elongated the prang into a **corncob–shaped tower**, rounding it off at the top and introducing vertical incisions around its circumference. The most famous example is Bangkok's Wat Arun, which though built during the subsequent Ratanakosin period is a classic Ayutthayan structure.

Ayutthaya's architects also adapted the Sri Lankan **chedi** so favoured by their Sukhothai predecessors, stretching the bell-shaped base and tapering it into a very graceful conical spire, as at Wat Phra Sri Sanphet in Ayutthaya. The **viharns** of this era are characterized by walls pierced by slit-like windows, designed to foster a mysterious atmosphere by limiting the amount of light inside the building; Wat Yai Suwannaram in Phetchaburi (see p.148) has a particularly fine example.

From Sukhothai's Buddha **sculptures** the Ayutthayans copied the soft oval face, adding an earthlier demeanour to the features and imbuing them with a hauteur in tune with the *devaraja* ideology. Like the Lopburi images, early Ayutthayan statues wear crowns to associate kingship with Buddhahood; as the court became ever more lavish, so these figures became increasingly adorned, until – as in the monumental bronze at Wat Na Phra Mane – they appeared in earrings, armlets, anklets, bandoliers and coronets. The artists justified these luscious portraits of the Buddha – who was, after all, supposed to have given up worldly possessions – by pointing to an episode when the Buddha transformed himself into a well-dressed nobleman to gain the ear of an emperor, whereupon he scolded the man into entering the monkhood.

Ratanakosin (eighteenth century to the 1930s)

When **Bangkok** emerged as Ayutthaya's successor in 1782, the new capital's founder was determined to revive the old city's grandeur, and the **Ratanakosin** (or Bangkok) period began by aping what the Ayutthayans had done. Since then neither wat architecture nor religious sculpture has evolved much further.

The first **Ratanakosin building** was the bot of Bangkok's Wat Phra Kaeo, built to enshrine the Emerald Buddha. Designed to a typical Ayutthayan plan, it's coated in glittering mirrors and gold leaf, with roofs ranged in multiple tiers and tiled in green and orange. To this day, most newly built bots and viharns follow a more economical version of this paradigm, whitewashing the outside walls but decorating the pediment in gilded ornaments and mosaics of coloured glass. The result is that modern wats are often almost indistinguishable from each other, though Bangkok does have a few exceptions, including Wat Benjamabophit, which uses marble cladding for its walls and incorporates Victorian-style stained-glass windows, and Wat Rajapobhit, which is covered all over in Chinese ceramics. The most dramatic chedi of the Ratanakosin era – one of the tallest in the world – was constructed in the mid-nineteenth century in Nakhon Pathom (see p.143), to the original Sri Lankan style.

Early Ratanakosin sculptors produced adorned **Buddha images** very much in the Ayutthayan vein, sometimes adding real jewels to the figures; more modern images are notable for their ugliness rather than for any radical departure from type. The obsession with size, first apparent in the Sukhothai period, has plumbed new depths, with graceless concrete statues up to 60m high becoming the norm (as in Bangkok's Wat Indraviharn), a monumentalism made worse by the routine application of browns and dull yellows. Most small images are cast from or patterned on older models, mostly Sukhothai or Ayutthayan in origin.

Painting has fared much better, with the *Ramayana* murals in Bangkok's Wat Phra Kaeo (see p.64) a shining example of how Ayutthayan techniques and traditional subject matters could be adapted into something fantastic, imaginative and beautiful.

Contemporary

Following the democratization of Thailand in the 1930s, artists increasingly became recognized as individuals and took to signing their work for the first time. In 1933 the first school of fine art (now Bangkok's Silpakorn University) was established under the Italian sculptor **Silpa Bhirasri**, designer of the capital's Democracy Monument and, as the new generation experimented with secular themes and styles adapted from the West, Thai art began to look

---

Art galleries and exhibitions

Bangkok has a near-monopoly on Thailand's **art galleries**. While the permanent collections at the capital's **National Gallery** (@www.thailandmuseum.com; see p.73) are disappointing, regular exhibitions of more challenging contemporary work appear at the huge, ambitious, **Bangkok Art and Cultural Centre** (@www.bacc .or.th; see p.109); the main art school, **Silpakorn University Art Centre** (@www .art-centre.su.ac.th; see p.73); the **Queen's Gallery** (@www.queengallery.org; see p.84); and at smaller gallery spaces around the city.

The excellent monthly **Bangkok Art Map** (@bangkokartmap.com), an annotated map of the capital galleries, carries exhibition listings and is available free from galleries. For a preview of works by Thailand's best modern artists, visit the virtual Rama IX Art Museum at @www.rama9art.org.

a lot more **"modern"**. As for subject matter, the leading artistic preoccupation of the past eighty years has been Thailand's spiritual heritage and its role in contemporary society. Since 1985, a number of Thailand's more established contemporary artists have earned the title **National Artist**, an honour that's bestowed annually on notable artists working in all disciplines, including fine art, performing arts, film and literature.

One of the first modern artists to adapt traditional styles and themes was **Angkarn Kalayanapongsa** (b. 1926), an early recipient of the title National Artist. He has been employed as a temple muralist and many of his paintings, some of which are on show in Bangkok's National Gallery, reflect this experience, typically featuring casts of two-dimensional Ayutthayan-style figures and flying *thep* in a surreal setting laced with Buddhist symbols and nods to contemporary culture.

Taking this fusion a step further, one-time cinema billboard artist **Chalermchai Kositpipat** (b. 1955) specializes in temple murals with a modern, controversial, twist. Outside Thailand his most famous work enlivens the interior walls of London's Wat Buddhapadipa with strong colours and startling imagery. At home his latest project is the unconventional and highly ornate all-white Wat Rong Khun in his native Chiang Rai province.

Aiming for the more secular environments of the gallery and the private home, National Artist **Pichai Nirand** (b. 1936) rejects the traditional mural style and makes more selective choices of Buddhist imagery, appropriating religious objects and icons and reinterpreting their significance. He's particularly well known for his fine-detail canvases of Buddha footprints, many of which can be seen in Bangkok galleries and public spaces.

Pratuang Emjaroen (b. 1935) is famous for his social commentary, as epitomized by his huge and powerful canvas *Dharma and Adharma; The Days of Disaster*, which he painted in response to the vicious clashes between the military and students in 1973. The 5m x 2m picture depicts severed limbs, screaming faces and bloody gun barrels amid shadowy images of the Buddha's face, a spiked *dharmachakra* and other religious symbols. Many of Pratuang's subsequent works have addressed the issue of social injustice, using his trademark strong shafts of light and bold colour in a mix of Buddhist iconography and abstract imagery.

Prolific traditionalist **Chakrabhand Posayakrit** (b. 1943) is also inspired by Thailand's Buddhist culture; he is famously proud of his country's cultural heritage, which infuses much of his work and has led to him being honoured as a National Artist. He is best known for his series of *33 Life of the Buddha* paintings, and for his portraits, including many of members of the Thai royal family.

More controversial, and more of a household name, **Thawan Duchanee** (b. 1939) has tended to examine the spiritual tensions of modern life. His surreal juxtaposition of religious icons with fantastical Bosch-like characters and explicitly sexual images prompted a group of outraged students to slash ten of his early paintings in 1971 – an unprecedented reaction to a work of Thai art. Since then, Thawan has continued to produce allegorical investigations into the individual's struggles against the obstacles that dog the Middle Way, prominent among them lust and violence, but since the 1980s his street cred has waned as his saleability has mushroomed. Critics have questioned his integrity at accepting commissions from corporate clients, and his neo-conservative image cannot have been enhanced when he was honoured as a National Artist in 2001.

Complacency is not a criticism that could be levelled at **Vasan Sitthiket** (b. 1957), Thailand's most outspoken and iconoclastic artist, whose uncompromising pictures are shown at – and still occasionally banned from – large and small galleries around the capital. A persistent crusader against the hypocrisies of establishment figures such as monks, politicians, CEOs and military leaders, Vasan's is one of the loudest and most aggressive political voices on the contemporary art scene, expressed on canvas, in multimedia works and in performance art. His significance is well established and he was one of the seven artists to represent Thailand at the 2003 Venice Biennale, where Thailand had its own pavilion for the first time.

Equally confrontational is fellow Biennale exhibitor, the photographer, performance artist and social activist **Manit Sriwanichpoom** (b. 1961). Manit is best known for his "Pink Man" series of photographs in which he places a Thai man (his collaborator Sompong Thawee), dressed in a flashy pink suit and pushing a pink shopping trolley, into different scenes and situations in Thailand and elsewhere. The Pink Man represents thoughtless, dangerous consumerism and his backdrop might be an impoverished hill-tribe village (*Pink Man on Tour*, 1998), or black-and-white shots from the political violence of 1973, 1976 and 1992 (*Horror in Pink*; 2001).

Women artists tend to be less high profile in Thailand, but in 2007 **Pinaree Sanpitak** (b. 1961) became the first female recipient of the annual Silpathorn Awards for established artists, sharing the honour that year with, among others, notorious bad boy Vasan Sitthiket. Pinaree is known for her interest in gender issues and for her recurrent use of a female iconography in the form of vessels and mounds, often exploring the overlap with Buddhist stupa imagery. She works mainly in multimedia; her Vessels and Mounds show of 2001, for example, featured installations of huge, breast-shaped floor cushions, candles and bowls.

Among the younger faces on the Thai art scene, **Thaweesak Srithongdee** (b. 1970) blends surrealism and pop culture with the erotic and the figurative, to cartoonlike effect. He is preoccupied with popular culture, as is **Jirapat Tatsanasomboon** (b. 1971), whose work plays around with superheroes and cultural icons from East and West, pitting the *Ramayana*'s monkey king, Hanuman, against Spiderman in *Hanuman vs Spiderman*, and fusing mythologies in *The Transformation of Sita (after Botticelli)*.

Books

W e have included publishers' details for books that may be hard to find outside Thailand, though some of them can be ordered online through Ⓦwww.dcothai.com. Other titles should be available worldwide. Those marked o/p are out of print but available through online booksellers. Titles marked 🏃 are particularly recommended.

Travel

Steve Van Beek *Slithering South* (Wind and Water, Hong Kong). An expat writer tells how he single-handedly paddled his wooden boat down the entire 1100-kilometre course of the Chao Phraya River, and reveals a side of Thailand that's rarely written about in English.

James O'Reilly and Larry Habegger (eds) *Travelers' Tales:*

Thailand. Absorbing anthology of contemporary writings about Thailand, by Thailand experts, social commentators, travel writers and first-time visitors.

William Warren *Bangkok.* An engaging portrait of the unwieldy capital, weaving together anecdotes and character sketches from Bangkok's past and present.

Culture and society

Michael Carrithers *The Buddha: A Very Short Introduction.* Accessible account of the life of the Buddha, and the development and significance of his thought.

🏃 **Philip Cornwel-Smith and John Goss** *Very Thai* (River Books, Bangkok). Why do Thais decant their soft drinks into plastic bags, and how does one sniff-kiss? Answers and insights aplenty in this intriguingly observant, fully illus-trated guide to contemporary Thai culture.

James Eckardt *Bangkok People* (Asia Books, Bangkok). The collected articles of a renowned expat journalist, whose encounters with a varied cast of Bangkok inhabitants – from construction-site workers and street vendors to boxers and political candidates – add texture and context to the city.

Sandra Gregory with Michael Tierney *Forget You Had A Daughter: Doing Time in the "Bangkok Hilton"*

– Sandra Gregory's Story. The frank and shocking account of a young British woman's term in Bangkok's notorious Lard Yao prison after being caught trying to smuggle 89 grams of heroin out of Thailand.

Roger Jones *Culture Smart! Thailand.* Handy little primer on Thailand's social and cultural mores, with plenty of refreshingly up-to-date insights.

Father Joe Maier *Welcome To The Bangkok Slaughterhouse: The Battle for Human Dignity in Bangkok's Bleakest Slums.* Catholic priest Father Joe shares the stories of some of the Bangkok street kids and slum-dwellers that his charitable foundation has been supporting since 1972 (see p.48).

Trilok Chandra Majupuria *Erawan Shrine and Brahma Worship in Thailand* (Tecpress, Bangkok). The most concise introduction to the complexities of Thai religion, with a much wider scope than the title implies.

Cleo Odzer *Patpong Sisters*. An American anthropologist's funny and touching account of her life with the prostitutes and bar girls of Bangkok's notorious red-light district.

Phra Peter Pannapadipo *Little Angels: The Real-Life Stories of Twelve Thai Novice Monks*. A dozen young boys, many of them from desperate backgrounds, tell the often poignant stories of why they became novice monks. For some, funding from the Students Education Trust (see p.48) has changed their lives.

Phra Peter Pannapadipo *Phra Farang: An English Monk in Thailand*. Behind the scenes in a Thai monastery: the frank, funny and illuminating account of a UK-born former businessman's life as a Thai monk.

Pasuk Phongpaichit and Sungsidh Piriyarangsan *Corruption and Democracy in Thailand*. Fascinating academic study, revealing the nuts and bolts of corruption in Thailand and its links with all levels of political life, and suggesting a route to a stronger society. Their sequel, a study of Thailand's illegal economy, *Guns, Girls, Gambling, Ganja*, co-written with Nualnoi Treerat, makes equally eye-opening and depressing reading.

Denis Segaller *Thai Ways*. Fascinating collection of short pieces on Thai customs and traditions written by a long-term English resident of Bangkok.

Richard Totman *The Third Sex: Kathoey – Thailand's Ladyboys*. As several *kathoey* share their life stories with him, social scientist Totman examines their place in modern Thai society and explores the theory, supported by Buddhist philosophy, that *kathoey* are members of a third sex whose transgendered make-up is pre-determined from birth.

William Warren *Living in Thailand*. Luscious gallery of traditional houses, with an emphasis on the homes of Thailand's rich and famous; seductively photographed by Luca Invernizzi Tettoni.

Daniel Ziv and Guy Sharett *Bangkok Inside Out* (Equinox Publishing, Jakarta). This A–Z of Bangkok quirks and cultural substrates is full of slick photography and sparky observations but was deemed offensive by Thailand's Ministry of Culture and so some Thai bookshops won't stock it.

History

Anna Leonowens *The English Governess at the Siamese Court*. The mendacious memoirs of the nineteenth-century English governess that inspired the infamous Yul Brynner film *The King and I*; low on accuracy, high on inside-palace gossip.

Michael Smithies *Old Bangkok*. Brief, anecdotal history of the capital's early development, emphasizing what remains to be seen of bygone Bangkok.

William Stevenson *The Revolutionary King*. Fascinating biography of the

normally secretive King Bhumibol, by a British journalist who was given unprecedented access to the monarch and his family. The overall approach is fairly uncritical, but lots of revealing insights emerge along the way.

William Warren *Jim Thompson: the Legendary American of Thailand* (Archipelago Press, Singapore). The engrossing biography of the ex-intelligence agent, art collector and Thai silk magnate whose disappearance in Malaysia in 1967 has never been satisfactorily resolved.

David K. Wyatt *Thailand: A Short History*. An excellent treatment, scholarly but highly readable, with a good eye for witty, telling details. Good chapters on the story of the Thais before they reached what's now Thailand, and on more recent

developments. His *Siam in Mind* (Silkworm Books, Chiang Mai) is a wide-ranging and intriguing collection of sketches and short reflections that point towards an intellectual history of Thailand.

Art, architecture and film

Steve Van Beek *The Arts of Thailand* (Periplus, Vermont). Lavishly produced and perfectly pitched introduction to the history of Thai architecture, sculpture and painting, with superb photographs by Luca Invernizzi Tettoni.

Susan Conway *Thai Textiles* (River Books, Bangkok). A fascinating, richly illustrated work which draws on sculptures and temple murals to trace the evolution of Thai weaving techniques and costume styles, and to examine the functional and ceremonial uses of textiles.

Sumet Jumsai *Naga: Cultural Origins in Siam and the West Pacific* (o/p). Wide-ranging discussion of water symbols in Thailand and other parts of Asia, offering a stimulating mix of art, architecture, mythology and cosmology.

Bastian Meiresonne (ed) *Thai Cinema* (Ⓦwww.asiexpo.com /boutique). Anthology of twenty short essays on Thai cinema,

published to accompany a film festival in France, including pieces on arthouse, shorts and censorship. In French and English.

Steven Pettifor *Flavours: Thai Contemporary Art* (Thavibu Gallery, Bangkok). Takes up the baton from Poshyananda (see below) to look at the newly invigorated art scene in Thailand from 1992 to 2004, with profiles of 23 leading lights, including painters, multimedia and performance artists.

Apinan Poshyananda *Modern Art In Thailand* (OUP, Singapore). Excellent introduction which extends up to the early 1990s, with very readable discussions on dozens of individual artists, and lots of colour plates.

Dome Sukwong and Sawasdi Suwannapak *A Century of Thai Cinema* (River Books, Bangkok). Full-colour history of the Thai film industry and the promotional artwork (billboards, posters, magazines and cigarette cards) associated with it.

Literature

M.L. Manich Jumsai *Thai Ramayana* (Chalermnit, Bangkok). Slightly stilted abridged prose translation of King Rama I's version of the epic Hindu narrative, full of gleeful descriptions of bizarre mythological characters and supernatural battles. Essential reading for a full appreciation of Thai painting, carving and classical dance.

Chart Korbjitti *The Judgement* (Howling Books). Sobering modern-day tragedy about a good-hearted Thai villager who is ostracized by his hypocritical neighbours. Contains lots of interesting details on village life and traditions and thought-provoking passages on the stifling conservatism of rural communities. Winner of the S.E.A. Write award in 1982.

Rattawut Lapcharoensap
Sightseeing. This outstanding debut collection of short stories by a young Thai-born author now living overseas highlights big, pertinent themes – cruelty, corruption, racism, pride – in its neighbourhood tales of randy teenagers, bullyboys, a child's friendship with a Cambodian refugee, a young man who uses family influence to dodge the draft.

Nitaya Masavisut (ed) *The S.E.A. Write Anthology of Thai Short Stories and Poems* (Silkworm Books, Chiang Mai). Interesting medley of short stories and poems by Thai writers who have won Southeast Asian Writers' Awards, providing a good introduction to the contemporary literary scene.

Kukrit Pramoj *Si Phaendin: Four Reigns* (Silkworm Books, Chiang Mai). A kind of historical romance spanning the four reigns of Ramas V to VIII (1892–1946). Written by former prime minister Kukrit Pramoj, the story has become a modern classic in Thailand, made into films, plays and TV dramas, with heroine Ploi as the archetypal feminine role model.

S.P. Somtow *Jasmine Nights* (Asia Books, Bangkok). An engaging and humorous rites-of-passage tale of an upper-class boy learning what it is to be Thai. Another of his works, *Dragon's Fin Soup and Other Modern Siamese Fables*, is an imaginative and entertaining collection of often supernatural short stories, focusing on the collision of East and West.

Khamsing Srinawk *The Politician and Other Stories.* A collection of brilliantly satirical short stories, full of pithy moral observation and biting irony, which capture the vulnerability of peasant farmers in the north and northeast as they try to come to grips with the modern world. Written by an insider from a peasant family, who was educated at Chulalongkorn University, became a hero of the left, and joined the communist insurgents after the 1976 clampdown.

Klaus Wenk *Thai Literature – An Introduction* (White Lotus, Bangkok). Dry, but useful, short overview of the last seven hundred years by a noted German scholar, with plenty of extracts.

Thailand in foreign literature

Dean Barrett *Kingdom of Make-Believe.* Despite the clichéd ingredients – the Patpong go-go bar scene, opium smuggling in the Golden Triangle, Vietnam veterans – this novel about a return to Thailand following a twenty-year absence turns out to be a rewardingly multi-dimensional take on the farang experience.

Mischa Berlinski *Fieldwork.* Anthropology versus evangelism, a battle played out over an imaginary hill tribe in the hills of northern Thailand by a fascinating cast of characters, as wrily and vividly told by an eponymous narrator.

Botan *Letters from Thailand.* Probably the best introduction to the Chinese community in Bangkok, presented in the form of letters written over a twenty-year period by a Chinese emigrant to his mother. Branded as both anti-Chinese and anti-Thai, this 1969 prizewinning book is now mandatory reading in school social studies' classes.

Pierre Boulle *The Bridge Over the River Kwai.* The World War II novel that inspired the David Lean movie and kicked off the Kanchanaburi tourist industry.

John Burdett *Bangkok 8.* Riveting Bangkok thriller that takes in

Buddhism, plastic surgery, police corruption, the *yaa baa* drugs trade, hookers, jade-smuggling and the spirit world.

Alex Garland *The Beach*. Gripping cult thriller (later made into a film) that uses a Thai setting to explore the way in which travellers' cease-less quests for "undiscovered" utopias inevitably lead to them despoiling the idyll.

Michel Houellebecq *Platform*. Sex tourism in Thailand provides the nucleus of this brilliantly provocative (some would say offensive) novel, in which Houellebecq presents a ferocious critique of Western decadence and cultural colonialism, and of radical Islam too.

Christopher G. Moore *God Of Darkness* (Heaven Lake Press, Bangkok). Thailand's best-selling expat novelist sets his most intriguing thriller during the economic crisis of 1997 and includes plenty of meat on endemic corruption and the desperate struggle for power within family and society.

Darin Strauss *Chang & Eng*. An intriguing imagined autobiography of the famous nineteenth-century Siamese twins (see p.98), from their impoverished Thai childhood via the freak shows of New York and London to married life in small-town North Carolina. Unfortu-nately marred by lazy research and a confused grasp of Thai geography and culture.

Food and cookery

Vatcharin Bhumichitr *The Taste of Thailand*. Another glossy introduc-tion to this eminently photogenic country, this time through its food. The author runs a Thai restaurant in London and provides background colour as well as about 150 recipes adapted for Western kitchens.

David Thompson *Thai Food*. Comprehensive, impeccably researched celebration of the cuisine, with over 300 recipes, by the owner of the first Thai restaurant ever to earn a Michelin star.

Language

Language

Thai

T‌hai belongs to one of the oldest families of languages in the world,
Austro-Thai, and is radically different from most of the other tongues of
Southeast Asia. Being tonal, Thai is extremely difficult for Westerners to
master, but by building up from a small core of set phrases, you should
soon have enough to get by. Most Thais who deal with tourists speak some
English, but once you stray off the beaten track you'll probably need at least a
little Thai. Anywhere you go, you'll impress and get better treatment if you at
least make an effort to speak a few words.

Thai script is even more of a problem to Westerners, with 44 consonants
and 32 vowels. However, street signs in touristed areas are nearly always written
in Roman script as well as Thai, and in other circumstances you're better
off asking than trying to unscramble the swirling mess of symbols, signs and
accents. For more information on transliteration into Roman script, see the
box on p.7.

Among **language books**, *Thai: The Rough Guide Phrasebook* covers the essential phrases and expressions in both Thai script and phonetic equivalents, as well
as dipping into grammar and providing a menu reader and fuller vocabulary in
dictionary format (English-Thai and Thai-English). Probably the best pocket
dictionary is Paiboon Publishing's (Ⓦwww.ThaiLao.com) *Thai-English, English-
Thai Dictionary*, which lists words in phonetic Thai as well as Thai script, and
features a very handy table of the Thai alphabet in a dozen different fonts.

The best **teach–yourself course** is the expensive *Linguaphone Thai* (including
6 cassettes), which also has a shorter, cheaper beginner-level version (with 4
CDs). *Thai for Beginners* by Benjawan Poomsan Becker (Paiboon Publishing)
is a cheaper, more manageable textbook and is especially good for getting to
grips with the Thai writing system; you can also buy accompanying CDs to
help with listening skills, or get the whole thing in CD-ROM format. For a
more traditional textbook, try Stuart Campbell and Chuan Shaweevongse's *The
Fundamentals of the Thai Language*, which is comprehensive, though hard going.
G.H. Allison's *Easy Thai* is best for those who feel the urge to learn the alphabet.
The **website** Ⓦwww.thai-language.com is an amazing free resource, featuring a
searchable dictionary of over 40,000 Thai words, complete with Thai script and
audio clips, plus a guide to the language and forums.

Pronunciation

Mastering **tones** is probably the most difficult part of learning Thai. Five
different tones are used – low, middle, high, falling, and rising – by which the
meaning of a single syllable can be altered in five different ways. Thus, using
four of the five tones, you can make a sentence just from just one syllable: "mái
mài mâi măi" meaning "New wood burns, doesn't it?" As well as the natural
difficulty in becoming attuned to speaking and listening to these different tones,
Western efforts are complicated by our habit of denoting the overall meaning
of a sentence by modulating our tones – for example, turning a statement into

a question through a shift of stress and tone. Listen to native Thai speakers and you'll soon begin to pick up the different approach to tone.

The pitch of each tone is gauged in relation to your vocal range when speaking, but they should all lie within a narrow band, separated by gaps just big enough to differentiate them. The **low tones** (syllables marked `` ` ``), **middle tones** (unmarked syllables), and **high tones** (syllables marked `´`) should each be pronounced evenly and with no inflection. The **falling tone** (syllables marked `ˆ`) is spoken with an obvious drop in pitch, as if you were sharply emphasizing a word in English. The **rising tone** (marked `ˇ`) is pronounced as if you were asking an exaggerated question in English.

As well as the unfamiliar tones, you'll find that, despite the best efforts of the transliterators, there is no precise English equivalent to many **vowel and consonant sounds** in the Thai language. The lists below give a simplified idea of pronunciation.

Vowels

a	as in d**a**d		e	as in p**e**n
aa	has no precise equivalent, but is pronounced as it looks, with the vowel elongated		eu	as in s**i**r, but heavily nasalized
			i	as in t**i**p
			ii	as in f**ee**t
			o	as in kn**o**ck
ae	as in th**e**re		oe	as in h**u**rt, but more closed
ai	as in b**u**y			
ao	as in n**o**w		oh	as in t**oe**
aw	as in **aw**e		u	as in l**oo**t
ay	as in p**ay**		uu	as in p**oo**l

Consonants

r	as in rip, but with the tongue flapped quickly against the palate – in everyday speech, it's often pronounced like "l"		k	is unaspirated and unvoiced, and closer to "g"
			p	is also unaspirated and unvoiced, and closer to "b"
kh	as in **k**eep		t	is also unaspirated and unvoiced, and closer to "d"
ph	as in **p**ut			
th	as in **t**ime			

General words and phrases

Greetings and basic phrases

When you speak to a stranger in Thailand, you should generally end your sentence in *khráp* if you're a man, *khâ* if you're a woman – these untranslatable syllables will gain goodwill, and are nearly always used after *sawàt dii* (hello/goodbye) and *khàwp khun* (thank you). *Khráp* and *khâ* are also often used to answer "yes" to a question, though the most common way is to repeat the verb of the question (precede it with *mâi* for "no"). *Châi* (yes) and *mâi châi* (no) are less frequently used than their English equivalents.

Hello	sawàt dii	My name is…	phŏm (men)/ diichăn (women) chêu…
Where are you going?	pai năi? (not always meant literally, but used as a general greeting)	I come from…	phŏm/diichăn maa jàak…
		I don't understand	mâi khâo jai
I'm out having fun/ I'm travelling	pai thîaw (answer to pai năi, almost indefinable pleasantry)	Do you speak English?	khun phûut phasăa angkrìt dâi măi?
		Do you have…?	mii…măi?
Goodbye	sawàt dii/la kàwn	Is…possible?	…dâi măi?
Good luck/cheers	chôhk dii	Can you help me?	chûay phŏm/ diichăn dâi măi?
Excuse me	khăw thâwt		
Thank you	khàwp khun	(I) want…	ao…
It's nothing/it doesn't matter	mâi pen rai	(I) would like to…	yàak jà…
		(I) like…	châwp…
How are you?	sabai dii reŭ?	What is this called in Thai?	níi phasăa thai rîak wâa arai?
I'm fine	sabai dii		
What's your name?	khun chêu arai?		

Getting around

Where is the…?	…yùu thîi năi?	east	tawan àwk
How far?	klai thâo rai?	west	tawan tòk
I would like to go to…	yàak jà pai…	near/far	klâi/klai
		street	thanŏn
Where have you been?	pai năi maa?	train station	sathàanii rót fai
Where is this bus going?	rót níi pai năi?	bus station	sathàanii rót mae
		airport	sanăam bin
When will the bus leave?	rót jà àwk mêua rai?	ticket	tŭa
		hotel	rohng raem
What time does the bus arrive in…?	rót theŭng…kìi mohng?	post office	praisanii
		restaurant	raan ahăan
Stop here	jàwt thîi níi	shop	raan
here	thîi níi	market	talàat
there/over there	thîi nâan/thîi nôhn	hospital	rohng pha-yaabaan
right	khwăa		
left	sái	motorbike	rót mohtoesai
straight	trong	taxi	rót táksîi
north	neŭa	boat	reua
south	tâi	bicycle	jàkràyaan

Accommodation and shopping

How much is…?	…thâo rai/kìi bàat?	Can you reduce the price?	lót raakhaa dâi măi?
I don't want a plastic bag, thanks	mâi ao thŭng	Can I store my bag here?	fàak krapăo wái thîi nîi dâi măi?
How much is a room here per night?	hâwng thîi nîi kheun lá thâo rai?	cheap/expensive	thùuk/phaeng
Do you have a cheaper room?	mii hâwng thùuk kwàa măi?	air-con room	hăwng ae
Can I/we look at the room?	duu hâwng dâi măi?	ordinary room	hăwng thammadaa
		telephone	thohrásàp
I/We'll stay two nights	jà yùu săwng kheun	laundry	sák phâa
		blanket	phâa hòm
		fan	phát lom

General adjectives

alone	khon diaw	easy	ngâi
another	ìik…nèung	fun	sanùk
bad	mâi dii	hot (temperature)	ráwn
big	yài	hot (spicy)	phèt
clean	sa-àat	hungry	hiŭ khâo
closed	pìt	ill	mâi sabai
cold (object)	yen	open	pòet
cold (person or weather)	năo	pretty	sŭay
		small	lek
delicious	aròi	thirsty	hiŭ nám
difficult	yâak	tired	nèu-ay
dirty	sokaprok	very	mâak

General nouns

Nouns have no plurals or genders, and don't require an article.

bathroom/toilet	hăwng nám	foreigner	fàràng
boyfriend or girlfriend	faen	friend	phêuan
		money	ngoen
food	ahăan	water/liquid	nám

General verbs

Thai verbs do not conjugate at all, and also often double up as nouns and adjectives, which means that foreigners' most unidiomatic attempts to construct sentences are often readily understood.

come	maa	go	pai
do	tham	sit	nâng
eat	kin/thaan khâo	sleep	nawn làp
give	hâi	walk	doen pai

Numbers

zero	sŭun	eleven	sìp èt
one	nèung	twelve, thirteen…	sìp săwng, sìp săam…
two	săwng	twenty	yîi sìp/yiip
three	săam	twenty-one	yîi sìp èt
four	sìi	twenty-two,	yîi sìp săwng,
five	hâa	twenty-three…	yîi sìp săam…
six	hòk	thirty, forty, etc	săam sìp, sìi sìp…
seven	jèt	one hundred, two	nèung rói, săwng
eight	pàet	hundred…	rói…
nine	kâo	one thousand	nèung phan
ten	sìp	ten thousand	nèung mèun

Time

The commonest system for telling the time, as outlined below, is actually a confusing mix of several different systems. The State Railway and government officials use the 24-hour clock (9am is *kâo naalikaa*, 10am *sìp naalikaa*, and so on), which is always worth trying if you get stuck.

1–5am	tii nèung–tii hâa	hour	chûa mohng
6–11am	hòk mohng cháo–	day	wan
	sìp èt mohng cháo	week	aathít
noon	thîang	month	deuan
1pm	bài mohng	year	pii
2–4pm	bài săwng mohng–	today	wan níi
	bài sìi mohng	tomorrow	phrûng níi
5–6pm	hâa mohng yen–	yesterday	mêua wan níi
	hòk mohng yen	now	diăw níi
7–11pm	nèung thûm–	next week	aathít nâa
	hâa thûm	last week	aathít kàwn
midnight	thîang kheun	morning	cháo
What time is it?	kìi mohng láew?	afternoon	bài
How many hours?	kìi chûa mohng?	evening	yen
How long?	naan thâo rai?	night	kheun
minute	naathii		

Days

Sunday	wan aathít	Thursday	wan pháréuhàt
Monday	wan jan	Friday	wan sùk
Tuesday	wan angkhaan	Saturday	wan săo
Wednesday	wan phút		

Food and drink

Basic ingredients

Kài	Chicken	Plaa mèuk	Squid
Mŭu	Pork	Kûng	Prawn, shrimp
Néua	Beef, meat	Hŏy	Shellfish
Pèt	Duck	Hŏy nang rom	Oyster
Ahăan thalay	Seafood	Puu	Crab
Plaa	Fish	Khài	Egg
Plaa dùk	Catfish	Phàk	Vegetables

Vegetables

Makěua	Aubergine	Taeng kwaa	Cucumber
Makěua thêt	Tomato	Phrík yùak	Green pepper
Nàw mái	Bamboo shoots	Krathiam	Garlic
Tùa ngâwk	Bean sprouts	Hèt	Mushroom
Phrík	Chilli	Tùa	Peas, beans or lentils
Man faràng	Potato		
Man faràng thâwt	Chips	Tôn hŏrm	Spring onions

Noodles

Ba mìi	Egg noodles	Kwáy tiăw/ ba mìi rât nâ (mŭu)	Rice noodles/egg noodles fried in gravy-like sauce with vegetables (and pork slices)
Kwáy tiăw (sên yai/sên lék)	White rice noodles (wide/thin)		
Khanŏm jiin nám yaa	Noodles topped with fish curry		
Kwáy tiăw/ ba mìi haêng	Rice noodle/egg noodles fried with egg, small pieces of meat and a few vegetables	Mìi kràwp	Crisp fried egg noodles with small pieces of meat and a few vegetables
		Phàt thai	Thin noodles fried with egg, bean sprouts and tofu, topped with ground peanuts
Kwáy tiăw/ba mìi nám (mŭu)	Rice noodle/egg noodle soup, made with chicken broth (and pork balls)	Phàt siyú	Wide or thin noodles fried with soy sauce, egg and meat

Rice

Khâo	Rice	Khâo niăw	Sticky rice
Khâo man kài	Slices of chicken served over marinated rice	Khâo phàt	Fried rice
		Khâo kaeng	Curry over rice
		Khâo tôm	Rice soup (usually for breakfast)
Khâo mŭu daeng	Red pork with rice		
Khâo nâ kài/pèt	Chicken/duck served with sauce over rice		

Curries and soups

Kaeng phèt	Hot, red curry	Hàw mòk thalay	Seafood curry soufflé
Kaeng phánaeng	Thick, savoury curry	Kaeng liang	Peppery vegetable soup
Kaeng khǐaw wan	Green curry		
Kaeng mátsàman	Rich Muslim-style curry, usually with beef and potatoes	Tôm khà kài	Chicken coconut soup
		Tôm yam kûng	Hot and sour prawn soup
Kaeng karìi	Mild, Indian-style curry	Kaeng jèut	Mild soup with vegetables and usually pork
Kaeng sôm	Fish and vegetable curry		

Salads

Lâap	Spicy ground meat salad	Yam plaa mèuk	Squid salad
		Yam sôm oh	Pomelo salad
Nám tòk	Grilled beef or pork salad	Yam plaa dùk foo	Crispy fried catfish salad
Sôm tam	Spicy papaya salad	Yam thuù phuu	Wing-bean salad
Yam hua plee	Banana flower salad		
Yam néua	Grilled beef salad	Yam wun sen	Noodle and pork salad

Other dishes

Hâwy thâwt	Omelette stuffed with mussels	Néua phàt nám man hâwy	Beef in oyster sauce
Kài phàt bai kraprao	Chicken fried with basil leaves	Phàt phàk bûng fai daeng	Morning glory fried in garlic and bean sauce
Kài phàt nàw mái	Chicken with bamboo shoots		
Kài phàt mét mámûang	Chicken with cashew nuts	Phàt phàk lǎi yàng	Stir-fried vegetables
		Pàw pía	Spring rolls
Kài phàt khǐng	Chicken with ginger	Plaa nêung páe sá	Whole fish steamed with vegetables and ginger
Kài yâang	Grilled chicken		
Khài yát sài	Omelette with pork and vegetables	Plaa rât phrík	Whole fish cooked with chillies
Kûng chúp paêng thâwt	Prawns fried in batter	Plaa thâwt	Fried whole fish
		Sàté	Satay
Mǔu prîaw wǎan	Sweet and sour pork	Thâwt man plaa	Fish cake
Néua phàt krathiam phrík thai	Beef fried with garlic and pepper		

Thai desserts (khanǒm)

Khanǒm beuang	Small crispy pancake folded over with coconut cream and strands of sweet egg inside	Khâo lǎam	Sticky rice, coconut cream and black beans cooked and served in bamboo tubes

Khâo niăw daeng	Sticky red rice mixed with coconut cream	Lûk taan chêum	Sweet palm kernels served in syrup
Khâo niăw thúrian/ mámûang	Sticky rice mixed with coconut cream and durian/mango	Săngkhayaa	Coconut custard
		Tàkôh	Squares of transparent jelly (jello) topped with coconut cream
Klûay khàek	Fried banana		

Fruit (phônlámái)

Faràng	Guava	Mánao	Lemon
Klûay	Banana	Mápráo	Coconut
Línjii	Lychee	Sàppàrót	Pineapple
Mákhâam	Tamarind	Sôm	Orange
Málákaw	Papaya	Sôm oh	Pomelo
Mámûang	Mango	Taeng moh	Watermelon

Drinks (khreûang deùm)

Bia	Beer	Nám plào	Drinking water (boiled or filtered)
Chaa ráwn	Hot tea		
Chaa yen	Iced tea	Nám sŏdaa	Soda water
Kaafae ráwn	Hot coffee	Nám taan	Sugar
Kâew	Glass	Kleua	Salt
Khúat	Bottle	Nám yen	Cold water
Mâekhŏng (or anglicized "Mekong")	Thai brand-name rice whisky	Nom jeùd	Milk
		Ohlíang	Iced coffee
		Thûay	Cup
Nám klûay	Banana shake		
Nám mánao/sôm	Fresh, bottled or fizzy lemon/orange juice		

Ordering

Phŏm (male)/diichăn (female) kin ahăan mangsàwirát/jeh	I am vegetarian/vegan	Khăw…	I would like…
		Saì/mâi saì…	With/without…
Khăw duù menu nóy?	Can I see the menu?	Khăw check bin?	Can I have the bill please?

Glossary

Amphoe District.

Amphoe muang Provincial capital.

Ao Bay.

Apsara Female deity.

Avalokitesvara Bodhisattva representing compassion.

Avatar Earthly manifestation of a deity.

Ban Village or house.

Bang Village by a river or the sea.

Bencharong Polychromatic ceramics made in China for the Thai market.

Bhumisparsa mudra Most common gesture of Buddha images; symbolizes the Buddha's victory over temptation.

Bodhisattva In Mahayana Buddhism, an enlightened being who postpones his or her entry into Nirvana.

Bot Main sanctuary of a Buddhist temple.

Brahma One of the Hindu trinity – "The Creator". Usually depicted with four faces and four arms.

Celadon Porcelain with grey-green glaze.

Changwat Province.

Chao ley/chao nam "Sea gypsies" – nomadic fisherfolk of south Thailand.

Chedi Reliquary tower in Buddhist temple.

Chofa Finial on temple roof.

Deva Mythical deity.

Devaraja God-king.

Dharma The teachings or doctrine of the Buddha.

Dharmachakra Buddhist Wheel of Law (also known as Wheel of Doctrine or Wheel of Life).

Doi Mountain.

Erawan Mythical three-headed elephant; Indra's vehicle.

Farang Foreigner/foreign.

Ganesh Hindu elephant-headed deity, remover of obstacles and god of knowledge.

Garuda Mythical Hindu creature – half-man half-bird; Vishnu's vehicle.

Gopura Entrance pavilion to temple precinct (especially Khmer).

Hamsa Sacred mythical goose; Brahma's vehicle.

Hanuman Monkey god and chief of the monkey army in the Ramayana; ally of Rama.

Hat Beach.

Hin Stone.

Hinayana Pejorative term for Theravada school of Buddhism, literally "Lesser Vehicle".

Ho trai A scripture library.

Indra Hindu king of the gods and, in Buddhism, devotee of the Buddha; usually carries a thunderbolt.

Isaan Northeast Thailand.

Jataka Stories of the Buddha's five hundred lives.

Khaen Reed and wood pipe; the characteristic musical instrument of Isaan.

Khao Hill, mountain.

Khlong Canal.

Khon Classical dance-drama.

Kinnari Mythical creature – half woman, half bird.

Kirtimukha Very powerful deity depicted as a lion-head.

Ko Island.

Ku The Lao word for prang; a tower in a temple complex.

Laem Headland or cape.

Lakhon Classical dance-drama.

Lak muang City pillar; revered home for the city's guardian spirit.

Lakshaman/Phra Lak Rama's younger brother.

Lakshana Auspicious signs or "marks of greatness" displayed by the Buddha.

Lanna Northern Thai kingdom that lasted from the thirteenth to the sixteenth century.

Likay Popular folk theatre.

Luang Pho Abbot or especially revered monk.

Maenam River.

Mahathat Chedi containing relics of the Buddha.

Mahayana School of Buddhism now practised mainly in China, Japan and Korea; literally "the Great Vehicle".

Mara The Evil One; tempter of the Buddha.

Mawn khwaan Traditional triangular or "axe-head" pillow.

Meru/Sineru Mythical mountain at the centre of Hindu and Buddhist cosmologies.

Mondop Small, square temple building to house minor images or religious texts.

Moo/muu Neighbourhood.

Muang City or town.

Muay thai Thai boxing.

Mudra Symbolic gesture of the Buddha.

Mut mee Tie-dyed cotton or silk.

Naga Mythical dragon-headed serpent in Buddhism and Hinduism.

Nakhon Honorific title for a city.

Nam Water.

Nam tok Waterfall.

Nang thalung Shadow-puppet entertainment, found in southern Thailand.

Nielloware Engraved metalwork.

Nirvana Final liberation from the cycle of rebirths; state of non-being to which Buddhists aspire.

Pak Tai Southern Thailand.

Pali Language of ancient India; the script of the original Buddhist scriptures.

Pha sin Woman's sarong.

Phi Animist spirit.

Phra Honorific term – literally "excellent".

Phu Mountain.

Prang Central tower in a Khmer temple.

Prasat Khmer temple complex or central shrine.

Rama/Phra Ram Human manifestation of Hindu deity Vishnu; hero of the Ramayana.

Ramakien Thai version of the Ramayana.

Ramayana Hindu epic of good versus evil: chief characters include Rama, Sita, Ravana, Hanuman.

Ravana see Totsagan.

Reua hang yao Longtail boat.

Rishi Ascetic hermit.

Rot ae/rot tua Air-conditioned bus.

Rot thammadaa Ordinary bus.

Sala Meeting hall, pavilion, bus stop – or any open-sided structure.

Samlor Three-wheeled tricycle.

Sanskrit Sacred language of Hinduism; also used in Buddhism.

Sanuk Fun.

Sema Boundary stone to mark consecrated ground within temple complex.

Shiva One of the Hindu trinity – "The Destroyer".

Shiva lingam Phallic representation of Shiva.

Soi Lane or side road.

Songkhran Thai New Year.

Songthaew Public transport pick-up vehicle; means "two rows", after its two facing benches.

Takraw Game played with a rattan ball.

Talat Market.

Talat nam Floating market.

Talat yen Night market.

Tambon Subdistrict.

Tavatimsa Buddhist heaven.

Tha Pier.

Thale Sea or lake.

Tham Cave.

Thanon Road.

That Chedi.

Thep A divinity.

Theravada Main school of Buddhist thought in Thailand; also known as Hinayana.

Totsagan Rama's evil rival in the Ramayana; also known as Ravana.

Tripitaka Buddhist scriptures.

Trok Alley.

Tuk-tuk Motorized three-wheeled taxi.

Uma Shiva's consort.

Ushnisha Cranial protuberance on Buddha images, signifying an enlightened being.

Viharn Temple assembly hall for the laity; usually contains the principal Buddha image.

Vipassana Buddhist meditation technique; literally "insight".

Vishnu One of the Hindu trinity – "The Preserver". Usually shown with four arms, holding a disc, a conch, a lotus and a club.

Wai Thai greeting expressed by a prayer-like gesture with the hands.

Wang Palace.

Wat Temple.

Wiang Fortified town.

Yaksha Mythical giant.

Yantra Magical combination of numbers and letters, used to ward off danger.

Travel store

Travel

Andorra The Pyrenees, Pyrenees & Andorra Map, Spain
Antigua The Caribbean
Argentina Argentina, Argentina Map, Buenos Aires, South America on a Budget
Aruba The Caribbean
Australia Australia, Australia Map, East Coast Australia, Melbourne, Sydney, Tasmania
Austria Austria, Europe on a Budget, Vienna
Bahamas The Bahamas, The Caribbean
Barbados Barbados DIR, The Caribbean
Belgium Belgium & Luxembourg, Bruges DIR, Brussels, Brussels Map, Europe on a Budget
Belize Belize, Central America on a Budget, Guatemala & Belize Map
Benin West Africa
Bolivia Bolivia, South America on a Budget
Brazil Brazil, Rio, South America on a Budget
British Virgin Islands The Caribbean
Brunei Malaysia, Singapore & Brunei [1 title], Southeast Asia on a Budget
Bulgaria Bulgaria, Europe on a Budget
Burkina Faso West Africa
Cambodia Cambodia, Southeast Asia on a Budget, Vietnam, Laos & Cambodia Map [1 Map]
Cameroon West Africa
Canada Canada, Pacific Northwest, Toronto, Toronto Map, Vancouver
Cape Verde West Africa
Cayman Islands The Caribbean
Chile Chile, Chile Map, South America on a Budget
China Beijing, China,

Hong Kong & Macau, Hong Kong & Macau DIR, Shanghai
Colombia South America on a Budget
Costa Rica Central America on a Budget, Costa Rica, Costa Rica & Panama Map
Croatia Croatia, Croatia Map, Europe on a Budget
Cuba Cuba, Cuba Map, The Caribbean, Havana
Cyprus Cyprus, Cyprus Map
Czech Republic The Czech Republic, Czech & Slovak Republics, Europe on a Budget, Prague, Prague DIR, Prague Map
Denmark Copenhagen, Denmark, Europe on a Budget, Scandinavia
Dominica The Caribbean
Dominican Republic Dominican Republic, The Caribbean
Ecuador Ecuador, South America on a Budget
Egypt Egypt, Egypt Map
El Salvador Central America on a Budget
England Britain, Camping in Britain, Devon & Cornwall, Dorset, Hampshire and The Isle of Wight [1 title], England, Europe on a Budget, The Lake District, London, London DIR, London Map, London Mini Guide, Walks In London & Southeast England
Estonia The Baltic States, Europe on a Budget
Fiji Fiji
Finland Europe on a Budget, Finland, Scandinavia
France Brittany & Normandy, Corsica, Corsica Map, The Dordogne & the Lot, Europe on a Budget, France, France Map, Languedoc & Roussillon, The Loire, Paris, Paris DIR,

Paris Map, Paris Mini Guide, Provence & the Côte d'Azur, The Pyrenees, Pyrenees & Andorra Map
French Guiana South America on a Budget
Gambia The Gambia, West Africa
Germany Berlin, Berlin Map, Europe on a Budget, Germany, Germany Map
Ghana West Africa
Gibraltar Spain
Greece Athens Map, Crete, Crete Map, Europe on a Budget, Greece, Greece Map, Greek Islands, Ionian Islands
Guadeloupe The Caribbean
Guatemala Central America on a Budget, Guatemala, Guatemala & Belize Map
Guinea West Africa
Guinea-Bissau West Africa
Guyana South America on a Budget
Holland see The Netherlands
Honduras Central America on a Budget
Hungary Budapest, Europe on a Budget, Hungary
Iceland Iceland, Iceland Map
India Goa, India, India Map, Kerala, Rajasthan, Delhi & Agra [1 title], South India, South India Map
Indonesia Bali & Lombok, Southeast Asia on a Budget
Ireland Dublin DIR, Dublin Map, Europe on a Budget, Ireland, Ireland Map
Israel Jerusalem
Italy Europe on a Budget, Florence DIR, Florence & Siena Map, Florence & the best of Tuscany, Italy, The Italian Lakes, Naples & the Amalfi Coast, Rome, Rome DIR, Rome Map, Sardinia, Sicily, Sicily Map, Tuscany & Umbria, Tuscany Map,

Venice, Venice DIR, Venice Map
Jamaica Jamaica, The Caribbean
Japan Japan, Tokyo
Jordan Jordan
Kenya Kenya, Kenya Map
Korea Korea
Laos Laos, Southeast Asia on a Budget, Vietnam, Laos & Cambodia Map [1 Map]
Latvia The Baltic States, Europe on a Budget
Lithuania The Baltic States, Europe on a Budget
Luxembourg Belgium & Luxembourg, Europe on a Budget
Malaysia Malaysia Map, Malaysia, Singapore & Brunei [1 title], Southeast Asia on a Budget
Mali West Africa
Malta Malta & Gozo DIR
Martinique The Caribbean
Mauritania West Africa
Mexico Baja California, Baja California, Cancún & Cozumel DIR, Mexico, Mexico Map, Yucatán, Yucatán Peninsula Map
Monaco France, Provence & the Côte d'Azur
Montenegro Montenegro
Morocco Europe on a Budget, Marrakesh DIR, Marrakesh Map, Morocco, Morocco Map,
Nepal Nepal
Netherlands Amsterdam, Amsterdam DIR, Amsterdam Map, Europe on a Budget, The Netherlands
Netherlands Antilles The Caribbean
New Zealand New Zealand, New Zealand Map

DIR: Rough Guide **DIRECTIONS** for short breaks

Available from all good bookstores

For more information go to www.roughguides.com

ROUGH GUIDES

Book Aid International
www.bookaid.org

Books change lives

Poverty and illiteracy go hand in hand. But in sub-Saharan Africa, books are a luxury few can afford. Many children leave school functionally illiterate, and adults often fall back into illiteracy in adulthood due to a lack of available reading material.

Book Aid International knows that books change lives.

Every year we send over half a million books to partners in 12 countries in sub-Saharan Africa, to stock libraries in schools, refugee camps, prisons, universities and communities. Literally millions of readers have access to books and information that could teach them new skills – from keeping chickens to getting a degree in Business Studies or learning how to protect against HIV/AIDS.

What can you do?

Join our Reverse Book Club and with your donation of only £6 a month, we can send 36 books every year to some of the poorest countries in the world. For every two pounds extra you can give, we can send another book!

Support Book Aid International today!

 Online. Go to our website at **www.bookaid.org**, and click on 'donate'

 By telephone. Start a Direct Debit or give a donation on your card by calling us on 020 7733 3577

Book Aid International is a charity and a limited company registered in England and Wales.
Charity No. 313869 Company No. 880754   39-41 Coldharbour Lane, Camberwell, London SE5 9NR
T +44 (0)20 7733 3577   F +44 (0)20 7978 8006   E info@bookaid.org   www.bookaid.org

Small print and
Index

A Rough Guide to Rough Guides

Published in 1982, the first Rough Guide – to Greece – was a student scheme that became a publishing phenomenon. Mark Ellingham, a recent graduate in English from Bristol University, had been travelling in Greece the previous summer and couldn't find the right guidebook. With a small group of friends he wrote his own guide, combining a highly contemporary, journalistic style with a thoroughly practical approach to travellers' needs.

The immediate success of the book spawned a series that rapidly covered dozens of destinations. And, in addition to impecunious backpackers, Rough Guides soon acquired a much broader and older readership that relished the guides' wit and inquisitiveness as much as their enthusiastic, critical approach and value-for-money ethos.

These days, Rough Guides include recommendations from shoestring to luxury and cover more than 200 destinations around the globe, including almost every country in the Americas and Europe, more than half of Africa and most of Asia and Australasia. Our ever-growing team of authors and photographers is spread all over the world, particularly in Europe, the US and Australia.

In the early 1990s, Rough Guides branched out of travel, with the publication of Rough Guides to World Music, Classical Music and the Internet. All three have become benchmark titles in their fields, spearheading the publication of a wide range of books under the Rough Guide name.

Including the travel series, Rough Guides now number more than 350 titles, covering: phrasebooks, waterproof maps, music guides from Opera to Heavy Metal, reference works as diverse as Conspiracy Theories and Shakespeare, and popular culture books from iPods to Poker. Rough Guides also produce a series of more than 120 World Music CDs in partnership with World Music Network.

Visit www.roughguides.com to see our latest publications.

Rough Guide travel images are available for commercial licensing at www.roughguidespictures.com

Rough Guide credits

Text editor: James Rice and Harry Wilson
Layout: Umesh Aggarwal
Cartography: Jasbir Sandhu
Picture editor: Emily Taylor
Production: Rebecca Short
Proofreader: Serena Stephenson
Photographers: Martin Richardson and
Karen Trist
Editorial: Ruth Blackmore, Andy Turner, Keith
Drew, Edward Aves, Alice Park, Lucy White,
Jo Kirby, James Smart, Natasha Foges, Róisín
Cameron, Emma Traynor, Emma Gibbs, Kathryn
Lane, Monica Woods, Mani Ramaswamy, Lucy
Cowie, Alison Roberts, Joe Staines, Peter
Buckley, Matthew Milton, Tracy Hopkins, Ruth
Tidball; **Delhi** Madhavi Singh, Karen D'Souza,
Lubna Shaheen
Design & Pictures: **London** Scott Stickland,
Dan May, Diana Jarvis, Mark Thomas, Nicole
Newman, Sarah Cummins; **Delhi** Ajay Verma,
Jessica Subramanian, Ankur Guha, Pradeep
Thapliyal, Sachin Tanwar, Anita Singh, Nikhil
Agarwal, Sachin Gupta

Production: Liz Cherry
Cartography: **London** Ed Wright, Katie Lloyd-
Jones; **Delhi** Rajesh Chhibber, Ashutosh Bharti,
Rajesh Mishra, Animesh Pathak, Karobi Gogoi,
Alakananda Bhattacharya, Swati Handoo,
Deshpal Dabas
Online: **London** Faye Hellon, Jeanette Angell,
Fergus Day, Justine Bright, Clare Bryson, Aine
Fearon, Adrian Low, Ezgi Celebi; **Delhi** Amit
Verma, Rahul Kumar, Narender Kumar, Ravi
Yadav, Debojit Borah, Rakesh Kumar, Ganesh
Sharma, Shisir Basumatari
Marketing & Publicity: **London** Liz Statham,
Louise Maher, Jess Carter, Vanessa Godden,
Vivienne Watton, Anna Paynton, Rachel
Sprackett, Laura Vipond; **New York** Katy Ball,
Judi Powers; **Delhi** Ragini Govind
Reference Director: Andrew Lockett
Operations Assistant: Becky Doyle
Operations Manager: Helen Atkinson
Publishing Director (Travel): Clare Currie
Commercial Manager: Gino Magnotta
Managing Director: John Duhigg

Publishing information

This fifth edition published March 2010 by
Rough Guides Ltd,
80 Strand, London WC2R 0RL
14 Local Shopping Centre, Panchsheel Park,
New Delhi 110017, India
Distributed by the Penguin Group
Penguin Books Ltd,
80 Strand, London WC2R 0RL
Penguin Group (USA)
375 Hudson Street, NY 10014, USA
Penguin Group (Australia)
250 Camberwell Road, Camberwell,
Victoria 3124, Australia
Penguin Group (Canada)
195 Harry Walker Parkway N, Newmarket, ON,
L3Y 7B3 Canada
Penguin Group (NZ)
67 Apollo Drive, Mairangi Bay, Auckland 1310,
New Zealand
Cover concept by Peter Dyer.

Typeset in Bembo and Helvetica to an original
design by Henry Iles.
Printed in Singapore
© Paul Gray and Lucy Ridout, 2010
Maps © Rough Guides
No part of this book may be reproduced in any
form without permission from the publisher except
for the quotation of brief passages in reviews.
272pp includes index
A catalogue record for this book is available from
the British Library
ISBN: 978-1-84836-261-1
The publishers and authors have done their best
to ensure the accuracy and currency of all the
information in **The Rough Guide to Bangkok**,
however, they can accept no responsibility for
any loss, injury, or inconvenience sustained by
any traveller as a result of information or advice
contained in the guide.

1   3   5   7   9   8   6   4   2

Help us update

We've gone to a lot of effort to ensure that the
fifth edition of **The Rough Guide to Bangkok**
is accurate and up-to-date. However, things
change – places get "discovered", opening hours
are notoriously fickle, restaurants and rooms raise
prices or lower standards. If you feel we've got it
wrong or left something out, we'd like to know,
and if you can remember the address, the price,
the hours, the phone number, so much the better.

Please send your comments with the subject
line "**Rough Guide Bangkok Update**" to ©mail
@roughguides.com. We'll credit all contributions
and send a copy of the next edition (or any other
Rough Guide if you prefer) for the very best
emails.
Have your questions answered and tell others
about your trip at ⊕www.roughguides.com

Acknowledgements

The **authors** would like to thank: Gade Taraksa; Bill Gray; Jack Grassby; Abigail Silver at London TAT; and Nikki Busuttil, Wannapa Rakkeo, Maria Kuhn and Marion Walsh in Bangkok.

Readers' letters

Thanks to all the readers who have taken the time to write in with comments and suggestions (and apologies if we've inadvertently omitted or misspelt anyone's name):

Carla Anderson, Julien Anseau, Luis F. Arévalogarcia, John Archibald, Jane Barnett, Alison Batley, Marcel Bokhorst, Paul Bonner, Michelle Brodie, Margo Burgers, Phil Cairns, Adam Cathro, Katie Clare, G. Clegg, John & Maggie Coaton, Ryan Collins, Cian Connolly, Diana Coode & Lee J Barnett, Melanie Cook, David Cunningham, Conrad Davies, Kieran Dignam, Chris Eichler, Mike Fletcher, Michael Gardham, Joanne Gardiner, David Gaukrodger, Chris Goward, Bernd Greiner, Kimberley Anne Gray, Pelle Gustafson, John & Shirley Harper, Anna Harrison, Paul Hie, Benjamin L Hilditch, Charlie Hogan, Andrew Hunt, Clare Johnson & Peter Lawrie, Steven Jolly, Grace Kenny, Helen Keynes, Majid Khan, A.G. Klei & Ruth Campbell-Page, Jan Kling, Viviana & Allister Levy, Jason Lewis, Rob van Loo, Bridget MacDonald, Aiden MacFarlane, Monica Mackaness & John Garratt, Anita & Hamish McFarlane, Jim McNalis, Regine De Naegel, Matt Nicholls, Jan van Oort, Megan Murphy O'Connell, James Newton, John, Phil & Sinead O'Reilly, John & Saw Payne, Jan Pennington, Por Fl Pharo, Allan and Margaret Rickmann, Paul Robson, Kimberley Ross, Simon Rowley, Vanessa Ryan & Russ Nash, Riccardo Sai, Beat & Anaida Schmid, Peter Searl, Keith Shaw, Alex Shields, Clayton Smith, Ray Smith, Andrea Spescha, Dave Stark, Jeff Stone, Vicky Stone, Sarah Stuteville, Will Swainson, Neal Teplitz, Robin & Matt Thomsen, Sue Thornton, Nick Trautmann, Wayne Turner, Charlotte Underwood, Gillian Walker, John Weldon, David Whiting, Moritz Winnen, Lisa Wortley.

Photo credits

All photos © Rough Guides except the following:

Introduction
Tuk-tuk driver © Ian Cumming/Axiom
Statues at the Grand Palace © Neil Emmerson/Robert Harding
Buddha feet © Peter Adams/PhotoLibrary
Thanon Sukhumvit at sunset © Pignatelli Massimo/SIME 4 Corners
Wat Phra Kaeo © Charles Graham/eStock Photo
The Golden Mount, Wat Saket © Walter G Allgawer/PhotoLibrary

Things not to miss
08 Modern Shopping in Bangkok © Ray Laskowitz/PhotoLibrary
09 Professional Thai kickboxing match in Bangkok © Chad Ehlers/PhotoLibrary
11 Cookery Classes in Bangkok © Courtesy of The Mandarin Oriental Hotel Group
12 Revellers at the Songkran festival © EPA/Corbis
16 Bike tours, Phraphadaeng district © Courtesy of ABC Cycling Tour - Real Asia Ltd
18 National Museum, 7th-8th century Buddha [detail] © Luca I. Tettoni/Corbis

Bangkok by Boat colour section
The Chao Phraya at night © Mark Harmel/Tips Images

Thai Cuisine colour section
Tom kha kai © Riou Riou/PhotoLibrary

Black and whites
p.194 Gay Pride, Bangkok © Paula Bronstein/Getty Images

Index

Map entries are in colour.

H

I

J

K

L

M

Map symbols

maps are listed in the full index using coloured text

– – – –	Chapter division boundary		✈	Airport
▬▬▬	Expressway		★	Transport stop
▬▬▬	Pedestrianized road		♦	Point of interest
═══	Road		♟	Museum
- - - - -	Path		⑤	Bank/ATM
▬●▬	Railway		@	Internet access
───	River/canal		ⓘ	Tourist information
───	Wall		ⓒ	Telephone office
⏝	Bridge		⊞	Hospital
▣	Accommodation		⊠	Post office
◉	Restaurants & bars		🎵	Market
🏔	Mountains		⏄	Temple
◖	Cave		⬭	Stadium
⊠	Gate		➕	Church
⌒	Arch		▮	Building
→	One-way street		⊞	Christian cemetery
⊙	Statue		▦	Park/forest

So now we've told you about the things not to miss, the best places to stay, the top restaurants, the liveliest bars and the most spectacular sights, it only seems fair to tell you about the best travel insurance around

WorldNomads.com
keep travelling safely

Recommended by Rough Guides

Nonthaburi

CHAO PHRAYA EXPRESS BOATS

(S)	BTS Skytrain station
★	Khlong Saen Saeb boat stop
(M)	Subway Station

Royal Barge Museum

Bangkok Info. Centre (i)

Siriraj Hospital & Museums

National Museum

Wat Mahathat

Patravadi Theatre

Wat Rakhang

Wat Arun

Museum of Siam

Wat Kanlayanamit

Santa Cruz

Wat Prayoon

THONBURI

Thonburi Train Station

National Library

National Gallery

National Theatre

Phra Sumen Fortress

BANGLAMPHU

KHAO SAN

Democracy Monument

Sanam Luang

Wat Phra Kaeo

Grand Palace

Wat Suthat

Wat Pho

CHINATOWN

Pak Khlong Talat

Wat Chakrawat

Vimanmek Palace

Dusit Zoo

DUSIT

Wat Benjamabophit

(i) TAT

Golden Mount

Tha Phan Fah

LAN LUANG

Khlong Saen Saeb

Wat Mangkon

Hualamphong Station

Wat Traimit

Hua Lamphong (M)

River City

SI PHRAYA

GPO

Oriental

Peninsula

SURIWONG

SILOM

Saphan Taksin (S)

Surasak (S)

TAKSIN BRIDGE

CENTRAL CHAO PHRAYA EXPRESS BOAT PIERS
Rush-hour no-flag boats stop at all piers.

(N15)	All-day orange flag special express boats stop here
(N12)	Rush-hour yellow flag special express boats stop here
(N9)	Rush-hour green-and-yellow flag special express boats stop here
(N10)	Rush hour blue flag special express boats stop here

(N15)	Thewet	(N7)	Ratchini (aka Rajinee)
(N14)	Rama VIII Bridge	(N6)	Saphan Phut/Memorial Bridge
(N13)	Phra Arthit	(N5)	Rachawongse (aka Rajawong)
(N12)	Phra Pinklao Bridge	(N4)	Harbour Department
(N11)	Bangkok Noi (Thonburi Railway Station)	(N3)	Si Phraya
(N10)	Wang Lang (Siriraj)	(N2)	Wat Muang Kae
(N9)	Chang	(N1)	Oriental
(N8)	Thien	(Central)	Sathorn

0   1 km

Krungthep Bridge

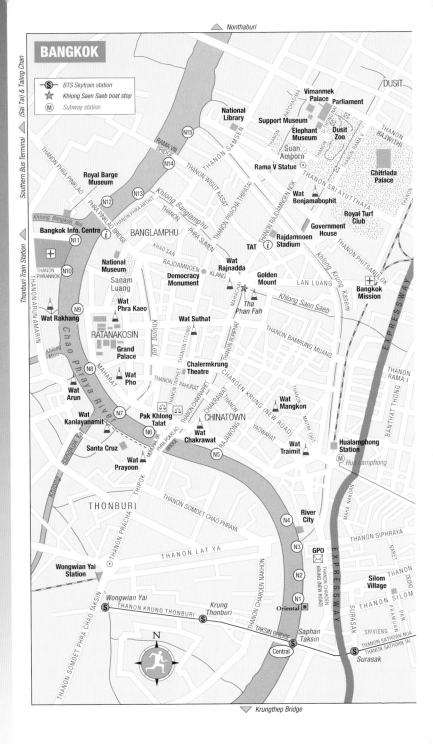

EXPRESS BOAT PIERS

N15	Thewet
N14	Rama VIII Bridge
N13	Phra Arthit
N12	Phra Pinklao Bridge
N11	Bangkok Noi (Thonburi Railway Station)
N10	Wang Lang (Siriraj)
N9	Chang
N8	Thien
N7	Ratchini (aka Rajinee)
N6	Saphan Phut
N5	Rachawongse (aka Rajawong)
N4	Harbour Department
N3	Si Phraya
N2	Wat Muang Kae
N1	Oriental
Central	Sathorn

Samsen Station

Ari

SOI ARI

THANON PHAHOLYOTHIN

Sanam Pao

THANON SAWANKHALOK

Phyathai Palace

THANON RAJWITHI

Victory Monument

Victory Monument

THANON YOTHI

THANON PHRAYATHAI

EXPRESSWAY

TOLLWAY

Siam City Hotel

Suan Pakkad Palace Museum

Phaya Thai

Phayathai (Airport City Line)

Phaya Thai

THANON RAJAPRAROP

Ratchaprarop (Airport City Line)

Rama IX (Phra Ram 9)

THANON ASOKE DINDAENG

Baiyoke II Tower

Pratunam Market

Ratchathevi

THANON PHETCHABURI

Jim Thompson's House

Tha Chitlom

Tha Pratunam

Tha Witthayu

THANON PHETCHABURI MAI

Phetchaburi

Makkasan City Air Terminal

TAT HQ

Tha Nana Nua

Bumrungrad

Tha Asoke

National Stadium

Siam (Central Station)

SIAM SQUARE

Chit Lom

SOI CHITLOM

THANON PLOENCHIT

British Embassy

SUKHUMVIT 1 (SOI NANA NUA)

SUKHUMVIT 3 (SOI NANA NUA)

SUKHUMVIT 13

SUKHUMVIT 15

THANON ASOK MONTRI (SOI 21)

SUKHUMVIT 23

MBK Shopping Centre

PHRAYATHAI

Ratcha-damri

Erawan Shrine

THANON HENRI DUNANT

SOI LANGSUAN

SOI TONSON

Phloen Chit

SOI RUAM RUDEE

Nana

Landmark

Ambassador

Ban Kamthieng

SUKHUMVIT 31

Chulalongkorn University

Royal Bangkok Sports Club

RAJDAMRI

THANON WITTHAYU (WIRELESS)

NZ & South African Embassies

SUKHUMVIT 2

Sheraton Grande

Asok

Sukhumvit

THANON SUKHUMVIT

DOWNTOWN BANGKOK

SOI SARASIN

American Embassy

EXPRESSWAY

SUKHUMVIT 4 (SOI NANA TAI)

Sam Yan

Queen Saovabha Institute

Lumphini Park

Suan Lum Night Bazaar

Emporium

Phrom Pong

SAP

SURIWONG

SILOM

PATPONG

THANA

CONVENT

SALADAENG

Sala Daeng

THANON RAMA IV

Canadian Embassy

Lumphini

Lumphini Stadium

THANON RATCHADAPISEK

Bangkok Christian

BNH

Chong Nonsi

JUSMAG

Australian Embassy

Khlong Toei

Queen Sirikit National Convention Centre (QSNCC)

SOI NGAM DUPHLI

SOI SUAN PHLU

Le Lys

SOI PHRA PINIT

Le Café Siam

NARATHIWAT RATCHANAKHARIN

Sarah Jane's

M. R. Kukrit's Heritage Home

| 0 | 500 m | 1 km |

BTS SKYTRAIN & SUBWAY

Don Muang Airport

Legend:
- (S) BTS Skytrain station
- (M) Subway station
- ★ Khlong Saen Saeb boat stop

N

Suvarnabhumi Airport

Northern Bus Terminal
Bangkok Butterfly Garden
Children's Discovery Museum
Mochit
Phahon Yothin (M)
Lat Phrao (M)
Bangsue
Kamphaeng Phet (M)
(S)(M) Chatuchak Park
Chatuchak Weekend Market
Ratchadapisek (M)
Saphan Kwai (S)
PRADIPHAT
Reflections
Sutthisan (M)
Samsen Station
THANON RAJWITHI
Ari (S)
Sanam Pao (S)
Huai Khwang (M)
Chitrlada Palace
Cambodian Embassy
Lao Embassy
PRACHA UTHIT
Siam Niramit
Victory Monument (S)
Victory Monument
EXPRESSWAY
Thailand Cultural Centre (M)
Thailand Cultural Centre
TAT
Democracy Monument (i)
Golden Mount ★
Tha Phan Fah
Phaya Thai (S)
Phayathai (Airport City Line)
Ratchaprarop (Airport City Line)
Rama IX (Phra Ram 9) (M)
Khlong Krung Kasem
Tha Saphan Hua Chang ★
THANON ASOK DINDAENG
Jim Thompson's House ★
EXPRESSWAY
Makkasan City Air Terminal
Tha Pratunam ★
Tha Chitlom
National Stadium (S)
Ratchathewi (S)
Siam (Central Station) (S)
Ratcha-damri (S)
Chit Lom (S)
Tha Witthayu ★
Tha Nana Nua ★
Phetchaburi (M)
Hualamphong Station
THANON PHETCHABURI
Wat Traimit
Hua Lamphong
Erawan Shrine
TAT HQ (i)
Tha Asoke
Khlong Saen Saeb
Tha Ekamai ★
Phloen Chit (S)
Nana (S)
Sam Yan (M)
Lumphini Park
Night Bazaar
Sukhumvit (M)
Samitivej Hospital
Sala Daeng (S)
Silom (M)
Asok (S)
EXPRESSWAY
Krung Thonburi (S)
THANON SILOM
Chong Nonsi (S)
Lumphini (M)
Phrom Pong (S)
Thong Lo (S)
THANON SUKHUMVIT
Saphan Taksin (S)
THANON SATHORN
Khlong Toei (M)
Queen Sirikit National Convention Centre (QSNCC) (M)
Eastern Bus Terminal
Ekamai (S)
Phra Khanong (S)
Surasak (S)
Wongwian Yai (S)
Chao Phraya
THANON RATCHADAPHISEK
On Nut (S)

0   1 km